CANADA AND THE AGE OF CONFLICT

C. P. STACEY

CANADA AND THE AGE OF CONFLICT

A History of Canadian External Policies

VOLUME I: 1867–1921

UNIVERSITY OF TORONTO PRESS
TORONTO BUFFALO LONDON

Toronto Buffalo London
Printed in Canada

ISBN 0-8020-6560-0 (paperback)

First published in 1977, and in paperback in 1979,
in both cases by The Macmillan Company of Canada

Canadian Cataloguing in Publication Data

Stacey, Charles P., 1906–
Canada and the age of conflict

Includes bibliographies and index.
Contents: v.1. 1867–1921.

1. Canada — Foreign relations. I. Title.
FC242.S73 327.71 C77-001317-1
F1029.S73

Cover illustration:
The British High Commisioners, Washington, 1871
(PAC, C-2422)

This book has been published with the help of a grant
from the Social Science Research Council of Canada, using
funds provided by the Canada Council.

CONTENTS

ABBREVIATIONS

CAB Cabinet
CAR *Canadian Annual Review of Public Affairs*
CHA Canadian Historical Association
CHR *Canadian Historical Review*
CID Committee of Imperial Defence
CO Colonial Office
CYB Canada Year Book
DCER *Documents on Canadian External Relations*
FO Foreign Office
MG Manuscript Group
PAC Public Archives of Canada
PC Privy Council (used in numbering orders-in-council)
RG Record Group

PREFACE

Since the Second World War, Canada's relations with the external world have interested both Canadian parliamentarians and the people they represent more than they ever did before. The subject has lately become important in the universities, and much valuable research has been done and is being done on special aspects of it. Yet it is a good many years since a serious attempt was made to write a general history of Canadian external policies. During those years the liberalization of public records policy and the increasing availability of important private papers have opened up many new sources of information. Experience in teaching the subject has made me aware of the need for a new history, and has encouraged me to make an effort to meet it. I hope the book now presented will serve both the student and the general reader.

My first intention was that the book should be only one volume, and that it should begin seriously in 1914, events before that date being covered in a single introductory chapter. As will be seen, things have turned out rather differently. The period from 1867 to 1914 has seemed to merit much more attention than I had proposed to give it; and the crowded and dramatic years from the outbreak of war in 1914 to the election of 1921 have demanded five long chapters. This volume concludes with the end of the decade of Conservative and Unionist rule that began in 1911, and the dawn of the day of Mackenzie King. The King era, and the new situation following the Second World War, will be the subject of a second volume.

I have profited by the labours of the many scholars who have been cultivating the field of Canadian external policy in recent years; they have made my task much easier. But I have myself had to do a great deal of research in the original sources, particularly in the Canadian records, both official and personal, preserved in the Public Archives of Canada. I have made much use of the copies of United Kingdom records which are also available in the PAC.

I must acknowledge assistance from many quarters. I have to thank Her Majesty the Queen for permission to use the British Prime Ministers' Cabinet letters to the Sovereign. Mr. Esmond Butler, Secretary to His Excellency the Governor General, kindly gave me access to several files of the Governor General's Office. I am grateful to the Literary Executors of the late W. L. Mackenzie King for access to Mr. King's diaries before they were generally opened. I owe a great debt to the staff of the Public Archives of Canada, and in particular to Miss Barbara Wilson, Mr. J. W. O'Brien, Mr. Peter Robertson, and Mrs. J. M. White. Mr. Arthur Blanchette, head of the Historical Division of the Department of External Affairs, has been most generous. Mr. Norman Hillmer of the Directorate of History at National Defence Headquarters has helped me a great deal at several points. Two of my colleagues at the University of Toronto, professors Robert Bothwell and Craig Brown, have taken time to read various chapters of the book and made most valuable comments. The students who have taken my graduate seminar in Canadian external policies have helped me a great deal; some of these debts are acknowledged in detail in the references. Much of the research for the book was financed by a grant from the Canada Council. The work was launched in 1970–71 with the assistance of a generous leave fellowship from the International Studies Programme of the University of Toronto. Finally, I thank most warmly Mrs. Audrey Douglas, who typed the manuscript, and Mrs. Diane Mew, my editor, who as usual has been most patient, painstaking, and skilful.

C.P.S.
Massey College in the University of Toronto

CANADA AND THE AGE OF CONFLICT

CHAPTER ONE

THE NEW 'NATION', 1867

DOMINION, EMPIRE, AND WORLD

The British North America Act, passed by the British Parliament in the early weeks of 1867, seems in many ways, at first glance, an unpromising foundation for the "great nationality, commanding the respect of the world"[1] which optimistic Canadian statesmen hoped to build upon it. It was intended for a somewhat limited purpose: to unite three British provinces—Canada, Nova Scotia, and New Brunswick—into a single federal state, and to provide for that state a workable form of government.

This purpose, on the whole, it performed admirably. It did nothing, however, to define the status of the new polity in the British Empire or the world. So far as the Act went, it had to be assumed that the "Dominion of Canada", with its population of over three million, which came into existence on July 1, 1867, stood no higher than the constituent colonies which it brought together or than any of the other British self-governing colonies around the globe.

No doubt this was the view of some people in the Colonial Office and other organs of the British government. But Canadian politicians saw things differently. They considered that the Confederation scheme they had invented had produced a community which was, or would shortly be, something more than a mere colony. John A. Macdonald had said, in the Confederation debates of 1865 in the Canadian legislature,

> Gradually a different colonial system is being developed—and it will become, year by year, less a case of dependence on our part, and of over-ruling protection on the part of the Mother Country, and more a case of a healthy and

cordial alliance. Instead of looking upon us as a merely dependent colony, England will have in us a friendly nation—a subordinate but still a powerful people—to stand by her in North America in peace or in war. The people of Australia will be such another subordinate nation. And England will have this advantage, if her colonies progress under the new colonial system, as I believe they will, that, though at war with all the rest of the world, she will be able to look to the subordinate nations in alliance with her, and owning allegiance to the same sovereign, who will assist in enabling her to meet the whole world in arms, as she has done before.[2]

There were British statesmen who were equally sanguine. The Colonial Secretary, Lord Carnarvon, moving the second reading of the British North America Bill in the House of Lords on February 19, 1867, said, "We are laying the foundation of a great State—perhaps one which at a future day may even overshadow this country."[3] And the last Governor-in-Chief of the colonies of British North America and first Governor General of the Dominion of Canada, Viscount Monck, argued in effect that Confederation had advanced Canada to something higher than colonial status. In the first instance he supported the proposal to term the new political unit a "Kingdom". The wish for the use of this term existing among the people of British North America was based, he said, "on a consciousness of their increasing importance, and a desire on their part to reconcile their highly prized position in reference to the Crown of England with the natural yearning of a growing people to emerge, at least in name, from the Provincial phase of existence".[4] This proposal was rapidly shot down by the Foreign Secretary, Lord Stanley (later fifteenth Earl of Derby), a spineless Little Englander who was far more interested in the probably adverse reactions of Americans than in the aspirations of colonials. "There is no idea of a new monarchy," he wrote to the British Minister in Washington, "and that may as well be explained. The Colonies will remain Colonies, only confederated for the sake of convenience. If they choose to separate, we on this side shall not object: it is they who protest against the idea. In England separation would be generally popular."[5]

Monck was sufficiently pertinacious to return to the attack on another question. The issue in itself was small enough, though it had large implications: whether the members of "the Queen's Privy Council for Canada" (a creation of the British North America Act) should be styled "Right Honourable" like British Privy Councillors or merely "Honourable" like great numbers of official people in the United States. The decision having been made that "Dominion" should be substituted for the dangerous term "Kingdom", Monck now argued that the former word itself carried a special connotation of status:

I would suggest that the analogy of other parts of H. M.'s Colonial Possessions does not apply to this case.

For the first time in the Colonial history of Great Britain a portion of her Colonial Empire has been elevated by H. M. from the rank of a Province to that of a distinct "Dominion".

I have reason to know that if peculiar local considerations had not in the opinion of some persons rendered it undesirable, the designation would have probably been that of "Kingdom".[6]

Canadian Privy Councillors remained mere "Honourables", as they remain to this day; but the point made by Monck has at least historical interest.

The British North America Act, omitting all reference to the *status* of the new Dominion, likewise had nothing to say about the conduct of foreign relations. The powers assigned to the Dominion Parliament under Section 91 do not include external affairs, simply because in 1867 those affairs were universally regarded, in both Canada and Britain, as the business of the British government. The relations of Canada with the nearby American republic were to be regulated by the Foreign Office in London and handled through the British Legation in Washington; the same procedures applied to dealings with every other foreign nation. Nevertheless, even in 1867 a thoughtful observer could hardly fail to conclude that this system was certain to undergo modification with the passing of the years. Self-government in internal affairs—which already existed in very full measure, even though a foreign observer would have had difficulty in finding this too in the text of the British North America Act—was bound to lead in due time to self-government in external matters. Those "national" aspirations which John A. Macdonald and others voiced in 1865 could not fail to issue in a desire for the control of foreign policy. The process by which the Dominion gradually acquired that control is one of the basic themes of this book. In this, as in other respects, the Act of 1867 is a milestone marking progress made and a starting-post for the next heat. What it said was not much; what it implied was a great deal.

FOREIGN POLICY BEGINS AT HOME

Inevitably, every nation's policy towards its neighbours is largely shaped by conditions within itself. It is fashionable to berate statesmen who speak of foreign questions in terms agreeable to domestic audiences; but particularly in democratic communities, a foreign policy that does not commend itself to the people on whose behalf it is advanced is likely to collapse at an early date.

In Canada it is not difficult to put one's finger on basic conditions that have helped to determine national attitudes towards problems of external policy. As early as 1867 it is possible to see within the country at least three regions with different interests whose influence was certain to be directed in somewhat diverse directions: the Maritime region, represented by the two provinces of Nova Scotia and New Brunswick, which themselves were not identical in their interests and views; the province of Quebec (the former Lower Canada), distinguished by its predominantly French-speaking population; and the inland province of Ontario (formerly Upper Canada), whose people's racial origins were found very largely in the British Isles. More regions and more diversities were in the making. The prairie West, the granary of the future, appears with the acquisition of the Hudson's Bay Company's territories in 1869 and the organization of the province of Manitoba the following year. In 1871 British Columbia entered Confederation, a remote community beyond the Rockies ("a million miles from Ottawa") with a Pacific outlook. In 1873 Prince Edward Island joined, and strengthened the Maritime interest. Except for the establishment of two new prairie provinces (Alberta and Saskatchewan) in 1905, this was the last provincial accession until Newfoundland entered the Canadian union in 1949, bringing another variant to the national pattern.

Geography is powerful; differences of blood are even more so. We have already mentioned the basic fact in this connection: the presence of a large French-speaking population in and around the St. Lawrence valley. The "French fact" has complicated and fundamentally influenced the formation of Canadian policy. We shall meet it constantly in the course of this study.

At Confederation the population of the Dominion, apart from the great Anglo-French division, was on the whole remarkably homogeneous. The first Dominion census (1871) covered the four original provinces only. The total population was 3,485,761. Of those, 2,110,592 reported their origin as the British Isles, the largest group being Irish (846,414) with English and Scottish following in that order. Canadians of French origin numbered 1,082,940, thus amounting to almost exactly half the British total. The only other national group with more than 100,000 members was the Germans, with 202,991, of whom 158,608 lived in Ontario. The balance did not change greatly until the first decade of the twentieth century, when there was relatively large immigration from central and northern Europe. By the census of 1911 the total population stood at 7,206,643. The British-origins group had risen to 3,896,985; it had been considerably reinforced by immigration, including some from the United States. The French community now stood at 2,054,890, its growth having been almost entirely by natural increase. The Germans were still the third-largest group (393,320); but there were now 107,535 "Scandinavians" (not including Finns), 75,681 "Hebrews", 74,963 "Ukrainians", and 43,142 "Russians", plus other considerable national bodies including 45,411 Italians.[7]

These changes were bound to affect the country's outlook on foreign affairs in some degree. It is questionable, however, whether the advent of these newer national bodies had any major influence before 1914. Their numbers were relatively small, their members were often low in the scale of wealth and education, they were dispersed on the land and remote from the seats of power. The disputes over the issues of national policy continued to be conducted mainly between what have often been called in recent times the two "founding races"—the "British" (or, more often, the "English") and the "French".

The attitudes of these two portions of the Canadian people towards their common country's policies will emerge in increasing detail as this study proceeds. Here some general remarks are in order. It was natural that the English-speaking part of the Canadian community should have a general sympathy for the aims of British policy and the interests of British power. The constant and sometimes large infusions of new immigrants from the British Isles certainly tended to strengthen this sympathy. It did not follow, however, that the British group thought as a bloc in these matters. There were, we shall see, infinite variations of opinion within it. No doubt the fact that the Irish were so numerous (they were finally outnumbered by the English only at the census of 1901)* had its own influence; but it must be remembered that the word

* "Racial" origins were not recorded in the census of 1891.

"Irish" itself had very wide variations of meaning. It might signify an origin in Ulster or in the South, and an individual with his roots in either might harbour opinions quite different from those traditionally associated with his own sector. But it is at least worth recalling that the most aggressive and best-organized "British" pressure-group in Canada—the Orange Order, very powerful politically in the province of Ontario—had Irish origins.

The French-Canadian community was certainly more homogeneous, though here, too, it is possible to exaggerate. Except for the Indians and the Eskimo, the French Canadians were the oldest-established Canadians. With comparatively few exceptions, they were the descendants of Frenchmen who had settled in the St. Lawrence valley in the seventeenth century; there had been very little immigration from France since that time. The cohesion of the community was greatly enhanced by its virtually universal allegiance to the Roman Catholic Church. (In 1871, out of a total population in Quebec of 1,191,516, no fewer than 1,019,850 were Roman Catholics.)[8]

Dangerous as it is to generalize, one may venture a few broad comments.

A recent historian writes, "When the French Canadian says '*Je me souviens*',* he not only remembers the days of New France but also the fact that he belongs to a conquered people. This fact is deeply embedded in his consciousness, although he may protest that New France was not conquered by the English but rather abandoned by the French. . . ."[9]

Perhaps it is possible to give a certain definition to French-Canadian attitudes in terms of three world capitals. For London, the seat of the conquering nation of 1759–60, the nineteenth-century French Canadian was likely to feel respect rather than affection. This was probably true even of Sir Wilfrid Laurier, in spite of his law degree from McGill and his deep regard for Gladstonian Liberalism. Paris? The France to which French Canada had once owed allegiance was separated from the Quebec of the Victorian age by both the memory of the abandonment of 1763 and the deep gulf of the Revolution of 1789; and early in the twentieth century the severance was worsened when the Third Republic abrogated Napoleon's concordat with the Papacy and separated Church and State: an unforgivable sin in the eyes of the French-Canadian clergy. Some sentimental attachment there was among Quebec intellectuals; there was no more.

* The motto of the province of Quebec.

For the average French Canadian of 1867, and of a good many decades to come—only in our own age have we seen the beginning of the triumph in Quebec of the materialism long dominant in English-speaking communities—Rome, the home of the Pope, probably commanded more honour and esteem than either London or Paris. In 1868 there was a rather remarkable evidence of this, when a small body of Pontifical Zouaves was raised in Quebec to help defend the Papacy against the Garibaldians. There were only 135 of them (though many more had offered), but 30,000 people saw them off from Montreal. They marched under a flag that bore the maple leaf and the beaver.[10] They did no fighting, but since Garibaldi was a hero to English-speaking communities, the affair emphasized the fact that Quebec saw the world in a rather different light from the rest of Canada and of North America. The contrast between the apparent readiness of many French Canadians to fight for the Pope, and their relative reluctance on later occasions to fight for the British Crown, is interesting. The question arises, however, whether they would have cared to be *conscripted* to fight even for the Pope.

EXTERNAL INFLUENCES AND PRESSURES: THE TRIANGLE

To an extraordinary extent the history of Canada is the history of relations with two other communities: the United Kingdom and the United States. The great republican neighbour won its independence from Britain in 1783, at the end of a long and bitter war. Canada, alone of important communities in the Americas, retained a political connection with a European mother state until the twentieth century, and through the Commonwealth she retains it still. Her modern story as reflected in this book is one of evolution, not revolution: evolution from self-government within the British Empire to independence within the Commonwealth. And throughout this development the giant presence south of the Great Lakes and the 49th parallel has been an infinitely complicating factor. American menaces, American pressures, American examples, and American friendship have all played their parts. Political, military, economic, and social threads have been woven into the curious and complex fabric of Anglo-American and Canadian-American relations.

The extraordinary thing about the North Atlantic Triangle—the phrase was invented by the late Bartlet Brebner[11]—is what a remarkably flexible figure it is: so much depends on the point of it at which you find yourself. It may not be true that from the East Block of the Parliament

Buildings in Ottawa on a clear day you can see Forever; but you can certainly see Washington; and even now you can see London too, though of course much depends on how hard you try. On the other hand, it is notorious that Englishmen have always had trouble descrying Canada through the murk that shrouds their island; and when they do see her the details are apt to be somewhat blurred (after all, even Lord Carnarvon, certainly a good friend of the Dominion, referred in that speech in the House of Lords already quoted to the conference held in 1864 at "Charlotteville"). As for Americans, normally they simply cannot see their northern neighbour at all, however brightly the sun may be shining. The plain fact is that only Canadians have any real awareness of the Triangle.

It is, of course, not at all difficult to see why Britain and the United States are such large objects on Canada's horizon, while Canada is such a small one on theirs. It is mainly a matter of simple statistics. While Canada's population, as already noted, was some 3,500,000 in 1871, that of the United States was nearly 41 million. Canada's had risen to 7,200,000 by 1911, but at the previous year's census the United States had had nearly 92 million people. The United States, then, continued to have roughly a dozen times Canada's population. In wealth the disparity was even greater. The situation concerning the United Kingdom was not very different. Its population was 31,484,000 in 1871, rising to 45,221,000 in 1911.[12] There was a rather less direct correlation of population with national power than in the case of the United States, but that the two things were related could not be doubted. When the British population curve began to level off (the population of England, Wales, and Scotland rose only from 40,831,000 to 42,769,000 between 1911 and 1921),* British power was beginning to wane. But even in 1921 Canada had only 8,788,000 people, and in wealth and power Britain still far outstripped her. (The United States, incidentally, had 105,710,000 people at the census of 1920.)

Canada, then, was a community with a large area (much of which however was, and remains, unproductive), but with few people. In so far as people are power, Canada was a weak state. A century has done little to change this fundamental fact. Let us turn to the political, military, and economic aspects of the country's situation.

* There was no Irish census in 1921. In 1926 the population of Northern Ireland, which had remained part of the United Kingdom, was 1,257,000.

In the early years of Canadian Confederation the Triangle was under unusually severe strain. The American Civil War had ended in 1865 and had left behind it a legacy of Anglo-American ill-will, the worst dispute being over the claims for the damage done by the Confederates' British-built cruiser *Alabama* and her sisters. There had nearly been war when a Northern warship took Confederate envoys off the British steamer *Trent* in 1861, and that crisis did great harm to Anglo-American relations. The tension was heightened when the Confederates made attempts to use Canada as a base against the North in 1864, and the situation was sufficiently menacing to have a definite if scarcely measurable influence upon the movement towards Confederation of the colonies. The end of the Civil War and the rapid disbandment of the great Union armies would have reduced Canadian apprehensions, but unfortunately these events were accompanied by the rise of the hostile Irish-American organization, or organizations, known as the Fenian Brotherhood, one wing of which chose to strike at England by striking Canada.[13]

In June 1866, this body actually attempted invasion on a considerable scale, and there was some bloodshed and enormous excitement before the effort collapsed. The United States government intervened to check the movement against Canada only belatedly and with evident reluctance; and although the Fenians never succeeded in organizing so extensive an attack again, it is important to realize that they were actively organizing aggression until 1871, and that throughout this period Canadian border communities were threatened with armed attack from the United States. There was another raid, on the Vermont border south of Montreal, in May 1870, and a minor incursion into Manitoba the following year. For six years the Fenians poisoned the atmosphere of relations between the British Empire and the United States.[14]

It is also important to remember that during these years Britain had a direct military involvement in Canada. Since about 1850 the Imperial government had been seeking to reduce its garrison commitment in British North America, a commitment for which the British taxpayer met the whole bill in spite of the large degree of self-government which the colonies enjoyed after 1847–48. The colonies, however, had no control of policy towards the United States; and it was arguable that if the mother country retained that control she had an obligation to protect them against the possible consequences of her policies. The Civil War, and particularly the *Trent* affair, led to large reinforcements of British troops being sent to British North America, and in 1866 the Fenian menace had a similar result. At Confederation there were over 15,000 British regulars stationed in the Dominion.[15]

For many reasons the British government was now resolved to end this situation; and Gladstone's Liberal ministry, which took office late in 1868, succeeded in doing so. In April 1869, Canada was told that there would be a large reduction in the garrison, and that although Halifax would continue to be "considered as an Imperial Station", the presence of British troops in Ontario, Quebec, and New Brunswick "must be considered a temporary arrangement". In February 1870, it was announced that after that year the Halifax garrison would be the only troops in Canada. These plans were carried through despite the opposition of the Queen, the Commander-in-Chief (the Duke of Cambridge), and the Canadian government. What is perhaps more to the point, continued Fenian threats and a crisis with the United States over the *Alabama* claims were not allowed to interfere with them. Mr. Gladstone and his colleagues were clearly determined to withdraw British forces from the interior of North America. There is ample evidence that they were powerfully influenced by the extent to which military commitments there paralysed British action in Europe. In November 1871, the fortress of Quebec was evacuated and British troops held no place in Canada* except the naval base of Halifax.[16]

One additional point should be made. It was specifically stated that these arrangements applied only under conditions of peace, and were "in no way intended to alter or diminish the obligations which exist on both sides in case of foreign war".[17] Britain, in other words, still recognized the obligation to defend all the Queen's possessions against American or other attack. But the withdrawal saved her a great deal of money; and it is an undoubted fact that many Britons believed that the removal of her troops from Canada improved the chances for permanent peace between the British Empire and the United States.

The continued Fenian threats, the American tolerance of them, the British government's evident reluctance to put strong pressure on Washington to end them, and the proposed withdrawal of the British troops, together bred strong resentment among Canadians against both the other points of the Triangle. After the Fenian raid of May 1870, the Canadian cabinet went on record as expressing "the deep sense entertained by the

* Over twenty years passed before a British garrison was established at the Pacific naval station of Esquimalt on Vancouver Island.

people of the Dominion of all shades of party, that they have not received from Her Majesty's Government that support and protection which, as loyal subjects of Her Majesty, they have a right to claim".[18] On June 3 the Toronto *Weekly Globe* printed three editorial articles attacking the United States, and two assailing British policy.

Canada, we have said, opposed and regretted the withdrawal of the British forces. But she took, on the whole, very little action of her own to replace them. It is true that the past fifteen years had witnessed great improvement of the Canadian militia. Beginning with the reduction of the regular garrison during the Crimean War (1855) a small force of volunteers had been superimposed upon the old paper militia, based on universal service, which had not been uniformed, armed, or trained. The Civil War and Fenian emergencies caused a steady enlargement and development of this force, and the Dominion of Canada in its first year of life spent $761,000 on its own defence, whereas before 1855 the old Province of Canada spent annually only about £2,000 and the Maritime colonies even less.[19] But the only concrete reaction to the departure of the British troops in 1871 was to organize two artillery batteries, in effect regular units, which would have the dual function of custody of the fortifications at Quebec and Kingston and instruction of the militia. This, with the maintenance of a small force in Manitoba and some other special items, raised the Dominion's militia expenditure to $1,779,000 for the fiscal year ending June 30, 1872, the highest point it was to reach for many years.[20]

It should be emphasized that the militia as it had been developed to that time was clearly intended to be a force auxiliary to the British regular army; and after that army disappeared from the Canadian scene the nature of the militia was not altered to meet the changed situation. It remained a force of horse, foot, and artillery, without the "departmental" or administrative corps—medical, supply and transport, etc.—which an army requires to enable it to take the field. Even engineers were almost entirely lacking. The British Army had formerly provided these elements; now they simply did not exist in Canada outside the fortress of Halifax. Except for the two artillery batteries—which were not supplemented by small cavalry and infantry units until 1883—there were no regular soldiers. The Canadian military organization consisted almost entirely of citizen troops, very inadequately trained and with increasingly obsolete equipment. The general efficiency of the force, fairly respectable in 1870 as a result of the Fenian troubles, declined once those troubles were over. The fact is that the new Canadian nation very largely lacked the apparatus of self-defence usually considered a necessary accompaniment of national existence.

The reasons for this are interesting to speculate upon. One obviously was the habit of relying upon the mother country, a habit which survived the withdrawal of the British troops; and, incidentally, Canadians certainly tended to over-estimate the mother country's power vis-à-vis the United States in North America. Another was the influence of an historical myth: the belief that the Canadian militia had played the major part in defeating the American attack on Canada in 1812–14, whereas the work had been mainly done by the British regular services. Canadians, moved by this legend, tended to believe that military preparation in advance of an actual crisis was unnecessary; that, in the words of the *Globe*, "Canadians can dispense with a standing army because they possess the best possible constituents for a defensive force in themselves. The finest soldiers are men whose own stake and interest in the conflict impel them to respond to a call to arms."[21] In actual fact, the successful defence of Canada in 1812 had been due mainly to the fact that the British defenders were trained and experienced professionals, supported by a naval force provided on the Great Lakes before war broke out; whereas the American attackers were in the main amateurs and the United States was ill-prepared for the conflict. It is fair to say that the Canadian people at the time of Confederation were unmilitary and essentially ignorant of military affairs; and they and most of their politicians continued to be so for a long time to come.

Speaking of legends, one of the most durable legends concerning Canadian-American relations began to acquire some historical substance only at the moment when British forces evacuated central Canada. It has often been assumed that the celebrated "unfortified frontier" existed from the end of the War of 1812, or at any rate from the acceptance of the Rush-Bagot Agreement of 1817 limiting naval armaments on the Lakes. It did not. Many fortifications were built on both sides of the border during the half-century following that agreement; the United States considerably improved its defences on the Great Lakes and Lake Champlain during the Civil War. But fort construction finally ended almost simultaneously with the British abandonment of Quebec in 1871.[22] The British, who had built and maintained the forts on the Canadian side, were gone; the Canadians were unwilling to spend money on such works and had little appreciation of their military value. The Americans, by nature the stronger party in North America, did not feel the need of artificial defences to make them stronger still; and by great good fortune—for the two things were really not connected—the British withdrawal from the interior coincided in time with the liquidation of the American grievances against Britain resulting from the Civil War.

We shall have something to say in the next chapter about the Treaty of Washington of 1871. Here it is enough to remark that it is the great watershed of Anglo-American and Canadian-American relations, separating the era of wars and threats of wars from that of gradually increasing friendship and co-operation. After that treaty there was a genuinely undefended border, in great part because the causes of tension between the two neighbouring communities had been removed. The boundary disputes in Maine and Oregon had been settled (though Alaska was still in the future). Also, the great internal disputes on both sides of the border which had invited external intervention had been disposed of. In British America the relationship of the colonies to the mother country had been peacefully settled by the concession of responsible government. In the United States the slavery question had been cleared away, though not without a great civil war. The way was open for friendly competition in the arts of peace.

One thus arrives naturally at the question of trade.

FOREST, FARM AND FACTORY

In 1867 external trade was already vital to the Canadian economy. And Confederation came at the end of a period in which British North American exporters were little hampered by tariff walls in approaching their chief markets. Here again we meet the Triangle: those markets were the United Kingdom and the United States. Britain had been a free-trade country since the late 1840s. Canadian goods no longer enjoyed tariff preferences there, as they had before the advent of free trade, but they could enter Britain freely if they could compete with their rivals for the market. Canada's greatest export to Britain in the first year of Confederation, and for long afterwards, was forest products—timber and lumber, for pulpwood and newsprint were far in the future. These exports amounted to $9,354,000 in 1867–68. Agricultural produce exported to Britain in the same fiscal year totalled only $4,056,000; the wheat economy had not yet come into existence. Total exports to the United Kingdom came to $17,905,000.[23]

In 1854 Lord Elgin's famous Reciprocity Treaty opened the United

States market to a wide variety of Canadian products. Between that date and the Civil War the United States was not far from being a free-trading community, thanks largely to the influence of the agricultural South in Congress. But in the same year in which the treaty was signed the Republican party was formed. Protection became an increasingly important plank in its platform; and after it won the presidential election of 1860, and the Southerners withdrew from Congress as a result of secession, the future of reciprocity was doubtful. Business was in the saddle now. Northern resentment against Britain and Canada resulting from the incidents of the Civil War presumably contributed to rendering the treaty unpopular; the United States denounced it in 1865, and it came to an end on St. Patrick's Day, 1866—a not unsuitable date in the year that marked the high tide of Fenianism. It was to be nearly seventy years before another general trade agreement came into effect between Canada and the United States.

In spite of this, trade for a time continued to follow the established channels. At Confederation, the United States was Canada's best customer; it bought $22,387,000 worth of Canadian merchandise as compared with the total of nearly $18,000,000 for Great Britain already noted. In the case of the United States, agricultural exports ($8,136,000) were slightly greater than those of forest products ($7,842,000). But in 1873–74 the proportion of exports as between the two great customers changed; the total to Britain rose to $35,769,000, while that to the United States was only $30,380,000. Except for two years in 1887–89, Britain thereafter was by far Canada's best customer for the rest of the century and long afterwards.[24]

It is a somewhat curious fact that roughly the reverse was true of Canadian imports from Britain (see Appendix A). At Confederation Canada was importing more from the United Kingdom than from the United States: respectively, $37,617,325 and $22,660,132 in the fiscal year 1867–68. But in 1875–76 the United States drew ahead, and by the end of the century (1899–1900) imports from Britain were only $44,279,983 as compared with $102,080,177 from the United States; this in spite of the fact that there had been a measurable increase in British imports since Canada introduced the British preferential tariff in 1897 (see below, page 53).[25]

Viewing the situation from the United States side, the figures of Canadian purchases from the U.S. are impressive, though Americans in general do not seem to have been really aware of them at any time. In 1870 the total of American export trade was $471 millions; of this more than half ($248 millions) went to Britain, by a large margin the United States' best customer. British North America absorbed $25 millions of U.S. exports, roughly one-third of the $79 millions that went to the Americas as a whole. Since that time American exports to Canada have increased steadily, both absolutely and relatively to other countries.

Looking far ahead, since the Second World War Canada has occupied the place as the United States' best customer once held by Britain. In 1957, American export trade as a whole was worth $20,810 millions; of this the Americas accounted for $8,720 millions, and of this in turn $3,905 millions went to Canada; Britain's purchases had fallen to $1,100 millions. Ten years later, in Canada's centennial year, U.S. exports to Canada had risen to $7,146 millions.[26] Yet how many Americans were or are aware of Canada as a customer to whom they sell annually far more than they sell to all the countries of South America put together, and roughly the same quantity of goods that is bought by the whole of Latin America? Their ignorance and lack of interest were painfully exemplified on September 16, 1971, when President Nixon said in a press conference that he had "found" that "Japan is our biggest customer in the world and we are their biggest customer in the world".[27] In this respect at least Nixon was a thoroughly typical American.

Part of the explanation for the American lack of awareness is the fact that to the United States, with its huge domestic market, foreign trade is a matter of somewhat marginal importance. For Canada, on the other hand, export trade is a matter of, one might almost say, life and death. Certainly in this generation wheat sales have affected the life or death of governments. For all countries economic policy is a vital aspect of foreign policy, simply because it affects the livelihoods of so many citizens. For Canada it is particularly vital, and much of this book must be concerned with economic matters.

At the time of Canadian Confederation, Great Britain, the homeland of the Industrial Revolution, was still the "workshop of the world", confident in the superior efficiency of her factories and feeling no need of protection for them. The business interest was now in control of British fiscal policy, and free trade was its gospel. But the United States was already challenging British industrial supremacy, and another challenge was soon to come from Germany. The tariff law passed during the Civil War had made the United States a protectionist country, and Bismarck was to do the same for the new German Empire in 1879. Canada was on a lower rung of the economic ladder than these much more populous and advanced countries; but it was already evident that the Canadian business community looked forward to an industrial future for the Dominion, that its conception of national fiscal policy was closer to the American than to the British model, and that it had much political support.

In 1858 and 1859 the Province of Canada had enacted tariff laws of a protectionist tendency, with rates high enough—particularly those of 1859—to attract angry notice both from English manufacturers and from American opponents of the Reciprocity Treaty. The primary object of these laws was to increase the province's revenue in a time of depression; but there was an active protectionist agitation going on and the government countenanced it. Alexander Galt, the minister responsible for the 1859 measure, said in introducing it, "it will undoubtedly be a subject of gratification to the Government if they find that the duties absolutely required to meet their engagements should incidentally benefit and encourage the production, in the country, of many of those articles which we now import".[28] The note thus struck was to be heard many times in the ensuing decades.

At Confederation the industries of Canada were all infants. Manufacturing business in Canada was little business. In the census year 1871, the total number of Canadians recorded as wage-earners in manufacturing was 187,942. The value of the product of their toil was $221,617,733—a figure which seems rather impressive at first glance. But food products accounted for $56,689,227 of this, and timber and lumber "and their remanufactures" for $41,065,971. These were the largest "industries"; the value of iron and steel products totalled only $13,928,855. Exports of manufactures to Britain that year were under a million dollars, and to the United States just over that figure.[29] The businessmen of Sheffield who had taken such umbrage at Galt's tariff of 1859 would have laughed at the idea of the products of Canadian factories finding their way to England; and indeed this did not happen on any scale until 1914–18, when shells from new Canadian steel plants fed the British guns on the Western Front. In 1867, and for a long time afterwards, the Canadians were a people who lived, predominantly, on and from the land and by selling its products. But some of them had ambitions to be more than just an agricultural, lumbering, and trading community. Among those of English speech, at least, many had their eyes on the two great business-dominated English-speaking industrial societies against which English-speaking Canadians have measured themselves ever since. Their country too, they told one another optimistically, would be an industrial giant.

CHAPTER TWO

MACDONALD AND THE PURSUIT OF NATIONAL POLICIES, 1867-1896

"DIPLOMACY IN LEADING STRINGS" THE WASHINGTON SETTLEMENT

The first task of the government of the new Dominion of Canada in 1867 was to round out the country, so far as might be, to its "natural frontiers". The Prime Minister, Sir John A. Macdonald, as he now became, addressed himself to it. On June 16, 1869 he wrote, "We hope to close our Session this week, and a very mountainous Session it has been! We have quietly and almost without observation annexed all the Country between here and the Rocky Mountains, as well as Newfoundland".[1] This was premature. Newfoundland, as we have already seen, did not come in for exactly eighty years; and the annexation of the Hudson's Bay Company territories between Lake Superior and the Rockies was not consummated without difficulties in which the fear of United States intervention was a serious complication.

Before Canada could establish its authority in the Red River Settlement, a provisional government headed by Louis Riel seized power there. The apprehensions of the local population were ultimately quieted by the concession of full provincial status for the territory. More dangerous were the annexationist views held by many people in Minnesota and in certain quarters in Washington. Hamilton Fish, President Grant's Secretary of State, was interested in the possibility of the United States getting possession of the Hudson's Bay Company lands, and indeed told the British minister that he believed that a large majority of Canadians favoured the annexation of their country to the United States. The Fenians presented a particular peril. These circumstances led Macdonald to feel that it was vital that any force sent from Canada to Red River should be a mixed force of British regulars and Canadian militia, to show that "England and

Canada are acting in complete accord and unity in the retention of British North America under British sovereignty".

When the Red River Expedition under Colonel Garnet Wolseley was dispatched in the summer of 1870, it was such a mixed force as Macdonald had desired; but as soon as it had established itself peacefully at Fort Garry the British element was hastily withdrawn by the orders of its government and the settlement was left under the protection of the Canadian volunteers alone. There had been a moment when the whole enterprise was jeopardized by the temporary refusal of Washington to allow the expedition's ships to pass through the American canal at Sault Ste. Marie, even though it had been intended that the troops and warlike stores should be landed and portaged across on the Canadian side of the river.[2] As it turned out, the expedition was a successful stroke of policy, effectively establishing Canadian possession of the great west. But the difficulties of communication between Ontario and Manitoba were such that that possession could not be said to be finally secure until the completion of a railway north of Lake Superior; and that did not happen until 1885.

On March 30, 1867 the United States signed a treaty agreeing to purchase Alaska from Russia for $7,200,000. It seems to have been a sudden act, the result of an unexpected opportunity and of the expansionist views of William H. Seward, Secretary of State under Lincoln and Andrew Johnson.[3] Thus the United States acquired a new frontier with British North America and a territory that severely limited future Canadian access to the Pacific. In other circumstances, Canada might herself have looked forward to the acquisition of Alaska. But there was no possibility of such a thing in 1867. It was inconceivable that Britain, at a moment when she was actively engaged in reducing her responsibilities in North America, should entertain any notion of the sort, even if Russia had been willing to sell to her. As for Canada (disregarding the fact that the sale to the United States took place three months before the Dominion came into existence) she had more than enough on her plate in acquiring and organizing for herself nearer territories already under the British flag.

American motivation in the purchase of Alaska, apart from the imperialism of Seward, is a matter of interest. Not surprisingly in the light of the general anti-British tone of the time, the idea that the acquisition of the territory would encircle the colony of British Columbia and thereby ensure its annexation was fairly prominent among the arguments for it presented in representative American newspapers. But it was much less prominent than two others: a feeling of friendship for Russia, which had showed sympathy for the North in the Civil War, and the view that Alaska at seven million dollars was a good bargain. These seem to have been the opinions that made possible the ratification of the treaty in 1867 and the appropriation of funds to implement it the following year.[4] When British Columbia entered the Canadian confederation in 1871, the territorial pattern of Northwestern North America assumed its final form—except for the disputed boundary which was to cause so much ill-feeling during the succeeding generation.

Before the union agreement with British Columbia was finally ratified by the colony's legislature and the Canadian Parliament, the Dominion had been concerned for the first time in a foreign diplomatic negotiation of great importance: the making of the Treaty of Washington with the United States. Two attempts at settlement of the dangerous Anglo-American issues left by the Civil War had failed, the second one (the Johnson–Clarendon Convention, 1869) after an attack in the U.S. Senate by Charles Sumner, who estimated the *Alabama* claims at an astronomical total. It was now agreed that the problem should be attacked by a Joint High Commission of five members from each party. The American delegation was headed by Mr. Secretary Fish, the British one by Lord de Grey and Ripon, Lord President of the Council in Gladstone's cabinet. Sir John Macdonald was one of the British commissioners. Obviously he was chosen because he was Prime Minister of Canada; the choice was a striking innovation and a recognition of Canada's new importance; yet he went to Washington not as a representative of Canada, but as an appointee of the British government. When the appointment was announced, Lord Monck, the former Governor General, an admirer of Macdonald, wrote to congratulate him:

> You have a great work committed to you, and if you succeed in accommodating all the different interests involved, you will extend the sphere, though you cannot increase the amount of your reputation—
>
> The man who has created a "Dominion" is to be trusted with the care of its external interests and I hope this experiment on your part of diplomacy in leading strings will convince you that you are nearly strong enough to walk alone.[5]

The letter is interesting: first, because it indicates Monck's belief that the Dominion's destiny was independence—and therefore control of its own external relations—at an early date; second, because of its recognition of the difficulties of Macdonald's task. He was the servant of two masters, and in fact he did not succeed in "accommodating all the different interests involved". His position at Washington was to be extremely embarrassing.

The understanding—it seems to have been first suggested by Secretary Fish, in a conversation with the British Minister in Washington, Sir Edward Thornton, on September 26, 1870[6]—was that the Joint High Commission was to attempt to settle all the issues outstanding between the United States and the British Empire. The supreme question was the *Alabama* claims. There was a minor but unpleasant boundary dispute, over the San Juan Islands between Vancouver Island and the American mainland, arising out of conflicting interpretations of the Oregon Treaty of 1846. This had caused a nasty crisis in 1859. Canadians assumed that there would be discussion of compensation for the Fenian raids. And there were a number of questions resulting from the demise of the Reciprocity Treaty. By this Americans had lost the privilege of free navigation of the St. Lawrence River, and Canadians that of free navigation of Lake Michigan.

Above all, there was the problem of the Canadian inshore fisheries. To sum this up quickly, in 1818 an Anglo-American convention had been signed excluding Americans "for ever" from fishing in the territorial waters of the Maritime provinces (though not on the south coast of Newfoundland, or on the coast of Labrador or of the Magdalen Islands).[7] In 1854 the Reciprocity Treaty opened the inshore Maritime waters to American fishermen, British subjects receiving similar privileges in U.S. waters as far south as the 36th parallel. The denunciation of the treaty restored the situation of 1818. Americans, however, continued to fish in Canadian inshore waters, and the Canadian authorities, after an interval during which they experimented with a licence system, fitted out cruisers to arrest vessels so engaged. The result was serious friction. In 1870 President Grant's annual message to Congress[8] made a famous and truculent reference to the problem and offered a studied insult to Canada. A *propos* of the affairs of Spanish America it remarked, "The time is not probably far distant when, in the natural course of events, the European political connection with this continent will cease." It then went seriously to work on Britain and Canada:

I regret to say that no conclusion has been reached for the adjustment of the claims against Great Britain, growing out of the course adopted by that government during the rebellion....

The course pursued by the Canadian authorities toward the fishermen of the United States during the past season has not been marked by a friendly feeling. By the first article of the convention of 1818, between Great Britain and the United States, it was agreed that the inhabitants of the United States should have forever, in common with British subjects, the right of taking fish in certain waters therein defined. In the waters not included in the limits named in the convention (within three miles of the British coast) it has been the custom for many years to give to intruding fishermen of the United States a reasonable warning of their violation of the technical rights of Great Britain. The imperial government is understood to have delegated the whole or a share of its jurisdiction or control of these in-shore fishing grounds to the colonial authority known as the Dominion of Canada, and this semi-independent but irresponsible agent has exercised its delegated powers in an unfriendly way. Vessels have been seized without notice or warning, in violation of the custom previously prevailing....

A like unfriendly disposition has been manifested on the part of Canada in the maintenance of a claim to exclude the citizens of the United States from the navigation of the St. Lawrence.... It is hoped that the government of Great Britain will see the justice of abandoning the narrow and inconsistent claim to which her Canadian provinces have urged her adherence.

Such was the atmosphere of Anglo-American and Canadian-American relations on the eve of the Washington negotiation. The importance of resolving the fisheries question is fairly evident.

It is perhaps unfortunate, however, that Canadian historians[9] have tended to write about the events in Washington almost entirely in terms of the fisheries. The British delegation had, as we have seen, many issues to deal with, and their basic task was really the restoration of good relations with the United States. To this the fisheries were important, but less important than the *Alabama* matter. To appreciate the British representatives' difficulties it is necessary to look at the whole negotiation and the whole treaty which resulted—a complicated document of forty-three articles.[10]

It is nevertheless true that the fisheries question was in practice the most difficult which confronted the commissioners. Statistically speaking, it took up seventeen of their sessions, whereas the various American claims against Britain took ten and the San Juan boundary four.[11] And the reason was that whereas the discussion of the other questions was essentially bilateral, that of the fisheries was triangular: Canada's position and interests were different from those of the other two parties, and Macdonald found himself in a permanent minority of one. The fact is, it is now pretty clear, that the Canadian government, and probably the Canadian people, overestimated the value of the fisheries as a bargaining tool. Their policy was to use them to obtain a renewal of the Reciprocity Treaty—or of something as close to it as possible. Macdonald's Minister of Finance, Sir Francis Hincks, wrote to him, "Our equivalent that should be pressed is full *reciprocal trade*. . . . We want reciprocity *as we had it*".[12] The Americans would not hear of it; the world, and Congress, had changed since 1854. What they were most prepared to consider was a cash payment for access to the fisheries; this idea, curiously enough, seems to have been first suggested to Sir Edward Thornton by the Governor General, Lord Lisgar, without consultation with his ministers.[13]

There is no point in describing all the details of the contention, which became very bitter between Macdonald and the other members of the British delegation. Each party was, inevitably perhaps, working behind the other's back: Macdonald communicating with his cabinet colleagues in Ottawa and receiving their "instructions" (usually along lines indicated by himself); de Grey cabling and writing to the Foreign Secretary without Macdonald's knowledge. In one of these letters de Grey went so far as to accuse Macdonald of "a pretty strong amount of treachery towards us".[14] Although Macdonald never knew it, he was himself the victim of an action perhaps more justly called treachery: the Governor General, Lord Lisgar, was carrying on a private correspondence with Sir Stafford Northcote, one of the British commissioners, in which he revealed Macdonald's confidential letters to himself and to members of the cabinet and abused his First Minister. "The letters," he wrote, "are the letters of a Huckster."[15]

The British government, with which Macdonald was able to communicate through Ottawa, was rather more disposed to support the Canadian attitude than were its commissioners in Washington; on March 11 it cabled the Governor General, "We never had any intention of selling the inshore fisheries of Canada without [Canada's] consent."[16] But in the end, after further sharp exchanges between Macdonald and his fellow commissioners, "consent" boiled down to a requirement that the Canadian Parliament should approve the fisheries articles; and the government in London, disregarding continuing Canadian objections, directed its representatives (April 21) "to negotiate on the basis of free fish* and arbitration or an additional sum".[17] The Americans had lately offered this. Macdonald, after considering resigning from the commission, stayed on and, justifying his action by the fact that he was a British representative and acting under London's instructions, signed the treaty with the other commissioners on May 8, 1871.

The fishery articles of the treaty granted American citizens the right to fish in the territorial waters of Quebec, Nova Scotia, New Brunswick, and Prince Edward Island, British subjects being given the same rights in American waters north of the 39th parallel. Fish and fish oil produced by the fisheries of Canada, Prince Edward Island, or the United States were to be reciprocally admitted into these countries free of duty. Additional compensation, if any, to be paid by the United States for access to the fisheries was to be settled by an international board of three commissioners, one named by Britain, one by the United States, and the third by agreement between the two, or failing this by the Emperor of Austria. These arrangements were to come into effect "as soon as the laws required to carry them into operation shall have been passed by the Imperial Parliament of Great Britain, by the Parliament of Canada, and by the Legislature of Prince Edward's Island, on the one hand, and by the Congress of the United States on the other". They were to last for ten years from the date they came into operation, and thereafter until two years after either Britain or the United States gave notice of a desire to terminate them.

The same time-limits applied to subsidiary arrangements: free navigation of Lake Michigan for British subjects; and bonding privileges for citizens of both parties in moving goods through each other's territory. The navigation of the St. Lawrence was conceded to Americans "forever", in exchange for similar freedom for British subjects on the Yukon, Porcupine, and Stikine rivers in Alaska; and the two contracting governments undertook to urge upon Canada and the American states respectively that British subjects and American citizens should be permitted to use the St. Lawrence and other canals in the vicinity of the border on a basis of equality.

On the great question of the *Alabama* claims, the treaty began with the statement that the Queen had authorized her representatives "to ex-

* That is, the free admission of Canadian fish to the American market.

press in a friendly spirit, the regret felt by Her Majesty's Government for the escape, under whatever circumstances, of the *Alabama* and other vessels from British ports, and for the depredations committed by those vessels". Having thus cleared the air, at some cost to British pride, the commissioners proceeded to provide for an international tribunal of arbitration to consider the claims and decide whether Britain was justly liable to make payments to the United States to discharge them, and if so what the amount should be. It was further agreed that the arbitrators should be governed by rules laid down in the treaty concerning the obligations of neutral governments, although the British government declined to accept these rules as a statement of principles of international law in effect during the Civil War. It is generally considered that by agreeing to arbitration under these rules the British government ensured an award against itself.

With respect to the San Juan boundary the treaty provided for another arbitration, this time by the Emperor of Germany. William I was to be invited to decide as between the British claim that the boundary should run through Rosario Straits, and the American claim that it should follow the Canal de Haro, "which of those claims is most in accordance" with the treaty of 1846. A compromise settlement was thus ruled out. Sir John A. Macdonald seems to have played little part in the San Juan discussion or indeed any part of the negotiations except that dealing with the fisheries; his recent biographer, Donald Creighton, does not even mention the San Juan question. Technically, of course, it was not a Canadian matter, for British Columbia was not yet part of Canada. But the union was to be completed long before the Emperor announced his award—which accepted the American contention and gave San Juan Island to the United States—in October 1872.[18]

There was nothing in the treaty about Canada's claim for compensation for the Fenian raids. The American commissioners had refused to admit that this lay within the Joint High Commission's terms of reference. As Macdonald expressed it,[19] they argued "that the correspondence only speaks of the mutual claims of British subjects and American citizens, and that the Fenian claims would be claims by the Governments of England and Canada".* The British clearly felt that they could not insist on

* The correspondence which formed the agenda of the Commission is in *Foreign Relations of the United States, 1871*, pp. 495-98. The record of the initial meeting of February 27 notes, "The commissioners further determined that the discussion

the point without wrecking the whole negotiation, which they could not afford to do. What they did do was suggest that Great Britain might compensate Canada for the Fenian claims. This idea would seem to have been in the air for a long time, for Gladstone had written to his Foreign Secretary in October 1870, "If we could sweeten the *Alabama* question for the United States by bringing in Canada (the fisheries), perhaps we might also sweeten the fisheries question for Canada by paying her compensation for the charges of the Fenian raids. It would perhaps be awkward to do this except as part of a final settlement with the United States."[20] It was a long time before London could be brought to agree that the compensation should take the form Macdonald desired—a guarantee of a loan for railways and canals. The offer, when it came, did "sweeten" the Washington treaty in the mouth of the Canadian Parliament, and made it easier to achieve the approval of the fishery clauses by a large majority.[21]

The Washington negotiation is an interesting, indeed a fascinating, episode, so important to our subject as to justify treating it at some length even in this short survey. It illustrated in a classic manner just how difficult the triangular relationship could be for the weakest of the three parties.

Macdonald at Washington took the attitude that Canada was being made a victim of the British determination to achieve a settlement. "I must say," he wrote to Sir Charles Tupper, "that I am greatly disappointed at the course taken by the British Commissioners. They seem to have only one thing on their minds—that is, to go home to England with a treaty in their pockets, settling everything, no matter at what cost to Canada."[22] And in one of those letters that aroused Lord Lisgar's scorn he wrote angrily, "There is a craven fear of the United States on the part of England."[23] When Lord de Grey argued that more than mere "commercial" considerations were at stake in the negotiation, Macdonald replied "that, while I admitted the importance to Canada, as well as to England, of friendly relations with the United States, I could not suppose that those relations were endangered by the maintenance of an undisputed right."[24] On their side the Englishmen were convinced that Macdonald's obstinacy was endangering a settlement that was at least as vital to Canada as it

might include such other matters as might be mutually agreed upon." Clearly, however, the Americans were not ready to "agree" to include the Fenian claims.

was to Britain. Lord de Grey told him "that Canada was more interested in the avoidance of unfriendly relations with the United States than any other portion of the British Empire, and would suffer most if those relations become hostile."[25] He might have added that if war came it was Britain who would bear the main weight of the defence of Canada.

It is fair to say that there was an unpleasant degree of truth in both the Canadian and the British assertions. On balance, however, in retrospect perhaps the British have somewhat the better of the case. Frightened they doubtless were; but they had reason to be. If Canada made sacrifices under the treaty, so did Britain; in the end she paid $15,500,000 to clear the *Alabama* claims. And although Canada's property was disposed of contrary to the declared wishes of her government, the bargain she got appears at this distance not too disadvantageous. When the Fishery Commission finally met in 1877 to decide the value of the concession she had been forced to make, it awarded her $5,500,000—a sum large enough to be severely criticized in the United States, and to contribute to the denunciation of the fishery clauses of the treaty by that country in 1885.[26]

As for the Americans, they held their usual winning cards in any serious dispute with Britain: their great local superiority in strength in North America, and the fact that Britain could never expect to confront the United States without encountering simultaneous trouble in Europe, and vice versa. The Foreign Secretary had written to the Queen in May 1869, "There is not the smallest doubt that if we were engaged in a Continental quarrel we should immediately find ourselves at war with the United States."[27] Knowing well that it was virtually impossible for Britain to go to war with them, and perceiving her urgent desire for a settlement in America that would leave her hands free in Europe, the Americans had only to be firm to achieve a diplomatic victory.

Though flowery things were said at the signing ceremony, it is doubtful whether any of the principal actors fully appreciated in 1871 just how important a landmark the Treaty of Washington was to be in the relations of the United States with Britain and Canada. Certainly, if one can believe his own copious record of the negotiation, John A. Macdonald does not seem to have lifted his eyes from the fisheries to look at the larger issues. But almost exactly a year elapsed between the signing day and the day—May 3, 1872—when Macdonald rose in his place in the Canadian House of Commons to move for leave to bring in a bill to carry the Canadian provisions of the treaty into effect. His language now was different from what he had said to his British colleagues in Washington.[28] In fact, he advanced the British arguments that he had scouted when they were put to him by Lord de Grey. The reader must judge whether he was activated by mere political expediency, or whether the passage of twelve months had given him a new perspective on events.

Macdonald reminded the House frankly of the fact that as long as there were dangerous difficulties between the United States and Britain, the latter could not "press or assert her opinions" in European matters with the freedom that was desirable:

It was in his opinion of greater consequence to Canada than [to] England that the *Alabama* question should be settled. (Cheers.) England had promised us, and we all placed faith in that promise, that in case of war between Canada and an enemy the whole force of the Empire should be exerted in our behalf. (Cheers.) But what would be the position of England, and what of Canada, if she was called upon to use the whole force of the Empire to defend us when engaged in a conflict elsewhere with some European nation? (Cheers.) Canada would be, as a matter of course, the battleground of the two nations. We should be the sufferers, our country would be devastated, our people slaughtered, our prosperity destroyed; and while England would under all circumstances, he believed, faithfully perform her promise to the utmost of her power, she would be greatly impeded in her desire by hostilities elsewhere....

... As an American statesman said to him, the rejection of this Treaty by the Senate meant war, not war to-day or to-morrow or at any given period but whenever England was so engaged elsewhere. (Hear, hear.) England's difficulty would be the United States' opportunity.

Macdonald proceeded to describe his own position and difficulties during this pioneer Canadian effort in diplomacy, in terms that many a Canadian statesman could have echoed during the century ahead:

They might therefore imagine the solemn considerations pressing on his mind as well as those of his colleagues if, by any unwise course or rigid adherence to one's own preconceived opinions or even to our own pecuniary interests, we would risk and destroy for ever all hope of a peaceful solution of the difficulty between two great nations. (Cheers.) Still, he did not forget he was selected from his acquaintance with Canadian politics, and supposed acquaintance with Canadian interests, and he had continually before his mind not only Imperial questions, but the interests of the Dominion, for whose defence he was specially there. The difficulty of his position was, that if he gave undue prominence to the interests of Canada, he might, firstly, be held in England, and by his colleagues at Washington, to be taking a purely Canadian, selfish, and narrow view, regardless of the interests of what was a whole, and of Canada as part, of the Empire. And on the other hand he had to guard against keeping his eye too closely on Imperial interests, that he should do all he was able for those of his country—Canada.

These statements present a much more balanced view of the treaty than Macdonald had taken, or at least expressed, during the negotiations. Canada had an interest in the fisheries and in obtaining reciprocal trade with the United States if she could; but she had a still greater interest in the restoration of good relations, and the maintenance of peace, between the United States and Great Britain. Macdonald was on sound ground when in his peroration he appealed to the House to accept the treaty "with all its imperfections . . . for the sake of peace"; and the House made a sound decision when it approved the bill on second reading by 121 votes to 55.[29]

One special point is worthy of exploration. It has been argued that the Washington treaty amounted in effect to United States recognition of the North American state system as it existed after Canadian Confederation —recognition of the Dominion of Canada and Canadian independence of the United States as accepted facts. Allan Nevins, in his excellent life of Hamilton Fish, says that Fish was inspired by "the ideal of not two but three great kindred democracies at peace, their differences justly settled, their paths stretching side by side into the remotest future".[30] How well founded is this flight of historical eloquence?

It is well established that Fish himself had earlier, as we have already noticed, formed a conviction that a majority of Canadians favoured separation from Britain; and he recorded that he approached the British Minister (September 18, 1870) with an inquiry as to whether the British government would "agree to submit the question of independence to the Provinces, and to open the fisheries in connection with a reference of the question of liability of Great Britain for the *Alabama*", to which Thornton replied that no such proposition could be made except on the colonies' own request.[31] This appears to have been the last of several occasions on which Fish spoke in such terms; and he proceeded shortly afterwards (above, page 20) to make the suggestion that led to the Joint High Commission.

The project for a Commission raised the question, what would be the attitude of Charles Sumner, Chairman of the Senate Foreign Relations Committee? As we have seen, he had attacked the Johnson–Clarendon Convention of 1869 in an intemperate speech which claimed that the *Alabama* and other British-built Confederate cruisers had doubled the duration of the Civil War and that Britain should be made to pay damages in proportion. He did not conceal his opinion that only the cession of British North America could settle the account. When Fish approached him in January 1871 with the scheme for a Commission, he made it clear that his views had not changed:

> The greatest trouble, if not peril, being a constant source of anxiety and disturbance, is from Fenianism, which is excited by the proximity of the British flag in Canada. Therefore the withdrawal of the British flag cannot be abandoned as a condition or preliminary of such a settlement as is now proposed. To make the settlement complete the withdrawal should be from this hemisphere, including provinces and islands.[32]

It was clear that Sumner would oppose such a settlement as the administration now hoped for; and in March it used its influence to have him deposed from his powerful committee chairmanship. There were other reasons, it is true, for this action—notably the bitter personal feud that had arisen between Sumner and President Grant over the latter's desire to annex Santo Domingo. But Sumner's eclipse removed a major obstacle to a rational Anglo-American arrangement and may be interpreted with some plausibility as involving the rejection of his ideas, which would have denied Canada the right of self-determination as a self-governing British state in North America.

Nevertheless, no historian has ever found a document in which an important American statesman of this period specifically accepted the new Dominion of Canada as a fact of international life. Nevins writes that under Fish's policies "the United States tacitly surrendered its demand for Canadian independence".[33] The fact is that, as always, Canada was not an object of great importance to Americans. When they thought of it at all, the majority of them probably thought that in due time it would quietly become part of the United States because that was of the natural order of things; who would not be an American if he could? In the meantime, the Washington treaty was good because it made for peace; and if it "tacitly" accepted the existence of a British Dominion of Canada nobody paid much attention.

From the Canadian viewpoint, however, and as seen in retrospect, these things were important. The danger of war receded; the Dominion was assured a period of tranquillity in which, in Macdonald's phrase, the gristle could harden into bone; and it was even possible that with the passing of the years and the quiet pursuit of peaceful and profitable commerce across the long frontier, the United States might come to regard its neighbour to the north—"the colonial authority known as the Dominion of Canada"—as a legitimate and permanent part of the North American landscape.

THE "NATIONAL POLICY"

In November 1873 John A. Macdonald fell from power as the result of a scandal concerning the projected Pacific railway, and a Liberal government headed by Alexander Mackenzie ruled Canada for the next five years.

In spite of Macdonald's disappointment in 1871, Canadians were still pursuing the *ignis fatuus* of reciprocity; and the Liberals clearly thought that they might succeed in regaining it where the Conservatives had failed. After all, the general international atmosphere was now much better. So George Brown, Liberal elder statesman and proprietor of the Toronto *Globe*, trundled off to Washington to try his hand. The plan was that a reciprocity agreement would take the place of the fisheries clauses of the Treaty of Washington. As part of the agreement, the inshore fisheries of Canada would be conceded to the Americans. While the negotiation proceeded, no action would be taken to set up the fisheries arbitration commission provided in the existing treaty. Brown made a preliminary reconnaissance in February 1874, talking to various politicians in Washington with what seemed to be encouraging results. The imperial government was then asked to provide him with credentials as a negotiator jointly with Sir Edward Thornton, who was still British Minister; and in March the two men called on Secretary Fish together. Fish recorded that Brown did "most of the talking", and that he himself told them "I doubt if any proposition could be made which would be accepted by the Senate and House". A long negotiation followed. Brown made concessions, agreeing to include among the items reciprocally free a considerable list of manufactured goods; these when published caused criticism in protectionist circles in Canada. As the discussions with Fish proceeded, Brown resumed his lobbying among congressional leaders and tried with some success, it seemed, to influence the American press. Finally, on June 18, 1874, a draft treaty was sent to the U.S. Senate.[34]

A *draft* treaty. It was not a signed treaty submitted with the President's recommendation for ratification, but a project submitted for advice. Fish subsequently explained its status stiffly for the benefit of the British chargé d'affaires: "the proposed draft of the treaty was not signed by me, and . . . it was presented by the President to the Senate as a draft of a treaty submitted to the Secretary of State by the plenipotentiaries of Her Britannic Majesty at Washington for the consideration of the President."[35] In these circumstances, as Fish and Grant were certainly aware, the "treaty's" chances of acceptance were nil. It was still in the hands of the Committee on Foreign Relations when the session ended on June 22. The results of further consideration in the next session were negative. On February 3, 1875 the Senate "resolved that it was not deemed expedient to recommend the negotiation of the treaty."[36]

It is hard to avoid feeling that Brown and the Canadian government had been made to look foolish. What is perhaps more important—and it is a point that has escaped notice—it had been demonstrated that a Canadian negotiator would not necessarily be more successful than an Englishman in dealing with the United States. This affair of 1874 was much less "diplomacy in leading strings" than the negotiations of 1871. The matters at stake were purely Canadian, the discussions were left largely to a Canadian statesman, and that statesman engaged in an intensive program of lobbying in Washington and New York, the sort of activity which Canadians were certainly apt to consider they understood better than the overwashed servants of the British Foreign Office. And the end result was exactly nothing. It was an experience which might have been sobering. Apart from this, it had only one practical effect. It set a useful precedent for procedure in the negotiation of future commercial treaties.

One achievement for which the Mackenzie administration is remembered is a modest widening of Canadian autonomy. Edward Blake, Minister of Justice from 1875 to 1877, obtained a change in the Governor General's Instructions which virtually ended the reservation of bills for the Queen's pleasure (in other words, for the consideration of the imperial government), and ensured that the prerogative of pardon would be exercised on the advice of Canadian ministers. The Supreme Court of Canada Act, 1875, contained an ineffective gesture in the direction of the abolition of appeals to the Privy Council. Blake, indeed, while out of the ministry in 1874, issued in his famous "Aurora speech" on "A National Sentiment" what amounted to a manifesto in favour of Canada insisting on a strong voice in the formation of foreign policy. The Canadians, he said, were "four millions of Britons who are not free": "To-morrow, by the policy of England, in which you have no voice or control, this country might be plunged into the horrors of a war." The remedy he advocated at this time was not independence but some form of imperial federation. The speech caused stir but no action. There was nothing to give the question urgency in 1874.[37]

Mackenzie had the misfortune to govern in a period of world depression. In these circumstances the failure to gain access to the American market was a serious political disadvantage. And in 1876 Macdonald and the Conservatives adopted a protectionist policy. The phrasing was cautious: "incidental protection", recalling 1859. But another phrase, more forthright and more effective, also appeared: the "National Policy".* In the general election of September 1878 this formula worked, and Macdonald returned triumphantly to power. He held it thereafter until his death in 1891.

The new tariff was duly erected in 1879.[38] In laying it before the House of Commons the Minister of Finance, S. L. Tilley (soon to be Sir Leonard), took a frankly protectionist line. The remedy for the country's economic troubles, he suggested, lay in "reducing the volume of our imports from all parts of the world". Since the abrogation of the Reciprocity Treaty Canada had continued to admit a large proportion of American imports free, hoping that this might produce "a more liberal spirit" in the United States. This had not happened, and now duties were to be imposed. In general, he explained, the government's policy was to place higher duties on goods that were or could be manufactured in Canada, leaving at lower rates those not made or likely to be made. In conclusion he said:

> . . . the time has arrived when we are to decide whether we will be simply hewers of wood and drawers of water; whether we will be simply agriculturists raising wheat, and lumbermen producing more lumber than we can use, or [than] Great Britain and the United States will take from us at remunerative prices . . . or whether we will inaugurate a policy that will, by its provisions, say to the industries of the country, we will give you sufficient protection; we

* Macdonald used this term in Parliament as early as April 26, 1870. Recent historians have sometimes used the phrase as a label for a triple Conservative policy, embracing protection, transcontinental railway construction, and western settlement; but Macdonald normally applied it simply to the tariff.

will give you a market for what you can produce; we will say that, while our neighbours build up a Chinese wall, we will impose a reasonable duty on their products coming into this country; at all events, we will maintain for our agricultural and other productions, largely, the market of our own Dominion....[39]

Consideration had been given to establishing a tariff giving a preference to the United Kingdom; but this was not done, partly because of fear of retaliation from the United States.[40] (There was a British preference on one item, salt: this had been the case since 1870.) The tariff was unitary, imposing the same rates against Britain, the United States, and everybody else. Macdonald told the Colonial Secretary, however, that it actually gave definite advantages to British manufacturers.[41] Moreover, the hope of American reciprocity had still not been abandoned. The new law provided[42] that animals, agricultural and dairy products, meat, and lumber might be imported into Canada duty free, or at lower rates than those set by the Act, if the same articles from Canada were admitted to the United States free or at similarly reduced rates. Another interesting point was the provision[43] that the whole or part of the thirty per cent duty imposed on wines might be remitted if France and Spain reduced their duties on Canadian imports. The fact was that Sir Alexander Galt was engaged in an attempt to work out commercial treaties with those countries. He had not been appointed Imperial Commissioner, as Brown had been in the United States in 1874, but was working with the British ambassadors in Paris and Madrid in the hope of arranging draft treaties for consideration in London and Ottawa. This was not achieved in either case at this period.[44]

The new Macdonald ministry did effect an innovation: the modest beginning of Canadian permanent representation abroad. Since 1869 Sir John Rose had been functioning informally as the Canadian government's man of business in London. It was now felt that the situation should be regularized and a proper office opened there, headed by an officer who could represent Canada as required not only before the British government but also on occasion on the Continent. The proposal somewhat alarmed the Beaconsfield (Disraeli) ministry in England; some officials were particularly unfavourably impressed by the title ("Resident Minister") which Macdonald and his colleagues proposed for the new appointment, and explained that the latter could not possibly be considered "diplomatic" or "quasi-diplomatic"—this would imperil the unity of the Empire in matters of foreign policy. It was with some reluctance that the

British ministers finally accepted the designation "High Commissioner for Canada in London". Sir Alexander Galt took up the office in the spring of 1880.[45]

Another appointment seems to have been instituted less formally and without consultation with the British government. From 1882 there was a Canadian *commissaire général** stationed in Paris; his duties were ill-defined and until 1912 he doubled as a representative of the Province of Quebec, which in fact first appointed him. In 1911, after an inquiry from the Colonial Secretary, Sir Joseph Pope investigated the records and reported that the office in Paris was in the beginning "regarded as purely an emigration and commercial agency, subordinate as regards the latter function, to the High Commissioner in London, and possessing no quasi-diplomatic character".[46] Both the *commissaire général* and the High Commissioner reported to the Secretary of State in Ottawa, though the High Commissioner corresponded with the Minister of Agriculture on immigration matters (which his instructions marked down as his first consideration) and with the Minister of Finance on financial matters.[47] In practice, the High Commissioner carried on an active personal correspondence with the Prime Minister.

It should be noted that even before Confederation the British North American colonies had had agents abroad to encourage immigration; and immediately after Confederation the Dominion set up offices for this purpose in Britain and on the Continent. Beginning in 1886 commercial agents were established abroad "to cultivate trade"; in 1907 they were renamed "trade commissioners". None of these people had diplomatic status.

While the small elements of a future diplomatic service were beginning to function abroad, at home the Macdonald government had launched the greatest of its projects. In October 1880 it made a contract with a new Canadian Pacific Railway Company to build the transcontinental line that had been promised to British Columbia back in 1871. The good iron spike that marked the completion of the enterprise was driven home in Eagle Pass just over five years later. The backbone of Canada was complete, and more than a century of imperial and national hopes had been realized. In 1876 the Intercolonial Railway had been finished, uniting the Maritime

* The French title seems to have been regularly used even in English-language documents; see, for example, the references in the Military Voters Act, 1917.

provinces with central Canada. Now a still larger dream had finally come true: speedy uninterrupted transport from the Atlantic to the Pacific, essentially unaffected by the seasons and wholly under Canadian control.[48]

In 1885, then, the way seemed open to a period of unlimited national prosperity. Unfortunately, however, the prosperity simply did not come. The hordes of immigrants whom Galt was to gather and whom the new railway was to carry into the new West did not appear. The good times that succeeded the bad ones of the seventies were modest and short-lived. The Canadian national revenue, which had been about $22 million in 1877, climbed close to $36 million in 1883 and then dropped again. (It did not reach $40 million until 1898; after that it soared.)[49] In the world at large the twenty-three years from 1873 to 1896 witnessed a "great downward sweep of prices"[50] and a general depression of trade. In these discouraging circumstances it is not suprising that economic questions continued to dominate discussions of Canadian external relations and particularly of relations with the United States.

THE FISHERIES AND "UNRESTRICTED RECIPROCITY"

There is a certain tiresome iteration about the question of the North Atlantic fisheries. As we have already noted (above, page 26) the United States denounced the fisheries clauses of the Treaty of Washington. This action, initiated by Congress, was taken as soon as the terms of the treaty allowed; it became effective in 1885. The result was that, just as in 1866 (above, page 20), the fisheries question was thrown back on to the basis of the Convention of 1818. The old song began again. Canadian cruisers arrested American fishing vessels—the *David J. Adams* (May 1886) was the most famous victim—and there were loud American diplomatic protests. Now, however, there was a dangerous variation. While American fishing ships were being seized by the Canadian authorities on the Atlantic coast, Canadian ones were being similarly treated by the Americans on the Pacific. Vessels from British Columbia had begun to engage in pelagic (ocean) sealing in the Behring Sea, and in 1886 and again in 1887 some of them were arrested by United States cutters while so engaged fifty miles or more from land. It is out of the question to describe all the diplomatic exchanges here.* In the course of them Edward Phelps, the

* The story is told in some detail in Robert Craig Brown, *Canada's National Policy, 1883-1900: A Study in Canadian-American Relations* (Princeton, 1964).

bellicose U.S. Minister in London, declared that his government could on no account "consent to be drawn, at any time, into a discussion of the subject with the Colonial Government of Canada".[51] But Phelps's chief, Thomas F. Bayard, Secretary of State under President Cleveland, was prepared to take a different view, and in May 1887 Sir Charles Tupper, the Canadian Minister of Finance, went to Washington by invitation for informal talks with him. Out of these came agreement for another Joint High Commission to settle the accumulated differences. The Canadian government was pleased, particularly as Bayard had written to Tupper that the only way to a satisfactory settlement was "by a straightforward treatment on a liberal and statesmanlike plan of the entire commercial relations of the two countries".[52] Once more it seemed that there was a possibility of using the fisheries to achieve reciprocity.

This time there were to be three commissioners on each side. In Britain the Conservative government of Lord Salisbury appointed as chairman a giant of British politics, Joseph Chamberlain, then out of office following his resignation from Gladstone's cabinet over Irish Home Rule. The second British negotiator, naturally enough, was the Minister in Washington, Sir Lionel Sackville-West. The third was to be a Canadian, and since Macdonald did not wish to repeat his experience of 1871 the choice fell on Tupper.[53] The American chairman was Bayard himself.

History did not entirely repeat itself. This was not a triangular negotiation. The Anglo-Canadian delegation stood staunchly together (though there were, inevitably, some disagreements within it) and in the last stages Tupper wrote that Chamberlain and West "could not have supported Canada with more untiring zeal than they have from first to last".[54] In other respects the Canadians found the negotiations less satisfactory. In effect, the American commissioners repudiated almost at once the offer of reciprocity implied in Bayard's letter to Tupper. The fact is that Cleveland's administration, though friendly to tariff reform, had no hope of getting a comprehensive reciprocity arrangement through the Republican-controlled Senate.[55] Moreover, the Canadian inshore fisheries were now less important to American fishermen and therefore still less powerful as a bargaining weapon. Chamberlain and his colleagues found themselves—as John A. Macdonald had glumly feared from the beginning—negotiating exclusively about the North Atlantic fisheries and the interpretation of the Convention of 1818. The Americans had refused to include the Behring Sea question in the agenda, and Macdonald agreed in thinking that it could best be settled separately.[56] On February 15, 1888 a treaty was signed. It conceded a considerable relaxation of the old Convention in favour of American fishermen, allowing them to purchase necessary supplies, etc., in Canadian ports; it also provided for a mixed commission to decide the precise geographical limits within which the Convention applied. Like the 1871 treaty, it gave reciprocal privileges in American waters to British subjects, and it allowed Canadian fish to enter the United States free.[57]

As it turned out, the most important part of the settlement was an incidental one. To provide against incidents that might occur before the treaty became effective, the British negotiators put forward a *modus vivendi*, to be an executive agreement not subject to ratification by the U.S. Senate. Under this, Canada would sell to U.S. fishermen licences that would permit them to purchase bait and other supplies, transship their catches in Canadian ports, and enjoy other privileges not allowed under the Convention of 1818. This arrangement was supposed to last only two years; in fact, the fisheries were to be conducted on the basis of it for over twenty years.

Although the "Chamberlain-Bayard Treaty" seems to have been generally regarded in Canada as another American diplomatic victory, it was approved by the Canadian Parliament in the spring of 1888. The United States Senate, however, rejected it in August by a strictly party vote; and it was left to the *modus vivendi*, so fortunately provided, to prevent trouble among the fishermen.[58]

The sequel in the United States is worth noting. Two days after the Senate acted, Cleveland, who had strongly recommended the treaty, sent an unexpected message to Congress asking for legislation authorizing the executive to suspend the transit of goods in bond across U.S. territory to or from Canada. It was widely considered that, with the presidential election approaching, this was an attempt by Cleveland to present himself to the voters as more anti-British than the Republicans. There was little danger of the latter taking up the President's program. The House of Representatives passed a Retaliation Bill but it failed in the Senate. There Senator John Sherman, now Chairman of the Committee on Foreign Relations, produced a program of his own. The only basis for a satisfactory settlement with Canada, he said, was political and commercial union with Canada; this, however, could only be secured by the free and hearty assent of both peoples, and the use of force would defeat the object.[59] Nothing came of all these words except some stirring of bad feeling between the two countries.

It is out of the question to tell in detail here the almost interminable story of the Behring Sea sealing controversy. It has been pointed out[60] that the British government was less subject to Canadian influence here than in the North Atlantic fisheries dispute. This was a question of events on the high seas; Canada's colonial status deprived her of any legal powers beyond her own territorial waters, and the defence of Canadian ships and rights on the open ocean was the business of the Royal Navy. As Canadians saw it, the Americans were harassing the Canadian pelagic sealers to prevent them from competing with the Alaska Commercial Company, which did its sealing on land on the Pribiloff Islands; and the British and Canadian governments pointed out that by arresting Canadian vessels far from land the American authorities were in effect claiming the Behring Sea as an American lake, contrary to the traditional United States doctrine of the freedom of the seas. The Americans on their side asserted that their concern was to avert the destruction of the seal herd. Negotiations in Washington in 1890 between James G. Blaine (Secretary of State in Harrison's Republican administration which had replaced Cleveland's) and Charles Hibbert Tupper (Sir Charles's son, and the Canadian Minister of Marine and Fisheries), who was acting as an "assistant" to Sir Julian Pauncefote, the British Minister, came to nothing, and Tupper and Pauncefote did not get on well.[61] However, further discussions the following year, which seem to have been closely supervised on the British side by Lord Salisbury, who was both Prime Minister and Foreign Secretary, resulted in an agreement to stop all sealing by land and sea in the Behring Sea for the 1891–92 season (except for 7,500 seals to provide food for the natives of the Pribiloff Islands); and in February 1892 Blaine and Pauncefote signed a treaty submitting to arbitration the question of jurisdiction in the Behring Sea and of regulations to protect and preserve the fur seal.[62]

Of the seven arbitrators, two each were to be named by Britain and the United States, and one each by the chiefs of state of France, Italy, and the Kingdom of Sweden and Norway. Britain named Lord Hannen, a British judge, and Sir John Thompson, the Canadian Minister of Justice. The tribunal reported in August 1893, deciding by majority votes that Russia had had no jurisdiction over the Behring Sea which could have passed to the United States with the purchase of Alaska, and that the United States had no rights of protection or property in the fur seals there outside the three-mile limit. Less satisfactory from the Canadian point of view were the regulations promulgated by the tribunal which forbade pelagic sealing within sixty miles around the Pribiloff Islands and established an annual close season (May 1 to July 31) on all pelagic sealing in the Behring Sea.[63]

The controversy was still not over. The claims of the Canadian sealing vessels seized by the United States remained to be dealt with. A procedure was not finally provided until 1896, when Britain and the United States signed a convention under which the claims would be referred to two commissioners, one appointed by each country. Britain appointed Mr. Justice George E. King of the Supreme Court of Canada. In accordance with the commissioners' award, in 1898 the United States paid the British Ambassador $473,151.26 to settle the damages.[64]

Enough has been said already to make it evident that economic relations with the United States very largely dominated Canadian domestic politics in the period we have been dealing with. Both political parties were anxious for a renewal of reciprocity; both tried to negotiate it, and both failed. In the late eighties, under the influence of the current depression, the question began to be discussed in Canada, and to some extent in the United States, under new labels: "Commercial Union" and "Unrestricted Reciprocity". The former involved the abolition of customs barriers between Canada and the United States, and the adoption of identical tariffs —decided, inevitably, in Washington—against third parties, including Great Britain. The latter, which seems to have been invented by James Edgar, proposed retaining the customs houses on the border and separate national tariffs against the rest of the world.

The two powerful arguments available for use against these schemes are evident. Both threatened with destruction such Canadian industries as had grown up under the protection of the National Policy, and the Canadian Manufacturers' Association said so, loud and clear. Both, but particularly commercial union, could be very plausibly represented as mere preliminaries to political absorption by the United States; Canadians devoted to the British connection—and they were legion—were quick to do this. If the Opposition in Parliament was going to embrace one of these schemes, then unrestricted reciprocity was clearly the less dangerous politically; and in 1888 the Liberal parliamentary caucus committed the party to a policy of complete free trade with the United States. On that platform the Liberals fought the general election campaign of 1891, the last in which Sir John A. Macdonald took part. The Old Chieftain routed them, largely by appealing to the old sentiment of loyalty to the Crown ("As for myself, my course is clear. A British subject I was born —a British subject I will die . . ."). Be it noted, however, that even now Macdonald declared himself ready to negotiate a reciprocity arrangement with the United States, as his government had tried to do in 1888.[65]

As soon as the election was over the divisions within the Liberal party on the question were brought fully into the open with the publication of Edward Blake's famous "West Durham letter". Blake made it clear that he considered that the distinction between commercial union and unrestricted reciprocity was artificial, and that commercial union would lead inevitably to political union. Rather characteristically, he managed to leave the impression that in his view the latter might itself be inevitable. The letter was Blake's farewell to the Liberal party of Canada (he shortly transferred his activities to Westminster, where he became an Irish Nationalist MP); and it almost certainly did the party great harm and contributed to its abandonment of the unrestricted reciprocity policy in 1893.[66] Macdonald had died soon after his electoral success of 1891, and without his leadership his party fell into disarray. In 1896 the Liberals, purged of the stain of "veiled treason", won a great victory, and Wilfrid Laurier became Prime Minister of Canada.

TROUBLES IN OTHER CONTINENTS BREAK IN

It is time to turn back to the consideration of Canada's place in the British Empire in the days of Macdonald.

The Britain of the 1860s was largely anti-imperial in spirit and in practice, more interested in contracting its responsibilities than in extending its imperial frontiers and developing its relationship to distant colonies. By the 1880s things had changed. Economic and territorial competition had become the rule in the world, and the colonies which even Disraeli had called "a millstone round our necks" in 1852, and "deadweights" in 1866,[67] suddenly became jewels in the crown. Whereas before 1870 Canadian governments had often been perturbed by anti-colonialism and separatism at "home", now they found themselves on guard against British projects that seemed to them to have centralizing tendencies. On the other hand, Canadians themselves (English-speaking Canadians at least) were moved by and responded to the urges of imperialism; and—something which has not always been recognized—their growing native nationalism found expression through imperial channels.

The period following the Franco-Prussian War of 1870–71 and the unification of Germany was one of increasing international tensions, culminating finally in the First World War. Gradually and spasmodically these troubles in other continents broke in upon the colonial isolation of Canada—whose foreign problems so far had been almost exclusively North American—and forced her government to take decisions concerning them. The first such occasion was the crisis of 1878, when Britain seemed to come close to war with Russia over the latter's advance towards Constantinople. There was fear of attacks by Russian cruisers. The Mackenzie cabinet now built the first, very rudimentary, defences at the western naval base of Esquimalt, and mounted some ancient guns at Atlantic ports; and military men and politicians discussed tentative plans for raising a division of 10,000 men in Canada in the event of war.[68]

Out of this scare, which extended far beyond Canada, came next year the Royal Commission on the Defence of British Possessions and Commerce Abroad (the Carnarvon Commission). John A. Macdonald testified before this commission confidentially in London in 1880, making two basic points: first, it was better to make military arrangements between the mother country and the larger colonies individually than to try to set up a general system of imperial defence; second, it would be unwise to attempt to negotiate any arrangements for the provision of colonial contingents at a time when war was not threatened. "I think if war were imminent," he told Carnarvon and his colleagues, "the spirit of the people themselves would force on the Legislature and the Government of the day the necessity for taking an active part in it."[69]

In these years the British government found itself more and more frequently involved in large-scale imperial military adventures, and the Canadian government for its part was subjected to a variety of internal and external pressures aimed at inducing it to take part. The first important incident of this sort took place in 1884–85. The British had gone into Egypt in 1882. Now they encountered problems in the neighbouring Sudan. General Charles Gordon was sent out to arrange the evacuation of the province—a task for which he was singularly unsuited—and was shortly surrounded and besieged in Khartoum. Mr. Gladstone, belatedly and reluctantly, authorized a relief expedition, and General Lord Wolseley was placed in command. Wolseley remembered the Red River Expedition of 1870 and the Canadian voyageurs who had taken its boats through the white water and over the portages of the arduous route between Lake Superior and the Lake of the Woods. He therefore asked for a contingent of such men to help his new expedition surmount the cataracts of the Nile.

When the request reached the Governor General (Lord Lansdowne) through the Colonial Office, Lansdowne at once consulted Sir John Macdonald, who it is evident saw no objection; and the Governor General put his staff to work on the task of raising the contingent. It was a strictly imperial project, carried out at British, not Canadian expense. The Canadian Voyageur Contingent when it sailed numbered 386 all ranks. Six were militia officers, who received the pay of their ranks; the others were civilian non-combatants who worked under a civil contract. The group was a microcosm of Canadian life, French-speaking and English-speaking, red men and white. Sixteen members of the contingent lost their lives on service. Some of the men were not experienced boatmen, and this led to criticism; but in general it seems clear that the contingent did valuable and at some points invaluable work. It was Canada's first small contribution to a British overseas war. The Voyageurs' share in the dramatic and unsuccessful attempt to rescue General Gordon is a unique episode in Canadian history.[70]

In the first week of February 1885 the matter entered a new phase. The outside world received tragic news. Wolseley's vanguard had got to Khartoum only a couple of days too late; the town had fallen and Gordon, the legendary hero, was dead. The report sent a shock wave across the British Empire, and it was powerfully felt in Canada. The result was a spate of offers of service pouring in upon Ottawa: hundreds of them, from individuals from the rank of major-general down to militia privates; from people anxious to raise units; from militia units offering their collective services. It was a remarkable phenomenon, reflecting doubtless both the current sentimental admiration for Gordon and the growing imperial enthusiasm of the time.[71]

The Canadian government's attitude to this popular military movement is interesting. At no time did it offer an official contingent, though this was not fully understood by newspaper writers and others in England. On the other hand, it had no objection to the British government raising a force in Canada at its own expense; this, after all, was what had just happened in the case of the Voyageur Contingent, which had been enlisted through the agency of the Governor-General's Office with the mere countenance of the Canadian authorities. Sir John Macdonald in fact made rather detailed suggestions on the procedures that might be followed in such a case. "It seems to me," he wrote to Lansdowne's secretary, "that the only Way to raise a Corps for foreign service will be for the War Office to authorize recruiting in Canada under the Mutiny Act, or rather under the present imperial statute* which has taken the place of the Mutiny Act."[72]

The situation was complicated almost immediately when New South Wales offered an official contingent, whose expense it was ready to pay. It seems fairly evident that the War Office was not enormously anxious for colonial help—after all, the crisis caused by Gordon's death was really emotional rather than military—but the offer was nevertheless accepted and the New South Wales force spent some time at Suakin on the Red Sea, though it saw little active service before the British government put an end to the operations. Other Australian colonies had made offers of troops which were politely declined. The Canadian High Commissioner in London (now Sir Charles Tupper) was extremely anxious that Canada should emulate New South Wales and offer her permanently embodied artillery batteries as a contingent. Macdonald had no intention of doing anything of the sort. The letter he wrote Tupper has rightly become celebrated:

> I have your notes . . . on the subject of sending Canadian troops to the Soudan. – I wrote you a hurried note the other day on this question and have both before & since talked it over with my Colleagues and we think the time has not arrived nor the occasion for our Volunteering Military Aid to the Mother Country—
>
> We do not stand at all in the same position as Australasia—The Suez Canal is nothing to us—and we do not ask England to quarrel with France or Germany for our sakes† —The offer of those Colonies is a good move on their part and somewhat like Cavour's sending Sardinian troops to the Crimea—Why should we waste money and men in this wretched business? England is not at War but merely helping The Khedive [of Egypt] to put down an insurrection and now that Gordon is gone the motive of aiding in the rescue of

* That is, the annual Army Act.

† The Australian colonies had complained of what they thought inadequate support from London against German activity in New Guinea and French activity in New Caledonia.

our Countryman is gone with him—Our men and money would therefore be sacrificed to get Gladstone and Co. out of the hole they have plunged themselves into by their own imbecillity [*sic*].

Again the reciprocal aid to be given by the Colonies and England should be a matter of treaty deliberately entered into and settled on a permanent basis—The spasmodic offers of our Militia Colonels anxious for excitement or notoriety have roused unreasonable expectations in England, and are so far unfortunate. I dare say that a Batallion [*sic*] or two of Venturous spirits might be enlisted but 7d a day will cool most men's warlike ardour.

Our Artillery Batteries are not enlisted for foreign service and could not be ordered to the Soudan. . . .[73]

The press, including the Conservative papers of Toronto, took much the same cool line; one is left wondering whether Macdonald had passed the word to the newspapers supporting his party. The Toronto *Mail*, in an editorial[74] which Lord Lansdowne sent to the Colonial Office, remarked, "If the Mother Country were in serious danger the Dominion would without doubt rush to her assistance with men and money if there were a reasonable prospect that our aid would mend matters. But just now Britain has an unlimited supply of both. . . ."

The whole episode is extremely interesting. The excitement in militia circles could easily have been fanned into a national outburst of imperial enthusiasm. Macdonald chose instead to damp it down. The "crisis" was largely spurious, and he knew it; therefore one should not perhaps make too much of the affair. Nevertheless it remains a landmark in the development of Canadian external policies. Macdonald's action, or inaction, reflects his conception of Canadian national interests, which made no provision for automatic participation in the resolution of secondary imperial problems in areas of the world where Canada had no concerns of her own. Canadian statesmen of later generations were to follow, not wholly unconsciously, the trail he had blazed. It would be difficult to discover two political characters more dissimilar than John Macdonald and Mackenzie King; yet the student of King's policies, turning back to the colonial simplicities of 1885 and reading Macdonald's testimony before the Carnarvon Commission and his letter to Tupper, finds himself in a curiously familiar atmosphere.

CONFERENCES IN LONDON AND OTTAWA

One of the potentially important phenomena of this period was the beginnings of what later came to be known as the Imperial Conference.

The first Colonial Conference was held in London in 1887, simultaneously with Queen Victoria's first Jubilee and apparently in part as the result of pressure from the Imperial Federation League, which had been founded in 1884. There was a certain casualness about the British government's invitation to the colonies, which were asked to send "any leading public man who may be at liberty to come to England next year" and who might be specially qualified to take a useful part. The primary business was to be "an attempt . . . to attain to a better understanding as to the system of defence which may be established throughout the Empire"; in this connection reference was made to the offers of the colonies in 1885 and to the recommendations of the Carnarvon Commission. A secondary topic was postal and telegraphic communications.[75]

The Canadian government's approach to the conference was at least equally casual. It coincided in time with the meeting of the Canadian Parliament; since no special invitation had been extended to colonial premiers, Macdonald did not go himself, nor did any other active Canadian minister. The Canadian representatives were Sir Alexander Campbell, newly appointed Lieutenant-Governor of Ontario and lately Postmaster General, and Sandford Fleming, builder of the Intercolonial Railway and original surveyor of the Canadian Pacific.[76]

The Canadian share in the discussion of defence consisted chiefly of describing the Canadian militia organization (the little Permanent Force had been expanded by the organization of cavalry and infantry units in 1883) and the work it had done in the North-West Rebellion of 1885; also in extolling the construction of the transcontinental railway as a contribution to national and imperial defence. The Canadian representatives had no power to make commitments and seem to have been asked to make none. The most concrete result of the conference was an agreement by the Australasian colonies to pay £126,000 annually towards the cost of a British naval squadron in their waters, while the British authorities on their side rather reluctantly agreed that they would not reduce the force in those waters without colonial consent.[77] On the communication question, Fleming represented strongly the desirability of a Pacific cable between Canada and Australia.[78]

The status of the next Colonial Conference, that of 1894, is unique and perhaps, as an imperial body, somewhat doubtful. It was called on the motion of the Canadian government and met in Ottawa. The Canadian order-in-council authorizing the invitations provided that they should go to the Australasian colonies, Fiji, and the Cape of Good Hope, and that the British government should be requested to take part by sending a delegate or by other means. Newfoundland was subsequently invited, but neither it nor Fiji sent a representative. The order indicated the purposes of the conference as being consideration of the trade relations between Canada and the Pacific colonies, and the means of securing "the construction of a direct telegraphic cable between those colonies and the Dominion of Canada".[79] No evidence has been found that the Canadian government consulted London before calling this conference. Downing Street can scarcely have been particularly well pleased with this colonial initiative, the less so as the agenda, Canadian in origin, made no reference to defence. The British authorities nevertheless put a good face on the matter and sent a representative, Lord Jersey, recently Governor of New South Wales. Jersey, however, was not a member of the British government, had no power to make commitments on its behalf, and did not vote.[80]

The results of the conference were certainly disagreeable to the imperial government in one respect. The discussions on trade were far-ranging and, from the British point of view, ambitious. Britain was still deeply committed to free trade; the colonies in this meeting showed themselves largely protectionist and, specifically, favourable to a measure of imperial preference. By a vote of five colonies to three (with Canada in the majority and New South Wales, New Zealand, and Queensland constituting the minority) the conference recorded

> its belief in the advisability of a customs arrangement between Great Britain and her colonies by which trade within the Empire may be placed on a more favourable footing than that which is carried on with foreign countries.

It was also resolved that, pending Britain's readiness to enter such an arrangement, it was "desirable that, when empowered so to do, the colonies of Great Britain, or such of them as may be disposed to accede to this view, take steps to place each other's products, in whole or in part, on a more favoured customs basis than is accorded to the like products of foreign countries". It was further decided, unanimously,

> That this conference is of opinion that any provisions in existing treaties between Great Britain and any foreign power, which prevent the self-governing dependencies of the Empire from entering into agreements of commercial reciprocity with each other, or with Great Britain, should be removed.[81]

It was quite clear that the reference here was to British treaties with Belgium (1862) and the German Zollverein (1865) which provided that goods from those countries entering British colonies should not pay duties higher than those on goods of British origin. Canada had protested against these treaties as early as 1882, and the Canadian Parliament in 1891 had passed an address to the Queen asking that they be denounced.[82]

The Colonial Secretary in Lord Rosebery's Liberal government was the Marquess of Ripon—that same Lord de Grey and Ripon who had found John A. Macdonald so difficult in Washington in 1871. This background perhaps did not render him especially sympathetic to colonial aspirations. It has been shown, however, that in addition he was surrounded by permanent officials, not so much in his own department as in the Foreign Office and the Board of Trade, who were strong free traders and hostile to the point of view expressed in the resolutions of the conference.[83] At any rate, in due course he informed the colonies concerned that the British government was unfavourable to a colonial preferential tariff arrangement as economically undesirable (he used the phrase "the evil results of a preferential policy"), and that the Belgian and German treaties would not be denounced, at least for the present. At the same time he read the colonies a lecture (since somewhat celebrated as the "Ripon Circular")[84] on the question of commercial treaties affecting them. A trifle gratuitously, it would seem, since the Ottawa conference had not suggested that the colonies assume independent powers of negotiation, he wrote, "To give the Colonies the power of negotiating Treaties for themselves without reference to Her Majesty's Government would be to give them an international status as separate and Sovereign States, and would be equivalent to breaking up the Empire into a number of independent States. . . ." The negotiation had to be conducted by the Queen's representative at the foreign court concerned; but "it would be desirable generally . . . that he should have the assistance, either as a second Plenipotentiary or in a subordinate capacity, as Her Majesty's Government think the circumstances require, of a Delegate appointed by the Colonial Government."

He passed on to deal in firm terms with a more relevant subject. It was obvious, he said, "that a Colony could not offer a foreign Power Tariff concessions which were not at the same time to be extended to all other Powers entitled by Treaty to most-favoured-nation treatment in the Colony." Since Britain had made a great number of most-favoured-nation treaties, this was important, and a considerable trammel on colonial freedom of action.* Ripon proceeded to state that "before any Convention or Treaty can be ratified" the British government must be satisfied that it fulfilled this condition.

These were not empty words. In 1893 Sir Charles Tupper had finally achieved that commercial treaty with France which Galt had failed to negotiate years before (above, page 33). In 1884 the Foreign Office had agreed that it would be suitable that in such negotiations the High Commissioner would be a plenipotentiary jointly with the British Ambassador, and that both should sign any treaty.[86] This procedure was now followed, Lord Dufferin and Tupper both signing.[87] But there were delays in implementation, first because members of the Canadian cabinet disliked parts of the treaty, then because the Colonial Office told Canada brusquely that the treaty (which the Canadian Parliament had finally sanctioned by an Act of 1894) would not be ratified until legislation was actually passed ensuring that countries so entitled under British most-favoured-nation treaties would receive its benefits. The first Canadian draft bill for the purpose was pronounced by London to be unsatisfactory; it was amended in accordance with detailed suggestions from the Colonial Office, and passed in July 1895.[88]

This whole episode seemed to indicate that progress towards complete colonial, and particularly Canadian autonomy in matters concerning commercial treaties had been abruptly and firmly checked. We shall see, however, that the check was very temporary. In the same year Lord Rosebery's government fell from power, and the incoming Conservative administration of Lord Salisbury took a different attitude.

THE CHRISTMAS CRISIS, 1895

The Salisbury government had to deal with one of the most bizarre incidents in the whole history of Anglo-American relations. The boundary between Venezuela and British Guiana had long been in dispute. Richard Olney, President Cleveland's Secretary of State, displeased with the British refusal of unrestricted arbitration of the question, sent a truculent dispatch to London on July 20, 1895.[89] Not content with dealing with the

* Under arrangements worked out between the Colonial and Foreign offices in London which may be said to have become effective in 1878, the major colonies were allowed to "contract out" of the operation of British commercial treaties made *after* that date.[85]

business in hand, and relating it to the Monroe Doctrine, he added some challenging and insulting generalizations:

> That distance and three thousand miles of intervening ocean make any permanent political union between an European and an American state unnatural and inexpedient will hardly be denied.... To-day the United States is practically sovereign on this continent, and its fiat is law upon the subjects to which it confines its interposition.

Salisbury took his time in replying to this remarkable document. When he did so, in December, he did not retreat from the position the British government had previously taken. The result was that Cleveland, in a special message to Congress of December 17, 1895,[90] made what amounted to a direct threat of war. In his opinion, he said, the time had come for the United States itself to determine "the true divisional line" between Venezuela and British Guiana:

> When such report is made and accepted it will, in my opinion, be the duty of the United States to resist by every means in its power, as a wilful aggression upon its rights and interests, the appropriation by Great Britain of any lands, or the exercise of governmental jurisdiction over any territory, which after investigation we have determined belongs of right to Venezuela.
>
> In making these recommendations I am fully alive to the responsibility incurred and keenly realize all the consequences that may follow.

The result in the United States, *The Times* of London told its readers, was a "passionate outburst" of nationalism in support of the President: "It was volcanic."[91] Immediately, however, the most potent voice in contemporary American popular journalism, that of Joseph Pulitzer's New York *World*, was heard on the side of peace; and while Pulitzer's formidable machine worked against the jingoes, other forces also made themselves felt. On Friday, December 20 the New York Stock Exchange experienced the worst crash since the panic of 1893. On Sunday, according to the *Times'* New York correspondent, "The pulpits of America spoke . . . for peace, and the great majority of them in New York, not only for peace, but in censure of the President's policy."[92] And on Monday evening the new commander of the United States Army, General Nelson A. Miles, mentioned at a dinner in Philadelphia that there were only three modern coast-defence guns mounted in the country: two at New York and one at San Francisco. "New York", he was quoted as saying, "is worth a hundred Canadas. It is true that we would invade and capture Canada if we wanted to, but there would be no special advantage gained as a result."[93]

Thus in the United States sober second thought began to appear. In Britain in the meantime—where probably not one person in a hundred had ever heard of the dispute with Venezuela before Cleveland threatened to make war about it—there was very little tendency to pick up the American gauntlet. Even in 1895, this was hardly the sort of issue on which the British public was disposed to fight. And almost at once its attention was diverted to a question in which it was much more interested. On December 29 the Jameson Raid was launched by Rhodesian police against the Transvaal, with which Britain had serious controversies but was at peace. The Boers quickly rounded up the raiders; and then the German Emperor sent President Kruger of the Transvaal a cable congratulating him on crushing the movement "without appealing to the aid of friendly powers". It was now Britain's turn to indulge in an outburst of nationalistic indignation, but the object was Germany, not the United States. The American quarrel slipped into the background; Lord Salisbury's cabinet colleagues, with their eyes on South Africa, pressed him to moderate his attitude to the United States,[94] and in due course Britain quietly agreed to arbitrate the dispute with Venezuela on terms agreeable to Washington.

In Canada, Cleveland's message came as a severe shock. Friendly relations along the border had seemed to be becoming traditional; and now suddenly a prospect appeared of its being a battlefield once more. There had been no general rearmament of the militia since the Fenian troubles at the time of Confederation. The government of Sir Mackenzie Bowell now took hasty action. A member of it later explained to the House of Commons, "there was a state of tension existing, and . . . it was very desirable . . . that the state of the armament of Canada should not be discussed in Parliament during the early part of this session"[95] (which began on January 2). But the Quartermaster General, Colonel P. H. N. Lake, was sent off to England, sailing from New York on January 4, to obtain new weapons through the War Office.[96] He quickly contracted for 40,000 long Lee-Enfield rifles, enough to rearm the infantry of the militia, 2,300 Lee-Enfield carbines for the cavalry, 24 12-pounder field guns with ammunition, and some Maxim guns.[97] By Canadian standards this was a very large measure of rearmament; and it is a notable fact that (disregarding a little paper planning) this was the last occasion when active military preparations were made in Canada for defence against the United States.

The scale of the action taken reflects the seriousness of the Canadian government's view of the crisis. Like many British observers, Canadians were particularly shaken by the strange lightheartedness, as it seemed to them, with which the American public approached the situation. The Toronto *Globe* remarked on December 23:

> One of the most disheartening developments in connection with what may be termed the war message which President Cleveland sent to Congress last week is the ostentatious exultation with which the great mass of the American public received the idea of war with England. It is not to be accounted for by mere jingoism. . . . The American mind takes no pleasure in the idea of the humiliation of France, Germany or Russia; it gloats on the idea of the humiliation of England. At the mere suggestion of a war with a country to whom they are everlastingly bound by ties of blood, religion and literature, a scream of delight is heard from one end to the other of the United States, softened only here and there by the warning voice of a soberer and truer patriotism. . . .
>
> We refuse to believe that there can be any other than a peaceful issue to the present controversy, but if the horrors of war break upon us the citizens of every quarter of the British Empire would enter upon the murderous contest with feelings of the most poignant regret that their adversaries should be their kinsmen of the United States. The Americans, on the contrary, discuss the possibility of such a struggle with the callousness and flippancy with which the details of a prize-fight are arranged, and are frankly jubilant that their antagonists should be their kinsmen of England.

It was evident that the time had scarcely arrived when war between the British Empire and the United States could be called unthinkable. The most encouraging aspect of the brief crisis had been the considerable reaction against Cleveland's irresponsible challenge which had gradually appeared among his countrymen.

The return of Salisbury to power in 1895 marked the beginning of a decade of Conservative rule in Britain. The following year the Conservative party of Canada, as already noted, met disaster in a general election. The Liberals came into office under Wilfrid Laurier, the Dominion's first French-Canadian prime minister. He was to rule for fifteen years. For the first seven of those years he would confront Salisbury's powerful and aggressive Colonial Secretary, Joseph Chamberlain.

CHAPTER THREE

LAURIER, NATIONALISM, AND IMPERIALISM

LAURIER AND CHAMBERLAIN

When Laurier formed his government in Ottawa in 1896, imperialism was fully in the saddle in London. Little England was, for the moment at least, a thing of the past. The representative figures of the new era were Joseph Chamberlain, the ex-radical and screw manufacturer turned imperialist who was Colonial Secretary from 1895 till 1903; Cecil Rhodes, born in Hertfordshire, the South African capitalist and politician who devoted himself to extending British rule in Africa; and Rudyard Kipling, the Anglo-Indian journalist who became the unofficial poet laureate of Empire.

Canada too had her "imperialists". An imperial-unity movement can be discerned at work in the country at least from 1867; and the latest and most thorough study of it is certainly right in concluding that "Imperialism was one form of Canadian nationalism."[1] The Canadian imperialists were not believers in humble dependence. They saw the Empire as a means by which to satisfy the strong and characteristic desire of English-speaking Canadians to play an important part in the world. For Canada, in their minds, "the imperial system was the vehicle through which she would attain nationhood."[2] Mr. Berger writes, it is true, "Imperial unity found no favour with the farmers or the working classes, and in French Canada it encountered indifference and hostility."[3] If this was the case—and with respect to French Canada it certainly was—it is nevertheless true also that imperialism, in the relatively innocuous sense in which Canadians used the word, was influential; and it is possible that its long-term influence was even greater than Mr. Berger allows.

Mr. Laurier (Sir Wilfrid from 1897) as a French Canadian was a nationalist of different stripe. The arguments of English-speaking imperialists like Sir George Parkin struck no responsive chord in him. But as a practical politician he had to take account of them, and even to pay a degree of lip-service to them. This ambivalence is reflected in his dealings with Chamberlain, notably in the Colonial Conference of 1897.

The most pressing external question confronting the Laurier ministry on its accession to power was the tariff. In 1893 a national convention of the Liberal party had adopted a platform denouncing protection as "radically unsound" and, while quietly dropping "unrestricted reciprocity", declaring in favour of a reduction of tariffs and specifically of reciprocity with the United States.[4] But the United States was in no mood for reciprocity. Following his inauguration in 1897, the new Republican President, William McKinley, called Congress into special session to deal with the tariff question. It proceeded to enact the Dingley Tariff, the highest the United States had yet had. If, as appears to be the case, the Canadian Liberals were not really anxious to defy the industrial community and abandon protection, here was their excuse. But they also had ready to hand the means of making at least a gesture towards both freer trade and the imperial spirit of the moment. There had already been much discussion of extending a preferential tariff to Britain (notably in the Ottawa Conference of 1894, above, pages 45–47). In 1897 such a tariff was adopted by the Canadian Parliament.

It was done, of necessity, in a rather peculiar way. The Act[5] makes no direct mention of British preference, but provides that goods from any country which admits Canadian products on terms "on the whole . . . as favourable to Canada as the terms of the reciprocal tariff herein referred to" shall enter at rates one-eighth (and after July 1, 1898, one-fourth) lower than those of the general tariff. Britain's free-trade policy ensured that she would receive the full benefit of this arrangement. But what about Belgium and Germany under their British treaties (above, page 47)? W. S. Fielding, Laurier's Minister of Finance, told the Canadian House of Commons on April 22, 1897 that, because the new law made no concessions to Britain specifically, but applied to all countries willing to establish "fair and reasonable trade relations" with Canada, the government (not without some doubts, he admitted) took the view that these treaties did not apply. When Sir Charles Tupper (now leading the Opposition) differed, and said that the treaties rendered the project of freer trade with Britain delusive, Fielding rejoined,

When I place these resolutions on the Table of this House to-night, they go into effect, and I speak with pride . . . when I say that to-morrow morning, at every custom-house in Canada from ocean to ocean, the doors will open on terms of preferential trade with the mother country.

Tupper's fears had some justification. Belgium and Germany immediately protested. The British Foreign Office took the view that the Governor General should be instructed to reserve the tariff bill unless it was amended to extend its benefits to countries having trade treaties with the United Kingdom. The imperial government referred the question to the Law Officers of the Crown, who reported that the treaties were binding (in other words, Canada was compelled to give Belgium and Germany the same treatment as Great Britain, without those two countries giving any reciprocal concession whatever). But the lives of the treaties were almost over. The Colonial Conference held in London in June and July 1897 was invited by Chamberlain to consider the matter. Following the precedent set by the conference of 1894, it "unanimously and earnestly" recommended denunciation of "any treaties which now hamper the commercial relations between Great Britain and her Colonies". Lord Salisbury then denounced the Belgian and German treaties immediately.[6] Thus victory finally crowned a long Canadian campaign.

This conference, like the first one in 1887, coincided with a great imperial celebration, that of the Queen's Diamond Jubilee. And Joseph Chamberlain used the occasion to place before the assembled colonial premiers—for this time it was the premiers who were invited—his triple program for the development of the Empire. *His* presentation, it is worth noting, was published to Parliament and the world; the colonial statesmen's comments remained confidential.[7]

Chamberlain dealt first with "political relations":

I feel that there is a real necessity for some better machinery of consultation between the self-governing colonies and the mother country, and it has sometimes struck me— I offer it now merely as a personal suggestion—that it might be feasible to create a great council of the Empire to which the Colonies would send representative plenipotentiaries—not mere delegates who were unable to speak in their name, without further reference to their respective Governments, but persons who . . . would be able, upon all subjects submitted to them, to give really effective and valuable advice. If such a council were to be created it would at once assume an immense importance, and it is perfectly evident that it might develop into something still greater. It might slowly grow to that Federal Council to which we must always look forward as our ultimate ideal.

The Colonial Secretary proceeded to note significantly that "with the privilege of management and control would also come the obligation and the responsibility. There will come some form of contribution towards the expense for objects which we shall have in common...."

Next came "defence"; and Chamberlain said he would be glad to hear the premiers' views concerning any contribution which the colonies might be willing to make to the naval defence of the Empire. On Canada specifically he made remarks which, in the light of some later events, are worthy of note:

... if Canada had not behind her to-day, and does not continue to have behind her this great military and naval power of Great Britain, she would have to make concessions to her neighbours, and to accept views which might be extremely distasteful to her in order to remain permanently on good terms with them. She would not be able to, it would be impossible that she should, herself control all the details of her own destiny; she would be, to a great or less extent, in spite of the bravery of her population and the patriotism of her people, she would still be, to a great extent, a dependent country.

Finally Chamberlain dealt with "commercial relations". Here his approach was rather tentative. He spoke of the German Zollverein. To form such a customs union would be "a matter of the greatest complication and difficulty", and yet in Germany the Zollverein had "made possible and encouraged the ultimate union of the empire". But Chamberlain emphasized that he was mainly asking for the views of the colonial premiers.

Sir Wilfrid Laurier was by all odds the leading colonial figure present, since he represented the only federated Dominion. (Australia, still unfederated, had sent the premiers of six states.) Laurier's biographer, O. D. Skelton, has comparatively little to say about his performance in this conference; but as revealed in the stenographic record it does not belie his reputation for verbal skill and urbanity. Three years later he said he had drafted the conference's resolution expressing the opinion "that the present political relations between the United Kingdom and the self-governing Colonies are generally satisfactory under the existing condition of things".[8] The record does not literally support this; but it does indicate that Laurier used these or similar words during the conference not once but repeatedly, and there can be little doubt that Chamberlain, framing the resolution on paper, borrowed the Canadian prime minister's phrase.

The speech[9] with which Laurier followed the Colonial Secretary's opening statement is worth quoting:

> We all feel pride in the British Empire. . . . At the present time, so far as I know, speaking at all events for the Colony which I represent, we are entirely satisfied with the relation that we have. We have our local autonomy, and that is the first thing with us. . . . The present relations are, as I said, satisfactory, but we all feel that something more must be done, and ought to be done, if not immediately, at least in the not distant future. A Federated Council has been suggested. That is an idea in itself we have all discussed, but the one thing that strikes me at the present time, is that all such views, all such methods of improving the relations which now exist between the Colonies and the mother land, must be preceded by grouping the different Colonies which now exist, wherever it is possible to group them. . . . Until this is done I do not see, for my part, how it will be possible to come to any terms of political council, and the only proposition which I should suggest for the present time would be, that the Conference here assembled views with great satisfaction and hopes that the proceedings now going on for the federation of Australia will come to maturity at their next conference. . . .

This was a clever piece of Fabianism. No one could doubt that Australian federation was vital to any advance in imperial organization (anyone reading the records of the 1897 Conference soon realizes that the presence of half a dozen Australian local premiers reduced the body's effectiveness). The conference limited its resolutions on political relations to three. The one already quoted which declared existing relations to be "generally satisfactory" was dissented from by R. J. Seddon of New Zealand and by Sir Edward Braddon of Tasmania (who said, "I am an Imperial Federationist").[10] A second favoured "periodical" conferences, "periodical" winning over "triennial" by a vote of six to five. The vote was not recorded in detail, but it is a fair assumption that Laurier was one of the majority. The third resolution favoured the federation of colonies which were geographically adjacent. Australia was in fact federated on January 1, 1901, and when the next Colonial Conference met the following year Laurier had been deprived of his strong short-term argument for delaying the Chamberlain program.

We used the word "ambivalence" in connection with Laurier's attitude towards the imperial movement of his time. It would be a pity not to quote another of his statements to the 1897 Conference:

I am quite satisfied with the condition of things as they are, but to imagine that will last for ever is a delusion. I venture from my heart to suggest that there is a good deal in representation. I conceive that it would be a good thing for the Colonies to be represented on the floor of Parliament. It would not be impossible that the representatives of the Colonies in the Imperial Parliament should be allowed as full-fledged members of that Parliament, the right to speak and not to vote, as is the case in America, where the representatives of certain territories have the right to speak, but not to vote. They are enabled in this way to bring matters which concern them to the attention of the public, and to form public opinion in regard to that in that way, and they are very effective in that way. Though that is practicable in America, I do not suggest anything of the kind in our case.[11]

The most important sentence here is presumably the last one. It is not surprising that many people found it difficult to fathom the nature of Laurier's real opinions.

On the matter of defence, Laurier said in 1897 that the question of a naval contribution had "not been discussed at all" in Canada; and he dwelt on the need for the colonies to spend great sums on public works, especially railways, as rendering it difficult for them to find money for military purposes.[12] As for commercial policy, the preferential tariff already enacted by Canada (which had been increased from 25 to 33 1/3 per cent in 1900) put him in a strong position. The conference's resolutions did little to further Chamberlain's activist program; a majority of the Australian premiers approved a continuance of their colonies' small naval contribution, and the premiers generally agreed to look into the possibilities of granting trade preferences to the United Kingdom.

THE SOUTH AFRICAN CRISIS

Before the next Colonial Conference met, the Empire had passed through a serious military emergency, the South African War of 1899–1902.

As war between Britain and the two Boer republics drew nearer, the possibility of military contributions by the self-governing colonies in other continents was increasingly canvassed. But the Canadian Prime

Minister avoided committing his government. On July 31, 1899 the Canadian House of Commons passed unanimously a resolution supporting Britain's cause in the South African controversy. Nevertheless Laurier told the Governor General, Lord Minto (1898–1904), that the case did not seem to be one for military assistance. He did this in spite of an earlier inquiry from Chamberlain (July 3) as to the possibility of Canadian participation in a "great demonstration of material force" to overawe the Boers.[13] As the situation developed, it was complicated, as in 1885, by offers of service by private individuals—notably by Lieutenant-Colonel Sam Hughes, an Opposition MP, who communicated not only through "normal channels" but also directly to Chamberlain. And again a further complication was offers, both official and unofficial, of troops from the Australasian colonies, beginning as early as July.[14]

As Minto recalled to Chamberlain later, the official discussion of a Canadian contingent began with the latter's private letter of July 3 to the Governor General informing him that a Canadian offer to take part in the proposed "great demonstration" would be welcomed. Minto's reply was a secret cable which Chamberlain received on July 20:

> Feel sure proposals made in yr letter of 3rd inst. wd. be received throughout Canada with enthusiasm, but my Premier, who seems personally lukewarm, points out the expense which wd. be incurred by Canada. Have told him that it wd. be expected that Canada shd. pay her own troops. Matters might be accelerated if you cd. give me some hint as to possible assistance from H[er] M[ajesty's] G[overnment]. . . .* Such info shd. only be used in replying to enquiries of my Ministers, & I wd carefully avoid appearance of bringing pressure to bear. Tho' doubtful of the approval of my Govt, I have consulted General [Hutton] as to the nature of the force. It wd. probably consist of one regiment of infantry, one battery, 100 mounted rifles—in all 1200 approximately.[15]

We have Minto's word for it[16] that although he informed Laurier of the portion of Chamberlain's letter of July 3 concerning an offer being welcomed, and allowed him to make a note of it, and although he subsequently had "frequent interviews" on the subject with the Prime Minister, who repeatedly promised a decision from the cabinet, nothing more happened until October 3.

On that date, with war clearly very close, the Colonial Secretary sent

* Passage garbled.

to the self-governing colonies a circular telegram, the text varying somewhat to suit the circumstances of each colony.[17] As sent to Canada, it acknowledged the "patriotic spirit of people of Canada shown by offers to serve in South Africa", and proceeded to furnish "information to assist organization of force offered into units suitable for military requirements":

> Firstly, units should consist of about 125 men; secondly, may be infantry, mounted infantry or cavalry: in view of numbers already available infantry most, cavalry least, serviceable. . . . fifthly, not more than one captain and three subalterns each unit. Whole force may be commanded by officer not higher than major. In considering numbers which can be employed, Secretary of State for War guided by nature of offers, by desire that each Colony should be fairly represented, and limits necessary if force is to be fully utilized by available staff as integral portion of Imperial forces; would gladly accept four units. Conditions as follows: Troops to be disembarked at port of landing South Africa fully equipped at cost of Colonial Governments or volunteers. From date of disembarkation Imperial Government will provide pay at Imperial rates, supplies, and ammunition, and will defray expenses of transport back to Canada, and pay wound pensions and compassionate allowances at Imperial rates. Troops to embark not later than October 31, proceeding direct to Cape Town for orders. Inform accordingly all who have offered to raise volunteers.

This communication still did not lead Laurier to think of offering a contingent. On the contrary, two days later he wrote privately to the editor of the Toronto *Globe* saying that he thought any "jingo spirit" should be discouraged and that he did not think it wise to take part "in all the secondary wars in which England is always engaged".[18] On October 7 he left to fulfil an engagement in Chicago.

While the Prime Minister was in the United States the situation developed dramatically. The sense of Chamberlain's dispatch of October 3 had reached the press in both England and Canada; the result was a campaign for military action by Canada, carried on with particular energy by the Montreal *Star*.[19] The Boers' ultimatum to Britain (October 9) added fuel to the flames. Laurier returned to Canada on October 11, having had long discussions of the question with his travelling companions. One of them, John Willison, editor of the *Globe*, later asserted in his memoirs that he had told the Prime Minister, then or perhaps earlier, that "he would either send troops or get out of office". But he remembered Laurier at Toronto as "still reluctant, unconvinced, and rebellious".[20] That evening in Ottawa the Minister of Militia, Dr. Frederick Borden, told a *Globe* correspondent, "The contingent that will be sent in the event of hostilities will be capable of being mobilized within a short time."[21] The political problem was more serious than Borden seems to have realized. The Canadian cabinet faced it when it met on the morning of October 12 with Laurier in the chair. War had now begun in South Africa; the Boers invaded British territory that day.

Laurier was receiving urgent advice from Minto. The Governor General, who was himself paying a visit to the United States, had sent him comments on Chamberlain's proposals on October 6. If troops were to go, he thought, it was far better that they should be raised by the government than by Colonel Hughes. Minto made another important suggestion:

> You will see from the cable that it is evidently intended that the Canadian troops on arriving in South Africa should be *attached* to the different units [arms?] which they represent, and that they should not remain constituted as a Canadian contingent. I think it would be better if troops are to be offered at all, that they should be offered as a Canadian contingent to act as such—and possibly this offer might still be made, and would appear to me more dignified, and also we could find a much better officer to command it, than if we accept the suggestion of small units, and an officer of the rank of major to command, which would cut out some of the best Canadian officers. . . .[22]

On October 12 (both Governor General and Prime Minister now being back in Ottawa) Minto sent a further note:

> In case I do not see you before Council meets—it seems to me . . . that if you decide to offer troops, it would probably be more in accordance with public sentiment here to offer a contingent of all arms, rather than to accept at once the proposal of 125 under a Major, which would cut out the best officers in Canada, and which makes no mention of the acceptance of artillery which is a particularly efficient arm here—It seems to me that if the offer of a contingent of all arms as originally intended by Dr. Borden, should be made, it would appear as an offer really worthy of Canada and that would find favour with the Canadian public. . . .[23]

The Laurier ministry was now faced with the gravest sort of internal crisis. World politics had impinged upon Canada's colonial isolation with a vengeance. The war that had broken out upon the African veldt forced a painful decision upon the cabinet in Ottawa. It was painful because the two great segments of the Canadian community, English and French, found themselves on opposite sides of the question to be decided. And the crisis remains unique in the country's history. Never since 1899 has the outbreak of a war found the national government so deeply and gravely divided. The *Globe*, loyally Liberal, assured its readers that reports that the cabinet was "not whole-minded on the subject" were "wholly unfounded"; the ministers spent some time "discussing certain minor details", but "the principle that the contingent should be sent was never a matter of doubt".[24] This was the reverse of the truth. The division was fundamental and grim.

Our information concerning the schism comes largely from the Governor General.* The basic division was English versus French; but in practice the situation was less simple than that. There were, it appears, three parties within the cabinet. The first, composed mainly of French Canadians but also apparently including Senator R. W. Scott, the Irish Roman Catholic Secretary of State, was opposed to sending a contingent on any terms; the second was in favour of acting on Chamberlain's proposals of October 3; while a third represented somewhat the same point of view which Minto had urged upon Laurier, asking for a Canadian contingent "preserving its individuality . . . & paid by Canada".[25] This third party was made up of ministers from Ontario.

The most violent opponent of sending troops was Israël Tarte, the Minister of Public Works. What Laurier reported, what Tarte said in print, and what Tarte told Minto directly,[26] indicates that Tarte based his opposition on constitutional grounds—the fact "that we are called upon to raise troops and to pay money without having any right whatever of representation in Imperial councils".[27] Laurier, in a conversation with Minto on November 16, attributed Tarte's opposition to the influence of Henri Bourassa, the independent young Liberal MP for Labelle. Minto wrote, "It appears, I think during Sir Wilfrid's absence in Chicago, that Mr. Bourassa brought all the influence he could to bear on Mr. Tarte against sending the contingent." Bourassa, Laurier told the Governor General, had no constitutional basis for his views; "He simply objects to sending a Contingent because he does not approve of a Colony being mixed up with the affairs of the Mother Country."[28] Nevertheless, since Bourassa made much of the constitutional argument later, Laurier may have been mistaken. During the two-day cabinet discussion, Laurier said,

* The Canadian cabinet began to keep a record of its proceedings only in 1944.

Tarte "vehemently" objected to the contingent proposal and threatened to resign: "his resignation was in doubt for two days, but he finally consented to accept the Government's policy."

At the opposite pole from Tarte was William Mulock, Postmaster General and member for North York (Ontario). He was as vehemently in favour of a contingent as Tarte was opposed; and early on the second day of the cabinet's deliberations he became so disgusted with the French opposition that he stormed out of the council chamber and had to be pursued and begged to return.[29] As for Laurier himself, his original reluctance to consider a contingent has already been adequately documented; but as Prime Minister his inevitable endeavour was to seek a compromise that would avoid a disruption of his cabinet and satisfy as many Canadians as possible. His own final views perhaps find expression in a strong letter which he wrote, just after the resolution of the crisis, to a Liberal editor in London, Ontario:

> What the Tories demand, what they will insist upon, is that we should equip, arm and send to South Africa and there maintain, at our own expense a contingent of about one thousand. This, I must tell you frankly, I am not prepared to do. . . . I question very much the advisability, even from an Imperial point of view, of a young country like Canada, launching into military expenditure. We have a great deal to do in this country to develop it to its legitimate expansion. Military expenditure is of such a character that you never know where it will end; I am not disposed in favour of it. We have done more in favour of Imperial defence in building the Intercolonial and the Canadian Pacific, than if we had maintained an army in the field in those last twenty years.
>
> We have resolved yesterday to equip and send to South Africa a force of one thousand on the terms asked by the Imperial Authorities themselves. More than this we could not do. . . .
>
> I must go a step more; I deem it my duty to tell you quietly but firmly that I am not disposed to go, at this moment, into such a military expenditure as your letter would imply. We have not reached that stage of development; there is no reason for such a waste of money on our part; there is no reason to play soldiering. Whilst we are quite willing to do our share as a part of the British Empire, we should not countenance any suggestion of Jingo bellowing. . . .[30]

Something of the course of the cabinet's discussions is indicated by a draft minute of council dated October 12 stating that the government had considered dispatching and maintaining a force under the General

Officer Commanding the Militia, but had refrained from doing so because of the suggestions made in the Colonial Secretary's communication and because such action would involve departure from past policy, consideration by Parliament and "reconsideration of the present relations" between Britain and the colonies. The evident intention is to act within the limits of Chamberlain's dispatch. This is what was finally done, but it was apparently considered undesirable to make so definite a reference to the rejected alternative.[31]

More definite evidence on the course of the crisis is found in a cable sent by Minto to the Colonial Office, evidently on the evening of October 12, and received the following morning:

Your telegram of third purporting to be reply to communication[s] received by H.M. Government my responsible advisers desire to know what were those communications and from whom and through what channels they were sent. Secret and confidential. Premier requests me to send the above. Have delayed replying sooner at request of my Govt. who are much annoyed at substance of your tel. of 3rd having appeared simultaneously in London press and here thereby increasing the enthusiasm which has nearly forced their hand. They believe also that irresponsible offers of troops have been made to W. O. [War Office] of which my Govt. have no knowledge and express determination to discover who have made them. Cabinet sitting all today arrived at no decision.

Chief opposition from Quebec; Premier personally opposed to offering troops because it would be new departure in Colonial responsibilities though he approves of Imperial action in S. Africa. All Ontario press with enthusiasm announce offer of troops as settled and public dissatisfaction as very great. Discussion in Cabinet extremely heated.

Newspapers stated that H.M.G. have asked for troops. Consider it important to dispel idea. Matter still under consideration....[32]

This telegram must have caused something of a flurry in Whitehall. It was promptly dealt with. John Anderson, a level-headed civil servant in the Colonial Office, drafted a reply for Chamberlain, which he covered with a minute:

No doubt they suspect that Genl. Hutton has been in communication with W.O. and wish to get an excuse for venting their irritation on him. He made no offer, of course, and we must keep him out of it.... They forget that today it is S. Africa, but the next time it may be N. America.[33]

The reply went off that evening. It explained that the telegram of October 3 referred to Hughes's offer, and to an offer by a "person in Br. Columbia" who had been referred to Minto by telegram, "as well as to numerous apparently authentic statements in press that volunteers were offering their services". No communication had been made to the British press concerning any telegram to Minto; "only statement issued referred exclusively to Australasian offers". Chamberlain proceeded:

> Yr Ministers shd clearly understand that H.M.G. do not ask for Canadian troops though any offer of such wd be highly appreciated as practical demonstration of unanimity throughout Empire as to importance & necessity of insisting on fair and equal treatment for Br. subjects and of maintaining interests of Empire in S. Africa or wherever they may be threatened.[34]

It is possible, though by no means certain, that this telegram, well suited to smooth the hackles that had been raised, reached Ottawa in time to contribute to resolving the battle in the cabinet. At any rate, resolved it was. That evening (the message was received at the Colonial Office early on the morning of October 14) Minto telegraphed to the Colonial Secretary:[35]

> Have shown Premier your Telegram of today and he is entirely satisfied. Much pleasure in telling you that my Government offers one thousand infantry on organisation proposed in your telegram of the 3rd October.*

The formula upon which ministers had finally reached agreement was recorded in a famous order-in-council (P.C. 1618 K, approved by the Governor General on October 14).[36] Like the draft considered on the 12th, it began by reciting the terms of Chamberlain's cable of October 3. It proceeded in terms that may well reflect the cable of the 13th:

> The Right Honourable Sir Wilfrid Laurier to whom the said despatch was referred, observes that the Colonial Secretary, in answer to the offers which have been sent to him from different parts of Canada expressing the willingness and anxiety of Canadians to serve Her Majesty's Government in the war which for a long time has been threatening with the Transvaal Republic and which, unfortunately, has actually commenced, enunciates the conditions

* As published in the Canadian Sessional Papers, the first sentence of this telegram was deleted. It should be noted that the published papers are incomplete (many being omitted) and that those published were heavily censored.

under which such offers may be accepted by the Imperial authorities. These conditions may be practically summed up in the statement that a certain number of volunteers by units of 125 men, with a few officers, will be accepted to serve in the British Army now operating in South Africa, the moment they reach the coast, provided the expenses of their equipment and transportation to South Africa, are defrayed either by themselves or by the Colonial Government.

The Prime Minister, in view of the well known desire of a great many Canadians who are ready to take service under such conditions, is of opinion that the moderate expenditure which would thus be involved for the equipment and transportation of such volunteers may readily be undertaken by the Government of Canada without summoning Parliament, especially as such expenditure under such circumstances cannot be regarded as a departure from the well known principles of constitutional government and colonial practice, nor construed as a precedent for future action. . . .

The Prime Minister therefore recommends that out of the stores now available in the Militia Department, the Government undertake to equip a certain number of volunteers not to exceed one thousand men, and to provide for their transportation from this country to South Africa and that the Minister of Militia make all necessary arrangements to the above effect. . . .

Thus a contingent was to go, but for the moment it was not called a contingent. In accordance with Laurier's financial scruples, it was to go very largely at British expense. As for the question of precedent, under strict construction the precedent which the action supposedly did not set was the expenditure of a modest sum of money without parliamentary sanction. But there can be little doubt that the country at large thought that the precedent involved was the dispatch of an expeditionary force to take part in an imperial war; nor can there be much doubt that Bourassa was right when he said later[37] that the precedent was the accomplished fact.

Though the worst of the crisis was over, this was not the end of the story. During the next few days the basis of the contingent was altered in important respects.

The order-in-council had represented only a partial victory for Minto and those Canadians who thought like him. The Governor General still hoped that the contingent might be a mixed force of all arms, whereas his message reporting his government's decision—though not the order-in-council expressing that decision—had stated that it was to be infantry. And along with the cable making the official offer Minto sent to the Colonial Office on the evening of October 13 a private message making important further suggestions:

I am requested by Premier to inform you privately that the general wish here is that troops offered should be kept together as Canadian Contingent. Organization as a small brigade of all arms most popular here.

Following has been thoroughly considered, one Battery one Regiment of Infantry of two small Battalions of four Companies each, one hundred mounted Rifles could be ready by the 31st.

Lieutenant Colonel [W.D.] Otter excellent officer to command. This represents the views of Hutton. If this is impossible, could troops now offered be kept together under Colonel Otter, he to sink rank to Major? Please submit this to War Office and inform me immediately, considering it private and in no way qualifying the offer officially made. Organization of your telegram of October 3rd caused disappointment as it cuts out best officers and Artillery the most efficient arm here.[38]

The Colonial Office proceeded to discuss the proposals received from Minto with the War Office. The discussion was notable for Chamberlain's firm minute of October 15 with reference to the fact that Canada had offered twice as many men as his cable of October 3 had suggested: "I will not accept a W. O. decision to decline the 1000 from Canada."[39] On the whole, however, both departments showed themselves sympathetic to Canadian views as interpreted by Minto. With respect to Minto's "personal" telegram, the War Office followed up an informal statement of October 15[40] with the suggestion that the reply should be in these terms:

War Office has agreed to accept offer as recommended by Hutton but Commander in Chief [Wolseley] wishes it to be clearly understood that he cannot guarantee that the Contingent ["Brigade" deleted] shall always be kept together during operations. General must be free to dispose of the force to the best advantage.[41]

No one could really take exception to this. The very small mixed force suggested by Hutton and Minto would have been difficult to find suitable independent tasks for, and a higher commander might have been faced with the choice of dividing its components or leaving it idle. It is worth mentioning that the infantry regiment of "two small Battalions" was something quite unknown to current British organization, and it is perhaps rather surprising that the War Office agreed to it.

The "small brigade of all arms", however, never came into existence, for there were further political developments. On October 16 Minto received from Chamberlain a cable approving the brigade organization and agreeing that the force should be kept together as far as practicable. Laurier was absent from Ottawa, and Minto discussed the matter with Scott and Dr. Borden.[42] They saw no reason why some artillery, at any rate, should not be sent.[43] Minto then again urged on Laurier the advantages of the brigade organization, emphasizing that the imperial government would still be paying the bill.[44] In spite of this assurance Sir Wilfrid was not pleased. His memory of the conversation on the evening of the 13th did not accord with Minto's. His displeasure was enhanced by the fact that his morning paper on October 17 announced that the War Office had accepted the Canadian view that the contingent should be one unit—the *Globe* said, a battalion, under Canadian officers. Laurier would have preferred a policy of "caution and silence".[45]

It appears that it was Scott who gave out such information as had been published, for he wrote to Laurier on the 18th, "The only information I gave to the public was the acceptance of the contingent to be kept together if practicable, and the statement that all Colonial troops were to be on the same footing. The effect on the public mind of giving this information has been a very much improved tone and has calmed the excitement."[46]

It seems likely that Laurier's pique affected the final decision concerning the composition of the contingent, which was evidently made on October 18, presumably by a cabinet meeting. Minto reported the rejection of his brigade organization as follows:

> After full consideration my Ministers have decided to offer a regiment of infantry, 1000 strong, under command of Lieut-Col. Otter.
>
> In reply to your telegram of today* I have to state that no artillery or Mounted troops will be sent.
>
> My Ministers hope that Canadian contingent will be kept together as much as possible but realize that this must be left to discretion of War Office and Commander in Chief.[47]

The only later modification of the organization was a minor one. On the same day Minto cabled secretly:

> We intend at present to organize Canadian Corps as two small battalions but we are anxious if possible not to make this public until last moment. Tarte's

* A cable formally accepting the brigade organization and stating the War Office reservations about a commitment to keep the contingent together.

opposition considerably complicates organization. He appears to be trying to render the contingent as little representative as possible. . . .[48]

At this distance, it is a little difficult to understand the importance attached to the two small battalions, or the nature of Tarte's alleged machinations, unless perhaps he was attempting to prevent the raising of troops in Quebec. The contingent was actually raised in eight companies in eleven centres across the Dominion from Charlottetown to Victoria, including one company each from Quebec and Montreal.[49] Before it went to South Africa the two small battalions quietly faded away, and it served as a unit conforming to British Army organization, designated the 2nd (Special Service) Battalion of the Royal Canadian Regiment of Infantry, the infantry component of the Canadian Permanent Force. The Royal Canadian Regiment has survived the policies of Mr. Hellyer and (to the time of writing) Mr. Trudeau; and it still carries the campaign honour "South Africa" and the battle honour "Paardeberg" to recall the part it played in those distant and exciting times.

Laurier and his colleagues had insisted on standing by their original decision of October 13, which in spite of the curious silence of the order-in-council had clearly envisaged an offer of infantry. Broadly speaking, they had conformed to the suggestions from London. The War Office—making perhaps its most legendary error of judgment—had said that infantry was what it wanted; and infantry was what it was going to get. The British authorities (influenced maybe by Minto's earlier comments) had decided to pay practically the whole bill, and Laurier was clearly delighted. Only on the vital points of strength and organization had there been a change. There were not to be four little units of 125 men scattered about the British army; instead, there would be 1,000 Canadians concentrated in a single unit. No doubt, this gave satisfaction to many other Canadians at home, though no doubt also there were some who were not pleased by the fact that Laurier's Canadian soldiers of 1899, like Mackenzie King's Canadian airmen of 1939, were to be paid by the British. (As in 1939, the Canadian government in 1899 finally paid the difference between British and Canadian rates of pay.)[50]

However accidental the decision to make the First Canadian Contingent a battalion of infantry may have been, in a national sense there seems no reason to regret it. As we have said, the Hutton–Minto plan of a small mixed brigade really was open to military objections (though if Hutton's hope of commanding this force combined with a similar one from Australia[51] had been realized the resulting body might have made more sense as a permanent formation). In the case of a battalion, on the other hand, the expressed hope that the unit might be kept together was really redundant; the only circumstance likely to have produced the dispersion of a battalion was its being hopelessly inefficient. And this the 2nd RCR was not (though its commanding officer remarked a trifle grimly in one of his reports, "The creation of the discipline, so imperative in a military body, was a more difficult matter than either that of drill or duties").[52] It is a rather remarkable fact that this battalion, which sailed for South Africa seventeen days after the order for its organization was issued, took its place in a British regular brigade on February 12, 1900 and fought with success in a major battle at Paardeberg about a week later. The brigade's reputation does not seem to have suffered by its colonial infusion; Arthur Conan Doyle, who was there, wrote later of "Smith-Dorrien's Nineteenth Brigade, comprising the Shropshires, the Cornwalls, the Gordons, and the Canadians, probably the very finest brigade in the whole army".[53] It may be remarked in passing that these achievements, though they doubtless owed something to the exceptionally good human stuff of which the battalion was made, probably owed more to the fact that the commanding officer and a fair proportion of his officers and men were experienced regular soldiers.

The dispatch of the Second Canadian Contingent can be briefly dealt with. It was offered (November 1, 1899) after the first British reverses in South Africa, and declined by the British government a few days later.[54] After the further defeats of "Black Week" in December, London changed its mind. This time mounted infantry and artillery were wanted. With respect to the former, the War Office again talked about units of 125 men commanded by captains.[55] Ottawa replied that before this suggestion was received action had already been taken to organize a regiment of two battalions; and this organization was left intact except that the regimental headquarters was dropped. The two battalions, each commanded by a lieutenant-colonel, served in South Africa under the names "Royal Canadian Dragoons" (that of the cavalry component of the Permanent Force) and "Canadian Mounted Rifles". The artillery, a "brigade division" of three batteries, also constituted a lieutenant-colonel's command. No attempt was ever made to bring all the Canadians in South Africa together as a self-contained body; they would not have been a "viable" military formation, quite apart from the fact that their personnel were enlisted at different times merely for "a term of six months, or longer if required".

But the units were never broken up, except that (as was not unnatural in the circumstances of the time) the three artillery batteries were separated.[56]

There were only two "official" contingents. Other units were raised in Canada later in the war, but entirely without expense to the Canadian taxpayer. The limited costs borne by the Canadian government in connection with the contingents, under the terms of the famous Chamberlain dispatch of October 3, 1899, were borne in the case of these units by the imperial authorities, or in one case, that of Strathcona's Horse, by a private individual. The status of all these units was thus defined by the Deputy Minister of Militia and Defence: "They were not, like the 1st and 2nd contingents, temporary corps in the Canadian Militia, but were temporary corps in the British army."[57] Including these units, and also the 3rd (Special Service) Battalion of the Royal Canadian Regiment, which was raised entirely at Canadian expense to relieve the British infantry garrison of Halifax, Canada's contribution to the war amounted to 8,372 soldiers of all ranks; the total cost to Canada was computed at the modest sum of $2,830,965.07.[58] The whole enterprise was remarkably small in scale in proportion to the national controversy it occasioned and the considerable outburst of national pride with which the troops' performance in South Africa was received.

Nevertheless, as we have suggested, the precedent was important. So was the controversy. The rift between French and English Canada caused by the great external crises of 1914–18 and 1939–45 is painfully foreshadowed in the events of 1899.

The affair is significant also in terms of national military policy. The rejection of little units scattered through the British army in favour of "a Canadian contingent to act as such"—a Canadian battalion under a Canadian colonel—is a small but nevertheless striking precedent. It was the beginning of a tradition that was to be carefully followed by Canadian governments and commanders in two world wars—or at any rate until the great aberration of 1943, when Mackenzie King's cabinet, somewhat against the Prime Minister's own better judgment, divided the First Canadian Army and insisted on sending a corps to Italy. This tradition rested on two foundations: the conviction that Canadians fought best and most effectively in their own organization and under their own commanders; and the evident fact that a small country contributing troops to the war effort of an empire or a coalition must keep its force concentrated if it wishes to exercise any effective control over it.

It is particularly interesting that the person who more than any other was responsible for initiating this healthy national tradition in 1899 was not a Canadian politician or soldier, but the Governor General, Lord Minto. As we have seen, there is evidence of some feeling in the cabinet in favour of a unified Canadian contingent, but it found no echo in the decision of October 13; both the order-in-council and Minto's "official" cable of October 13 reporting the decision accept the organization of the Chamberlain telegram, in units of 125 men. Minto, as his letters prove, had worked hard to convince Laurier that this was not sound policy. It seems highly probable that the Premier's opinion, reported in Minto's "private" cable of October 13, in favour of keeping the troops together, was arrived at after a final verbal argument from Minto. Here, as on some other occasions, one is impressed with Minto's rugged common sense and with the fact that he was a rather remarkably "good Canadian".[59]

Mr. Norman Penlington has suggested that there was a close relationship between Canadian difficulties with the United States at the end of the nineteenth century and Canadian participation in the war in South Africa. The Alaska boundary dispute, as we shall see shortly (below, page 86) became an active question following the discovery of gold in the Klondike in 1896. The argument is that Canada, urgently needing British support in this controversy, sent troops to South Africa to build up a credit of goodwill; that, in fact, she did what Sir John A. Macdonald alleged the Australian colonies had done in 1885 when they thought themselves menaced by French and German imperialism in the Pacific (above, page 43). The idea is plausible, but there really is not much evidence for it. It is true that both General Hutton, the General Officer Commanding the Militia, and Lord Minto used the Alaska controversy as an argument in urging a Canadian contribution in South Africa; it was used also by people like Colonel George T. Denison in pressing the government to act.[60] But the Canadian public does not seem to have been very conscious of this aspect of the matter. Few Canadians thought in terms of war, or of any type of power clash, with the United States over Alaska; indeed, in the recent war between the U.S. and Spain (1898) Canadian sympathy had been very actively enlisted on the American side. Mr. Penlington admits that "Whether Laurier saw the demand for participation as insurance for Britain's protection against the United States is doubtful."[61]

One thing which unfortunately there is no doubt about is the conflict of opinion between French and English Canada over the dispatch of troops to South Africa. It is true that the English-speaking parts of the country were not absolutely united on the issue. A student of the contemporary press finds "a current of opposition to the war among farmers, radical labour, protestant clergy and Anglophobic Canadians of Irish and German descent". Nevertheless, "English" Canada for practical political purposes was a bloc in favour of the war.[62] French Canadians on the other hand felt some sense of kinship with the Boers and no obligation or desire to fight them. Within the cabinet, we have seen, the minority's battle against participation was fought mainly by Israël Tarte; in the House of Commons it was carried on by the eloquent and formidable young Henri Bourassa, grandson of Louis-Joseph Papineau, the rebel of 1837. Bourassa resigned his seat in protest against the decision to send the First Contingent; he was promptly re-elected without a contest.

On March 13, 1900 there was a memorable exchange between Bourassa and Laurier in the Commons. Bourassa interpreted the late events as the result of the machinations of the imperial government and its agents or dupes in Canada. Chamberlain and his disciples, he said, were "leading us towards a constitutional revolution, the consequences of which no man can calculate". Things had been done which could only have been justified if Canada had had a share in imperial decision-making, which could only have been properly authorized by the Parliament of Canada, representing the free opinion of the people. If there were to be changes in Canada's relation to Great Britain, they must be approved by Parliament—and afterwards, "our present constitution being an agreement between the various provinces of British North America", by a plebiscite in which "a majority of the people of each province" was required for approval. Bourassa thought the government's declaration that the action taken involved no precedent "a frail barrier to oppose to the current of noisy militarism": "It is that fear which I expressed in my letter to the Prime Minister when I said: 'The precedent, Sir, is the accomplished fact.' "

Laurier in reply said that the government had only carried out the obvious will of the people: "What would be the condition of this country to-day if we had refused to obey the voice of public opinion?" He spoke with pride of the Canadians' bravery in South Africa, and said with considerable hyperbole that events there had "revealed to the world that a new power had arisen in the west". He pointed out too that both "branches of the Canadian family" were represented among those who had fought and fallen. And he made a remark about imperial consultation which for ambivalence deserves to stand beside his remark about parliamentary representation at the 1897 Colonial Conference (above, page 57), and which he must have lived to regret many times:

... If we were to be compelled to take part in all the wars of Great Britain, I have no hesitation in saying that I agree with my hon. friend [Bourassa] that, sharing the burden, we should also share the responsibility. Under that condition of things, which does not exist, we should have the right to say to Great Britain: If you want us to help you, call us to your councils; if you want us to take part in wars let us share not only the burdens but the responsibilities and duties as well. But there is no occasion to examine this contingency this day. My hon. friend forgets one thing which is essential to this discussion, that we did not use our powers as a government to go into that war.... We simply provided the machinery and expenses for the two thousand young men who wanted to go and give their lives for the honour of their country and the flag they love....

Bourassa divided the House, and only nine members, all from Quebec—five Liberals and four Conservatives—voted with him. It is fair to assume that a good many more Quebec members sympathized silently.[63]

As for Laurier's own views, Lord Minto gave Chamberlain a severely practical assessment of them:

Sir Wilfrid's own inclination toward an Imperial Federation of any sort is in my opinion extremely doubtful.... His speech in the House was very eloquent and the "call us to your councils" phrase appears to have been accepted as indicating a wish to be called—the very last thing Sir Wilfrid would wish and the speech itself did not justify that interpretation of it.... I should say that seriously he is devoid of the British feeling for a United Empire—that it has no sentimental attraction for him and that a closer connection with the Old Country he would consider from the utility point of view and nothing more.[64]

The accuracy of Minto's opinion was supported by an exchange shortly afterwards. Chamberlain, believing optimistically (as nearly everyone did after the successes in February and March 1900) that the war was virtually over, inquired whether Canada would wish to have a voice in the peace settlement; he also raised again the question of a Colonial or Imperial Council. To the first inquiry Laurier replied, "I would not favour the idea of Canada asking to take part in those conferences, but if Canada were invited by Great Britain to attend, I have no doubt that the invitation would be cordially received and accepted." There seems to have been no invitation. On the question of a council, Laurier observed that the chief object of such a body would presumably be action "in the direction of organizing a general plan of defence of the Empire"; and he felt that Canadian assistance in time of need was "more likely to be given voluntarily than under any detailed plan of military organization which would impose on the Colonies fixed financial obligations".[65]

The tide of popular opinion that carried Canada into the South African War was accurately described by Laurier's biographer in a preliminary sketch written in 1915:

> The real source of the demand that Canada should . . . take a part lay in the new-born imperial and national consciousness. The crisis served to precipitate the emotions and opinions which had been vaguely floating in the Canadian mind. The Jubilee festivities and the British preference had increased imperial sentiment; and, with returning prosperity and rapid growth, national pride was getting the better of colonial dependence. A curious element in this pride was the sense of rivalry with the United States, which had just won more or less glory in a little war with Spain. All these sentiments, fanned by vigorous newspaper appeal, led to the wish to do something tangible to show that the day of passive loyalty was over and the day of responsible partnership had begun.[66]

The influence of English-Canadian "nationalism" in producing participation in the war is as evident as the influence of French-Canadian "nationalism" in opposition to it.

CONFERENCES WITH CONSERVATIVES AND LIBERALS

The Colonial Conference which assembled in London in the summer of 1902 was an immediate aftermath of the South African War, and Joseph Chamberlain, still Colonial Secretary, clearly approached it in the hope that the military enthusiasms of the war period could be used to effect some permanent measures of imperial reorganization. Once more he confronted Laurier, the champion of the status quo. The six Australian premiers were now replaced by one Prime Minister of the Commonwealth, Sir Edmund Barton.

Chamberlain made a strong plea for advance in the three areas of policy which he had indicated in 1897: political relations, commercial relations, and defence. Under the first head, he recalled the resolutions of 1897:

Well, then, gentlemen, what I put to you is. Can we make any advance to-day upon these proposals? I may be considered, perhaps, to be a dreamer, or too enthusiastic, but I do not hesitate to say that, in my opinion, the political federation of the Empire is within the limits of possibility.

He went on, nevertheless, to strike a note of caution. Nothing should be done prematurely.

We have had, within the last few years, a most splendid evidence of the results of a voluntary union without any formal obligations, in the great crisis of the war through which we have now happily passed.... it would be a fatal mistake to transform the spontaneous enthusiasm which has been so readily shown throughout the Empire into anything in the nature of an obligation which might be at this time unwillingly assumed or only formally accepted. ...And, therefore, upon this point of the political relations between the Colonies and ourselves, His Majesty's Government, while they would welcome any approach which might be made to a more definite and a closer union, feel that it is not for them to press this upon you. The demand, if it comes, must come from the Colonies. If it comes it will be enthusiastically received in this country.

Chamberlain now made his most dramatic appeal. He used as his text Laurier's already too-famous remark, "If you want us to help you, call us to your councils":

Gentlemen, we do want your aid.... The weary Titan staggers under the too vast orb of its fate. We have borne the burden for many years. We think it is time that our children should assist us to support it, and whenever you make the request to us, be very sure that we shall hasten gladly to call you to our councils. If you are prepared at any time to take any share, any proportionate share, in the burdens of the Empire, we are prepared to meet you with any proposal for giving to you a corresponding voice in the policy of the Empire. And the object, if I may point out to you, may be achieved in various ways.... I have always felt myself that the most practical form in which we could achieve our object, would be the establishment or the creation of a real Council of the Empire... the Council might in the first instance be merely an advisory council.... But although that would be a preliminary step, it is clear that the object would not be completely secured until there had been conferred upon such a Council executive functions, and perhaps also legislative powers, and it is for you to say, gentlemen, whether you think the time has come when any progress whatever can be made in this direction.[67]

No progress was made. The assembled Prime Ministers did not meet Chamberlain even half-way. The fact is that his political propositions were not discussed, except to the extent of a unanimous resolution to the effect that it would be advantageous if conferences "were held, as far as practicable, at intervals not exceeding four years". (New Zealand proposed three years; Laurier had discouraged the idea of a fixed period.)

The visitors had presumably not failed to note the specific statement that the British government considered that it was for the colonies to initiate action towards political changes, and may well have thought to themselves that Chamberlain's colleagues had imposed this condition upon him. Indeed, the retiring Prime Minister, Lord Salisbury, in his last important speech (May 7, 1902) had uttered what seemed clearly a warning to Chamberlain against a premature attempt at imperial federation.[68] At any rate, none spoke up in reply to the Colonial Secretary's urgent appeal.

Laurier maintained his usual unvarying politeness. Differences in conditions, he told Chamberlain,

compel us, I believe, at all events compel me as far as I am concerned, to take views upon many of the subjects to which you have referred which perhaps in the end may be a little at variance with those which you have yourself expressed. But whilst I say this, at the same time I express my sincere conviction that this Conference must do a great deal of good, even though no more results are obtained and reached under it than those which were reached at a previous Conference, which, though they did not amount to much in the way of concrete results, effected a great deal in opening the space for future development of the ideas which were there expressed.

This was not at all what Chamberlain wanted.

On commercial policy, Chamberlain said, "Our first object . . . is free trade within the Empire . . . But when I speak of free trade it must be understood that I do not mean by that the total abolition of Customs duties as between different part of the Empire."[69] He recognized the fact that the colonies' revenue was raised largely from customs duties. But he called the results of the Canadian preference "disappointing"; Canadian trade with "foreigners" had increased far more since 1897 than trade with the United Kingdom.

He was told in reply that Canada could not dispense with her "moderately protective" tariff. W. S. Fielding, who was present, said, "We do not profess that we want to introduce British goods to displace the goods made by the manufacturers of Canada. That is a point upon which we must speak with great frankness. Whether or not it was a wise policy for Canada to foster her manufacturers by high duties is a point hardly worth discussing now; we must deal with things as we find them." If Britain did not value the preference, then perhaps it should be done away with; it had its critics in Canada.

The conference, while recognizing that imperial free trade was "not practicable" under present circumstances, went on record as favouring preferential treatment by the colonies for British goods, while the overseas Prime Ministers urged on the British government "the expediency of granting in the United Kingdom preferential treatment to the products and manufactures of the Colonies either by exemption from or reduction of duties now or hereafter imposed." This movement towards preference was spearheaded by Laurier and Fielding, who were pursuing the object of an exemption for Canadian wheat under the small "corn duty" lately levied by the British government.

It was on the question of defence that Canada and the mother country differed most firmly. Chamberlain had said that Canada's military expenditure per head was "about one-fifteenth of that incurred by the United Kingdom". The Admiralty wanted the colonies to contribute to the support of the Royal Navy; the War Office (and New Zealand) wanted them to earmark special land contingents for service in an "Imperial Reserve". Canada had no use for either scheme. Laurier brought out the old argument about the cost of public works; but in a memorandum of August 11 explaining why they could not accept the Admiralty and War Office suggestions, the Canadians went to the heart of the matter: "The Ministers desire to point out that their objections arise, not so much from the expense involved, as from a belief that the acceptance of the proposals would entail an important departure from the principle of colonial self-government." They were ready to improve the Canadian Militia and were now "prepared to consider the naval side of defence as well". Lord Selborne, the First Lord of the Admiralty, argued, cogently enough from the strategic viewpoint, "The sea is all one, and the British

Navy therefore must be all one"; but the most he could report from his discussions with Laurier was that the Canadian Prime Minister had told him that the Dominion was "contemplating the establishment of a local Naval force in the waters of Canada". Some years were to pass before anything came of this.

Generally speaking, the Dominion government's attitude continued to be, just as in 1897, that the existing situation was satisfactory. If changes had to be made, they should be made cautiously and control should remain in Canadian hands. Laurier's preference for the status quo was admirably exemplified on July 30 in a discussion on treaties affecting colonial interests:

> I might say that so far as Canada is concerned we have no fault to find or no complaint to make as to the way in which we have been treated in the matter of treaties in the last years. . . . In all matters in which we have been primarily concerned, as in our relations with our neighbours, the United States, not only have we been consulted, but we have been directly given a preponderating voice in the discussions and in the treaty making. So far as that matter is concerned we are quite satisfied with the conditions of things.

The 1902 Colonial Conference must have been the gravest possible disappointment for Joseph Chamberlain. But there was a glimmer of light in one quarter. Some progress towards effective imperial unity seemed possible in the field of commercial policy, the one in which Chamberlain had seemed least interested in 1897. The colonies, led by Canada, had sought to push the mother country towards a policy of imperial preference—a policy indeed of protection. Had the time come for a movement away from the free-trade policy that Britain had made her own since the days of Peel? Chamberlain was beginning to think so.

After the conference he corresponded with Fielding on the subject; and he raised it in the cabinet. On November 19, 1902, the new Prime Minister, A. J. Balfour, informed the King, the cabinet decided that "as at present advised, they would maintain the Corn Tax; but that a preferential remission of it should be made in favour of the British Empire". It seemed that the Colonial Secretary had triumphed; but the real victory was to go to the traditional free traders. Their voice had been heard in a memorandum which the Chancellor of the Exchequer, C. T. Ritchie, had written on November 15: "Let us first be quite clear what preferential treatment involves. It involves the imposition of a charge on the taxpayers of the United Kingdom, in order to benefit our kith and kin beyond the sea." Ritchie prevailed on the cabinet to reverse itself; and in his budget brought down on April 23, 1903 he remitted the Corn Duty.[70]

This was the beginning of the disruption of Balfour's government. In September Ritchie and other free traders were dropped from it; but it seemed evident that the country was not ready to accept a tax on food, and Chamberlain himself resigned simultaneously in order to conduct an educational campaign for tariff reform.[71] The ultimate result was the Unionist (Conservative) debacle in the general election of 1906. By that time Balfour had resigned, and the election confirmed in power the new Liberal ministry of Sir Henry Campbell-Bannerman. It left no doubt that the British people were still free traders and still hostile to taxes on food; and it seemed to indicate that the high tide of imperialism was past. In the same year the great imperialist Chamberlain was struck down by paralysis, and never returned to the political stage.[72] With his career a phase, if not an era, of imperial history drew to a close.

The defeat of imperial preference in Britain did not lead to the principle being dropped in Canada. In 1907 the Canadian tariff assumed the form it has held ever since, in three columns:* a general tariff, the British preferential tariff, and an intermediate tariff, intended to apply to foreign countries having reciprocal trade arrangements with Canada.[73] In this same year—after an interval of five years, not four—another Colonial Conference was held.

The atmosphere of this 1907 conference, held under Liberal auspices, was rather different from those over which Chamberlain had presided.[74] The pressure was lower. The chairman was again the Colonial Secretary, now Lord Elgin (born in Canada during his father's famous tenure as Governor General), a much less dynamic personality than Chamberlain. (His Parliamentary Under-Secretary, Winston Churchill, predictably did a good deal of talking.)[75] At the opening session (April 15) the Prime Minister, Campbell-Bannerman, struck the keynote. He thought, he said, that the views taken of the relations of the colonies and the mother country in connection with expenditure on armaments, had been, "of late, somewhat modified":

* One concrete example from the tariff of 1907 may be given: iron and steel rails paid $4.50 per ton under the British preferential tariff, $6.00 under the intermediate tariff, and $7.00 under the general tariff. It is worth remarking that "Spirits, Wines and other Beverages" obtained no advantage under the British preference; they paid the same rates under all three tariffs.

We do not meet you to-day as claimants for money, although we cordially recognise the spirit in which contributions have been made in the past, and will, no doubt, be made in the future. It is, of course, possible to over-estimate the importance of the requirements of the over-sea dominions as a factor in our expenditure; but however this may be, the cost of naval defence and the responsibility for the conduct of foreign affairs hang together.

This gathering witnessed considerable discussion on the conference as an institution. The phrase "Imperial Council" had been mooted in the correspondence before the meeting, but Canada had discouraged it; and Alfred Deakin, now Prime Minister of Australia, said that after seeing Laurier's dispatch, "We accepted the term 'Imperial Conference' instead of 'Imperial Council'." The resolution finally passed provided that the conference should in future be called the Imperial Conference, and that it should be "between His Majesty's Government and His Governments of the self-governing Dominions beyond the seas".* (The word "Dominions" as a term for the self-governing colonies thus came into official use.)

It was also agreed that henceforth the Prime Minister of the United Kingdom, not the Colonial Secretary, should preside. The latter, however, would be an ex officio member of the conference. This change was agreeable to the Dominion representatives, who had certainly not relished the situation exemplified under Chamberlain by the famous photograph of the conference of 1897,[76] with the Colonial Secretary seated while the colonial premiers stand around him. "This Conference", said Laurier, "is not, as I understand it (I give my own views) a Conference simply of the Prime Ministers of the different self-governing Colonies and the Secretary of State, but it is, if I may give my own mind, a conference between government and governments; it is a Conference between the Imperial Government and the Governments of the self-governing dependencies of England."[77]

In previous conferences Laurier had contended for the right of a colonial premier to be accompanied by one or more of his cabinet colleagues,

* For the Canadian Minute of Council (November 13, 1905) suggesting "Imperial Conference" as a more suitable term than "Imperial Council", see Maurice Pope, ed., *Public Servant: The Memoirs of Sir Joseph Pope* (Toronto, 1960), pp. 169-700. It also discouraged a British suggestion for associating with the conference a "permanent Commission" parallel to the Committee of Imperial Defence. The minute was based on a memorandum by Joseph Pope.

and there had been some opposition to the idea. It was now agreed that additional ministers might attend, "it being understood that, except by special permission of the Conference, each discussion will be conducted by not more than two representatives from each Government, and that each Government will have only one vote".

The conference also considered the question of some form of permanent secretariat to lend continuity to its proceedings, and on this there was wide difference of opinion. Laurier clearly would have preferred no secretariat at all, whereas Deakin (an old foe of the Colonial Office) would have liked to see one erected quite independent of the Office and responsible to the British Prime Minister. Campbell-Bannerman would not accept this last idea; the Colonial Office naturally fought for its own position; and the plan at last adopted, with Laurier's support, was that there should be "a permanent secretarial staff, charged, under the direction of the Secretary of State for the Colonies, with the duty of obtaining information for the use of the Conference, of attending to its resolutions, and of conducting correspondence on matters relating to its affairs".[78]

Defence still loomed large in the proceedings of the conference of 1907. As a result of the South African War, there had been important improvements in British military organization: notably, the institution of a General Staff and of the Committee of Imperial Defence. As early as 1903 Sir Frederick Borden, the Canadian Minister of Militia and Defence, had attended a meeting of the CID. The result was not altogether happy, as there was some disagreement as to just what had been decided.[79] Inevitably, the British authorities thought of the committee as a means of maintaining influence over the Dominion military organizations; the Canadians, just as inevitably, tended to mistrust it as an instrument of centralization. An attempt was now made to fit these innovations into the imperial pattern. It was agreed that the colonies might refer to the CID, through the Colonial Secretary, any local questions on which expert assistance "is deemed desirable"; and that "whenever so desired" a representative of the colony seeking advice "should be summoned to attend as a member of the Committee during the discussion of the questions raised". On the other question, it was resolved that the conference,

> without wishing to commit any of the Governments represented, recognises and affirms the need of developing for the service of the Empire a General Staff, selected from the forces of the Empire as a whole, which shall study military science in all its branches, shall collect and disseminate to the various

Governments military information and intelligence, shall undertake the preparation of schemes of defence on a common principle, and without in the least interfering in questions connected with command and administration shall, at the request of the respective Governments, advise as to the training, education and war organisation of the military forces of the Crown in every part of the Empire.[79]

Sir Frederick Borden, who attended the conference with Laurier, had accepted the Imperial General Staff as "a purely advisory body", adding, "but it really seems to me we should have our own General Staff responsible to the Canadian Government". In fact the Imperial General Staff as such was destined to be virtually stillborn, though the British government's senior army adviser carried the imposing title of Chief of the Imperial General Staff until 1964.

As Campbell-Bannerman had indicated, the British representatives this time refrained from pressing the colonies for contributions to naval defence. Lord Tweedmouth, the First Lord of the Admiralty, said, "We want you to give us all the assistance you can, but we do not come to you as beggars." But there was an incident which is worthy of note. A representative of Cape Colony, Dr. T. W. Smartt, moved a resolution to the effect that the conference considered it to be "the duty of the Dominions beyond the Seas to make such contribution towards the upkeep of the Navy as may be determined by their local legislatures", in the form of a grant of money, the "establishment of local Naval defence", or otherwise. Laurier dissented very strongly, referring yet once more to the extent of Canadian expenditure on public works: "For my part, if the motion were pressed to a conclusion, I should have to vote against it." The matter was hastily dropped and not revived during the conference. But defence was to become a pressing problem in the near future, and hard decisions lay ahead for Canada.

On the question of trade and imperial preference, there was nothing to be done in London in 1907. The British electorate had spoken, and the Liberal government was delighted with the decision. Free trade had been confirmed as the British gospel. The conference reaffirmed the resolutions of 1902 on imperial preference but the British government "was unable to give its assent" to the reaffirmation in so far as it implied "that it is necessary or expedient to alter the fiscal system of the United Kingdom". Years would have to pass, and the world would have to change radically, before a British minister would again be able to speak of Great Britain setting up a preferential tariff.

In the meantime, Canada, with the benevolent countenance of the mother country, proceeded to enlarge her commercial contacts with foreign countries. In 1906 the British Ambassador in Tokyo had signed a treaty with Japan whereby the provisions of a treaty of commerce and navigation and a supplementary convention made between Britain and Japan in 1894 and 1895 were "applied to the intercourse commerce and navigation between the Empire of Japan and the British Dominion of Canada"; this was duly "sanctioned" by a statute passed by the Canadian Parliament the following year.[80] The Dominion government now let it be known that it wished to negotiate a new trade treaty with France, and also one with Italy. Sir Edward Grey, Campbell-Bannerman's Foreign Secretary, in effect turned the whole negotiation over to Canadian ministers. In a dispatch to the British chargé d'affaires at Paris he recalled the "Ripon Circular" of 1895 (above, pages 47-48) but went on to say that he did not "think it necessary to adhere in the present case to the strict letter of this regulation, the object of which was to secure that negotiations should not be entered into and carried through by a Colony unknown to and independently of his Majesty's Government":

> The selection of the negotiator is principally a matter of convenience, and, in the present circumstances, it will obviously be more practical that the negotiations should be left to Sir W. Laurier and to the Canadian Minister of Finance, who will doubtless keep you informed of their progress.
>
> If the negotiations are brought to a conclusion at Paris, you should sign the Agreement jointly with the Canadian negotiator, who would be given full powers for the purpose.[81]

A similar letter went to the British Embassy at Rome. In the event, the French treaty was signed on September 19, 1907 by the British Ambassador in Paris, Sir Francis Bertie, and two Canadian ministers, W. S. Fielding and L. P. Brodeur. A wide range of Canadian products, including fish and grains, were given the benefit of the French minimum tariff. Many French products were brought under Canada's new intermediate tariff (above, page 79); and some, including sparkling wines and books, were given the benefit of a special tariff.[82] The Italian project produced no results for the moment.

By 1907, it is evident, Canada was essentially a free agent in the negotiation of commercial treaties, the imperial representative's involvement being largely a formality. Commercial treaties—treaties directly affecting the making of money by Canadians—were the sort of treaty in which the Canada of that period had most interest. And the country with the greatest money-making potential for Canadians was clearly the "great republic" next door.

CHAPTER FOUR

LAURIER AND THE AMERICANS, 1896-1909

TARIFFS AND ALASKA

The problems besetting Canada's relations with her North American neighbour as the Victorian age drew to a close were, as they almost always are, in great part economic; but they also included the last of the great and formidable boundary disputes.

On the tariff question as the Canadian Liberals found it on their accession to power in 1896 we have already said something. Their electoral victory nearly coincided with a victory of the Republican party—the high-tariff party—in the United States, William McKinley being elected President. In February 1897 Laurier sent Louis Davies, Minister of Marine and Fisheries, to Washington to spy out the land. He was pleasantly received, but his mission had no solid results; and the Dingley Tariff (above, page 53), finally enacted in the United States in July of that year, expressed "an aggressive spirit of protection"[1] and hit Canadian produce exports hard (see Appendix B). Fear of reaction from the business community had led Laurier to appoint Fielding as his Minister of Finance instead of the notable free trader Sir Richard Cartwright, who had held the portfolio under Alexander Mackenzie. Fielding made dutiful bows to free trade and to the Liberal platform of 1893; but in the circumstances of 1897 all he *did* for free trade was to produce the modest British preferential tariff already described. In his budget speech of April 22, made when the Dingley Bill was still before the U.S. Senate, he advised, with respect to the United States, a policy of "wait and see": "it is the part of prudence that we should to-day hold our hands and not extend to that country the measure of tariff reform which we would be anxious to extend if they would meet us on liberal lines." With the Dingley Act in effect, United States products remained subject to Canada's general tariff, that is, the highest rates.

About the same time that Laurier came to power, the boundary between Canada and Alaska became a pressing question. The background of the trouble—the American purchase of Alaska from Russia in 1867—we have already glanced at. The difficulty lay in a still more remote diplomatic transaction, the Anglo-Russian treaty of 1825 defining the boundary. The United States had inherited Russia's rights under this treaty, and unfortunately the document's language was uncertain. In particular, did a line "parallel to the sinuosities of the coast" mean a line drawn across the mouths of the deep inlets or around their heads? If the former, Canada's Yukon Territory had access to the sea; if the latter, it was landlocked. From 1884 onwards there were sporadic attempts to settle the question. It received some attention from the Joint High Commission of 1887–88 (above, pages 36–37). In 1892 a joint survey was agreed on and it was completed in 1895. Then in 1896–97 gold was found in the Yukon, prospectors poured in, and the whole problem assumed a new importance. It was now a question of access to the goldfields.[2]

By 1897 there was again a long list of issues outstanding between Canada and the United States. The arrangement of 1893 (above, page 38) had not ended the trouble over the Behring Sea seal fishery; the North Atlantic fisheries were still making difficulty; Canadians still hoped for reciprocity in tariffs; all this in addition to the Alaska boundary. In November 1897 Laurier and Davies (now Sir Louis) went to Washington and suggested a joint commission to settle the accumulated problems. While this was still under consideration war broke out between the United States and Spain (April 1898) and this added another question to the catalogue: the possibility of revising the Rush-Bagot Agreement of 1817 to permit the United States to build warships on the Great Lakes. There were also some less contentious matters. The fact that in the crisis with Spain the British Empire appeared to be the United States' only friend among the nations made an arrangement easier to arrive at; and by the early summer of 1898 the three parties concerned had agreed on the reference to a Joint High Commission generally similar to those of 1871 and 1887–88.[3]

The final agreement on the composition of the Commission provided for six members on each side. On the British side only one, the chairman, came from the United Kingdom. He was Lord Herschell, a distinguished lawyer who had been Lord Chancellor under Gladstone and Rosebery. There were four Canadians: Laurier himself, Davies, Cartwright, and John Charlton. (The contrast with the two earlier High Commissions is marked.) Finally there was Sir James Winter, Premier of Newfoundland, a late addition. The decision concerning the instructions to the commissioners likewise reflected changing times. The Foreign Office's advice to the Colonial Office (which was followed) seems a model of common sense.[4] Several of the questions to be discussed, it remarked, "are of a purely local character, about which this Department at least is without information on which any instructions to the British Representatives on the Commission could usefully be framed":

> In these circumstances it appears to Lord Salisbury that the direct representation of Her Majesty's Government on the Commission might be confined to Her Majesty's Ambassador at Washington, and that the Canadian representatives while being appointed by Royal Commission should take their instructions from the Dominion Government.*

The American chairman was Senator Charles W. Fairbanks. Among his colleagues were Representative Nelson Dingley of tariff fame (who actually proved tractable on the reciprocity issue, but unfortunately died while the commission was sitting) and John W. Foster, a former Secretary of State. The commission began its sittings at Quebec in August 1898 and subsequently moved to Washington. It worked hard and made good progress on a number of questions—notably the Behring Sea sealing and the Rush–Bagot Agreement—and there seemed to be some prospect of a satisfactory general settlement.[5] But the whole negotiation foundered on the rock of the Alaska boundary.

The crux of the question here was the deep inlet called the Lynn Canal. If the Canadian contention were accepted, the boundary would cross this waterway low down, and Canada would own its upper reaches. At the head of it, however, were two well-established American communities, Dyea and Skagway, and it was widely held even in Canada that the Dominion could scarcely expect to take them over. The Americans had a good claim based on effective occupation. Nevertheless the United States members of the commission were for a time disposed to recognize the force of Canada's desire for an outlet to the sea via the Lynn Canal.

* The decision to substitute Herschell for the Ambassador came later. Note that Lord Salisbury was his own Foreign Secretary.

Herschell suggested that the United States might be left in possession of Dyea and Skagway but that Canada might be given the neighbouring port of Pyramid Harbor and a strip of land connecting it with the interior. The Americans were ready to accept this, subject to Pyramid Harbor remaining under nominal U.S. sovereignty, Canada agreeing not to fortify it and the concession being limited to a term of fifty years. This last provision was unacceptable to the Canadians. It seemed, however, that a settlement was in sight. Then, most unfortunately, news of the proposed arrangement leaked out. There was a roar of protest from the Pacific Coast states, and the American representatives felt obliged to modify and then to withdraw their offer.[6]

Reluctantly, the commissioners turned to consider arbitration. They met an impasse. The British suggested a tribunal of three arbitrators, one from each party to the dispute and one appointed by a European power. This was the sort of arbitration which the United States had successfully pressed on Britain with respect to the boundary between Venezuela and British Guiana (above, page 50). The Americans, however, proposed a tribunal of six, three from each party. Canada would not accept this, nor would she accept the idea of a Latin American third party; and there the matter rested. What is more, the whole negotiation came to an end. The Anglo-Canadian delegation took the view that if the most important issue, the Alaska boundary, could not be settled, they did not wish to proceed with discussion of the lesser ones. In February 1899 the Joint High Commission adjourned—officially, to meet again in Quebec in August. It never did meet again. A particular misfortune contributed to its total failure. Shortly before the adjournment Lord Herschell fell on an icy street in Washington and was severely hurt. He told Lord Salisbury that he hoped that while detained in Washington he could still achieve a diplomatic settlement of the Alaska question. His Canadian colleagues had formed a high opinion of Herschell, and he might conceivably have worked out an arrangement mutually satisfactory to the parties. But his injury proved fatal; and with him died the hope of an immediate settlement.[7]

For months to come the Canadian government declined all proposals made to it either for a resumption of the work of the High Commission or for an Alaskan settlement. One of the suggestions refused was a British one, based on discussions with the U.S. Ambassador in London, that the Alaska dispute should be referred to an arbitration board of seven with a neutral umpire, with Dyea and Skagway reserved to the United States in all circumstances. Canada would not agree unless Pyramid Harbor was similarly reserved to Canada (although there was no Canadian community there). Colonial Office officials regarded the Canadians' attitude with alarm, feeling that "the consequences of delay in a settlement appear to be more serious for them than for the U.S. who are in possession". Chamberlain pressed these views upon the Governor General, Lord Minto, but without notable effect upon the Canadian ministers. The only achievement of 1899—apart from the U.S. abandonment, after British representations, of a plan to establish a military garrison at Pyramid Harbor—was a fortunate agreement upon a *modus vivendi* by which the parties to the dispute accepted as a provisional boundary, pending a settlement, a line at the summits of the White, Chilkoot, and Chilkat passes.[8]

The fact is that Canada and her government were in a mood of rather extravagant self-confidence. The long depression had lifted, very luckily for Laurier, almost simultaneously with his advent to power. Prosperity was flooding in, and it had its due effect. Laurier remarked in the House of Commons on March 21, 1899, "I think I am not making too wide a statement when I say that the general feeling in Canada to-day is not in favour of reciprocity":

> There was a time when Canadians ... would have given many things to obtain the American market; there was a time not long ago when the market of the great cities of the union was the only market we had for any of our products. But thank heaven! those days are past and over now. We are not dependent upon the American market as we were at one time. Our system of cold storage has given us a market in England which we had not before.* Some few years ago we had no market except the cities of the union. Those days are over, and I recognize that fact; though I admit without any hesitation that there are yet quite a number of articles concerning which the American market would be of great advantage to Canada.

In the view of one historian, Canadian intransigence in the Alaskan affair "was based on three miscalculations: on time being on Canada's side, on the country's strength, and on British imperial power".[9] There is con-

* Thanks to a government-assisted program involving mechanical refrigeration on steamships, railway refrigerator cars, and cold storage in creameries, Canada's share of the British butter market increased from 1.38 per cent in 1895 to 7.19 per cent in 1902 (*Statistical Year-Book of Canada for 1902*, pp. 153-4). But this was hardly as important in the national economy as Laurier here implies. See also Appendix B.

siderable evidence that the electorate was not in a mood for concessions to the United States, and that Laurier and his colleagues feared that such concessions would be politically disadvantageous.[10] The parliamentary Opposition criticized them, not for breaking off the negotiation through the Joint High Commission, but for not taking a still tougher line.[11] Time, however, would reveal that with respect to the Alaskan question, at least, the new Canadian self-confidence was ill-founded.

Certain diplomatic developments of 1900 and 1901 were calculated to foster doubts in Canadian minds. In 1850 Britain and the United States had signed the Clayton–Bulwer Treaty concerning the possibility of a Central American canal connecting Atlantic and Pacific. The treaty bound both parties not to seek "exclusive control" over such a canal if built, and not to fortify it; on the contrary, they undertook to guarantee its neutrality and to ensure that its use would be available to all countries on equal terms. After the war with Spain in 1898 the United States, now an imperial power, felt the naval need for an inter-oceanic canal more than ever before; and it was in no mood to share the control of it in the manner provided in the Clayton–Bulwer Treaty, which nevertheless was still binding. Late in 1898 the United States, eager to get on with building a canal, raised with Britain the possibility of a modification of the treaty; and Pauncefote, the British Ambassador,* rapidly worked out with John Hay, the new American Secretary of State, a convention that would permit the United States to proceed independently with a canal (January 1899). Lord Salisbury, however, insisted on consulting Canada, and the Laurier government in its turn insisted that before the Clayton–Bulwer Treaty was modified there should be agreement on arbitrating the Alaska boundary in accordance with the Venezuelan precedent, as well as some consideration for the damage being done to Canadian trade with the former Spanish colony of Puerto Rico by American coasting laws. The British cabinet accepted these conditions, the United States was advised of them, and for the moment no action was taken on the new convention.[12]

The United States, however, was not disposed to wait, and in 1900 a bill providing for the construction of an isthmian canal in total disregard of the Clayton–Bulwer obligations seemed likely to pass Congress. More-

* Until 1893 Congress had always refused to give any American mission abroad a rank higher than legation, but in 1893 it was mutually agreed that the legations in Washington and London should become embassies.

over, the British position had been weakened by the outbreak of the war in South Africa and the early defeats there. On Janury 19 Pauncefote wrote personally to Salisbury, "America seems to be our only friend just now & it would be unfortunate to quarrel with her."[13] Itself under pressure from the U.S. State Department, the British government now put pressure on Canada. The Colonial Office explained the hard facts of the American situation as London saw them, and proceeded:

> Her Majesty's Government are deeply conscious of the valuable support received from Canada in the present [South African] crisis and would reluctantly abandon any point which might be effectively pressed in pursuance of the wishes of your Ministers.
>
> There is little hope however of an early agreement in the boundary question and it is recognized by public opinion here that claim of United States for the revision of the Clayton-Bulwer Treaty is legitimate.
>
> If Her Majesty's Government further delay or refuse to proceed with Convention, such refusal would be regarded as an affront to United States Government, and would tend to shake position of President [McKinley] whose friendly attitude is in the present condition of public affairs of great importance.
>
> I need not point out what would be the consequences of such a result to Canadian interests, and I trust that your Ministers will recognize that in the interests of the Dominion as well as in those of the rest of the Empire it is necessary that Her Majesty's Government should agree to sign at once. Telegraph reply as soon as possible, as the matter is very urgent.[14]

Canada really had no choice, and her government accepted the situation. The Americans would probably have gone ahead with their canal plan whether or not the British agreed to revise the treaty of 1850; the British would probably have agreed whether or not Canada concurred. But by accepting the revision without a *quid pro quo* London abandoned its only diplomatic weapon of any force on the Alaska boundary. And further trouble was in store. When Hay and Pauncefote dug out their draft convention of January 1899 and signed it as a treaty (February 1900) the U.S. Senate took exception to it, particularly because it still forbade the United States to fortify the canal; and it amended it in this and other respects, with the consequence that the British government declined to proceed with it. Nevertheless, when in the spring of 1901 John Hay produced a new treaty that said nothing about fortification and seemed likely to satisfy the Senate, Salisbury and his colleagues shortly accepted it.

This was more than could be said for two treaties on Canadian matters which Hay put forward simultaneously. One proposed the settlement of the Alaska question by a tribunal of "six impartial jurists of repute", three from each side; the other dealt with most of the other problems that had been before the Joint High Commission of 1898–99. Laurier declined to have anything to do with either. The Alaska document, he said, as the Canadian members of the commission had said, could not produce a final settlement. On the other treaty, he maintained the attitude taken in 1899: the Alaska boundary must be settled before other matters could be dealt with.[15] Canada was continuing to take a high line. But bitter disappointment lay ahead.

"THE BEST OF A BAD JOB"

The resolution of the Alaska question was certainly not helped when President McKinley's life was ended by an assassin's bullet in September 1901. Canada had been urged to make concessions to strengthen the hand of the conciliatory McKinley. Now he was gone, and his successor was Theodore Roosevelt, noted more as a jingo than a conciliator.

In the Alaska affair Roosevelt was to live up to his reputation. On many occasions he declared that the Canadian case was non-existent, that Canada had not a leg to stand on. However, it never occurred to him that in these circumstances the United States could afford to submit its case with confidence to impartial judicial decision. On the contrary, he disliked the very idea of arbitration, and in the first instance took the attitude that the most he would agree to was a tribunal which would record, not a judicial verdict, but merely its members' "reasoned opinions".[16]

That Roosevelt later changed his opinion somewhat seems to have been due in part to information that Sir Wilfrid Laurier had changed his. While in England for the Colonial Conference of 1902 Laurier had conversations both with the U.S. Ambassador, Joseph H. Choate, and the First Secretary to the Embassy, Henry White. Choate subsequently (September 1, 1902) told the British Foreign Secretary that Laurier had said to him that the Canadian government, "earnestly desiring that the boundary question should no longer remain unsettled, would probably not object to an arbitral tribunal composed of six members, three on each side, in spite of the objection which had previously been urged to a Commission so constituted". Laurier is also reported as saying that whatever a tribunal might decide, Canada would not wish to take over the American towns of Dyea and Skagway. This latter point is similarly recorded in a letter by White (June 28, 1902), who says that Laurier told him that in the event of a decision favourable to Canada, the Dominion would be "entitled to compensation elsewhere, either in land or in *money*, for the Skagway district".* These conversations were of course at once reported to Washington and to the President.[17]

Clifford Sifton, Laurier's Minister of the Interior, told a confidant at the time that before Laurier went to England he had assured a group of concerned colleagues that he would not yield to any pressure for an even-numbered tribunal. Nevertheless, on his return in October he told them that he had no option but to accept such a tribunal.[18] What were the considerations that made him change his mind? An American scholar has suggested that they may have been connected with Newfoundland. The island colony was desirous of undertaking an independent reciprocity negotiation with the United States, and Laurier feared that if this took place Newfoundland might be drawn into the American orbit, and the possibility of her confederating with Canada, to which he attached importance, might go glimmering. Therefore, it is argued, he made concessions to Britain on the boundary question in the hope that she would discourage the Newfoundland negotiation.[19] This seems a little far-fetched. It would seem rather more likely that he yielded to strong pressure from British ministers representing the vital imperial importance of a settlement of the boundary. But no real evidence on the point has been brought to light.

After his return to Canada Laurier, who was in poor health, went to Hot Springs, Virginia, to recruit. According to his biographer, while there he had, "by request", an interview with Roosevelt and his Secretary of State.[20] Whether this meeting really took place seems doubtful, for no reference to it has been found in either Canadian or American records.† If it did happen, Laurier may well have said to the President much what he had already said to Choate. Some months later, John Hay

* These events were unknown to Laurier's biographer, O. D. Skelton, who denied that the Prime Minister made any concessions while in England; see his review of John W. Dafoe's life of Sifton in *Queen's Quarterly*, February 1932. But the documents are too specific to leave any serious doubt.

† There seems to be nothing in the Laurier or Minto Papers. The latter contain a letter from Laurier to Minto written from Hot Springs on December 18, 1902, stating that he is leaving the next day for St. Augustine, Florida; there is no reference to Roosevelt or Hay. The Roosevelt and Hay Papers in the Library of Congress have been examined without result; and the newspapers of December 1902 make no mention of a meeting. Minto's memorandum of his first conversation with Laurier after the Prime Minister's return from the South (the interview was on January 8, 1903) likewise make no such reference.

was to write, "... I have heard from Laurier, and Pauncefote, directly, *that they know they have no case.*"[21] He might have been referring to this supposed interview, or to contacts he is known to have had with Laurier through an intermediary. At any rate, in the words of Skelton, "Finally, the President was won over" (that is, Roosevelt condescended to accept the sort of settlement the United States had been demanding for years).

By December 18 the new British Ambassador in Washington, Sir Michael Herbert, completed with Hay a draft treaty very similar to Hay's proposal of 1901 (above, page 92). It did not use the dangerous word "arbitration", though to Roosevelt's indignation the phrase "arbitral tribunal" got into the preamble of the draft, but the important parts of its Article I ran as follows:

> A Tribunal shall be immediately appointed to consider and decide the questions set forth in Article IV of this Convention. The Tribunal shall consist of six impartial jurists of repute, who shall consider judicially the questions submitted to them, each of whom shall first subscribe an oath that he will impartially consider the arguments and evidence presented to the Tribunal, and will decide thereupon according to his true judgment. Three members of the Tribunal shall be appointed by His Britannic Majesty and three by the President of the United States. All questions considered by the Tribunal, including the final award, shall be decided by a majority of all the members thereof....

Simplifying the matter as far as possible, it may be said that the vital questions the tribunal was directed to settle under the terms of the treaty of 1825 were, in order of importance, first, was it the intention of that treaty that Russia should have "a continuous fringe or strip of coast on the mainland" separating the British possessions from the sea and its inlets? If the answer to this question was negative, then a further decision would be required as to how Russia's actual strip should be measured. Secondly, with respect to the extreme southward end of the Alaska "panhandle", what channel was the Portland Channel mentioned in the treaty, and where did the boundary run in this area?

A striking feature of the Hay–Herbert Convention was the extraordinary haste with which it required action to be taken. The written case of each party was to be presented not more than two months after the convention was ratified.[22] And the British government was in a tearing hurry to get it ratified. Strong pressure was again put on Canada to accept the draft, and reluctantly the Laurier cabinet did so. (The Prime Minister told Minto on January 19 that there was "opposition in Council", particularly from W. S. Fielding, but that he himself was "quite determined" that the treaty should be accepted.) On January 24, 1903 Hay and Herbert formally signed the convention. It was slipped through the U.S. Senate. The President then proceeded to make three extraordinary appointments. After hearing of these, but before informing Canada of them, A. J. Balfour's government in Britain had the King ratify the convention.[23]

Few American scholars have tried to defend Roosevelt's choice of "impartial jurists". One of the three, Elihu Root, was an eminent lawyer and a man of stature, but he was Roosevelt's Secretary of War. Henry Cabot Lodge, the anglophobe senator from Massachusetts, and ex-Senator George Turner of the State of Washington, had both committed themselves publicly against the Canadian claim, and neither could be said to have much status as a jurist. Inevitably, when the names were announced there was an outburst of criticism in Canada, and the Dominion government made a strong protest to London, suggesting in effect that if the United States persisted in these appointments the whole arrangement should be broken off. Laurier, clearly appalled, now made an attempt at personal diplomacy, by-passing the normal channel through the Governor General and pointing out in letters to both Herbert and Hay that Canada had been led to believe that the United States would appoint eminent judges.[24] He got no satisfaction. Herbert (who died later in the year) replied in terms worthy of quotation at length, for the letter illustrates both the difficulty of dealing with Roosevelt and the insoluble dilemma that confronted Canada in any serious crisis with the United States:[25]

Feb. 23, 1903

PRIVATE & SECRET

Dear Sir Wilfrid Laurier,

I write this to supplement my telegram of to-day.

You are not quite correct in stating in your letter that my correspondence with Lord Minto put forth that the American jurists *were* to be the Chief Justice of the U.S. and two other Judges of an equally high character.

Nothing was put in writing by Hay and he never stated definitely that the Chief Justice would be appointed. The Chief Justice's name was, however, mentioned between us, and Hay certainly led me to understand that at least two of the American Jurists would be taken from the Supreme Court. Of course his excuse now is that the Judges of the Supreme Court all refused to sit. He says he spent an hour with Justice White, who would have been an admirable appointment, trying to get him to re-consider his decision. The Alaska Question is so universally regarded here as a political question, that I imagine the Judges of the Supreme Court did not want to run the risk of having to give a decision against the U.S.

I saw Mr. [John] Charlton* a day or two ago and asked him to tell you what I feel about the whole matter. He thought it inadvisable to protest and stated somewhat cynically that whatever Americans had been appointed the result would have been the same.

Deeply as I sympathize with you I should strongly deprecate Canada breaking off. The President's appointments are all approved here, and such action on the part of Canada would create a political outcry agst. her throughout the U.S. and make the President more popular than ever. The modus vivendi would probably be denounced, and the consequences would be too grave to contemplate.

Yrs very sincerely
Michael H. Herbert.

While the American appointments were still being discussed between London and Ottawa, the Canadian government received another blow. Britain exchanged ratifications of the convention with the United States.† Laurier considered this hasty action a "slap in the face" and a grave discourtesy, and it is hard not to agree with him. But there seemed to be nothing to do now but go ahead with the tribunal.[26]

John Hay had hoped that only one Canadian would be appointed to it; Herbert recommended that there be none, but the Colonial Office would give no countenance to this suggestion. Two Canadians were appointed: Sir Louis Jetté, Lieutenant-Governor of Quebec and formerly a member of that province's Supreme Court, and A. B. Aylesworth, an eminent lawyer who had declined appointment to the Supreme Court of Canada. Aylesworth replaced Mr. Justice J. D. Armour of that court, who died when the tribunal was about to assemble. The third representative on the Anglo-Canadian side was the Chief Justice of England, Lord Alverstone. These

* A Canadian Liberal MP with exceptional connections in Washington. Cf. above, p. 87.

† Balfour wrote to the King about the appointments, "The Americans have behaved ill over this. . . . The Canadians naturally object. But the Cabinet were unanimous in thinking that to break off the treaty now would be in the highest degree inexpedient; and that all we could do was to make the best of a bad job." He did not mention the exchange of ratifications.

appointments were recommended by the Canadian government and approved by the British cabinet.[27]

The story of the tribunal and its award can be very briefly told. Roosevelt was not content with packing the court; he sent instructions to the three American "impartial jurists" which included the sentence, "In the principle involved there will of course be no compromise." And before and during the sittings of the tribunal in London in the autumn of 1903, he wrote not one but a succession of letters to the American commissioners and others which it is quite clear were intended to be shown or reported to members of the British government who (Roosevelt equally clearly expected) would put pressure on Lord Alverstone. These communications were to the general effect that if the tribunal failed to agree the United States would make no further effort at negotiation but would seize and hold the area in dispute by force. One quotation must suffice; if there were "captious objections" on the part of the English, Roosevelt wrote to Turner, "I am going to send a brigade of American regulars up to Skagway and take possession of the disputed territory and hold it by all the power and force of the United States." These tactics had their due effect. No Englishman left any record of the transactions that has come to light; but the Americans left a great deal, and there is no doubt that Roosevelt's threats duly reached and impressed Balfour, the British Prime Minister, and very little that he in his turn made known to Alverstone the urgent need that the tribunal should agree.[28] Henry White spent a weekend with Balfour early in October, and briefed him thoroughly on Roosevelt's views. White wrote later to Hay, "I never heard directly whether he did anything nor if so what; but two days afterwards his confidential secretary, Sanders [Sandars], who is a friend of mine, let me know very confidentially that he [evidently Sandars] had had two interviews with Lord Alverstone."[29]

The net result was that the United States won its case. Alverstone voted with the three Americans; the two Canadians (who had observed for some time that the Chief Justice had ceased to discuss issues with them and had been closeting himself with the other side) refused to sign the award. That Alverstone should have voted against Canada on the question of the "continuous fringe or strip of coast" running round the heads of the inlets was not perhaps surprising. What shocked Jetté and Aylesworth and other Canadians was his attitude on the question of the Portland Channel. Here Canada seemed to have a strong case, and in the early sessions of the tribunal Alverstone took the view that four disputed islands in the channel should go to Canada. In the end, however, he agreed with the Americans in accepting an arrangement no one had previously suggested, giving two of the islands to each country. This seemed clearly a diplomatic compromise rather than a judicial decision such as the tribunal was pledged to render, and in Canada it was made a special grievance against Alverstone.[30] The Chief Justice had been in an extraordinarily uncomfortable position. The two Canadian jurists, though no one had "instructed" them, seem to have been just as much devoted to their own country's case as the Americans were to theirs; and there was some force in Lord Minto's remark with respect to Alverstone, "personally I believe his to have been the only judicial mind on our side".[31] He might well have said, "on either side". Yet the evidence indicates rather strongly that in the end Lord Alverstone, who had been Attorney General in three Conservative administrations, reverted to type and under pressure from his government acted the part of a politician rather than a judge.

Sparked by the fact that the Canadian commissioners not only refused to sign the award but issued a public statement attacking it,[32] the Canadian press burst out in anger against it. The remarks of the Ottawa *Evening Journal* on October 22 may serve to indicate the tone:

> Apparently most of the British newspapers think Lord Alverstone was right.
>
> It is precisely because such a course as Lord Alverstone's finds wide favor in the old country that the Alverstone case is serious. As an episode in itself, it would count for little. As an indication of the English habit of mind towards the United States, Canadians are compelled to consider that it counts for a great deal.
>
> Cut loose from Britain, we would of course be robbed by the United States whenever opportunity occurred, and bullied if we protested. But we are that now. The only difference now is that Englishmen inform us that it is justice and have the right to compel us to accept it as justice.
>
> And as Canada shouts "stop thief" while Brother Jonathan is disappearing with the goods, the British press sings "For He's a Jolly Good Fellow" and deplores that we don't join in.

The Toronto *News*'s comment was likewise typical: "The Alaskan treaty, like the Treaty of Washington, seems to be a sacrifice of Canadian interests to the paramount desire of Great Britain to cultivate the good opinion of the United States."[33] The heaviest burden of the complaints was directed against Britain rather than against the United States—though today, with all the evidence we are ever likely to see before us, it might seem difficult to differentiate responsibility as between the power that made naked threats of force and the power that yielded to the threats. Laurier himself on the morrow of the award (October 23, 1903) spoke in the House of Commons in terms that expressed the mood of the country:

> I have often regretted, Mr. Speaker, and never more than on the present occasion, that we are living beside a great neighbour who, I believe I can say without being deemed unfriendly to them, are very grasping in their national acts, and who are determined upon every occasion to get the best in any agreement which they make. I have often regretted also that while they are a great and powerful nation, we are only a small colony, a growing colony, but still a colony. . . .
>
> The difficulty, as I conceive it to be, is that so long as Canada remains a dependency of the British Crown the present powers that we have are not sufficient for the maintenance of our rights. It is important that we should ask the British Parliament for more extensive power, so that if ever we have to deal with matters of a similar nature again we shall deal with them in our own way, in our own fashion, according to the best light that we have.

Laurier implied that what Canada would seek was "the treaty-making power". This alarmed Minto, who remarked that "such an arrangement would really mean independence".[34] He need not have worried, for Laurier, rather characteristically, made no move to follow up his words with action.

The *News* was right in drawing an analogy with the Treaty of Washington. There is an obvious parallel between the two incidents. The triangular relationship was under strain, just as it had been in 1871. One parallel was lacking, however. In 1903, unlike 1871 (above, page 22), there was no provision for approval by the Canadian Parliament either of the convention setting up the tribunal or of the tribunal's award. In the same debate in the Commons that has just been quoted, Robert Borden, the leader of the Conservative opposition, assailed the Laurier government for accepting the treaty "without the consent of parliament, and without a provision for ratification by parliament". There is no evidence that Laurier had sought such a provision; the facts suggest that neither the British nor the Americans would have entertained such a request for a moment; and the absence of any requirement for parliamentary approval certainly relieved the government of what would have been a grave embarrassment after the award.

Just as in 1871, however, we are faced with the question, where did the paramount interests of Canada lie? And they certainly did not lie in the possession of small islands in the Portland Channel, important as these were made to seem at the time.* They consisted in a basis being found for a sure and lasting peace between Great Britain and the United States. The circumstances of the Alaska settlement were in many ways, to put it mildly, unfortunate; Roosevelt's behaviour was irresponsible and offensive to international decency; but it was fortunate that the settlement was made. In retrospect it appears as an essential part of a general Anglo-American rapprochement by which Canada, in the long run, was the greatest gainer. To British policy as it contributed to this result we must now turn our attention.

To anyone who gave careful thought to Britain's strategic problems it had long been clear that, with the growth of American power, her military position in North America was becoming increasingly untenable. We have already mentioned this in connection with the Treaty of Washington. Nor was the British dilemma entirely a matter of American power. The United States did not need a navy as large as Britain's to cut British communications with Canada, provided only that Britain had trouble elsewhere. And by the turn of the century it was clearer than ever that Britain would never be free of the threat of trouble elsewhere. Her "splendid isolation" (George Foster's phrase) was becoming increasingly uncomfortable. The Franco-Russian alliance of 1894 was the great bugbear of this period. In a few years the German menace would supplant it. The moral that British statesmen and strategists came to draw from this situation was that friendship with the United States had to be cultivated at virtually any price. It is impossible to quote a cabinet decision, or to fix a precise moment when this became British policy; but the Hay–Pauncefote Treaty, abandoning Britain's rights in an isthmian canal without compensation, may well be considered the turning point. An American canal, the British knew, would double the power of the United States Navy at a time when its strength was in any case being rapidly increased. In the words of one careful student of the period, the treaty of 1901 "committed Great Britain to naval inferiority in American waters and therefore to friendship with the United States".[35] In January 1901, when the canal question was being discussed by the cabinet, the

* It was said that they commanded the sea approach to Port Simpson, which was being considered as the terminus of the Grand Trunk Pacific Railway.

First Lord of the Admiralty (Lord Selborne) urged his colleagues to think of the "two-power standard" of naval strength in terms only of France and Russia, leaving other powers, including the United States, out of consideration. In the following April he wrote, "I would never quarrel with the United States if I could possibly avoid it," and went on to point out that the Americans if they chose could well afford to build a navy as large as Britain's and even larger.[36] Dr. Bourne remarks, "Certainly by the end of 1902, when Salisbury had finally retired, a special attitude towards the United States seems clearly to have been adopted by British statesmen generally." This "special attitude" was in evidence in the Alaska case. It amounted to this: that Britain was determined not to risk war with the United States over any Canadian question, or for that matter over any question whatever. The War Office (though not the Admiralty) nevertheless continued to go through the motions of planning for the contingency of war with the United States until May 14, 1908, when the Committee of Imperial Defence in effect decided that such activity should cease.[37] No one told Canada about this; but her government could scarcely have objected, for Sir Wilfrid Laurier had said in the House of Commons on February 8, 1907, "Now, we have come to this position in our relations with the people of the United States—we can never conceive of war between us, or of war between Great Britain and the United States. We mean to settle all our difficulties with that nation by peaceful means, by diplomatic action, by negotiation, but never by the arbitrament of war."

Such was the "rise of Anglo-American friendship", the development of "Anglo-American understanding", which became the theme of historians of this period. On the British side, it is evident, the essential element was a hard practical assessment of interest and power; the Empire's interests in America, including those of Canada, were to be sacrificed for the sake of security and influence nearer home. An element of Anglo-American sentiment was not lacking, but it was secondary. On the American side, there were people (John Hay seems to have been one of them) who believed that an Anglo-American rapprochement would serve the interests of both countries and of mankind; but there were also many who still cultivated the "ancient grudge". In the period we have been describing, as in earlier ones, American policy profited largely by the embarrassments of Britain. Nevertheless, the better understanding that came about in these years was destined to be enduring, and with the passage of time it would be increasingly accepted on both sides as a vital and fundamental feature of national policy. Canada would find in it a source of security and satisfaction, and might even come to regard the Alaska award, so bitterly resented in 1903, as not too high a price to pay for the benefits of the new era.

In the meantime, however, the Alaska crisis left much bitterness behind it. The Canadian image of the grasping and threatening American was refurbished, and the conciliatory attitude which we shall see the United States adopting in the diplomatic exchanges of the next few years probably did little to remove it from Canadian minds. The effect on Laurier himself is well documented (below, pages 105–06). It is more than likely that the Canadian voters' rejection of reciprocity in 1911 owed a good deal to memories of 1903.

On certain minds the British actions in the Alaska case left an especially deep imprint. Here we find ourselves confronting in particular the figure of Clifford Sifton. Laurier's Minister of the Interior had been designated under the Hay–Herbert convention as British "Agent" to "attend the Tribunal" and in fact to superintend the preparation of the British case. Sifton thus observed the proceedings in London at close range. Even before the tribunal met, the manner in which the convention had been rammed through had made a most adverse impression upon him. At this time he wrote to John W. Dafoe, whom he had brought to Winnipeg in 1901 to serve as editor of the *Manitoba Free Press*:

> As you have no doubt already sized the matter up, the British Government deliberately decided about a year ago to sacrifice our interests at any cost, for the sake of pleasing the United States. All their proceedings since that time were for the sake of inveigling us into a position from which we could not retire. I am bound to say that we have been pretty easy prey, but the result would probably have been the same in any event, as it simply gets down to a very narrow question. The United States would not recede, and England would not take any chances of a quarrel.
>
> It is, however, the most cold-blooded case of absolutely giving away our interests, without even giving us the excuse of saying we have had a fight for it, which I know of, and I do not see any reason why the Canadian press should not make itself extremely plain upon the subject. My view, in watching the diplomacy of Great Britain as affecting Canada for six years, is that it may just as well be decided in advance that practically whatever the United States demands from England will be conceded in the long run, and the Canadian people might as well make up their minds to that now.[38]

These, be it remembered, were the views of a Canadian cabinet minister, with access to some confidential information. As we have seen, they are not very different from the interpretations of modern scholars who have sifted the records. They were only strengthened by Sifton's experiences in London. He came back to Canada angry with Alverstone and with the British government. Small things had reinforced the effects of great: the Canadian official party had not received much hospitality in England (Minto wrote to the Colonial Secretary, about a week after a long interview with Sifton, "Also I hear that the wives were not sufficiently taken care of!").[39] In the opinion of Dafoe, the episode left Sifton "essentially nationalist in spirit and outlook".[40] He resigned from the Laurier ministry in 1905, and never held office afterwards. But he remained influential; he was the proprietor of the most powerful newspaper in western Canada; and we shall meet him, as Sir Clifford Sifton, later in the story.

CLEANING THE SLATE

The adjournment of the Joint High Commission in 1899 (above, page 88) left unsettled a long list of issues between Canada and the United States. After the Alaska boundary was settled at the point of Theodore Roosevelt's pistol the others still remained. Laurier's attitude was that it was for the Americans to take the initiative for further negotiation.[41] In Canada there was now a new governor general, Albert, fourth Earl Grey, son of Queen Victoria's private secretary and grandson of Lord Grey of the Reform Bill. Grey, whose term ran from 1904 to 1911, was an enthusiastic lightweight; his zeal for the twin causes of imperial unity and Anglo-American cooperation was as notable as his gallantries among the ladies of Ottawa. He had been an associate of Cecil Rhodes, and he lost no opportunity, as he said, of "preaching the Rhodes Gospel of devoting all one's energies to the service of one's country on lines ultimately leading to a race federation".[42] He made it one of his great objects to settle the outstanding Canadian-American questions, and in this matter he found a kindred spirit in Elihu Root, who succeeded John Hay as Roosevelt's Secretary of State in 1905.

On April 3, 1906 we find Grey writing Laurier from New York, "The iron is malleable & now is the time to strike." Next day in Washington Grey and the British Ambassador, Sir Mortimer Durand, had a long talk with Root, and Grey reported to Laurier that the Secretary of State was "ready and anxious for a Treaty or series of Treaties on all outstanding questions". "He recognises," Grey continued, "that the national sentiment of Canada like that of the U.S. has to be considered. He will prepare a list of questions which his Govt. propose should become the subject of negotiations, and hopes you will also prepare your list." Root was as good as his word. On May 3, 1906 he sent to Durand a twenty-one-page document[43] rehearsing the history of the matter since 1898 and proposing a concerted attack upon the unsettled issues:

> My proposal is that we should take up the outstanding questions between Canada and the United States where the conferees of May, 1898,* left them, and proceed to dispose of those questions by direct negotiation so far as practicable, utilizing for that purpose the incomplete results secured by the discussion and negotiation of the Joint High Commission so far as they are preserved in the reports, correspondence and records of the Commission and its committees; and that we should further supplement the work of the conferees and the Commission by disposing in like manner of such questions as have arisen subsequently.

To a rather remarkable extent this ambitious program was carried out to the letter.[44]

The whole story cannot possibly be told here, but it is in order to list the topics that Root enumerated: the fur seals in the Behring Sea; the Atlantic and Pacific and inland fisheries; the delimitation of the Alaska boundary; transit of merchandise across the other country's territory (the "bonding system"); transit of merchandise from one country for delivery at points in the other; alien-labour laws; mining rights of one country's citizens within the territory of the other; reciprocity in customs duties; revision of the agreement concerning naval vessels on the Lakes; "complete definition and marking" of any part of the international boundary not already adequately marked; conveyance of persons in custody of one country's officers through the territory of the other; reciprocity in wrecking and salvage rights. To these twelve topics Root added "as subsequently arising" uses and disposition of international waterways including the protection of Niagara Falls; logging booms on the St. John River; pecuni-

* Pauncefote and Davies on behalf of Britain and Canada, and John W. Foster and John A. Kasson on behalf of the United States, the group who prepared the agenda for the Joint High Commission.

ary claims on both sides; and "some minor items in which citizens of Canada are interested", including exemption from head tax for Canadians temporarily entering the United States, and relief of vessels from Canadian Atlantic ports from having to produce bills of health.

Extraordinarily few of these topics were not covered in the series of agreements made between Britain (in the closest consultation with Canada) and the United States during the half-dozen years following Root's memorandum. The Rush–Bagot agreement on naval armaments was not revised at this period; and the questions of transit of merchandise, alien labour laws, and mining rights were not dealt with in treaties or conventions. Tariff reciprocity was, as ever, a political question and must be treated by itself. But it can be said that well before the outbreak of the First World War the slate had been cleaned; no serious controversy remained unsettled between Canada and the United States.*

To this result a great contribution was made by James (afterwards Viscount) Bryce, British Ambassador in Washington from 1907 to 1913. Bryce, the author of *The American Commonwealth* and other celebrated books, was very successful in his contacts with the American people. He was scarcely less successful in Canada, which he visited repeatedly and where he may be said to have lifted to some extent the cloud that overhung the reputation of British diplomacy on the morrow of Alaska. He worked hard to advance the project of Grey and Root. Not quite so much can be said for the Prime Minister of Canada. Laurier was growing old and was unwell; time had dimmed such enthusiasms as he had ever had, and experience had decidedly tempered the warmth of his feelings for the United States. In conversation with Grey in December 1907, he "referred . . . with much bitterness" to the American appointments to the Alaska Boundary Tribunal;† and at a moment of some strain in 1908,

* It is a telling comment on American attitudes that Philip C. Jessup's *Elihu Root*, 2 vols. (New York, 1938) devotes some 250 pages to Root's career as Secretary of State, and that only seventeen of these can be spared for his rather remarkable Canadian achievements; while of these in turn all but two and a half deal with the Atlantic fisheries.

† It was evidently during Root's visit to Ottawa in this year that Laurier gave him "a piece of my mind" on this subject. "I sd. we are a small ctry. & cannot resist, you can force us but it is not fair or just—Root said nothing in reply—He said nothing." (Mackenzie King's diary, conversation with Laurier, September 16, 1912.) This must have somewhat marred the harmony of a rather famous occasion.

Mackenzie King recorded that the Prime Minister regarded Americans as "selfish, self-seeking and . . . caring only for Canada in so far as it may serve their own purpose to be friendly". The paper, the work of Pope, which Laurier submitted in response to Root's, was belated and a bit thin. In these dealings with Washington his natural tendency to procrastination is much in evidence. Nevertheless, he mildly encouraged the process of conciliation.[45]

There is no need to review all the negotiations of this period; we must, however, take note of the most important of them, and we may begin by summarizing what amounted to the final settlement of the North Atlantic fisheries and the Behring Sea difficulties. In January 1909 Bryce and Root signed a special agreement providing for an arbitration tribunal chosen from the list of members of the Permanent Court of Arbitration at The Hague (established in 1899) to interpret the famous Convention of 1818 concerning the Atlantic fisheries. Canada at this stage took the position that the question was more important to Newfoundland than it was to her; and both Canada's Minister of Justice, A. B. Aylesworth, and Newfoundland's, James M. Kent, were in Washington to assist Bryce* in the final negotiation with Root. The tribunal of five judges when constituted included a United States judge and Sir Charles Fitzpatrick, Chief Justice of Canada. It handed down its award, a very long document, in September 1910.[47] It provided, among other things, for two Permanent Mixed Fishery Commissions, one for Canada and one for Newfoundland, to decide questions "as to the reasonableness of future regulations"; these were each to consist of three members, one nominated by Britain and one by the United States, while the third, not a national of either party, was to be nominated by agreement between the two countries or, failing this, by the Queen of the Netherlands. The comment of Laurier's biographer seems on the whole fair: "It was gratifying that on every important phase the Canadian contention was sustained, but still more welcome were the evidences of friendliness and of an honourable desire on both sides to ensure a strictly fair and legal decision." American remarks about the result are rather less gushing;[48] but it is evident that the contending parties approached the question in a spirit different from that of twenty years before.

* "I think I ought not to let the opportunity pass without saying that in my opinion Mr. Bryce is entitled to the gratitude of Canada for what he has accomplished." (Aylesworth to Lord Grey, February 9, 1909).[46]

To the same happy period belongs the final settlement of the Behring Sea fur-seal controversy. The treaty, award and claims commission of 1892–98 had not laid this question to rest. Humanitarians in the United States and elsewhere argued that the killing of mother seals at sea involved the death by starvation of their pups on the islands. It was again asserted that the seal herd was threatened with destruction, and after 1900, when the Japanese began pelagic sealing on a large scale, this was pretty clearly the case. The Canadian government was slow to respond to American arguments forwarded through British diplomatic channels; it demanded adequate compensation for those engaged in the trade if pelagic sealing were ended. Finally, a satisfactory basis of agreement was found, and in February 1911 Britain and the United States signed a treaty providing that pelagic sealing by their subjects and citizens should be prohibited while it remained in force. The United States agreed to deliver to Canada one-fifth of the sealskins taken annually in the Pribiloff Islands. The treaty was not to become effective until parallel restrictions were accepted by Japan and Russia.[49] The consequence later in the same year was a quadripartite conference in Washington at which the British representatives were Bryce and Joseph Pope, Under Secretary of State in the new Canadian Department of External Affairs. Pope acted as a Canadian delegate under the instructions of the Canadian government.[50] He had his troubles, though not with Bryce. He reported that on one occasion when he took an initiative, "My offer was received almost contemptuously," the Americans being apparently the worst culprits.[51] In the end, however, a treaty satisfactory to Canada was achieved. All four powers agreed to prohibit pelagic sealing in the North Pacific. Japan was to receive from the United States the same compensation the previous treaty had already allotted to Canada; Russia was similarly to compensate Canada and Japan, and Japan to compensate the United States, Canada, and Russia, from the sealskins taken on these two countries' islands. Great Britain undertook to make similar compensation to the United States, Japan, and Russia in the event of any seal herd resorting to British (i.e., Canadian) islands or shores. Pope signed the treaty along with Bryce. He reported to Laurier that it was "Thanks primarily to the good offices of His Majesty's Ambassador" that so good an agreement had been obtained.[52]

Root, it may be recalled, had included in his list of outstanding problems "the complete definition and marking" of the international boundary at any points where it might be liable to dispute. On April 11, 1908 Bryce and Root signed a treaty (which had been duly considered and agreed to by the Canadian government) providing for the precise demarcation of the various sections of the boundary by a series of international commissions.[53] Article I of this treaty dealt with the only area where there was likely to be serious dispute—Passamaquoddy Bay; and provision was made for arbitration if agreement here could not be otherwise reached. Actually, arbitration was not required, but there was a tiresome and complicated negotiation before this very minor boundary dispute was laid to rest by a separate treaty signed by Bryce and President Taft's Secretary of State, Philander C. Knox, on May 21, 1910.[54]

AN INTERNATIONAL JOINT COMMISSION

Another of Root's list of problems, the "uses and disposition of international waterways", requires more extended discussion, for out of the consideration of it emerged the modern International Joint Commission. The story cannot, however, be told in all its detail.

It may be said to have begun in 1895, when the National Irrigation Congress,* a United States body, held its annual meeting at Albuquerque, New Mexico. Representatives from Canada were invited, not for the first time; Mexico also appears to have been represented; and the Congress passed a resolution asking "for the appointment of an International Commission to act in conjunction with the authorities of Mexico and Canada in adjudicating the conflicting rights which have arisen, or may hereafter arise, on streams of an international character". The Canadian government by an order-in-council of January 8, 1896 asked the British Ambassador in Washington to inform the United States authorities of the Dominion's readiness to co-operate in the manner suggested; but the Americans did not close with the offer.[55] Perhaps the atmosphere created by the recent Venezuela incident (above, pages 48–51) was inimical to such an exercise. However, in the summer of 1902 the U.S. Congress passed an act inviting the British government to join in an International Waterways Commission of six members, three representing the interests of Canada and three from the United States. On April 27, 1903 the Canadian cabinet approved such action. The United States proceeded to

* Later, but not at this time, it came to be called the International Irrigation Congress.

appoint its three commissioners. It was another bad moment for international co-operation, relations having been soured by the Alaska boundary negotiations. On December 3, 1903 the Dominion government appointed *one* commissioner. In spite of continued pressure from Washington and London, the other two were not appointed until January 7, 1905. The commission was at last ready for business. Its real activity as an instrument of Canadian policy may, however, be said to have begun in the following November, when (the first chairman of the Canadian section, James P. Mabee, having been made a judge), George C. (later Sir George) Gibbons, a lawyer of London, Ontario, was appointed in his place.[56]

When Root drew up his comprehensive program in 1906 he noted that the two national sections of the International Waterways Commission were working on the question of the preservation of Niagara Falls.[57] Gibbons, however, and his superiors in Ottawa, had more comprehensive ideas. It is difficult from the available correspondence to decide precisely how far these originated with Gibbons and how far they were Laurier's or someone else's. One is left with the general impression that Gibbons had a high degree of responsibility. An energetic, determined, and apparently sometimes thorny personality, he fought consistently against a piecemeal approach to boundary water problems and for a permanent international commission which, unlike the International Waterways Commission whose functions were merely investigative, would have genuine power to deal with those problems. Thus we find him writing to one of his U.S. colleagues in April 1906:

> We shall not come to a satisfactory "entente cordiale", unless your Government consents to an investigation of all the problems connected with all the International Waterways from the Atlantic to the Pacific, so that the one Treaty shall settle the Preservation of the Falls as well as all causes of difference on all International Rivers.

After a visit to Washington in February 1907—during which he formed an adverse opinion of Root which he afterwards revised—he wrote to Laurier:

> It is evident that we are going to have trouble coming to any effective conclusion with these people; it may be accomplished by a persistent effort.
>
> My own idea, growing stronger every day, is that there is only one way in which we will get fair play, and avoid a conflict with them, and that is by

a permanent joint Commission which will play the game fairly, and whose conclusions will be so justified by public opinions, even in the United States, as to compel their acceptance.[58]

Gibbons also seems to have resented having to work through the British Embassy. People in Washington doubtless sometimes found him difficult. Nevertheless he gradually made progress. In June 1907 Root submitted to the British Embassy a draft treaty dealing with the equitable apportionment of the waters of two related international streams in the west, the St. Mary and Milk rivers.[59] These had been the subject of a long-standing dispute. The Canadian government was in no hurry to deal with this. On December 13, 1907, however, Bryce sent to Root a quite different draft treaty which Gibbons had drafted in consultation with George Clinton, one of the U.S. members of the commission, and which apparently carried Laurier's approval.[60] It proposed a new joint commission of members, three from each side, with powers to consider and decide questions relating to the use of boundary waters. It laid down general principles, one of which was that, broadly speaking, navigation was paramount to all other rights; another was equality in the use of surplus water for power; and another the prohibition of pollution in one country to the injury of health or property in the other. It provided that the commission could deal not only with boundary waters, but also with all other matters which the two governments might choose to submit to it for decision. And it included a provision that "for all the purposes of these Articles the Dominion of Canada shall be deemed to represent His Brittanic [sic] Majesty". In sending the draft to Root, Bryce made the comment that it would render his own draft treaty concerning the Milk and the St. Mary unnecessary, as this business would fall naturally to the new commission.

Root disliked these developments. On January 3, 1908 he told Bryce that the Clinton–Gibbons treaty "in its present form went too far and could not be recommended by his Government to the Senate". It gave too much power to a permanent commission. "He added that it was not the Anglo-Saxon habit to deal in an abstract fashion with principles before the cases they were intended to cover had arisen and been examined. . . ."[61] In June 1908 Root and Gibbons went over the ground again, and in the tactful words of the British *chargé d'affaires* the discussion became "somewhat animated".[62] The fact is that Root blew up. As reported by Gibbons to Sir Wilfrid Laurier:

... He broke out and talked for fifteen minutes about the unfriendly attitude that had been displayed by Canadians generally towards the United States for many years, not only in the Press, but on the floor of the House and at public banquets. He said that one party seemed to vie with the other in saying nasty things and all seemed to imply that the American people had always overreached them heretofore and were lying in wait to do so again.

He spoke about the freedom with which people, who had not resumed [sic] "responsibilities" of a nation, were able to talk. He said that it was unbearable; denied that we had been put to any unfair advantage by the Alaska award or by the Webster–Ashburton Treaty.[63]

Laurier refused to get excited about this. He replied to Gibbons, "Do you think that our friend in the State Department was serious when he made that little display, or was it simply a piece of bluff?"[64]

This momentary storm seems to have actually cleared the air. Laurier supported Gibbons, using as his text the fact that in 1906 the International Waterways Commission had recommended a general treaty defining the use of boundary waters.[65] On August 25, 1908 Gibbons told Laurier that he and Chandler P. Anderson (who was Root's special assistant in Canadian matters) were working on a draft treaty "following the lines for which we have all along contended". Though its wording was not that of the Clinton–Gibbons treaty, its content was very similar.* Root apparently had warmed to that document's principles. Referring to the new draft's proposal to appoint the proposed Joint Commission "a Permanent Board of Arbitration" to deal with all disputes that might be referred to it, Gibbons wrote:

Mr. Anderson says that it is Mr. Root's desire to dispense with the Hague Tribunal as far as possible in connection with matters between themselves and Canada and set an example to the world by the creation of a judicial Board as distinguished from a diplomatic and partisan one to deal with all these matters.[66]

Thus in the end the Canadians got their way. On January 11, 1909 Bryce and Root signed the Boundary Waters Treaty.[67] This instrument, it is

* The most substantive change, suggested by Anderson, was the device of providing that damages caused by diversions of waters flowing across the border should be dealt with as though they had occurred in the country where the diversion had taken place. This avoided the dangerous imputation that American sovereign rights were being delegated to an international agency.

true, dealt specifically with two waterways, the Niagara, and the St. Mary and Milk rivers; but it also laid down general principles applicable to all waters on or flowing across the boundary. It provided that interference or diversions on either side of the border, causing injury on the other side, would "entitle the injured parties to the same legal remedies as if such injury took place in the country where such diversion or interference occurs". It forbade works in one country which would raise the level of waters in the other unless they were approved by the commission created by the treaty; and it laid down that boundary waters "shall not be polluted on either side to the injury of health or property on the other". Above all, the treaty created an International Joint Commission of six members, three to be appointed by the President of the United States and "three on the part of the United Kingdom appointed by His Majesty on the recommendation of the Governor in Council of the Dominion of Canada". This body was charged with decision in cases involving use, obstruction, or diversion of boundary waters, and was given power to subpoena witnesses and take evidence on oath; if it failed to agree on any question, the two countries would then refer the matter to an umpire chosen in accordance with the Hague Convention of 1907. The treaty, indeed, permitted the United States and Canada (with the consent of the U.S. Senate and the Governor General in Council) to refer to the commission for decision "any question or matters of difference arising between the High Contracting Parties involving the rights, obligations, or interests of the United States or of the Dominion of Canada either in relation to each other or to their respective inhabitants"; in other words, the commission might be used if desired not merely in matters affecting boundary waters but in any matter of dispute.

At the last moment the treaty was placed in jeopardy by the United States Senate insisting upon adding to it a rider protecting "existing territorial, or riparian rights" at the rapids of the St. Mary's River between lakes Superior and Huron. Sir Wilfrid Laurier was disposed at this point to "decline the Treaty". However, the Minister of Justice, A. B. Aylesworth (a veteran, it will be remembered, of the Alaska Tribunal) very strongly urged that it should be accepted, with the Senate's rider, "as a fair and just international agreement in which the interests of Canada have been kept in view and are honourably conserved".[68] On March 25, 1910 Laurier informed Bryce that his government was satisfied and that the letters of ratification of the treaty could be exchanged.[69]

Two points should be made about this rather famous treaty. First, although it was signed in the usual way by the British Ambassador in Washington, it was negotiated almost entirely by a Canadian representative and, more important, the machinery which it set up was on the British side entirely under Canadian control. Britain, in effect, made the treaty and withdrew; the British government would have nothing to do with the Canadian appointments to the International Joint Commission or with the commission's work. This would have the useful effect, from the British Embassy's point of view, of relieving it of a great mass of detailed Canadian business which it was not well equipped to do. Secondly, the treaty was largely a product of Canadian initiative. The "slate-cleaning" program of 1906 was an Anglo-American project initiated by Grey and Root and advanced by Bryce; in general, Canada was simply a willing concurrent in most of the treaties that carried it out. But the Boundary Waters Treaty was mainly shaped by Canadian ideas which were carried into effect in the face of considerable American opposition. And in its permanent results it was probably the most important of the whole series. The International Joint Commission has continued to exist to the present day, has a considerable record of useful work, and appears in our time to be playing a valuable part in Canadian-American border relations.

ASIATIC IMMIGRATION AND YOUNG MR. KING

This chapter has been concerned with widening Canadian international contacts and increasing Canadian autonomy in external relations. It remains to say a little about a touchy question which affected Canadian relations with countries both inside and outside the Empire and which serves to introduce an individual who will be prominent in later chapters.

Immigration from Asia—chiefly from China, Japan, and the Indian Empire—had long presented Canadian governments with a troublesome problem. They had to handle the matter with care; for Japan was an ally of Britain, China had treaty relations with Britain, and India was part of the dominions of the Crown. On the other hand, few Canadians in those days were much in favour of the admission of orientals to the country, and the people of British Columbia were in general violently hostile to the idea. The result was what may be called a legislative feud between British Columbia and Ottawa. As early as 1884 the Pacific province passed an act to prevent the immigration of Chinese, which the Dominion government disallowed under section 90 of the British North America Act. Down to 1908 a succession of British Columbia acts directed against the admission of Chinese and other Asiatics suffered the same fate.[70] In 1907 there were anti-Japanese riots in Vancouver. The person sent from Ottawa to investigate was a rising young civil servant (aged thirty-two) named William Lyon Mackenzie King. King had university degrees from Toronto and Harvard and a well-documented interest in social questions. He had been recruited by Sir William Mulock for the new Department of Labour and became its deputy minister. Later in 1907 the Postmaster General, Rodolphe Lemieux, was dispatched to Japan on behalf of the Canadian government and with the help of Joseph Pope and the friendly cooperation of the British Ambassador negotiated a "gentleman's agreement" by which the Japanese government would limit emigration to Canada to four hundred persons a year. The final agreement was concluded in Ottawa in January 1908.[71]

On February 5, 1908 James Bryce addressed to the British Foreign Secretary, Sir Edward Grey, a "Most Confidential" dispatch of which a copy was sent to Sir Wilfrid Laurier.[72] Four days before, he said, "Mr. Mackenzie King, Deputy Minister of Labour in the Government of Canada" had called on him by appointment. King told him that he had come to Washington the previous week on a personal invitation from President Roosevelt received through a friend* who had told the President of a report which King had lately written on Asiatic immigration into British Columbia. King had not called at the Embassy because, he said, he knew that Bryce was absent. Roosevelt told King the situation in the Pacific states concerning Japanese labourers was extremely serious. He added that he had sent the U.S. fleet to the Pacific because of the failure to obtain assurances from the Japanese government about restrictions on emigration. He even talked of the possibility of a secession movement in the Pacific states if the situation continued, a movement which might involve British Columbia. The President asked that King, if he should be in England, should explain the American position to the government there in the hope that if her British ally made a friendly exposition to Japan of the strength of American views it would help in the preservation of peace. At Roosevelt's request King also discussed the matter with Secretary Root.

King went back to Ottawa and reported to Laurier. Sir Wilfrid, as Bryce put it, "found difficulty in believing that the President could have intended to send a message of this sort in this way". He sent King back

* J. J. McCook. King had apparently cleared the visit with Sir Wilfrid Laurier. It had a merely social appearance—an invitation to lunch at the White House.

to Washington "and requested him to tell the President that he concurred in the opinion that there was a common interest in this question, but that Canada had now settled the matter to her own satisfaction". He desired King to ask Roosevelt more precisely whether he desired any assistance "and to tell him that anything that was fit to be done could only be done after full consultation with the Governor General of Canada". On returning to Washington King saw Root and subsequently lunched with the President. Both were pleased with Laurier's message. Root told King that Japan had now given the United States very satisfactory assurances concerning restriction of emigration. It remained to be seen how they were carried out; if they were not, "there would be trouble". Roosevelt again said that he would like to have the British government informed that while anxious to "save the face of" the Japanese, the U.S. were "determined to obtain exclusion at all costs". He asked King to go and see Bryce and tell him the story, "which," says Bryce, "it need hardly be said Mr. King had already determined to do". King spent the whole of the following morning with Bryce, and thereafter they both had lunch with the President. Roosevelt made "what under the form of an explanation was in substance an apology for the way in which things had been done", and then repeated much what he had said to King previously about Japanese-American relations. Bryce said that he saw no objection to King, on his coming visit to England, reporting what he had seen in British Columbia. He himself would inform the Foreign Secretary of what Roosevelt had said; on the President's suggestion he telegraphed in addition to writing. Bryce was too large a man to complain of the corners that had been cut during the affair, though he was obviously very much aware of them. It is quite clear that Roosevelt was trying to by-pass the Ambassador.

This was not the whole story. After this second trip of King to Washington, Roosevelt wrote Laurier a letter which made it appear that the initiative in suggesting that King should visit England had come, not from the United States, but from Canada, and that the U.S. would be glad to come to Canada's assistance in her immigration troubles! King then made a third journey to the American capital, carrying a reply from Laurier which refrained from expressing the Prime Minister's considerable disgust with these suggestions ("a smart Yankee trick" was his private comment); and in March he was duly sent to England, ostensibly to discuss Canada's Asiatic immigration problems with the British government, actually to pass on to British ministers what he had heard in

Washington. Sir Edward Grey told his cousin, the Governor General, that he had said "very explicitly" to King that there was no basis for any suspicion that Britain would not support Canada in the unlikely event of serious trouble with Japan over immigration.[73] The episode may be concluded with two comments on young Mr. King. The last sentence of Bryce's original dispatch to Sir Edward Grey[74] ran:

> I wish to add that in all this somewhat singular and delicate business Mr. King appears to me to have acted with a tact and judgment which do him the utmost credit. He is a man of undoubted capacity and likely to be conspicuously useful in the public service.

Lord Grey added his own observation to Bryce's: "I share his favourable opinion of M. King and his belief that a career of growing usefulness and distinction awaits him if he keeps both his health and his modesty."[75] These were King's first visits to the White House; there would be many more, and many more missions to London. And he kept his health. About his modesty, to borrow a phrase of Winston Churchill's, there might be two opinions.

Before 1908 was over, King was a member of Parliament (and on his way to the cabinet); but before he actually took his seat he was sent on another mission in connection with Asiatic immigration. After a short visit to London he went on to Shanghai to represent Canada in the International Opium Conference being held there. En route he discussed immigration with the government of India (where Lord Minto was now Viceroy); that government did not wish to limit emigration in the Japanese manner, and considered that recent Canadian legislation (including a requirement for continuous voyage from the country of which the immigrants were citizens) would be quite sufficient safeguard. After Shanghai, King went to Peking for similar discussions with the Chinese government. He sought to promote an agreement like that with Japan, but in the end did not succeed. Canada continued to limit Chinese immigration by means of a $500 head tax; originally thought of as constituting virtual exclusion, this ultimately came to mean that the Chinese entered Canada much more easily than the people of the Empire's Japanese ally or the King's Indian subjects.[76]

The Dominion government and Parliament were no doubt more liberal-minded than the race-rioters of Vancouver, but the difference was only of degree. When R. B. Bennett told a British Columbia audience in 1907 that "British Columbia must remain a white man's country"[77] he was proclaiming doctrine with which at that time the vast majority of Canadians as well as the vast majority of British Columbians agreed. And as in other aspects of external policy, in immigration matters there was no point in attempting to legislate policies with which the voters did not agree.

BEGINNINGS OF A FOREIGN OFFICE

This chapter ends with a development which appears more important today than it did at the time: the creation in 1909 of the Canadian Department of External Affairs.

The first person to suggest such a department seems to have been W. Sanford Evans, a Winnipeg journalist later active in public life, in his book on the South African War called *The Canadian Contingents and Canadian Imperialism* (Toronto, 1901). "It would," he wrote, "be a movement toward the rounding-off of our system of self-government, and yet would be neither a challenge for independence in these matters, nor a submission to continual dependence. It would simply be the supplying of defects in the present machinery." It is possible that Evans had noted the fact that the constitution for a federated Australia enacted by the British Parliament in 1900 provided for a Department of External Affairs. It is difficult to say whether his suggestion contributed to the ultimate result. That result was slow in coming; but it certainly arose from consciousness of "defects in the present machinery", and it was in fact a by-product of the Grey-Root-Bryce slate-cleaning operation.

The first person in the government service to call attention to the need for better arrangements for dealing with (to use his words) "what I may term, for want of a better phrase, the *external affairs* of the Dominion" was Joseph Pope (Sir Joseph from 1912), sometime private secretary to Sir John Macdonald and since 1896 Under-Secretary of State. On May 25, 1907 Pope addressed a memorandum to a Royal Commission on the Civil Service pointing out that under the existing system dispatches relating to external matters might be referred to any one of several departments, and that the terms in which it was subsequently dealt with were normally left to the department to which it was first referred; "there is no uniformity of system or continuity of plan." Moreover, this custom resulted in no department possessing a complete record of the correspondence on any external subject. The implication (Pope did not fully spell it out) was that there should be a single bureau concerned specifically with external affairs, possessing complete records of international questions with which Canada had been concerned, and staffed by officials trained in the preparation of dispatches on such questions.[78]

This was the opening gun in the campaign. It was James Bryce who continued the bombardment.[79] Whether he knew of Pope's ideas on the subject is not clear, but it is by no means impossible that the two men had a talk during Bryce's first visit to Ottawa in March–April 1907, which was a few weeks before Pope's memorandum was written. It is improbable that Bryce's own experience had given him any firm notions on Canadian organization at this early date. But before the end of 1907 he was discouraged by the failure of the machine in Ottawa to work faster on the slate-cleaning operation with the United States. He wrote to Lord Grey,

> I need only ask you to be kind enough to continue to apply a little gentle pressure, of course as from yourself, to get your Ministers to move a little faster. Considering what a brisk and go ahead country Canada has now become, I am surprised at the long delays before I get answer to my requests for expressions of the views of your Ministers. Even when I ask for a reply by telegraph it doesn't come. . . . I am practically now handling all these questions directly with Canada, and expected in that way to get on faster. But they don't move. We may not always have as good conditions as we have now. . . .[80]

By February 1908, when he made another visit to Ottawa, Bryce was not only convinced of the need for a Canadian Department of External Affairs, but he wrote to the Foreign Secretary that Laurier and Lord Grey both approved the plan.[81]

The Colonial Office in London, however, not unnaturally entertained doubts about it. Would it not involve the Dominion's taking over some of those functions which were properly the business of the Foreign Office? Foreign policy was an imperial concern. Bryce, it is evident, soothed these fears. Sir Francis Hopwood, the Permanent Under-Secretary of State for the Colonies, was sent to Canada to discuss this among other matters. Bryce wrote to Lord Grey from London in August 1908,

> The C.O. has been uneasy as to this, lest it should relax the connection with C.O. and F.O., but they now appear to see that it is indispensable, and that in the form not of a separate Ministerial Department but of a secretariat

attached to the Prime Minister it need not do any harm. I trust you will get Laurier to establish it before the general election. When does that come?[82]

Grey replied:

... we cannot look forward to the creation of a new Dept of External affairs, the object of wh. will be to keep the PM fully informed as to the exact position of all outstanding questions with the U.S., until after the next Genl. Election. Sir W. says an Act of Parlt. will be necessary. He excuses himself for not having passed an Act last Session by pleading inability to do so. Under the existing rules of the House, he found it impossible to get through the urgent business under 8 mths. He has however promised to take up this question at the beginning of next session.[83]

The general election came on October 26, and Laurier won it. He had already told Pope that the cabinet had decided to set up a Department of External Affairs and make Pope its permanent head. Pope proceeded to draft a bill to go before the first session of the new Parliament. The draft provided that the First Minister should preside over the new department, "with the title of Secretary of State for External Affairs". The duties of the office were thus described:

The Secretary of State for External Affairs shall be charged with the direction of all matters relating to the external affairs of the Dominion, including the conduct and management, in so far as appertains to the Government of Canada, of such international and intercolonial negotiations as are now pending, and others which may from time to time, arise.[84]

Before being presented to Parliament in the spring of 1909 this draft was altered. The Secretary of State (once called Secretary of State for the Provinces) replaced the Prime Minister as the member of the cabinet who doubled as Secretary of State for External Affairs; and the most important paragraph relating to his duties, as passed by Parliament, read:

3. The Secretary of State, as head of the department, shall have the conduct of all official communications between the Government of Canada and the Government of any other country in connection with the external affairs of Canada, and shall be charged with such other duties as may, from time to time, be assigned to the department by order of the Governor in Council in relation to such external affairs, or to the conduct and management of

international or intercolonial negotiations so far as they may appertain to the Government of Canada.[85]

Nobody in Parliament attempted to represent the measure as involving constitutional change, and it passed all its stages without a division. The new department had taken a shape somewhat different from what Bryce had anticipated. It was not, in form at least, a mere secretariat, but a "separate Ministerial Department", even though its minister held another portfolio as well. In practice it was to be a secretariat, and remained so for a good many years. Its first humble quarters were above a barber shop on Ottawa's Bank Street—a strange contrast with the heavy Egyptian splendour of the building it occupies today. But the wording of the act establishing it could have been interpreted as giving it much wider functions, and Lord Grey, who presumably had not been shown the final draft (though Pope's original one had been sent to his office) considered that it encroached upon the prerogatives of the Governor General. His objection was to the word "conduct", which he thought should have been "care". He spoke to Sir Wilfrid Laurier on the subject, and Sir Wilfrid undertook to have the necessary amendment made before the bill was finally passed; but, whether by dilatoriness or design, this was not done. The Prime Minister now said that the act could be amended at the next session, and protested against what he called the "impression somewhere" that there was a "sinister motive" behind the wording:

> Nothing will suffer until November, and our action in bringing [in] an amendment will certainly emphasise that we have no such thought as interfering with the well settled principle that the Governor General has the conduct of foreign & Imperial relations.[86]

Grey in reply expressed his "great disappointment", and added: "Until an amending act is passed I feel that I shall occupy a more or less false position."[87] The Colonial Secretary (now Lord Crewe) approved Grey's action in assenting to the bill "on the understanding that the Act will be amended next Session in the sense indicated in your correspondence with Sir Wilfrid Laurier".[88] Nevertheless, in spite of Laurier's assurances, the Act was not amended. In 1912, when an amendment intended to put the Department of External Affairs under the Prime Minister was before Parliament, the Colonial Office instructed the Governor General (the

Duke of Connaught now) to inform the Prime Minister (Robert Borden) of the promise given by Laurier in 1909. Borden's reply was strongly reminiscent of Laurier himself:

> As no inconvenience or embarrassment has arisen or been occasioned during three years in which the existing Statute has been in force, it is probable that none may be seriously apprehended. However, I shall be glad to consider at another session any suggestion as to a desirable amendment in respect of the consideration to which Your Royal Highness has alluded.

The Duke in reporting this to the Colonial Secretary made the comment that merely substituting "care" for "conduct" would "reduce the Department to the position of a storehouse for documents". At that point the matter seems to have lapsed.[89]

Whatever interpretation may be put upon this tiff over the wording of the act, it is evident that Laurier had to be pushed into setting up the department, and that the pushing was mainly done by the British Ambassador in Washington. It is equally evident that the department was not in any significant degree an expression of a Canadian desire for a larger share in the control of foreign policy. In the eyes of its originators, it was not a foreign office, but an expedient for the more efficient dispatch of business under the existing arrangements; Bryce and Grey certainly saw it as a means of keeping Laurier up to the mark, of overcoming the effects of his poor memory and his notorious procrastination. One recalls Grey's remark that the object was "to keep the PM fully informed as to the exact position of all outstanding questions with the U.S." Pope, who had worked hard to bring the department into existence, when he became its permanent head made little attempt to become a maker of policy. He devoted himself to building up a complete set of records and to ensuring that incoming dispatches were handled with promptness and efficiency.[90] In the future, after a world war and under another permanent head, the Department of External Affairs would become a true Canadian foreign office and would play, for a time, a dominant role in the Ottawa bureaucracy. But in 1909 that future was far away.

CHAPTER FIVE

EXTERNAL RELATIONS AND THE FALL OF LAURIER

THE CANADIAN SITUATION IN 1908

In 1908 Sir Wilfrid Laurier won his fourth successive general election. Before his old administration appealed again to the electorate serious issues of external policy were to arise, and the election of 1911 was to be dominated by such problems to an extent hitherto unknown.

So far as relations with the United States were concerned, the situation in 1908 appeared to be very satisfactory. The nasty confrontation of 1903 over the Alaska boundary was apparently receding into history, and both American and British governments seemed concerned to speed it on its way. A contemporary comment of 1907 struck the keynote of the new era: "Canadian relations with the United States took on quite a new form in 1907. Instead of Canadian delegates and Ministers going to Washington asking tariff or treaty favours the United States Secretary of State [Elihu Root] paid a formal visit to Ottawa; instead of the British Ambassador in Washington looking on at Canadian affairs from a philosophical distance, Mr. Bryce came to see the Dominion and its concerns for himself."[1] We have watched the process of "cleaning the slate" of outstanding Canadian-American disputes; by 1908 it was well advanced, and the fact that Canadian representatives were playing an increasingly direct part in the negotiations was contributing to the general goodwill.

In the background, nevertheless, there still lurked a persistent and essentially unsolved problem: that of trade relations. An attempt at producing a bold solution here was to be the most important factor in ending Laurier's long tenure of power.

Very different was the European outlook. The clouds of the dreadful storm that was to burst in 1914 were already gathering. Britain was becoming more and more directly involved in European international politics; her old policy of isolation was a thing of the past. Its abandonment was marked by the signing of the Anglo-Japanese Alliance early in 1902. Two years later a thing the Germans had believed could never happen came to pass: Britain made an *entente* with France. In 1907 the diplomatic revolution was completed when she made an arrangement settling outstanding issues with Russia. The country which had so feared the Franco-Russian alliance of 1894 (above, page 100) had now aligned itself with France and Russia. There was no formal alliance with either nation, but in effect a new power bloc had been formed, and the successive European crises that followed merely served to solidify it. Germany, which had rejected British overtures for an alliance in the days of Chamberlain, found herself facing what began to look like a formidable coalition; and she made her situation worse by steadily building up her navy, a policy she had followed since the turn of the century. The strongest land power on the Continent now seemed to be challenging British superiority at sea; and the island country whose industrial prosperity and very existence depended upon the secure importation of raw materials and food thought itself gravely menaced.

In the circumstances of those days, no one in England yet thought seriously of consulting the self-governing colonies about the fundamental changes in British foreign policy that we have outlined. These changes were nevertheless to have fateful effects on the life of those communities. In the long run they were to embroil them in the First World War, with all its incalculable costs and consequences. In the somewhat shorter run, they produced the Naval Question, which in Canada particularly was to dominate and complicate domestic politics for years.

Laurier's years of power witnessed two revolutionary developments in the export trade by which Canada so largely lived and lives: the advent of the wheat boom, and the beginning of the newsprint industry.

A sudden rise in wheat prices, following a long period in which they had been preternaturally low, encouraged the faster settlement of the West; and shortly new early-ripening strains of wheat (the first being Red Fife, by 1900) increased prairie productiveness. From about 1898 Canadian wheat exports shot up. Totals varied annually with the state of the crop and the market; but the value of wheat sent abroad, which was only about $2,100,000 in the 1891 fiscal year, rose fairly steadily to about $45,800,000 in 1911 and far higher thereafter (see Appendix B). Much the largest customer was the United Kingdom, whose dependence on imported food had lately vastly increased. From those days to the present time the selling of wheat has been a major factor in Canadian economic welfare and a major concern of Canadian trade policy.

The pulp and paper business may be said to have spread into Canada from the United States. As American forest resources began to be depleted, Canada increasingly took on the task of satisfying the enormous demand of the American newspapers for newsprint—exporting wood or wood pulp to be manufactured into paper across the border, or (partly under the impulsion of provincial legislation) finished newsprint paper made in Canada. Plentiful timber, cheap electric power, proximity to the American centres of population, and, in due course, free access to that great market, were the foundations of the Canadian pulp and paper industry. Before the end of the twentieth century's first quarter it would be the country's greatest industry by any standard. It was still far from this position when Laurier fell, but it was growing fast in both economic and political importance. Four-fifths of Canada's pulp and paper exports went to the United States, just as a comparable proportion of her wheat exports went to the United Kingdom. Wood pulp first appears in official Canadian export statistics in 1906, with a value of under $3,500,000; ten years later it was about $10,300,000. Newsprint is first listed in 1911 ($3,000,000); by 1921 it was up to about $79,000,000.[2] Modest as the figures for Laurier's time are, we shall see that newsprint was playing a significant part in international economic politics in his last years of power; and we have already noted that to increase wheat sales was a major object of his government in dealings with Great Britain as early as 1902 (above, page 77).

The rise of these two new export trades, and particularly that in wheat, exemplified and was to a large extent responsible for the previously unparalleled Canadian prosperity of the Laurier years. The statistics of the national revenue reflect the change in the country's economic situation; the total rose from $38,500,000 in 1891 to $117,700,000 in 1911.[3] And as we have seen, the buoyancy of the economy was reflected in the political climate; both government and electorate were under the influence of a confidence more sanguine than the facts fully supported.

NAVAL POWER AND POLITICS

The growing naval rivalry in Europe had consequences for British naval policy in the outer seas. Almost inevitably it led to increased concentration of force in European waters and a reduction on more distant stations. One of those stations was North America. As we have seen, the British government had come by 1902 to the conclusion that British security required a policy of peace with the United States at almost any price. A natural consequence was the reduction of British naval forces in North American waters and the abandonment of British naval bases in Canada. While the unilateral decision to have no war with the United States in any circumstances whatever freed British forces from America for transfer to the European danger-zone, in the Far East the Anglo-Japanese alliance simultaneously served a similar purpose, and the Admiralty strongly supported it accordingly. An historian of the alliance writes, with specific reference to the renewal and revision of it in 1905, "so long as Japan remained Britain's ally, Britain could afford to leave the naval defence of her far-eastern interests to Japan".[4] She would have preferred not to have to do this, for it was to be assumed that Japan would protect British interests only as long as it suited her own interests to do so; but Britain simply did not have the resources to maintain naval supremacy all across the world.

In 1871, as already noted, the British Army was withdrawn from the interior of Canada; the only British garrison then remaining was that at the still-important naval port of Halifax. In 1893 the British and Dominion governments made an agreement for the joint defence of the Pacific base of Esquimalt on Vancouver Island. By the turn of the century batteries had been constructed there and a small British garrison was in occupation, the cost being shared between the two countries.[5] A larger imperial force remained at Halifax, the provision of a Canadian battalion there during the South African War having been a merely temporary arrangement.

On October 21, 1904 Admiral Sir John Fisher became First Sea Lord at the Admiralty and launched a famous campaign of naval reforms. One of his measures was the scrapping of a great number of old and weak ships. Another was the redistribution of the fleet. The program was announced in December. Its most important element was a large reduction of the battleship force on the China station; but from the Canadian viewpoint the most significant changes were the abolition of the Pacific Squadron (based on Esquimalt) and the North America and West Indies Squadron. The latter, which had utilized Halifax, was now replaced by a "Particular Service Squadron" which it was proposed should make occasional cruises to the West Indies but was to be based at Devonport in England. On December 15 the Admiralty informed the Colonial Office that the naval establishments at Halifax, Jamaica, Esquimalt, and Trincomalee (Ceylon) would be reduced to cadres on which no money would be spent in peacetime.[6]

The result of this decision was the withdrawal of the British garrisons from the Canadian fortified ports. The British authorities had been hinting for some time that they would be glad to have Canada take over the protection of them. In fact, both Halifax and Esquimalt now appeared unimportant to War Office and Admiralty alike, and it is evident that if Canada had declined to garrison them they would simply have been abandoned. Canada, however, was never told this. Providing garrisons for the two ports could be and was represented in the Dominion as a suitable Canadian contribution to imperial defence and a natural assumption of national responsibilities. In January 1905 Lord Grey conveyed to the British government his ministers' formal request to take over the two places. During 1905 and 1906, accordingly, the British troops were withdrawn, and the little Canadian Permanent Force, somewhat enlarged for the purpose, replaced them at Halifax and Esquimalt. The actual transfer of the naval dockyards at the two places was carried out in a more leisurely manner, the legal formalities not being completed until 1911. The British order-in-council making the transfer, expressing terms agreed on between the two governments, required Canada to maintain the existing properties in a state of efficiency or to provide "conveniences at least equal in character" at the same ports, and to extend storage and other facilities to the Royal Navy.[7]

In the meantime international tensions in Europe had grown worse, and technical developments had heightened the naval rivalry between Britain and Germany. In 1906 the Royal Navy, under Fisher's inspiration, produced the battleship *Dreadnought*, the first "all-big-gun"* ship, far

* She mounted ten 12-inch guns and no others except small weapons for use against torpedo craft, whereas earlier battleships normally mounted four 12-inch and heavy secondary armaments. The *Dreadnought* was also the first battleship to be driven by turbines.

more powerful than any other war vessel afloat and faster than any other capital ship. All battleships except the *Dreadnought* suddenly became obsolete, Britain's previous great superiority in this class of ship was nullified, and all the great naval powers started virtually "from scratch" in the construction of dreadnoughts. The Germans plunged into the new competition, and Britons viewed the German threat with still greater alarm than before.

Early in 1909 there was a genuine panic in England, caused by reports (now known to have been exaggerated) of a secret acceleration of the German dreadnought program. It was suggested that Germany might actually outnumber Britain in dreadnoughts by 1912. There was dissension within the cabinet, and by the end of February the matter was being aired in the press. On March 16 there was a tense debate in the House of Commons. The Conservative opposition to the government of H. H. Asquith was now demanding the immediate construction of eight more dreadnoughts ("We want eight, and we won't wait."). In July, after news came of Austrian and Italian dreadnought construction, all eight proposed ships were authorized.

Inevitably these events had echoes in Canada. Their effect was strengthened by others: the long and dangerous European crisis initiated by Austria's annexation of Bosnia and Herzegovina (contrary to the Treaty of Berlin of 1878) in October 1908, and naval measures taken in the Antipodes. In Australia Alfred Deakin's government disliked the system of money contributions to the Royal Navy and had committed itself to the principle of an Australian naval force. In New Zealand this idea had less appeal; but on March 22, 1909, in the midst of the scare in England, that Dominion's government offered the mother country the gift of a dreadnought, and of a second if required.[8]

Against this background the Canadian Parliament for the first time seriously confronted the problem of naval defence. On March 29, 1909 George E. Foster, a leading and eloquent member of the opposition, moved the following resolution in the House of Commons:

> That in the opinion of this House, in view of her great and varied resources, of her geographical position and national environments, and of that spirit of self-help and self-respect which alone befits a strong and growing people, Canada should no longer delay in assuming her proper share of the responsibility and financial burden incident to the suitable protection of her exposed coast line and great seaports.

Foster pointed out that his motion had been on the order paper since the beginning of the session and was therefore not the mere product of recent events. He added that it was not conceived in any party spirit, and that he hoped the matter could be dealt with "outside of party politics and party contention". And it may be said that so far as that day's debate was concerned he had his wish.

Like many Canadian utterances of that age, Foster's combined the national with the imperial theme. "The most sublime figure in all history," he said, was "the figure of the old mother empire, the great-hearted mother who has given birth to the young nations that circle the globe, the great-hearted mother that has gone outside of her own kith and kin and has mothered nation after nation, people after people, continent after continent, brought them out of darkness and slavery and set them upon the path of a better civilization." But he had an equally sanguine vision of the new Canadian nation:

> Sir, into this world of trouble, of uncertainty, amongst this world of nations, Canada has pushed forward to her place. She has taken a position which is important now, which will become more and more important as the years advance. Her ship of state is launched on the world's waters, it is open to every storm, it is exposed to every danger. She cannot escape the common burden, she cannot neglect the common duty, she cannot ignore the common responsibility. I do not believe that she wishes to. . . .

Canada had done something in the way of providing land defence; for naval defence as yet she had done nothing, and action was overdue. Foster discussed the forms such action might take. For "the policy of a fixed annual contribution in money to the British government or the British admiralty" he had little enthusiasm; he thought it not national enough; it ignored "the necessities and the aspirations and the prospects of a great people such as the Canadian people are destined to become". He preferred to think in terms of Canadians themselves assuming "the defence of our own ports and coasts, in constant and free co-operation with the imperial forces of the mother country," though he admitted that a Canadian naval service would have to have modest beginnings and would be at first wholly dependent upon British assistance. But at the end of his speech he spoke of the current crisis and the action of Australia and New Zealand:

> Let me say to my right hon. friend [Sir Wilfrid Laurier] that if, after careful consideration, he proposes to this parliament a means for meeting that

emergency adequately, by the gift of Dreadnaughts [*sic*] or the gift of money, this side of the House will stand beside him in thus vindicating Canada's honour and strengthening the empire's defence.

Laurier spoke immediately after Foster. It is evident that he had given much thought to his reply, and that the old procrastinator (has there ever been a successful prime minister of Canada who was not a procrastinator?) had come to the conclusion that the time had come when some form of naval defence had to be provided. The suggestion of offering a dreadnought he sidestepped without specifically rejecting it. The policy which commended itself to the government he defined in these words: "We should consult with the naval authorities of the British government . . . and after having organized a plan, we should carry it out in Canada with our own resources and out of our own money." And he produced as a substitute for Foster's motion a more elaborate one which he hoped Foster would accept:

This House fully recognizes the duty of the people of Canada, as they increase in numbers and wealth, to assume in larger measure the responsibilities of national defence.

The House reaffirms the opinion, repeatedly expressed by representatives of Canada, that under the present constitutional relations between the mother country and the self-governing dominions the payment of any stated contribution to the imperial treasury for naval and military purposes would not, so far as Canada is concerned, be a satisfactory solution of the question of defence.

The House has observed with satisfaction the relief afforded in recent years to the taxpayers of the United Kingdom through the assumption by the Canadian people of considerable military expenditure formerly charged upon the imperial treasury.

The House will cordially approve of any necessary expenditure designed to promote the organization of a Canadian naval service in co--operation with and in close relation to the imperial navy, along the lines suggested by the admiralty at the last Imperial Conference, and in full sympathy with the view that the naval supremacy of Great Britain is essential to the security of commerce, the safety of the empire and the peace of the world.

The House expresses its firm conviction that whenever the need arises the Canadian people will be found ready and willing to make any sacrifice that is required to give to the imperial authorities the most loyal and hearty co-operation in every movement for the maintenance of the integrity and the honour of the empire.

The leader of the opposition, R. L. Borden, followed the Prime Minister. He too sounded the note of nationality, and reminded the house that "a national status implies national responsibility". He said that on the matter of naval defence he was "entirely at one" with Laurier: "I am entirely of opinion . . . that the proper line upon which we should proceed in that regard is the line of having a Canadian naval force of our own. I entirely believe in that." But he had some amendments to suggest. He particularly asked for the inclusion of "some word which would indicate an intention to act promptly". He suggested omitting the sentence concerning the relief afforded the British taxpayer. And, most significant of all in the light of later events, he also suggested that the paragraph rejecting "the payment of any stated contribution" should be deleted:

> The day might come—I do not know that it will come—the day might come; it might come to-morrow, it might come next week, it might come next month, when the only thing we could do in the absence of preparation in this country would be to make some kind of contribution.

Some weeks later Borden explained to a correspondent in England that his object was "to leave open the door to a money contribution in time of peril, as a sudden emergency might arise in which the most effective assistance for the time being could be given in that form". In the same letter he said that there had been "many private conferences" between Laurier and himself before the resolution reached its final form.[9] It is evident that these consultations must have taken place while the backbenchers talked in the later stages of the debate. In the end, the amended resolution which Laurier laid before the Commons and which the House adopted unanimously had the same first and final paragraphs as his original one. The intervening portion of it read as follows:

> The House is of opinion that under the present constitutional relations between the mother country and the self-governing dominions, the payment of regular and periodical contributions to the imperial treasury for naval and military purposes would not, so far as Canada is concerned, be the most satisfactory solution of the question of defence.
>
> The House will cordially approve of any necessary expenditure designed to promote the speedy organization of a Canadian naval service in co-operation with and in close relation to the imperial navy, along the lines suggested by the admiralty at the last imperial conference, and in full sympathy with the view that the naval supremacy of Britain is essential to the security of commerce, the safety of the empire and the peace of the world.

Thus Laurier had consented to eliminate the reference to relief to the British taxpayer, and had accepted the idea of a commitment to prompt ("speedy") action. He had not cut out the paragraph concerning a "stated contribution", but it had been amended to state that "regular and periodical contributions" would not be "the most satisfactory solution". These concessions had made possible the achievement of unanimity on a great question of national policy. They also opened the door to a breakdown of unity at a later stage.

It is important to note that both parties were deeply divided on the naval issue. The divisions centred largely in French Canada, where very few people actively favoured Canada's taking a share in naval defence in any form, and many were actively hostile either to a contribution or to a Canadian service. And French Quebec was a vital factor in both parties' calculations. It was the chief stronghold of Laurier's political power (he had taken 54 of its 65 seats in the Commons in 1908) and it was of course only too obvious that the naval question offered possibilities for sapping his authority there. In English-speaking Canada there was division; the rural voter was less enthusiastic than the city man about naval defence, as he was about imperialism, and in many cases people who did favour the idea preferred a contribution to the Royal Navy over the idea of creating a Canadian fleet.

Here tradition and colonial thinking had their influence. No imperial institution impressed the colonist so much as the navy,

> Whose flag had braved a thousand years
> The battle and the breeze.

The Canadian Militia might be allowed to take over the local responsibilities of defence on land; but it was hard for colonial thinkers to envision setting up a Canadian navy. A navy—*the* navy—was something that existed, that had existed for aeons; not something that could be invented. The same line of thought led Canadians, including Laurier,[10] to believe that the German naval threat was exaggerated because Germany had no great naval tradition and navies supposedly could not be created in a limited time (a notion which the events of 1914–18 showed to be a gross error). This view also led them to think that the establishment of an effective Canadian naval force would be the work of many years. They could not believe that Canadian energy and address were equal to performing the task with any rapidity. What was worse, they felt called upon to ridicule any such attempt.

Such colonial thinkers were numerous in Borden's party, and the argument that there was an emergency which made an immediate contribution to the Royal Navy desirable lay ready to their hands. Four Conservative provincial premiers, Richard McBride (British Columbia), Rodmond Roblin (Manitoba), Sir James Whitney (Ontario), and J. D. Hazen (New Brunswick) all argued for a contribution. Roblin seems to have popularized, though he probably did not coin, for the policy of a Canadian fleet the phrase "tin-pot navy", which was to follow the Royal Canadian Navy about for many years.[11] At the same time the Quebec wing of the party was determinedly hostile to any naval expenditure whatever. Furthermore, Borden's own position was shaky. He lacked the long-established prestige of Laurier, and especially in Quebec his leadership was questioned. His situation as the parliamentary session of 1910 drew on was embarrassing.

In the meantime there was an imperial conclave in London. The 1907 Imperial Conference had accepted the idea of "subsidiary conferences" on special topics being held from time to time as might be desirable. On April 30, 1909 the Colonial Secretary suggested that, in view of the resolution passed by the Canadian House of Commons and the proposals made by Australia and New Zealand, such a conference, dealing with the "general questions of naval and military defence of the Empire", should be held that July. It assembled accordingly, with Sir Frederick Borden and L. P. Brodeur, Minister of Marine and Fisheries, representing Canada.[12] Perhaps the conference's most solid achievement was agreement, with respect to land forces, on the principle of maintaining general uniformity throughout the Empire in organization, training, and equipment. Sir Frederick Borden fully accepted this. "We believe," he said, "that local defence and Imperial defence are very largely one and the same thing . . . the moment attack is made upon Canadian territory by any other nation, then at once Canada becomes the scene, the theatre of a war in which immediately the Empire is interested, and Imperial troops would be necessary. So that it seems to me it is only common sense which would lead us to so organise our local defences that they could co-operate with an Imperial army and be really and genuinely a part of that army." Borden went on to look at the question from the other side, the possibility of Canada co-operating with imperial forces in a war abroad:

> May I say that there is nothing in any of these recommendations which suggests in any way any change in our method of raising our troops . . . we are

left absolutely to ourselves. Under the militia law of Canada the Governor-General in Council has power to mobilise the whole of our forces, and if a war is imminent and Parliament is not in session, Parliament may be called within 15 days, and Parliament will then decide, and Parliament can alone decide whether we will take any part in that war, whatever it may be. . . . If . . . we maintain forces which are organised on a common principle and in co-operation and in co-ordination with those of Great Britain, then we are ready, if we see fit, to take part in any war in which the Empire is interested. That is the whole point, that we shall be ready if we wish to take part; but we are not bound to take part if we do not wish to do so. We shall be able to do so if we desire it. . . .[13]

Dominion autonomy and freedom of action were fully protected. Nevertheless the principle that had been established was of great importance. The plan for (to use the words of Mr. Asquith in the British House of Commons on August 26, 1909) "the formation of units, the arrangements for transport, the patterns of weapons, &c., being as far as possible assimilated to those which have recently been worked out for the British Army"[14] provided the basis for the smooth and effective co-operation of Dominion and British forces in two world wars.

The discussion of naval defence (now the matter of greatest immediate interest to the Canadian representatives) began with the presentation of a memorandum of proposals by the Admiralty.[15] It remarked wistfully, and truly, "If the problem of Imperial naval defence were considered merely as a problem of naval strategy it would be found that the greatest output of strength for a given expenditure is obtained by the maintenance of a single navy with the concomitant unity of training and unity of command." In these circumstances contributions by all parts of the Empire to the maintenance of the British navy would produce "the maximum of power". But it was recognized now that "other considerations than those of strategy alone" had to be taken into account. And in the view of the Admiralty a Dominion government "desirous of creating a navy" should aim at forming "a distinct fleet unit". Such a unit would be built around one of the new dreadnought armoured cruisers (the term "battle cruiser" had not yet come into use) and include also lighter cruisers, destroyers, and submarines. It is evident that the Admiralty was thinking in terms of the establishment of Dominion fleet units—including a Canadian one—in the Pacific, where they would compensate for the recent withdrawal of British units and perhaps permit a still greater concentration of the Royal Navy in European waters. As Admiral Fisher pointed out, "the full power of the British fleet could readily be brought to bear in the Western Atlantic in case of need".[16]

The Canadian representatives, with political considerations clearly in mind, replied that to concentrate all of Canada's naval force on one of her two coasts would not be satisfactory. Furthermore, said Frederick Borden, they were obliged to work within the limits of the Commons resolution of March 29, which spoke of a navy "along the lines suggested by the admiralty at the last imperial conference", and a statement by the First Lord of the Admiralty to the conference of 1907 had spoken of small vessels "such as torpedo boats or submarines", not of major units. The Admiralty now produced two different schemes for forces of light cruisers and smaller craft, which would be divided between the two coasts, and said that it would endeavour to comply with a request of the Canadian ministers to provide a cruiser or cruisers and instructors for training purposes.[17]

On the basis of these discussions the Laurier government framed a program which it placed before Parliament on January 12, 1910, when the Prime Minister introduced the Naval Service Bill. The bill made legal provision for a naval service which would include a naval college for the training of officers. Laurier explained that it was proposed to implement the larger of the two schemes put forward by the Admiralty, involving a force of five light cruisers and six destroyers. Under normal conditions the new service would be as much under Canadian control as the militia; but there was provision for special action in time of war:

> In case of an emergency the Governor in Council may place at the disposal of His Majesty, for general service in the Royal Navy, the Naval Service or any part thereof, any ships or vessels of the Naval Service, and the officers and seamen serving in such ships or vessels, or any officers or seamen belonging to the Naval Service.

Laurier emphasized that such action would not be automatic. He took his stand, as Sir Frederick Borden had in London, on the principle that Parliament would decide what part, if any, Canada would take in an imperial war. Moving the second reading of the bill on February 3, he said, "The position which we take is that it is for the parliament of Canada, which created this navy, to say when and where it shall go to war." He went on to use words that were quoted long after Sir Wilfrid himself was dead:

If England is at war we are at war and liable to attack. I do not say that we shall always be attacked, neither do I say that we would take part in all the wars of England. That is a matter that must be determined by circumstances, upon which the Canadian parliament will have to pronounce and will have to decide in its own best judgment.

The formula "Parliament will decide" would serve another Liberal Prime Minister well a generation later.

Robert Borden for his part had to make up his mind as to the attitude he would take towards this program. As we have seen, he had kept his options open during the debate of 1909 to the extent that he could advocate a policy of contribution without being accused of total inconsistency. But could he justify destroying the precious unity that Parliament had then achieved? One Conservative elder statesman thought not. Sir Charles Tupper, Borden's predecessor as party leader, wrote to him from England on November 20, 1909:

Under existing circumstances it was of immense importance to have Sir Wilfrid Laurier and his party committed to the policy which secured the unanimous consent of the House of Commons on a question of such vital importance and a great responsibility will rest upon those who disturb that compact.[18]

This responsibility Borden now took. His motives remain uncertain. We have seen that he was under pressure from extremists within his party. His decision to oppose the Laurier naval policy was fateful. It was the beginning of a train of events which made him Prime Minister. On the other hand it also had the ultimate effect of preventing Canada from making any material addition to the collective naval strength of the Empire, either through a Canadian force or a contribution, previous to the outbreak of the First World War.

Borden, it is true, strove to maintain an appearance of consistency. He said in the debate of January 12:

I say to my right hon. friend the Prime Minister, so far as my words have any weight with him: Go on with your naval service. Proceed slowly, cautiously and surely. Lay your proposals before the people and give them if necessary opportunity to be heard, but do not forget that we are confronted with an emergency which may rend this empire asunder before the proposed service is worthy of the name. In the face of such a situation immediate, vigorous earnest action is necessary. We have no Dreadnought ready; we have no fleet unit at hand. But we have the resources and I trust the patriotism to provide a fleet unit or at least a Dreadnought without one moment's unnecessary delay. Or, and in my opinion this would be the better course, we can place the equivalent in cash at the disposal of the admiralty to be used for naval defence under such conditions as we may prescribe. In taking this course we shall fulfill not only in the letter, but in the spirit as well, the resolution of March last, and what is infinitely more important we shall discharge a great patriotic duty to our country and to the whole empire.

On the second reading on February 3 Borden moved an amendment opposing Laurier's plan, requiring that "no permanent policy" should be undertaken "until it has been submitted to the people and has received their approval", and proposing that Canada offer the imperial authorities immediately "as a free and loyal contribution" a sum sufficient to provide two dreadnoughts.

Laurier was already in serious trouble in Quebec. Henri Bourassa, who was not at this time in the House of Commons, had decided to make the naval question an issue against him, and at the beginning of 1910 he founded the newspaper *Le Devoir* which gave him an effective mouthpiece and at once became very influential in nationalist and clerical circles. In its editorial columns and elsewhere Bourassa thundered against Laurier's measure as a capitulation to imperialism that would result in Canada being dragged into British wars around the globe:

It is the most complete backward step Canada has made in half a century.

It is the gravest blow our autonomy has suffered since the origin of responsible government.[19]

Bourassa was seconded, in effect, by F. D. Monk, formerly the federal conservative leader in Quebec, who now resumed that position. On February 3 in the House of Commons Monk moved a sub-amendment to Borden's amendment, reading as follows:

This House, while declaring its unalterable devotion to the British Crown, is of opinion that the Bill now submitted for its consideration changes the relations of Canada with the empire and ought in consequence to be submitted to the Canadian people in order to obtain at once the nation's opinion by means of a plebiscite.

When the vote was taken on March 9 only eighteen members voted for this sub-amendment; Borden's amendment was likewise voted down (by

74 to 129), and in due course the Naval Service Bill became law.[20]

It was painfully clear, however, that a divisive national issue had been raised. It was South Africa all over again. As in 1899, Laurier had sought to adopt a middle-of-the-road policy which might attract the support of the greatest possible number of Canadians. Now as then, the extremists on both sides raged against him. In 1899 his government, young and vigorous, had survived. Now, old and shaky, it was to fall a victim to the naval issue combined with other circumstances. The shape of things to come was clearly delineated in a famous Quebec incident of November 1910, the Drummond-Arthabaska by-election. A Nationalist, anti-navy candidate, with both Bourassa and Monk campaigning for him, defeated a Liberal who had Sir Wilfrid's personal blessing.[21] The possible effect on Laurier's fortunes of an alliance between Nationalist isolationists and Conservative imperialists was beginning to be evident.

THE IMPERIAL CONFERENCE OF 1911

Before the crash came Laurier attended his last Imperial Conference, in London in May and June 1911. This meeting was notable for a bumbling attempt by Sir Joseph Ward, the New Zealand Prime Minister, to obtain approval for the formation of an "Imperial Parliament of Defence"—a version of the old dream of Joseph Chamberlain. Ward seems to have been influenced by the imperialist group in England called the Round Table, though its members had not favoured any such *démarche* at this time. His proposal was anything but clear, but it evidently implied the existence of a superior authority which would spend money contributed by the countries of the Empire without the formality of their legislatures' consenting. Laurier called it "absolutely impracticable", and in the end Ward himself admitted that he was in "a minority of one" and withdrew his motion.[22]

Although the spectre of war with Germany was now only too evident, there was virtually no discussion of defence in the sessions of the Imperial Conference of 1911. The reason is simple; this discussion took place concurrently in the strictly secret meetings of the Committee of Imperial Defence. The fact is that the secretaries of the CID (Rear-Admiral Sir Charles Ottley and Captain Maurice Hankey) were conducting what amounted to a campaign to have their committee take over some important functions of the Imperial Conference;[23] and in 1911 there was progress in that direction.* The Dominion Prime Ministers attended three meetings of the committee. At the first of these, on May 26, the Foreign Secretary, Sir Edward Grey, gave them a detailed account of the international situation as seen from the Foreign Office; this was a quite new development in imperial history. Grey explained the motives behind it:

> . . . the creation of separate Fleets has made it essential that the Foreign Policy of the Empire should be a common policy. If it is to be a common policy, it is obviously one on which the Dominions must be taken into consultation, which they must know, which they must understand, and which they must approve. . . .

After describing the manner in which the existing situation in Europe had come about, Grey went on to interpret the British position in case of some power or group of powers attempting "what I would call the Napoleonic policy":

> . . . I may say at once we are not committed by entanglements which tie our hands. Our hands are free, and I have nothing to disclose [as] to our being bound by any alliances, which is not known to all the world at the present time. But I do feel this very strongly, that if such a situation should arise, and there was a risk of all the Powers [*sic*], or a group of Powers, acquiring such a dominating position in Europe it would be the arbiter not only [of] peace and war, but of the diplomacy of all the other Powers of Europe, and if while that process was going on we were appealed to for help and sat by and looked on and did nothing, then people ought to realize that the result would be one great combination in Europe, outside which we should be left without a friend.

Everything Grey said about Britain's hands being free was technically correct. He did not mention the famous "military conversations" which had taken place with France, and which are seen in retrospect as a very

* However, Stephen Roskill, *Hankey, Man of Secrets*, vol. I (London, 1970) is in error in stating that Ottley and Hankey acted as secretaries of the conference. The secretariat from the Colonial Office remained in charge. The minutes indicate that Hankey never attended a meeting of the conference, though his chief, Ottley, was present on several days.

considerable practical entanglement; they were known at this time only to the inner circle of the British cabinet.*

During this day's meeting there was specific if superficial consultation with the Dominion Prime Ministers on one important point of foreign policy: the question of extending the existing Anglo-Japanese alliance (due to expire in 1915) to 1921. Dominion attitudes were curiously different from those that were to appear on the same issue ten years later. The Australians, while not opposing the extension, made it clear that the treaty was unpopular in their country and that there was much fear of Japan. Sir Wilfrid Laurier, on the other hand, hailed the alliance as "one of the happy events of the last century" and applauded the extension. It was assumed that any difficulty with the United States would be precluded by the proposed addition to the treaty of a provision stating that it would not require either of the parties to go to war with a power with which it had a general arbitration treaty; such an arbitration treaty was then under discussion between Great Britain and the United States. The Committee of Imperial Defence adopted a formal conclusion favouring the extension of the alliance on these terms:

> The Committee approves of negotiations being entered into with the Japanese Government for the prolongation of the existing Alliance for a period of ten years from this date and on its present basis subject to a condition that it shall not be inconsistent with the provisions of any Treaty of General Arbitration which may hereafter be concluded.

At the second committee meeting, on May 29, the naval question was discussed, and there was something of an encounter between Laurier and the First Lord of the Admiralty, Reginald McKenna. The committee's secretariat, showing less than the invariable efficiency with which its admirers like to credit it, had come up with a paper defining the relationship of the British and Dominion fleets in terms precisely the reverse of the Canadian Naval Service Act. All the fleets, it suggested, would be "sister members of the King's Navy":

* No evidence has been found to indicate that any information about these quasi-commitments was given to Canada or the other Dominions after the whole of the British cabinet was let into the secret after the Agadir crisis later in 1911.

In time of war the Admiralty of the United Kingdom to control the whole of the King's Navy. A Dominion Government to be at liberty to withdraw its fleet from membership with the King's Navy before joining in hostilities.

Laurier took "very strong exception to this language". "The spirit of our Act," he said, "is that in time of peace our navy is under our own control, but in time of war we may place it at the disposal of His Majesty the King." A somewhat incoherent discussion followed concerning the position of Canada in a time of war. Laurier made himself less clear than usual, but it is evident that while recognizing that Canada was legally at war when Britain was at war, he was attempting to make the point that active participation in hostilities was another matter:

It is the policy which would bring Canada in to take part in all wars that I object to.... The point I make, and the point of policy of our Act is that we are going to war only when the Canadian Parliament has so determined. The point you have taken is that we cannot help being at war and taking part in a war the moment war is declared between Great Britain and some other Power. If war were declared with Germany probably our duty would be to go to war at once, but I can conceive there are many smaller nations who might be at war with Great Britain in which war we should take no part whatever, and that is the reason we have framed our policy as we have framed it. This point is, however, clear that we do not hold ourselves bound to take part in all the wars in which Great Britain may be engaged.... The way you put it is that you have the right to depend upon our assistance, and to make your calculations accordingly, and at the last moment we may withdraw and thus make your calculations all wrong, which would make it a position infinitely weaker than the position in which we want to regard it... what I want to impress upon the Conference here is, that so far as we are concerned in Canada, we must stand by the principle that we have the control of our own fleet until we place it in the hands of His Majesty.

Asquith observed that the paper would have to be recast, and it appeared in revised form at the third Committee meeting on May 30:

In time of war when the Dominion Fleets, in whole or in part, have been placed under the control of the Imperial Government, the ships to form an integral part of the Imperial Fleet, and remain under the control of the Admiralty of the United Kingdom, and be liable to be sent anywhere during the continuance of the war.

In this third meeting Asquith accepted Canada's co-operation upon Canada's terms ("We would have preferred to have it in another form, but that is a matter for you to decide"). He emphasized the legal fact that if Great Britain went to war, the whole Empire was at war. Laurier took no exception to this, but he did give vent to his feelings on militarism and military expenditure:

> You people in Great Britain, if I may say so, do not appreciate the different conditions in which we stand in the Dominions beyond the seas compared with the centre of the Empire here. All the nations of Europe to-day, in my humble estimation have gone, if I may say so, mad. I think Great Britain would willingly limit her armaments but every nation in Europe to-day is spending I suppose one-half of its revenue in military precautions against its neighbours. We are not in a position to do that in Canada....

This meeting discussed the relationship of the Dominions to the Committee of Imperial Defence. Asquith made it clear that the British government would welcome a closer association than heretofore. There was discussion of what sort of person would be the best representative, and general doubt about the suitability of the Dominion High Commissioners. Finally the committee approved another Conclusion on the subject:

> 1. That one or more representatives, appointed by the respective Governments of the Dominions, should be invited to attend meetings of the Committee of Imperial Defence when questions of naval and military defence affecting the Overseas Dominions are under consideration.
> 2. The proposal that a Defence Committee should be established in each Dominion is accepted in principle. The constitution of these Defence Committees is a matter for each Dominion to decide.

It should be noted that the Dominion representatives were not to attend all meetings of the CID. The committee could still discuss any matter—including, if it chose, matters concerning the Dominions—behind their backs. And the CID was not a genuinely "imperial" body but a creature and an arm of the British government. The only body owing its existence to the Empire governments collectively was still the Imperial Conference.[24]

Discussions at the War Office and the Admiralty during this conference produced significant decisions in matters of detail. A committee "to discuss Defence (Military)", over which the Chief of the Imperial General Staff, General Sir William Nicholson, presided, produced an agreed report[25] which among other things provided for the continuance on a larger scale of the attendance of Dominion officers at the British staff colleges at Camberley and Quetta, on the understanding that their governments would contribute about £200 per head per year.* Talks at the Admiralty designed to provide a basis for the new navies being created in Canada and Australia resulted in a tripartite agreement[26] between the United Kingdom and the two Dominions which had long-term consequences. This agreement began by recognizing that the Canadian and Australian naval forces would be "exclusively under the control of their respective governments", but that (as agreed with respect to land forces in 1909) their training and discipline would be "generally uniform" with those of the Royal Navy. The still undoubted control of foreign policy by the United Kingdom was reflected in the provision that Dominion ships in foreign ports would report their proceedings to the British Commander-in-Chief of the station or to the Admiralty, and while remaining there would obey any instructions received from the British government, "the Dominion Government being informed". One paragraph deserves special note:

> 9. When a ship of the British Admiralty meets a ship of the Dominions, the Senior Officer will have the right of command in matters of ceremony or international intercourse, or where United action is agreed upon, but will have no power to direct the movement of ships of the other service unless the ships are ordered to co-operate by mutual arrangement.

In 1914, as we shall see, the Canadian naval service, such as it was, was placed at the disposal of the Admiralty. In 1939 this was not done; instead, it was ordered to "co-operate" with the ships of other Commonwealth navies.[27] No definition of "co-operation" was given. In practice, however, this was interpreted to mean that when ships of different Commonwealth countries were acting together the senior officer took com-

* John Gooch, "The Creation of the British General Staff 1904-1914" (*Journal of the Royal United Services Institute for Defence Studies*, June 1971) suggests mistakenly that an intervention by Sir Frederick Borden led to this paper being withdrawn, and to the end of any possibility of the War Office controlling the development of Dominion general staffs. The paper was not withdrawn, but was approved by the committee and subsequently by the conference. The slip is corrected in Mr. Gooch's book *The Plans of War: The General Staff and British Military Strategy c. 1900–1916* (London, 1974).

mand. It seems evident that the origin of this arrangement is to be found in the naval agreement of 1911.

TARIFFS AND POLITICS

When we last looked at the tariff relationship of Canada and the United States, we saw Laurier, in 1899, proclaiming that "the general feeling in Canada to-day is not in favour of reciprocity" (above, page 89). It might have been well for Sir Wilfrid had he continued to act upon that opinion; but for what seemed good and sufficient reasons at the time he consented to revive the question of reciprocity in 1911 with unfortunate results for his party and himself.

In both countries there were noisy low-tariff agitations in 1910. Like McKinley in 1897, President William H. Taft, immediately upon taking office in 1909, called the United States Congress into special session in order to enact a new tariff law. This, it was generally understood, would incorporate a downward revision; but the Payne–Aldrich tariff of that year "still showed an extremely intolerant attitude on foreign trade".[28] As a result, many Americans, particularly in the Middle West, felt betrayed; and one powerful special interest, the newspaper press (anxious for cheap newsprint from Canada) devoted itself to campaigning for more liberal tariff relations with the Dominion.[29] In Canada Laurier, making a swing through the prairie west and British Columbia in the summer of 1910, came under heavy pressure from farm organizations demanding tariff cuts and reciprocity; and that December—after reciprocity negotiations had actually begun—a large and aggressive group of farmers descended on Ottawa with similar requests.[30] On both sides of the border, it seemed, tariff reform might be good politics.

At one moment an actual tariff war seemed possible as the result of the Payne–Aldrich law. This provided for the imposition of a "maximum" tariff, higher than the normal one by twenty-five per cent of the value of the imported articles, against countries which the President considered to be "unduly discriminating" against the United States. Action was required by March 31, 1910. Canada's treaty with France (above, page 83) was regarded by the President's advisers as constituting such discrimination. Canada was very unwilling to make to the United States, merely because of a threat, concessions which France had purchased by concessions of her own. President Taft, however, was glad to accept a gesture as enough; and after a series of direct conversations in Ottawa,

Albany, and Washington (initiated through the British Embassy in the American capital, which however played no actual part in them), Canada granted the United States its intermediate tariff rates on thirteen articles of no great importance, ranging from prunes to window glass. Parliament then incorporated these lower rates in the general tariff, to which American goods remained subject. In the words of O. D. Skelton, "a phantom concession had been made to remove an invented grievance."[31]

These discussions did more than head off an impending crisis. They set the United States and Canada on the road to reciprocity. This was pretty clear after the dramatic meeting at Albany on March 19–20. President Taft had had for some weeks an engagement to speak to the University Club there. Apparently on the prompting of the Rev. J. A. Macdonald, editor of the Toronto *Globe*, who was in touch with him, the President suggested to the club that it should invite Lord Grey, the Governor General—thus keeping the imperial authority in the picture; and the President himself, having ascertained that Laurier would not be available, invited W. S. Fielding, the Canadian Minister of Finance, to come to Albany also. The occasion turned into something of a love-feast. At the University Club Grey made one of his speeches on the Anglo-Saxon theme: "I never visit the United States without entertaining a feeling that Canadian and Americans are related by the closest ties of a common ancestry, and that we are, so far as the real [*sic*] big things of this world are concerned, practically one people." The President in reply spoke warmly of Canada, saying, "We must be as close friends as possible for mutual benefit." The serious business, of course, was done not by Grey but by Fielding. On Sunday, March 20, he and Taft "were in conference in respect to the tariff . . . for several hours". Final agreement was not reached at Albany, but later in the month Fielding was a guest at the White House and the last details of the arrangement to prevent a tariff war were then hammered out.

The Albany meeting, however, also made it evident that on the American side the omens were very favourable for a wider agreement. Among those present was the "amateur diplomat", as Skelton calls him, J. A. Macdonald; and on the Monday morning following the meeting he published in the *Globe* a quite unprecedented message from the President to the Canadian people, which Taft had evidently given him verbally. After stating his hopes for a satisfactory solution of the immediate difficulties, Taft went on to declare it his deliberate purpose "to promote, in such ways as are open to me, better trade relations between the United States and Canada than at present exist":

I am profoundly convinced that these two countries, touching each other for more than three thousand miles, have common interests in trade and require special arrangements in legislation and administration which are not involved in the relations of the United States with nations beyond the seas. We may not always have recognized that in the past, but that must be our viewpoint in the future. Say that for me to the people of Canada, with all the earnestness and sincerity of my heart.[32]

After some delay, during which the Americans showed themselves anxious to get negotiations under way before the congressional elections on November 8, serious discussions began in Ottawa on November 5, and after an interval were resumed in Washington in January 1911. On January 26 agreement was announced.

Throughout, the American negotiators had been prepared to go further than the Canadians, whose consciousness of political obstacles was obvious. The Americans would have been glad to obtain free exchange of a range of manufactures including farm machinery; the Canadians would not go so far. The final agreement provided for reciprocal free trade across the border in a wide range of natural products, particularly agricultural products. The reciprocal free list also included a few manufactured goods, such as cream separators, typecasting and typesetting machines, and barbed wire. Similarly, there were identical reciprocal lists of goods on which both countries would reduce their duties: these included meat, fish and some other natural or agricultural products, and a certain number of manufactured articles. Prominent among the latter were agricultural implements, on which each country was now to levy fifteen per cent *ad valorem*. (The Canadian tariff of 1907 charged such things coming from the United States various rates from 17½ to 25 per cent; ploughs, for instance, paid 20 per cent, hay-loaders 25 per cent.) There were in addition two short lists which were not identical, the United States undertaking to accept from Canada at specified rates certain items beginning with aluminum, while Canada on her side agreed similarly to take from the United States items beginning with Portland cement and including peanuts. Free importation of wood pulp or newsprint into the United States was made dependent, in effect, on Canadian provincial action. It was to apply only if no export duty or other export prohibition of any sort had been applied to these products; and Ontario had in fact forbidden the export of pulpwood cut on Crown lands, in the interest undoubtedly of encouraging papermaking within the province.

The agreement was to be made effective, not by treaty as in 1854, but by concurrent legislation: that is, after an exchange of notes each country would enact the proposed tariff changes by statute, making their effect dependent upon the other country's enacting its half of the agreed schedules. This was done primarily upon Canadian insistence.[33]

Such was, for the moment, the sequel of the meeting at Albany. Almost inevitably, one's mind goes forward thirty years, to the similar meeting of Franklin Roosevelt and Mackenzie King at Ogdensburg in 1940. That was a turning-point, the beginning of a *rapprochement* in Canadian-American relations whose effect, for good or ill, has been evident ever since. If conditions had been right, that *rapprochement* might have begun at Albany. But conditions in 1910–11 were not right, the time was not ripe. The hand of friendship which President Taft extended in such evident honesty and simplicity at Albany was to be struck aside.

When the reciprocity agreement went to the United States Congress, there was a certain amount of trouble. Farmers and papermakers in particular attacked it as inimical to their interests, and a considerable parliamentary battle took place. Nevertheless, in the end the President triumphed; the bill passed unamended and he signed it into law on July 26, 1911.[34]

The story in Canada was different. It is true that when the agreement was unveiled in Parliament on January 26 the first reaction was "strongly favourable", and the view has been expressed that if the government had dissolved Parliament as soon as opposition began to gather the verdict of the constituencies would have been favourable also.[35] But the appeal was too long delayed; Parliament was not dissolved until July 29, and when the people voted on September 21 Laurier and reciprocity were rejected.

The events of the campaign are familiar and need not be described in detail here.[36] The special interests whose opposition had given the Canadian government pause during the negotiations with the United States fought the measure tooth and nail; industry, organized in the Canadian Manufacturers' Association, declared that it would be ruinous. Though the agreement covered only a few manufactured articles, it was argued that this was the "thin end of the wedge"; colour was given to this by the fact that the final section of the American statute "authorized and requested" the President to negotiate agreements with Canada for "the further reciprocal expansion of trade and commerce". There were secessions from the Liberal party, the most important being those of Sir Clifford Sifton (still a Liberal MP though no longer a minister), who played a great part in organizing the anti-reciprocity campaign, and a group of eighteen prominent Toronto businessmen. But the economic arguments were less important than the political ones. It was widely contended that reciprocity was a mere preliminary to annexation, and that what was at stake was in fact Canada's position as a unit of the British Empire. In many cases those who took this line were undoubtedly burningly sincere; in others it is fair to presume that the Union Jack was being used to cover special and sordid interests. Canadian anxieties were fanned by stupid utterances in the United States. The most stupid of all was that of Champ Clark, Speaker-designate of the House of Representatives, who said of reciprocity, "I am for it, because I hope to see the day when the American flag will float over every square foot of the British-North American possessions clear to the North Pole." Taft immediately repudiated this remark; but the President used an almost equally unfortunate phrase himself, and more than once: "Canada stands at the parting of the ways." In context it was harmless, indicating merely that Canada had to choose between being an isolated country and one trading freely with her neighbour; but inevitably it was torn from this context and represented as regarding her as faced with a choice between the British and American systems.[37]

While in English-speaking Canada, and above all in Ontario, the battle raged over reciprocity, in Quebec (and, it may be said, in Quebec alone) the election turned mainly on the naval question. And the Conservative "imperialists", avid for power after fifteen years in the wilderness, were ready to work in the province with the anti-Laurier, anti-imperial, anti-navy nationalists. The Conservative election platform tactfully refrained from mentioning the navy; and Borden's personal manifesto briefly attacked Laurier's naval policy, but said nothing of a contribution to the Royal Navy. Long afterwards Mackenzie King, who was one of the Liberal ministers personally defeated in 1911, spoke bitter words in Montreal about the affair:

> I saw Sir Wilfrid defeated by an unholy alliance between the Nationalists of this province and the Tories of the other provinces of Canada. I saw all that grew out of that ignoble and treacherous plot.... It will be for all time a blot of shame on the pages of our country's history.[38]

The alliance seems to have actually existed; at any rate, C. H. Cahan, one of the English-speaking Conservatives in Quebec, averred (many years later) that at Borden's request he approached Bourassa, Armand Lavergne, and other Nationalists and obtained their co-operation against Laurier.[39] Certain it is that the Conservatives refrained from opposing Nationalist candidates, and the Conservative leader in the province, Monk, was himself one of the strongest Nationalists. The net result was that on September 21 Laurier, while still retaining a majority of the Quebec seats in the House of Commons, found his strength there reduced from the 54 of the 1908 election to 38. At the same time British and industrial Ontario, which had given the Liberals 37 in 1908, now gave them only 13 and returned 73 Conservatives. In the west Saskatchewan and Alberta were strongly Liberal, but Manitoba and British Columbia went to Borden. The Maritime provinces were divided. Overall, Conservatives and Nationalists got 134 seats to the Liberals' 87.[40]

Why did these things happen? Explaining elections is a guessing game. Part of the explanation, doubtless, was the normal swing of the electoral pendulum against a government long in power. Part of it was the powerful intervention of wealthy vested interests that felt themselves menaced. Part of it was the isolationist prejudices of Quebec, where so many French-Canadian voters turned against the French-Canadian Prime Minister in this crisis. Part of it was that same feeling of national self-confidence that we have seen at work in the days of the Alaska Boundary difficulties, the product largely of the unprecedented prosperity Canada had been enjoying since 1896; reciprocity, the goal of so many Canadian governments since Confederation, now seemed to be something the country could do without. And much of it was inherited or remembered grievances against the United States, the fruit of old slights and old aggressions. It was nearly a hundred years since Americans had burned the legislative buildings at Little York during the War of 1812, but the holocaust was not entirely forgotten in the modern city of Toronto, the centre of the opposition to reciprocity. Nor had Canadians lost their memory of American tolerance of the Fenian menace. And it is fair to assume that the treatment Canada had received over the Alaska question in 1903 loomed much larger in Canadian minds than the admirably conciliatory disposition which Washington had shown more recently. When President Taft at Albany said, in effect, that there should be a special relationship between the United States and Canada, adding, "We may not always have recognized that in the past, but that must be our viewpoint in the future," one suspects that a good many Canadians were skeptical. They knew about the unhappy past; as for the future, time would tell.

One final point. The crisis of 1911 was widely interpreted at the time as a victory for the spirit of imperial unity over the spirit of continentalism. Certainly a friendly American approach had been rebuffed. The British allegiance of English-speaking Canada, and its suspicion of the United States, had been strikingly reaffirmed. It was clear in September 1911 that reciprocity was dead. But the great imperial issue that had lately been under discussion had not been resolved in the manner that an outsider might have expected. With the passage of time it would become evident that a Canadian contribution to imperial naval power, in any shape or form, was for the moment just as dead as reciprocity.

CHAPTER SIX

THE FIRST YEARS OF BORDEN, 1911-1914: A NEW DIRECTION

A TURNING POINT

It is evident in retrospect that when Robert Borden's ministry took office in Ottawa on October 10, 1911 Canadian external policies were about to take a new direction.

The decade of Conservative and Unionist rule beginning in 1911 was to be more complicated and arduous than any that modern Canadians had lived through. The new policies were the product, in great part, of outside pressures: the First World War and the period of growing tension that preceded it. But other factors were also at work. Since 1900 Laurier had been increasingly dependent on Quebec; it was the evident citadel of his political power.[1] It was equally clear, as we have seen, that the new government's citadel was Ontario (above, page 148). A government dependent on Quebec was, and is, certain to have an isolationist bias; a government dependent on Ontario was, in those days, bound to have an imperialist tinge. The trend of the times was reflected in and influenced by the great contemporary immigration from the British Isles; there were 144,000 arrivals from there in 1911.[2]

Laurier and Borden were both nationalists; but their nationalisms were of very different orders. Laurier had spent his fifteen years in power defending the imperial status quo, politely resisting those at home and abroad who favoured measures tending to centralize or institutionalize the Empire, and fighting a determined, unending rearguard action against what now seems the inevitable tendency of world events to intrude upon Canada's happy isolation and force her to take unwonted steps to help ensure her own security and her friends'. Borden, on the other hand, represented the readiness of many English-speaking Canadians to see their country play an active part in world politics, as one of the daughter-nations of the Empire. Unlike Laurier, he was happy to contemplate the Dominion making a contribution to "imperial defence", but only on condition of its being conceded a "voice" in the formation of imperial policy. On the basis of this principle, Dominion autonomy was to make remarkable progress during the ten years ahead. "If you want us to help you, call us to your councils"; so Laurier had said back in 1900, simultaneously explaining that he didn't mean it. The phrase is a good epitome of Borden's policies, and he acted on it.

THE UNITED STATES: "HARMONY AND NOT DISCORD"

The omens did not seem good for Canadian-American relations after the election of 1911 and the Canadian rejection of reciprocity. Nevertheless, Borden's administration was not a time of strain in those relations, and he took pains to ensure that it should not be. In a speech in Halifax in November 1911, soon after coming to power, he said, "Canada's voice and influence should always be for harmony and not for discord between our Empire and the great Republic and I believe that she will always be a bond of abiding friendship between them."[3] Borden, in fact, was an early adherent of what has come to be known as the "linch-pin" theory of the relations between the states composing the North Atlantic Triangle—the theory that argues that Canada has a special role to play in bringing and keeping the United States and Great Britain together.*

Tranquillity was encouraged in the years after 1911 by the fact that the "slate-cleaning" process dealt with in an earlier chapter was virtually complete when Borden took office, although one of its tutelary geniuses, James Bryce, remained at the Washington Embassy until 1913. He took justifiable pride in the fact that while there he had signed "either eleven or twelve treaties" of which, he told a Canadian audience, nine related to the affairs of Canada:

> By those nine treaties we have, I hope, dealt with all the questions that are likely to arise between the United States and Canada—questions relating to boundary; questions relating to the disposal of and the use of boundary

* The actual phrase "the linch-pin" may have been first used by Winston Churchill, in an article in the *Saturday Evening Post* of February 15, 1930.

waters; questions relating to the fisheries in the international waters where the two countries adjoin one another; questions relating to the interests which we have in sealing in the Behring Sea, and many other matters, which it would take too long to go into at this moment—and I am happy to say that I do not think your relations with the United States ever stood upon a better footing than they do now.[4]

Borden was able to make the first appointments to the new International Joint Commission's Canadian section. Sir George Gibbons' contribution to the Boundary Waters Treaty of 1909 (above, chapter 4) would have entitled him to the chairmanship, and Laurier had in fact belatedly nominated him; but Gibbons, as his papers show, was an active Liberal partisan. What happened is reflected in a letter from Laurier to Gibbons:

Unfortunately, the Imperial authorities had not issued the Commission before our fall and, therefore, the new Government took advantage of this delay to push on their own men . . .

I agree with you it is better to make no fuss about it.[5]

The chairman Borden appointed was Thomas Chase Casgrain, a Conservative who, Laurier observed in the same letter, was a suitable person. The American members had already been appointed, with Thomas H. Carter as chairman. The commission, though not idle, was not overwhelmed with business in its early years. One issue which was making trouble before it was set up, and long continued to do so, never came before it. This was the diversion of water from Lake Michigan by the Chicago Sanitary Commission. The treaty of 1909 provided (article 8) that its provisions should not "apply to or disturb any existing uses of boundary waters on either side of the boundary". Laurier had in fact sought to insert a clause covering the Chicago diversion, but yielded to the opinion of both Gibbons and Bryce that insistence on this would result in the American Senate refusing to ratify the treaty.[6]

In due course American unilateral action took the fire out of another very bitter issue—the tariff. In 1912 a liberal Democrat, Woodrow Wilson, erstwhile President of Princeton University, was elected President of the United States, with majorities behind him in both houses of Congress. The result, in 1913, was the Underwood tariff. "For the first time in half a century, the tariff was materially reduced." Canada, it has been said, obtained most of the advantages she had forfeited by rejecting reciprocity.[7] In particular, she gained unconditional free trade in newsprint. This was a victory for the American Newspaper Publishers' Association, but also for the provinces of Ontario and Quebec, which in the face of mild opposition from the federal government had set up export restraints designed to ensure that their pulpwood would be manufactured into paper within their borders, not in the United States. The effect on the pulp and paper business in Canada was revolutionary. Within a few years the Underwood tariff made that business the greatest of Canadian manufacturing industries.[8] And it seems clear that it materially improved the general atmosphere of Canadian–American relations. (See Appendix B.)

In the years before the great explosion of 1914 international idealism was active in North America, and one of its favourite themes was the lesson which that admirably peaceful continent could teach to turbulent and backward Europe. For nearly a century Britain and Canada on one side, and the United States on the other, had contrived to keep the peace. It seems to have been Mackenzie King who suggested a celebration of the one hundredth anniversary of the Treaty of Ghent. Committees came into existence in all three countries, and in 1912 Premier Borden gave support to an unofficial "Canadian Peace Centenary Association". The year 1914 was called "Peace Year" at the Canadian National Exhibition in Toronto. The outbreak of the greatest war in history a few months before the actual anniversary came round put something of a crimp in the celebrations; but it was still possible to point the moral of the superiority of what one of the most active Anglo-Saxon propagandists of the time, the Rev. James A. Macdonald, called "the North American Idea".[9]

A VOICE IN THE COUNCILS

Rather more important than Borden's policies towards Canada's American neighbour were his views on the Dominion's place in the British Empire.

These views had formed themselves in Borden's mind before he came to power, probably in the course of the naval controversy. In the House of Commons on November 24, 1910, during the debate on the Address, and in connection with the naval question, he said:

> I think the question of Canada's co-operation upon a permanent basis in imperial defence involves very large and wide considerations. If Canada and the other Dominions of the empire are to take their part as nations of this empire in the defence of the empire as a whole, shall it be that we, contributing

to that defence of the whole empire, shall have absolutely, as citizens of this country, no voice whatever in the councils of the empire touching the issues of peace or war throughout the empire? I do not think that such would be a tolerable condition. I do not believe the people of Canada would for one moment submit to such a condition. . . .

This was said as part of a definition of what the Conservatives' policy would be if they came to power, and was joined with a declaration that the permanent defence policy when developed would be submitted to the decision of the people. It was a deliberate and considered statement, for Borden had already said almost the same thing in the House on November 21. It was not particularly brilliantly phrased, for Borden was not a phrase-maker like Laurier; but it expressed the heart of the imperial policy which he would follow during his administration.

He was, however, in no great hurry to present his naval policy to Parliament and the country. He was not likely to forget the part that the anti-naval nationalists in Quebec had played in electing him; and Frederick Monk had entered his cabinet as Minister of Public Works. There was no reference to naval matters in the Speech from the Throne when the new Parliament assembled in November 1911. The government's policy was not defined until after the Prime Minister and several of his colleagues had visited England to consult with ministers there; and they did not set out until late in June 1912. It is quite probable that by that time Borden had already decided to propose a money contribution to purchase dreadnoughts for the Royal Navy—the plan which he had suggested in February 1910; but even this cannot be proved.[10]

While in London Borden listened from the gallery of the House of Commons on July 22 to what he called in his diary a "debate which will be historical". The British Prime Minister, Asquith, made a statement which in spite of Borden's enthusiasm seems notably cautious. Referring to the naval discussions with the Canadians, he said in part:

I will add—although I will not make any detailed statement upon that point at this moment—that side by side with this growing participation in the active burdens of the Empire, on the part of our Dominions there rests with us undoubtedly the duty of making such response as we can to their obviously reasonable appeal that they should be entitled to be heard in the determination of the policy and in the direction of Imperial affairs. . . . I do not say in what shape or by what machinery that great purpose is to be obtained. Arrangements like that cannot be made in a day . . . but without committing ourselves in any degree to particular forms in the matter, we share with our great Dominions the feeling . . . that . . . we ought more and more to be conscious partners with one another.

"Such response as we can." It was really not a very hopeful phrase.

The Canadian ministers attended two meetings of the Committee of Imperial Defence, evidently held primarily for their benefit. The second of these, on August 1, was perhaps the more important. Asquith, who as usual presided, referred back to the meeting of May 30, 1911, with its agreed conclusion relating to Dominion representation on the Committee (above, page 141). His remark is interesting:

Although this conclusion was unanimously accepted by the representatives of the Dominions at the 113th meeting of the Committee of Imperial Defence, it was never included in any published record of the proceedings, as some of the representatives of the Dominions (particularly Sir Wilfrid Laurier) did not think this expedient; and in view of Sir Wilfrid's attitude this resolution has not been communicated formally to the Government of any Dominion.

Laurier's "attitude" had in fact made the conclusion, at least so far as Canada was concerned, a dead letter; and no action had been taken either to associate Canada with the committee or to set up a parallel Defence Committee in Canada. (During the 113th meeting Louis Brodeur had in fact said that Canada already had such a committee.[11] He was mistaken. Canada actually did not set up a Cabinet Defence Committee until 1936; and even then it was an ineffective body compared with the British CID.)

Replying to Asquith, Borden confirmed that he and his colleagues had been ignorant of the action taken in 1911. He showed himself sympathetic to the proposals then approved, but said that before expressing a final opinion he would wish to consult his cabinet. He wrote in his diary, "Spoke my mind as to display of flag* and as to representation." His recorded remarks on the latter subject seemed to look forward to still larger policies:

. . . the representation of Canada upon this Committee does not perhaps on the surface seem likely to carry into effect what will probably have to be considered

* "We have felt in the past that the British flag has been withdrawn a little too much from our coasts, both on the Atlantic and on the Pacific . . . we desire to see the flag displayed by a British fleet upon our coasts . . . whenever it is possible to do so."

in the very early future. As we are speaking here in confidence I venture to speak quite frankly. At the present time we have in the Dominion of Canada about 8 millions of people; we have a boundary line between Canada and the United States of nearly 4,000 miles; and the people on each side of the line are very similar in their habits, their ideals, and their mode of government, civic, municipal, and otherwise. On one side of the line the people have a direct and immediate voice in the government of their country in every respect, including all matters of foreign policy; on the other side of the line that is not the case. While we do not know that that particular difference has impressed itself very strongly upon the imagination of the Canadian people up to the present time, it will undoubtedly begin to do so in the very early future, especially as the country advances in wealth and population and resources, and more especially as it advances in its conception of what a national spirit demands. So that I think it will be necessary in the very early future to give a little study and consideration as to the larger outlook to which I have called attention. No one is more seriously impressed with all the difficulties of working out anything of the kind than I am. What I suggest at the moment is that, if this proposal is carried out as a temporary measure, we must not lose sight of the importance of studying and considering the larger questions to which I have alluded. I need not say that it is obviously impossible that the present relations in respect of such matters can continue in respect of Canada after she will have a population of 20 millions or 25 millions of people. It may take some years—it will take some years—before that status shall have been acquired; but in the meantime the spirit to which I have alluded is one that I think will demand consideration not only by our own Government but by the Imperial authorities as well.[12]

One almost finds oneself wondering, had Borden remembered Edward Blake's Aurora speech (1874)? "A National Sentiment." "Four millions of Britons who are not free." It was very different talk from what the people in London had grown accustomed to hearing from Laurier, who had said yet once more, as recently as the 1911 conference, "I have the happy privilege of representing here a country which has no grievances to set forth and very few suggestions to make. We are quite satisfied with our lot."[13] The British government had not been fond of Laurier's attitudes; but there was obviously going to be serious food for thought in Borden's as well.

No one present at the Committee of Imperial Defence on August 1 made any comment on Borden's speaking of his mind. It is a fair presumption that Asquith was taken aback and that no other British minister felt disposed to make a remark in the absence of any from him. At a somewhat later stage C. J. Doherty, the Canadian Minister of Justice, suggested that the British and Dominion governments should "agree upon the formation of some species of committee or commission for the purpose of studying the question of how we could deal with such matters so as to give the Dominions a means of exercising their influence and of taking part in the direction of foreign affairs." Neither Borden nor Asquith encouraged pursuing the matter, and there is little doubt that the British government found the suggestion distasteful. Lewis Harcourt, the Colonial Secretary, explained to his officials later, "No one has paid the slightest attention to Mr. Doherty's suggestion . . . and I do not think we shall hear any more of it."[14]

The main object of Borden's visit to England was to consult the Admiralty, now presided over by Winston Churchill. That department, whose concurrence in 1909 in the policy of a separate Canadian navy had certainly been reluctant, was delighted with the Canadian change of heart. Borden and Churchill met on Borden's second day in London (July 5), and on July 11 Churchill discussed the naval situation in detail in a meeting of the Committee of Imperial Defence. He made it quite clear that the German navy was considered a serious menace; and he pointed out that the fact that Austria-Hungary and Italy were now building dreadnoughts complicated the British position and rendered it much more serious. There was an immediate need, and "if it is the intention of Canada to render assistance to the naval forces of the British Empire, now is the time when that aid would be most welcome and most timely." This was quite apart from the question of a permanent Canadian naval policy, which would require careful consideration. In further discussions Churchill undertook to furnish Borden with two memoranda, one secret for the information of the government, the other suitable for publication, making the case for an immediate emergency contribution by Canada. These were forwarded in mid-September, by which time Borden and his party had returned home.[15]

The Canadian Prime Minister had visited the offices of the Committee of Imperial Defence and "had a most interesting and instructive interview with Capt. Hankey and Major Grant Duff". More important, he had had conversations with several members of the British cabinet, and one of the topics was the means of giving Canada, and the other Dominions, a voice in foreign policy. On July 30, before the committee meeting at which this matter was discussed, he wrote to the Governor General:

A great deal of discussion has been on the very difficult question of representation. It may be that one of our Ministers without portfolio will become a member of the Imperial Defence Committee and will live in London part of the year in close touch with the Foreign office and with the Colonial Secretary. This of course would only be a temporary expedient until a more carefully prepared system of Empire organization could be discussed after consultation with all the Dominions.[16]

On returning to Ottawa, Borden proceeded to embody his "emergency" (as distinct from his "permanent") naval policy in draft legislation. This "Naval Aid Bill" proposed to provide a sum not exceeding $35 million to be "used and applied under the direction of the Governor in Council in the construction and equipment of battleships or armoured cruisers of the most modern and powerful type." These ships were to be placed "at the disposal of His Majesty for the common defence of the Empire". This draft went before the cabinet in October 1912. Frederick Monk felt that he could not support it unless it was referred to the electorate in a plebiscite; other ministers would not agree and Monk resigned. When Parliament met in November and Borden consulted his French-speaking supporters, only six of the Conservatives and Nationalists from Quebec were prepared to vote for the bill.[17]

On December 5 Borden introduced his bill into the House of Commons. He placed before the House the publishable memorandum from the Admiralty, which ended with much the same words as the secret one:

The Prime Minister of the Dominion having inquired in what form any immediate aid that Canada might give would be most effective, we have no hesitation in answering after a prolonged consideration of all the circumstances that it is desirable that such aid should include the provision of a certain number of the largest and strongest ships of war which science can build or money supply.[18]

The government, Borden said, proposed to contribute three capital ships, "the three most powerful battleships in the world". (Had these been built, they would presumably have been of the *Queen Elizabeth* class, the best battleships of the coming war.) On permanent future policy he had little to say; but he did speak scornfully of those who talked of building up "a great naval organization in Canada": "In my humble opinion, nothing of an efficient character could be built up in this country within a quarter or perhaps half a century. Even then it would be but a poor and weak substitute for that splendid organization which the Empire already possesses. . . ." He had already stated that Laurier's Naval Service Act of 1910 would in due course be repealed. He did, however, attach importance to the creation of a naval shipbuilding industry in Canada, and expected the Admiralty to help. He wrote to Churchill on November 2, 1912, "Your promised letter as to the encouragement of shipbuilding in connection with dockyards and naval bases in this country has not yet arrived." Nothing serious in this respect happened before war broke out.[19]

The Prime Minister's exposition dwelt at length on the connection between naval aid and foreign policy. During his visit to Britain, he said, he had "on many public occasions" propounded the principle "that the great dominions, sharing in the defence of the Empire upon the high seas, must necessarily be entitled to share also in the responsibility for and in the control of foreign policy." Not only the British government but the opposition leaders had "explicitly accepted this principle" and the urgency of finding means of constitutionally accomplishing it. Borden described the Committee of Imperial Defence, and went on,

> I am assured by His Majesty's Government that, pending a final solution of the question of voice and influence, they would welcome the presence in London of a Canadian minister during the whole or a portion of each year. Such minister would be regularly summoned to all meetings of the Committee of Imperial Defence, and would be regarded as one of its permanent members. No important step in foreign policy would be undertaken without consultation with such a representative of Canada. This seems a very marked advance, both from our standpoint and from that of the United Kingdom. It would give to us an opportunity of consultation, and therefore an influence which hitherto we have not possessed. . . .

He admitted—and this passage doubtless reflects the misgivings of British statesmen with whom he had talked—that the "final solution" would be difficult to reach: but "however difficult the task may be, it is not the part of wisdom or statesmanship to avoid it. And so we invite the statesmen of Great Britain to study with us this, the real problem of Imperial existence."

Before pursuing the sequel as to Borden's imperial policies generally, it is best to note briefly the *débâcle* of his naval policy in particular. The Naval Aid Bill became the centre of one of the fiercest parliamentary battles in Canadian history. The Liberals in the House of Commons fought it tooth and nail, and resorted to obstruction. The government finally had recourse to closure—never before used in the Canadian Parliament—and after receiving second reading on this basis the measure passed its third reading in the Commons on May 15, 1913. But there was still a Liberal majority in the appointed Senate, and on May 29 it passed an amendment to the effect "that this House is not justified in giving its assent to this bill until it is submitted to the judgement of the country."[20] Borden was not prepared to appeal to the people on the issue. On June 6 he announced the policy (as stated in his diary) "that before additional ships to be laid down by G. B. are completed we will introduce a bill to pay for them and take them over."* In the event, neither party's naval policy was carried out. There was no contribution to the Imperial fleet. At the same time, there was virtually no Canadian navy. The Naval Service Act of 1910 remained on the statute book, the two old cruisers that had been purchased remained in Canadian possession but were neglected and only partially manned; no new ships were built and no personnel recruited. When war broke out in 1914 Canada depended for the defence of her coasts upon British, Australian, and Japanese ships. A Japanese battleship and two armoured cruisers were sent to reinforce the west coast of North America during the period when Admiral von Spee's German squadron was loose in the Pacific.[21] At this juncture the Anglo-Japanese Alliance paid Canada a considerable dividend, justifying Sir Wilfrid Laurier's warm approval of it in 1911 (above, page 139).

In the light of these and other facts, Borden's naval policy cannot be considered anything but a national disaster. There is no point in discussing his motives further than we have already done. His policy destroyed the unity of Parliament on the fundamental question of na-

* The British government refused to have anything to do with this idea. Borden had explained that he could not dissolve Parliament until 1915, after passage of a redistribution bill. Asquith told the King on June 5 that a cabinet meeting the day before had rejected the idea of going ahead with the three additional ships on Borden's assurance that Canada would ultimately pay the bill; this would be "in the nature of a gambling transaction, and would be construed in Canada as a direct intervention by the Imperial Government in her party controversies." Instead the cabinet decided to accelerate construction of three British ships which had not been scheduled to be begun before March 1914. "If this is done, the ships will be ready at least as early as those proposed in the rejected Canadian Bill, and in the meanwhile time will be given to ascertain whether or not Canadian opinion is really in favour of or opposed to Mr. Borden's policy. The additional burden thrown on the present financial year will be about £500,000."

tional defence; it produced the bitterest of controversies but no ships. The affair damaged Canada's reputation in the Empire and would have done more harm had it not been followed so quickly by the outbreak of war. Like most Canadian politicians, Borden was totally ignorant of military matters, and he was evidently incapable of forming any effective independent judgments about them. If he really believed that an efficient navy could not be built up "within a quarter or perhaps half a century", he was grotesquely wrong; Australia, starting from scratch in 1909, had created by 1914 (admittedly with much assistance from the Royal Navy) a small fleet that was able to play a valuable part in the early months of the war.[22] Laurier was militarily just as ignorant as Borden; but there is no reason to believe that his policy would not have been as effective in Canada as the same policy was at the Antipodes.

DOUBTS AND UNCERTAINTIES, 1912–1914

We must look now at the fortunes of Borden's imperial policies between his visit to England in 1912 and the outbreak of war in 1914.

British ministers were the authors of the theory that there was a connection between Dominion contributions to imperial naval defence and a "voice" in foreign policy. We have seen Joseph Chamberlain in 1897 noting that "the privilege of management and control" implied also obligation and responsibility, and in 1902 grasping eagerly at Laurier's "call us to your councils" speech and proclaiming that Britain was prepared to offer "a corresponding voice in the policy of the Empire" if the colonies would assume "any proportionate share" of the imperial burden (above, pages 55, 75). We have seen the Liberal Campbell-Bannerman in 1907 noting rather more cautiously that naval defence and responsibility for foreign affairs "hang together" (above, page 80). Asquith in 1911 was still more cautious. On the second day of the discussion of Ward's motion concerning constitutional relations (above, page 137) he made a pronouncement which had evidently been carefully considered:

> ... what does Sir Joseph Ward's proposal come to? I might describe the effect of it without going into details in a couple of sentences. It would impair if not altogether destroy the authority of the Government of the United Kingdom in such grave matters as the conduct of foreign policy, the conclusion of treaties, the declaration and maintenance of peace, or the declaration of war and, indeed, all those relations with Foreign Powers, necessarily of the most

delicate character, which are now in the hands of the Imperial Government, subject to its responsibility to the Imperial Parliament. That authority cannot be shared, and the co-existence side by side with the Cabinet of the United Kingdom of this proposed body—it does not matter by what name you call it for the moment—clothed with the functions and the jurisdiction which Sir Joseph Ward proposed to invest it with, would, in our judgment, be absolutely fatal to our present system of responsible government.[23]

The situation is, in a sense, rather comical. The Conservative government in the United Kingdom had offered some share in imperial decisions to the Dominions in return for contributions to imperial defence, and Canada, represented by the Liberal Laurier, had resisted the suggestion in the name of colonial responsible government. Now the Conservatives in Canada, through the mouth of Borden, were offering to accept Chamberlain's terms; and the new Liberal government in Britain was shying away on the ground that such an arrangement would derogate from responsible government in the mother country. The reaction in England to Borden's speech introducing the Naval Aid Bill had not been uniformly laudatory. Some Liberals had doubts both about the constitutional respectability of the Committee of Imperial Defence and the constitutional propriety of people with no responsibility to the British Parliament meddling with the control of British foreign policy.* In the official British response to Borden there were undertones of both alarm and annoyance. The Canadian Prime Minister had omitted to tell Whitehall that his colleagues in Ottawa had accepted the formula proposed in the Committee of Imperial Defence, and it would seem that his easy declaration that if a Canadian minister went to London no important step in foreign policy would be taken without consultation with him struck the British ministers as committing them to something more sweeping than they had intended to

* "... some English Liberal organs, while fully recognising the munificence of the gift [of battleships], regarded with misgiving the momentous new departure which it might entail in the development of the British Empire. The *Manchester Guardian* feared that if the Canadian representatives on the Imperial Defence Committee had only advisory power, the Dominion would not have the share in naval policy contemplated by its Parliament; but the Defence Committee, unless purely advisory, itself involved a break with the theory of control by Parliament of foreign policy; the Dominion would become a power behind the Cabinet in naval and foreign policy, and the Committee an Imperial Bundesrat. Analogous views were expressed in the *Nation*, and indicated by Mr. Gibson Bowles in *The Times*" (*Annual Register*, 1912, p. 255). Bowles was a Liberal MP.

agree to. At any rate, five days after Borden's speech a circular dispatch which had been considered by the cabinet went by cable from the Colonial Secretary to the Dominions.[24] It described the proceedings in the CID on May 30, 1911 and August 1, 1912, and after noting Borden's provisional acceptance of the 1911 formula proceeded:

> Mr. Asquith and I had, subsequently, several private conversations with him at which he expressed the desire that the Canadian and other Dominions Ministers who might be in London as members of the Committee of Imperial Defence, should receive in confidence, knowledge of the policy and proceedings of the Imperial Government in foreign and other affairs. We pointed out to him that the Committee of Imperial Defence is a purely advisory body and is not, and cannot under any circumstances become, a body deciding on policy, which is and must remain the sole prerogative of the Cabinet, subject to the support of the House of Commons. But at the same time we assured him that any Dominions Ministers resident here would, at all times, have free and full access to the Prime Minister, the Foreign Secretary and the Colonial Secretary for information on all questions of Imperial policy.

Harcourt went on to quote a recent public speech in which he had referred to the Canadian desire for more consultation and co-operation. There was no need, he said, to think of imperial federation and the problems of taxation and representation that had rendered that policy a dead issue. "But speaking for myself, I see no obstacle, and certainly no objection, to the governments of all the Dominions being given at once a larger share in the executive direction in matters of defence and in personal consultation and co-operation with individual British Ministers whose duty it is to frame policy here. I should welcome a more continuous representation of Dominion Ministers, if they wish it, upon the Committee of Imperial Defence. . . ." This, he said, represented "the views and intentions" of the British government.

Several points call for comment. First, the British, partly perhaps with an eye on domestic critics, were choosing to depreciate the importance of the Committee of Imperial Defence. Harcourt's description of it as a purely advisory body was technically quite correct, but, as is well known, less correct in practice;[25] indeed, no committee presided over by the Prime Minister and attended regularly by some of his senior colleagues can fail to be in some degree a policy-forming body. Second, Borden's speech in Parliament specifically suggested that Dominion representatives would have the right to attend *all* meetings of the CID, and not only those at which defence questions affecting the Dominions were under discussion, as stated in the 1911 formula. And both that speech and Harcourt's cable seem to suggest that Borden had asked for consultation on foreign affairs outside as well as inside the CID. Finally, Harcourt's carefully worded message suggested (a) that Dominion representatives would be welcomed at meetings of the CID (some meetings? all meetings? he does not say); and (b) that they could have a "larger" part in "the executive direction in matters of defence" (note that foreign policy is not mentioned) and in "personal" consultation with "individual" British ministers. To the present writer this phrasing suggests that defences were being set up against a possible Dominion demand for admittance to meetings of the British cabinet. The fear of such a demand might well have stemmed from Borden's remarks at the CID meeting of August 1, 1912.

Harcourt's dispatch was published, and doubtless further disturbed those British Liberals who were troubled by the prospect of Dominion politicians interfering in policy which was the proper sphere of a body responsible to the British House of Commons. W. S. Fielding, who was in England, reported to Laurier in March 1913 that a group of backbench MPs were agitating along these lines, and that he was encouraging them. Borden had no sympathy with these critics who thought that his proposals would abnegate the people's control of foreign policy through their representatives: "This argument seems to proceed upon the assumption that the people who can properly be entrusted with such control reside wholly within the United Kingdom. The people are undoubtedly entitled to control foreign policy but there are at least fifteen millions of them outside the United Kingdom and by 1930 there will probably be thirty millions." A couple of days after Borden wrote these words two of Fielding's friends, Philip Morrell and Arthur A. W. H. Ponsonby, raised the question in the British House of Commons during the discussion on Churchill's navy estimates. They expressed disquiet over the talk of a "voice" for Canada in foreign policy, suggested that it would have been better if the Dominion had stood by the policy of a separate navy, and implied in effect that Churchill had been interfering in Canadian domestic politics.[26] The matter was not pressed to a division, but it certainly contributed to further embittering the debate in Canada.

Harcourt's dispatch had ended by inquiring of the Dominion governments whether they wished to adopt "some such method" as had been suggested "of more continuous connection in Naval and Military affairs with the Committee of Imperial Defence". Borden made no haste to reply; indeed, Canada does not appear to have replied. The reasons can only be conjectured. Borden had made it quite evident on August 1 (above, pages 155–56) that he was looking forward to something more than admission to the CID; and Harcourt had made it quite clear that what the imperial authorities were offering was some association with defence policy, not a share in making foreign policy. There was nothing here to get excited about. No action was taken; and as the months slipped by and war came closer, there appears to have been no consultation between Westminster and Ottawa on foreign problems. However, in the summer of 1913 two Canadian ministers, Thomas White (Finance) and Martin Burrell (Agriculture) were in England; and Harcourt inquired by cable whether Borden would wish them to be summoned to attend a meeting of the CID which was to take place on August 5. Borden assented warmly, and they did attend. The meeting dealt with no matters of Canadian interest, and neither Canadian minister spoke.[27]

It has been suggested[28] that in 1914, previous to the outbreak of war, the Canadian government appointed George Perley, a Minister without Portfolio, to represent it on the Committee of Imperial Defence. This is not altogether the case. Perley went on a mission to London, but all the evidence indicates that attendance at the CID was a merely incidental part of his duties there. The order-in-council authorizing the mission refers to "important matters . . . which require the attention of a Minister in London during the present summer; among others, discussion with His Majesty's Government of proposed amendments of the British North America Act, 1867, and . . . selection of a site for a suitable building to accomodate [*sic*] the Canadian Offices in London." Perley was to go to London in connection with these matters "and any others in which he may be specially instructed".[29] The order makes no reference to the CID. A copy of it was sent to Harcourt, and Borden then wrote further:

> Mr. Perley during his visit to London will discharge the duties of Acting High Commissioner.
>
> He will also discuss so far as may be necessary the question of defence with you and with Mr. Churchill, and particularly the question of Canada's participation in the naval defence of the Empire.
>
> If it should be thought desirable by His Majesty's Government that Mr. Perley should be summoned to attend any meetings of the Imperial Defence Committee which may be held during his visit to London, I would be pleased to have him attend. His good judgment and discretion may be absolutely

relied upon and he has my complete confidence as to the policy which we shall pursue in the future on this important question.

It is probable that in the early future I shall write to you further in relation to these matters. . . .[30]

It appears that there were no further important developments before the outbreak of war less than two months later. It is interesting, however, that Perley did attend the 128th meeting of the Committee of Imperial Defence on July 14, 1914.

We have already mentioned in passing that in 1912 a new Department of External Affairs Act[31] was passed. The direction of the department was no longer to rest with the Secretary of State of Canada:

The Member of the King's Privy Council for Canada holding the recognized position of First Minister shall be the Secretary of State for External Affairs. . . .

The change suggests the advent of a more active external policy, and the Prime Minister's intention that he should himself play the leading part in it. It also suggests that the Department of External Affairs was no longer to be a mere post office, but that it was to have some share in the making of policy. In fact, the amendment opened large vistas of influence for the permanent staff of External. The Under-Secretary of State for External Affairs would now have direct and automatic access to the Prime Minister, who would be his own minister. Thanks in part to this, O. D. Skelton, Under-Secretary from 1925 to 1941, would be perhaps the most powerful civil servant in Canadian history.

The impression that External was now to contribute to policy-making is heightened by the one important appointment that Borden made to the department. The aging Sir Joseph Pope remained its permanent head, the staff remained tiny; but it was reinforced in 1913 by a Legal Adviser, Loring Cheney Christie. This brilliant young graduate of Acadia University, born at Amherst, Nova Scotia, in 1885, was to become a legendary figure in External Affairs and to travel through a remarkable odyssey of personal opinions before he died as Canadian Minister to Washington in 1941. He studied at the Harvard Law School and edited the *Harvard Law Review*; and he practised law for a year in New York City, in the firm founded by Elihu Root. In 1910—on condition of beginning procedure for naturalization—he was appointed an attorney in the United States

Department of Justice, and in 1911–13 he was Assistant to the Solicitor General of the United States.[32] He clearly wanted, however, to work in Canada, in one of the metropolitan cities; but he failed to obtain on his own account a place in a Toronto law firm. Later his friend Alfred Mitchell Innes, Counsellor in the British Embassy, wrote to Borden about him. Innes described him as "one of the two cleverest young men in Washington and . . . a particular friend of mine and [Lord Eustace] Percy's" and asked whether Borden would use his influence to get him into a leading Toronto or Montreal firm. Borden did better; he hired him for the Department of External Affairs, and Christie took up his appointment there in April 1913.[33] He shortly became, in effect, Borden's confidential assistant in external matters, and remained at his elbow for the rest of his administration.

Christie was far better educated in a formal sense than Borden—the Prime Minister, though a qualified lawyer, a King's Counsel, and a well-read man, had never seen the inside of a university—and he had a far more theoretical mind. Very "good on paper", he was well equipped to turn Borden's firm but general notions on policy into pungent, closely argued memoranda. He could do this all the better because of the fact that his ideas on imperial policy, at this stage, ran along lines generally similar to Borden's: generally but not completely. In a memorandum of December 1913[34] he depicted the Canadian situation as he saw it:

1) That the Canadian people must sooner or later assume a control over foreign policy (i.e., over the issues of peace and war) no less effective than that now exercised by the people of Britain or by the U.S.A.

2) That they can only do so

A) By separating their own foreign policy from that of the Empire and by controlling it through their own Dominion Government.

B) or by insisting that the foreign policy of the Empire be separated from the domestic affairs of Britain and entrusted to a Government responsible no less to Canadian than to British voters.

At a day still far distant, Christie was to become convinced that the policy he labelled (A) was the only possible one for Canada. At the moment, he clearly considered that the only possible one was (B). He was in fact an imperial federationist, and joined the Round Table group in Canada and, later, in England.[35]

Borden, I think, would certainly have called himself an imperialist, in the limited and special sense in which the word was used in the Canada of those days. That is to say, he believed in the maintenance and, within the limits of Dominion autonomy, the development of the imperial connection. He thought of the Empire mainly in terms of the United Kingdom and the self-governing Dominions. When, in his diary for July 13, 1912 which describes his first interview with King George V, he wrote of the King, "Great Imperialist", he clearly implied approval. But Borden was too much the practical politician to be an imperial federationist. During this same visit to England he consented to attend a discussion arranged for him by the Round Tablers in a country house at Newmarket. They got little encouragement from him. His diary records laconically, "Stated my views plainly. They were appreciated." He adds, "[Lionel] Curtis had scheme of preference in investments. Impracticable...."[36] As we have seen, Borden was in agreement with Christie's proposition (1); but he would not have accepted either (2A) or (2B). He was feeling his way towards some intermediate mechanism of consultation that would not involve the destruction of the autonomy of the individual countries of the Empire such as would inevitably result from the creation of an imperial Parliament or an imperial executive. This was the goal; how it was to be reached he did not know.

Christie seems never to have lost his regard for Borden or his respect for his judgment. With the passage of time, however, he would lose all touch with the conceptions that he helped Borden to promulgate. We shall encounter him frequently as he pursues his extraordinary intellectual pilgrimage. He left behind him a considerable mass of letters and papers which serve as marking buoys for those who are interested in charting the course of

> . . . a mind for ever
> Voyaging through strange seas of Thought, alone.

CANADA ON THE EVE, 1914

In 1912 Stephen Leacock published perhaps the best of his many books, *Sunshine Sketches of a Little Town*. His Mariposa, he explained, was not a real town: "On the contrary, it is about seventy or eighty of them. You may find them all the way from Lake Superior to the sea, with the same square streets and the same maple trees and the same churches and hotels, and everywhere the sunshine of the land of hope."

Leacock's Little Town is no bad symbol of Canada as it was just before the people of the land of hope found themselves, unbelievably, deeply engaged in a world war. It is a simple and isolated place, unutterably remote from the quarrels of the chancelleries of Europe which are so soon to plunge Canadians into death, mutilation, private misery, and political disruption. Its people work hard to earn modest livings. A less military community could scarcely be imagined. There is only one soldier in *Sunshine Sketches*—Neil Pepperleigh, the judge's son, who went to South Africa with the "Third Contingent" and left his bones there. It may be significant that the town's only soldier was also the town drunk —though it is quite incredible that he can have been the only drunk. The Canadian militia had been materially improved since the South African days; during the four years preceding the outbreak of war with Germany the annual expenditure upon it increased from under $6 million to nearly $11 million, but this volunteer army had only the merest rudiments of training.[37] By European standards Canada was still what she had been in 1867, a country utterly without military power. It is extraordinary to think that by 1915 the men from Mariposa were crossing bayonets with the Prussian Guard.

The sunshine that streamed down on Mariposa in 1912 was not unrelated to long-continued economic prosperity. We have seen that the late Victorian depression lifted almost simultaneously with the Liberal election victory in 1896 and, generally speaking, the Laurier era was an era of good times. To the chagrin of the Conservatives, the good times ended soon after they came to power in 1911. Things turned sour in 1913; in particular, the Western "land boom", with its unrealistically inflated prices, suddenly collapsed, and British capital investment in Canada declined steeply. "Boom gave way to depression as the price level of Canadian export staples fell in world markets and the effects of a growing volume of unemployment were felt throughout the economy."[38] The state of things was reflected in the national government's revenue: $168.7 millions (a new peak) in 1912, $163.2 millions in 1913, $133 millions in 1914. Clouds obscured the sun, and it was a less prosperous Canada that went to war with Germany. Only in 1915 did the activity resulting from the war begin to reverse the trend.[39]

The English-speaking town of Mariposa, which has been plausibly identified as Orillia, Ontario, characteristically showed no awareness of it; but Canada on the eve of Armageddon was still painfully divided. The French and English sections of the Dominion had stayed together chiefly by remaining apart. They had comparatively little consciousness of each other, except when some crisis reminded one section of the other's existence and of its ingrained undesirable tendencies. The South African War, we have seen, had been such a crisis; a greater one was now on the way. In the meantime, unpleasant internal tensions were building up between French Quebec and English Ontario. The issue was a cultural one which had already made much trouble in modern Canada: the relationship of education and the "race question". French Canadians in increasing numbers were settling in eastern and northern Ontario. They showed an alarming disposition to continue speaking French; and in 1912 the Ontario Department of Education reacted with Circular of Instructions No. 17 (usually called "Regulation 17"), which limited French both as a language of instruction and a subject of study. French-speaking Ontarians reacted bitterly in their turn, and they received voluble and violent support in the province of Quebec, notably from Henri Bourassa. As war approached, this domestic question was threatening serious damage to the country's shaky unity.

The population of Canada in the summer of 1914 is estimated to have been a little less than eight million, of whom considerably over two million were of French origin. Those who have read this book thus far will realize that these two million and the four million whose ancestors came from the British Isles would view the impending crisis rather differently. When war came, and the British Empire and the French Republic stood together as allies against Germany, some English-speaking Canadians simple-mindedly thought that their French compatriots would be moved by the peril of the French motherland, as they themselves, in general, were drawn by inherited sentiment to support Great Britain. But not many French Canadians were so moved. Twentieth-century France and twentieth-century Quebec had little in common. Indeed, as we have seen, the Third Republic's action in 1905, when it abrogated the concordat with the Papacy made by Napoleon I, had considerably widened the gap. Many admirable Roman Catholic priests in Quebec saw the war of 1914 as a divine chastisement visited upon godless France.[40] Sad divisions were coming in Canada.

There were also, however, to be very remarkable achievements. The year 1914 is the real beginning of Canadian "nationhood". The Fathers of Confederation had made a plan and laid foundations. A different group of nation-builders, men in ill-fitting khaki, who seldom thought of themselves as people of much consequence, were now to carry the work forward. Borden's three dreadnoughts, which he had regarded as the key to gaining influence for Canada in imperial councils, had sailed away into the mists of fantasy, never to return. But the Canadian Corps that fought in Europe was a grim reality, as the Germans found. Canadian battles in the Flanders mud, and Canadian political initiatives which those battles made possible, were to do much to transform the British Empire into the British Commonwealth, a new polity, not quite like anything seen before. The introductory portion of this history ends with the earliest shots of the First World War.

CHAPTER SEVEN

THE WORLD EXPLODES, 1914-1916

THE STATE OF CANADIAN POLICY, 1914

The first three years of Borden's administration—we must now call him Sir Robert, for he accepted a GCMG, rather reluctantly, in June 1914—had not been a time of triumph for his policies. Relations with the United States were satisfactory, but he could not claim great credit for this nor was it a matter of enormous contemporary interest. The country's boasted prosperity had collapsed like a pricked balloon; this was not his fault, but inevitably he was blamed for it. Above all, the imperial policy that had been announced with such pride and fanfare had produced no tangible results.

This policy had indeed been defeated, for the moment at least, by opponents at home and abroad. The contribution to imperial defence in the Empire's time of need, which Borden had intended should purchase for Canada a voice in imperial councils, had been blocked by the Liberals in the Senate of Canada; and the Liberals in power in London, while willing enough to accept battleships if Canada would give them, were backward about conceding that share in the direction of foreign policy which sanguine Canadians thought so magnificent a gift would warrant. Since the gift in fact was not forthcoming, Borden was in no position to press the matter. In the early summer of 1914, Canada's credit and reputation in England were certainly much lower than they had been when he made his great gesture in December 1912.

They might have remained low but for the outbreak of war in August. Thereafter the Dominion made much more than gestures for the common cause, and a new basis was available to support Borden's claims. But the same men still ruled in Whitehall, and until H. H. Asquith fell Canada, and her sister Dominions with her, were communities that gave without receiving.

READY, AYE, READY

"The spring and summer of 1914 were marked in Europe by an exceptional tranquillity."[1] It was on troubled Ireland that British eyes, at least, were focused. Even when the Archduke Francis Ferdinand of Austria was murdered in Sarajevo on June 28, the danger of a European war was not appreciated. Least of all was it appreciated in distant Ottawa. The Prime Minister's rather exiguous personal diary had recorded on the 24th that he spent the day at Petawawa Camp watching manoeuvres by citizen soldiers "between two opposing forces of 5000 each", a tremendous military occasion by Canadian standards; but he made no note of the assassination four days later. The Canadian government's chief worry during July was what Borden called the "Hindoo question": a very critical phase of the Asiatic immigration problem which we have seen had been troublesome for years. A ship called the *Komagata Maru* had arrived at Vancouver carrying a large number of Sikh would-be immigrants, most of whom were, under recent orders-in-council, refused permission to land; there was violence, and the vessel was finally escorted out of Canadian waters by HMCS *Rainbow* on July 23.[2] Only on July 27 did the Prime Minister (then holidaying in Muskoka) make the first reference to the European crisis in his diary: "War declared by Austria agst Servia and stock markets in panic." Next day he wrote that a general European war seemed "exceedingly probable", adding, "Almost impossible for us to keep out if France is involved." "Us" undoubtedly meant the British Empire. On the 30th he decided to return to Ottawa at once.[3]

During the month of July, when the British Foreign Secretary, while never losing sight of the virtual obligations that had been assumed towards France (above, pages 138–39), was doing his utmost to keep the peace, there is no evidence of any consultation between the British and Canadian governments, nor even of Whitehall sending the Dominions information on the development of the situation. Borden and his colleagues got their knowledge of it from the newspapers, and in the circumstances of the day this does not seem to have been resented. The one established channel for anything like consultation was the Committee of Imperial Defence, which met seldom. George Perley, we have noted, attended the meeting of July 14, 1914, the last before the outbreak; but it did not discuss the situation on the Continent. At that point the British government was still not gravely disturbed. The cabinet did not consider the European crisis until July 24. Asquith's letter to the King about that meeting spoke of the Austrian ultimatum to Serbia with rather surprising detachment: "the greatest event for many years past in European politics; as it may be the prelude to a war in which at least 4 of the Great Powers might be involved."

On August 1 the Austro-Serbian conflict widened into a European war, when hostilities began between Germany and Russia. Britain had not declared herself, and the British cabinet was divided. Borden returned to Ottawa that morning, and was shown a telegram from the King's Private Secretary to the Governor General to the effect that the situation was most serious but there was "a faint hope of peace". The cabinet met at 11 a.m. and again in the afternoon. Parliament was not in session and nobody seems to have suggested that it should be consulted. After all, there was no need to decide whether or not Canada should go to war; that was decided by the existing constitution of the Empire. What did require decision was whether or not the Dominion should take an active part in the war; and this the cabinet felt quite equal to settling. Two important telegrams went off to London from the Governor General on August 1. One in effect offered an expeditionary force:

> In view of the impending danger of war involving the Empire my advisers are anxiously considering the most effective means of rendering every possible aid and they will welcome any suggestions and advice which Imperial naval and military authorities may deem it expedient to offer. They are confident that a considerable force would be available for service abroad. . . .

The other cable was intended for immediate publication:

> My Government desire me to send you the following: My advisers while expressing their most earnest hope that peaceful solution of existing international difficulties may be achieved and their strong desire to co-operate in every possible way for that purpose, wish me to convey to His Majesty's Government the firm assurance that if unhappily war should ensue the Canadian people will be united in a common resolve to put forth every effort and to make every sacrifice necessary to ensure the integrity and maintain the honour of our Empire. . . .

Canada, in her own small way, had given the British government a blank cheque at a moment when it was still striving to make up its mind. But there is no reason to believe that Ottawa's action had any effect upon London's subsequent decision. (Perhaps it is worth while to remark that the British Prime Minister's reports to the King on cabinet meetings in August 1914 contain no reference to Canada and only one to the Dominions at large: on August 18 Asquith told King George that the cabinet had decided that, in view of the danger of unemployment, every effort should be made "to encourage the placing of orders here by France & the Dominions".)[5]

In Whitehall the decisive day was August 2, and the German threat to Belgium brought essential unity to the cabinet (though two ministers resigned) and to the country. On August 4 Britain sent an ultimatum to Germany, demanding that her forces withdraw from Belgium, and when no answer was received by eleven o'clock (London time) that night, Britain—and the Empire—was at war.[6] In Ottawa, the cabinet had been meeting most of the day, with the Governor General (the Duke of Connaught) sitting with them. At 8:55 p.m. came Lewis Harcourt's telegram announcing war. Borden recorded,

> Summoned Parlt for 18 Aug. & placed Naval Service at disposal of King. Great excitement in all Canadian Cities. Crowds on streets cheered me.[7]

No Canadian ceremony was required to effect the change from peace to war. On August 5 an extra of the *Canada Gazette* gave the nation the official word:

> His Royal Highness the Governor General received a telegraphic despatch from the Secretary of State for the Colonies at 8.45 this evening [August 4] announcing that war has broken out with Germany.[8]

There was a moment of delay before the British government closed with the Canadian offer of an expeditionary force. On August 6, however, Harcourt cabled gratefully accepting,* and on the 8th Perley

* The delay was presumably due to the fact that, as Asquith's letter to the King on August 6 records, it was only on that day that the British cabinet sanctioned the dispatch of "an Expeditionary force" to France. On the course of events, see G. M. Trevelyan, *Grey of Fallodon* (London, 1937), pp. 317-18.

reported an interview with the new Secretary of State for War, Lord Kitchener, who clearly knew he would need all the troops he could get: "Hopes you can send him full division of twenty to twenty five thousand. Says he can use all you think best to send."[9] The Canadian cabinet had already on the 6th authorized placing on active service a force of unspecified size; on the 10th another order-in-council set the strength of the expeditionary force at 25,000 men.[10]

In his election manifesto of November 1917 Sir Robert Borden was to assert, "Canada, as became a partner nation in the British Commonwealth, entered the struggle by the decree of her Parliament."[11] By 1917 there had been important constitutional developments, as indeed the use of the phrase "British Commonwealth" indicated. Borden was thinking in terms of 1917—one might say, of a future beyond 1917—rather than of 1914. His statement was certainly not factually true. The executive government had fully committed the Dominion to an extensive war effort before Parliament was even called. When the national legislature met on August 18 for a "special war session" that lasted only until the 22nd, it had but to confirm the action of the cabinet and provide financial and other means of carrying it out. This it certainly did, to borrow another phrase from Borden's manifesto, "without a single dissenting voice". There was no criticism of the measures the government had taken. On August 4, before Britain's actual declaration of war, Sir Wilfrid Laurier, the leader of the opposition, recalled that he had "often declared that if the mother country were ever in danger, or if danger ever threatened, Canada would render assistance to the fullest extent of her power", and he called for "a truce to party strife". In an eloquent speech in the Commons on August 19 he approved the government's action. "When the call comes," he said, "our answer goes at once, and it goes in the classical language of the British answer to the call to duty: 'Ready, aye, ready'."[12]

Nevertheless, even though not a single word of criticism was spoken in Parliament, it is clear that the unity of the country was not quite complete. L. G. Power, a Nova Scotia senator, was reported as saying that Canada should "await developments before undertaking to send troops to Europe"; and in Quebec some voices were raised in favour of a policy of home defence only.[13] Clearly also there was some dissatisfaction that did not reach the public prints. On August 19 Borden recorded a conversation with Laurier: "He told me privately that he is having trouble with some of his men & will hold a Caucus tomorrow."[14] It would be interesting to know what happened in that caucus. As the war proceeded the divisions in the country would grow and become only too evident.

In the meantime enthusiasm for the cause—the enthusiasm of a nation which had scarcely the faintest idea of the nature of the ordeal ahead—was unbounded. Militiamen and others (including many recent immigrants from Britain) pressed forward to volunteer. On October 3 a convoy of thirty transports carrying 31,200 Canadian soldiers sailed for England from Gaspé harbour. It was the largest military force that had ever crossed the Atlantic as a unit.[15] Yet, contrary again to the expectations of many people at the time, it was only the vanguard of a much greater host. And what lay ahead was very different from the sham battles of Petawawa.

THE FIRST YEAR, 1914–1915

Throughout the war Canadian assistance to the common cause was centred on the army. In October 1914 an informal inquiry to the Admiralty concerning the possibility of naval aid was met with the reply that ships took too long to build and the suggestion that Canadian help should be concentrated on the military forces.[16] The Canadian naval service accordingly remained small. Canada had no air force of her own during the struggle, though Canadians served, many of them with great distinction, in the British flying services.[17] But the expansion of the Canadian Expeditionary Force began with the offer of a second contingent while the first was on the ocean,[18] and it was to be a long process.

Before the 2nd Canadian Division reached England the British government began to ask for further efforts. So far, Canada had made offers without any request or suggestion from the mother country; but in May 1915 the War Office wrote Sir George Perley (he had been knighted at the New Year) asking on behalf of Kitchener whether it might be possible to provide "even a larger army than already provided or contemplated":

> It is difficult for us to place a limit upon the numbers of men that may be required in this devastating war. No numbers which the Dominion Government are willing and able to provide with arms and ammunition would be too great for His Majesty's Government to accept with deep gratitude.[19]

The following month, by which time the 2nd Canadian Division was in great part in England, the War Office suggested, "should the Dominion

Government find it practicable to do so, that endeavours should be made to raise a third division of like composition and strength to those which have already been furnished".[20] The United Kingdom, itself making great efforts,* was prepared to ask the Dominions to extend themselves also. It should be noted, however, that the British military authorities had been shown, many weeks before, a letter in which Colonel Sam Hughes, the Canadian Minister of Militia, had advocated a force of three divisions. It is interesting that Perley—who, it is perhaps relevant to recall, represented a Quebec constituency in Parliament—had already suggested to Borden that Canada should not provide more divisions than she could reinforce: "Practical difficulties in this connection are necessarily great and question is whether two full divisions with reserves say twelve or fifteen thousand will not be all you can in practice keep up to full strength at such distance from Canada." In July 1915 the Deputy Minister of Militia and Defence, Colonel Eugène Fiset (also incidentally a Quebecker) gave similar advice: "Having regard to what war wastage means, it would be better to concentrate effort on the raising and training of reinforcements, than to go on adding to the number of units at the front."[22] Nevertheless the expansion of the overseas force continued. The decision to form the 3rd Division was taken even before Fiset wrote his memorandum. Late in 1915 the British authorities asked whether Canada could provide twelve battalions for service in Egypt, either in addition to the 3rd Division or by deferring its formation. The Canadian government, preferring to keep its forces together, offered instead to provide both the 3rd and a 4th Division for the Western Front, and this was agreed to.[23]

The story has been circumstantially told that the British War Office proposed in the beginning to break up the 1st Canadian Division and scatter its battalions among British formations; and that this was prevented only by the determined intransigence of Sam Hughes. The tale (which rests entirely on one individual's memory set down twenty years after the supposed event) seems to be unfounded; it may have had its origin in a recollection of an entirely sensible proposal, which was duly

* At the peak of its effort, late in 1917, the United Kingdom had raised seventy-five divisions in addition to eight cavalry divisions. Of the seventy-five divisions, fifty-two were in France (five of these were later sent to Italy) and eight were retained in Britain and Ireland for home defence. The others were in other theatres, with three in garrison in India. In terms of divisions provided in proportion to population, the British effort was about three times that of Canada.[21]

carried out, to give Canadian battalions some initial knowledge of trench warfare by attaching them temporarily to experienced British brigades.[24] The War Office plan of 1899, which Lord Minto had so objected to (above, pages 59–71), was not revived in 1914. Generally speaking, the Canadian field force fought as a national unit throughout; and in 1918 a danger of the Canadian divisions being separated from each other was averted.

The 1st Canadian Division was commanded in the first instance by a British regular officer, Lieutenant-General E. A. H. Alderson, who had had Canadians under his command in South Africa. Colonel Hughes had shown a rather marked willingness to take the command himself, but this was discouraged by the War Office. The fact is that there was no Canadian in sight possessing the experience necessary for the command of a division in the field; and since Hughes took the view that Alderson was the best-qualified British officer, Kitchener appointed him. The division had its baptism of fire in France under dramatic and fearful circumstances: those of the first German gas attack, in April 1915. This terrible weapon routed French colonial troops on the Canadians' left, leaving a great gap in the line. Sir John French reported later, "In spite of the danger to which they were exposed the Canadians held their ground with a magnificent display of tenacity and courage; and it is not too much to say that the bearing and conduct of these splendid troops averted a disaster which might have been attended with the most serious consequences."[25] This Second Battle of Ypres made the Canadians' reputation; it also introduced their countrymen at home to those dreadful lists of casualties with which they were to live for the next three and a half years. After that month of April the Canadian world would never be quite the same again.

In September 1915, when the 2nd Division reached France, a Canadian Corps was formed, still under General Alderson. In May 1916 Alderson was succeeded (on the nomination of Sir Douglas Haig, now the British Commander-in-Chief) by Lieutenant-General Sir Julian Byng, also a British regular. The 3rd Division arrived in France early in 1916, the 4th in August of the same year. The first occasion when the Corps attacked with all four divisions under command was in the famous action of Vimy Ridge in April 1917. A 5th Division was formed in England in 1916–17, but in spite of British pressure it did not go to France, except for its artillery and certain other special units. The Canadian government did not now believe that it could find the men to reinforce five fighting divisions. Early in 1918 the division was broken up to provide additional men for units in the field.[26]

This quick glance at Canada's deepening military commitment to the war in France has carried us beyond our period, and we must now return to consideration of other aspects of the Canadian government's international problems in the early months of the war.

Economic difficulties were the first to arise. Canada's chief source of revenue, customs duties, were suddenly cut in half by war conditions, and her government had to raise money in England at short notice; this was done with little difficulty, partly by loans from the British government, partly by private borrowing.[27] Other troubles were not so easily dealt with. The first effect of the war was further to damage the already depressed Canadian economy, and very shortly Sir Robert Borden was complaining of the fact that the British and French governments were purchasing in the United States material which could well have been obtained in Canada. On November 26 a very bitter message went to Perley, citing particularly the failure to buy wagons from the Canadian industry:

> Not only the people of Canada as a whole but individuals are making sacrifices hitherto undreamed of to support Empire in this war. A very painful and even bitter feeling is being aroused throughout the Dominion. Men are going without bread in Canada while those across the line are receiving good wages for work that could be done as efficiently and as cheaply in this country. You cannot emphasize too strongly the considerations set forth in this message. Public opinion is being so seriously aroused as to most gravely affect our future action.[28]

Reverting to his prewar interest in British encouragement to a Canadian shipbuilding industry, Borden urged the Admiralty through Perley to give contracts for submarines and destroyers to the Canadian Vickers yard established at Montreal in 1911.[29] In fact, that firm was about to undertake the construction of submarines, but in circumstances which gave Borden and his colleagues little satisfaction.

In November 1914 the Bethlehem Steel Corporation contracted with the British Admiralty to build twenty submarines at the Electric Boat Company's yard in Connecticut. The United States government scotched this arrangement on the understandable grounds that it was a breach of neutrality; and Bethlehem and the Admiralty quickly effected a new one. The components for ten submarines would be shipped to Canada and assembled at the Vickers yard at Montreal.[30] The extraordinary thing about this plan was that there had been no consultation whatever with the Canadian government, even though it involved stopping work on two vessels (an icebreaker and a dredger) which Vickers were building for that government. The new agreement was made in London in mid-December, but the first intimation of it reached the Canadian government in a "vague and partially inaccurate" telegram sent by the British Ambassador in Washington to the Governor General on January 6, 1915.[31] This does not seem to have registered with Borden, who got his first real knowledge of the situation from Canadian Vickers on the 15th. The following day the Colonial Office, on behalf of the Admiralty, finally sent a relatively full account of the matter, explaining,

> Bethlehem Steel Corporation still remain responsible contractor for supply of materials, work of construction, completion and delivery, Admiralty and Vickers Canadian Company's representative in London having arranged for permission for use of Vickers Canadian Company yard.

It was hoped that the "inconvenience" of interference with the vessels being built for Canada would be "excused".[32] Five days later Ottawa replied that while the government welcomed and appreciated the use of a Canadian shipyard they would be grateful for earlier information in such matters; there was reference also to the labour difficulties created by bringing workmen from the United States.[33] Borden was undoubtedly displeased, though there is little comment on the matter in his private diary.

Borden either did not understand or chose to disregard the real nature of the Vickers–Bethlehem submarine transaction. When the contract was nearing completion in April 1915 he pointed out that this would put over two thousand men out of work and urged that the Admiralty should give Canadian Vickers a "reasonable share" of future orders for submarines, destroyers, or cruisers. "We have never understood," he cabled Perley, "why the Admiralty should have given orders for submarines in first instance to United States when every facility was available in Canada at Montreal and elsewhere for constructing them." A few days later he telegraphed, "The wonderful expedition with which submarines have been constructed at Montreal must convince Admiralty that they can be constructed here as speedily as anywhere on this continent."[34] The fact is, however, that the Admiralty had turned to the U.S. because Bethlehem Steel and its subsidiaries had built submarines before and had the plant, the staff, and the experience that the task required. In spite of the large use of Canadian labour, it was undoubtedly these elements that enabled the job to be done with such "wonderful expedition". Even so, what was done in Montreal was a considerable achievement. Subsequently the same American firms supplied components for eight submarines which were constructed by Canadian Vickers for Italy; and six hulls were built at Montreal for Russia.[35]

Another question which produced a certain amount of acrimony between Canada and the United Kingdom was that of the requisitioning of ships. (It is interesting that the government in Ottawa had more difficulty with the Admiralty under Churchill than with any other British government department. It would be unfair however to blame this on the First Lord personally; his eye was on larger questions, including those of Allied strategy.) There was a great deal of correspondence about requisitioning. Thus on March 23, 1915 the Governor General cabled that his advisers were convinced that the requisitioning of so many of the best vessels from the principal lines would cause serious interference with Canadian trade:[36]

> Only three cargo and one passenger vessel now left to Canadian Pacific Steamship Company. The best steamships of Allan line have been taken. Canadian Northern line all taken.

It should be remembered that vessels like those of the Canadian Pacific, though Canadian-owned, were registered in Britain; this was doubtless the justification for the Admiralty dealing with them as unceremoniously as with other British ships. Yet it did not hesitate on occasion to take Canadian-registered ships too, and in 1917 a Canadian order-in-council asserted that while there might be legal power in the British government to take ships of any British subject for defence purposes, as a matter of "constitutional right" the requisitioning of Canadian registered vessels by the British government "conflicts with the constitutional autonomy of Canada in the present stage of its development".[37] As a result, a generally satisfactory settlement of the long difficulty was reached. The British government agreed that the last word as to requisitioning should rest with the government in whose country the vessel was registered; while where a United Kingdom vessel was engaged in coastal trade in a Dominion, in trade between two Dominions, or in other activity which

Dominion governments stated to be vital, the British government would consult the Dominion government before requisitioning, the Dominions giving similar assurances with respect to their ships.[38]

Sir George Perley had thought it desirable to explain to Borden at some length the British government's difficulties in the matter. The shortage of shipping was "really the most serious difficulty we have to face in connection with this war", and the Admiralty, at its wits' end for tonnage, had had to be tough; Canada was not the only sufferer. Borden on his side complained particularly of the absence of consultation: "I do not think it can fairly be said that just recognition has been accorded; indeed the Admiralty officials have sometime adopted towards our representations an attitude of suspicion and arbitrariness that might perhaps be appropriate in dealing with a private firm but is scarcely to be expected or tolerated by the Government of one of the Dominions of the Empire. Such difficulties no doubt largely arise from the present anomalous constitutional organization (or lack of it) of the Empire."[39]

STILL SEEKING FOR A VOICE

The words about the constitution of the Empire just quoted, written by Sir Robert Borden in October 1916, express dissatisfaction and frustration that had been growing in the Prime Minister since a few months after the outbreak of war. In the excitement of the outbreak, when the first troops were being raised and dispatched, matters of constitution and status were pushed into the background; nobody suggested that terms should be made before Canada made a contribution to the common cause. Before the end of 1914, however, as Canada raised larger and larger forces and the war showed no sign of an early end, Borden began to talk once more of that connection between a contribution to the defence of the Empire and the formation of the Empire's policy which he had proclaimed during the naval controversy. Early in December, making his "first public appearance outside of Parliament since the war broke out",[40] he made speeches at Toronto and Montreal. To the Canadian Club of Montreal, on the 7th, he spoke of the consolidation of the Empire:

> In one respect only the evolution has not attained its full development. The citizens of the self-governing dominions do not directly participate through their Ministers or through their Parliament [s] in the councils of the Empire which determine the issues of peace and war.
>
> It would be rash to predict the method by which that great problem will be

solved; but of this I am convinced, that the events of this war will powerfully assist in hastening its wise solution. Let me add that the presence of a member of the Government as Acting High Commissioner in London during the past four months has been of inestimable advantage to Canada. As a Minister of the Crown he occupies a unique position among those who represent in London the great Dominions.[41]

The same day, in a speech at McGill University, he again referred to the question of foreign relations. The day must come, he said, "when the men of Canada, Australia, South Africa and the other dominions will have the same just voice in these questions as those who live within the British Isles. Any man who doubts that will come, doubts that the Empire will hold together."[42]

Shortly Borden began asking London questions. Evidently as a result of a press report of a meeting of the Committee of Imperial Defence in January, he cabled Perley inquiring whether he had attended.[43] A hasty consultation between Perley and Hankey followed. After speaking to Asquith and Harcourt, Hankey wrote Perley at length on January 15.[44] The war, he explained, had greatly changed the situation of the CID. There had been no meeting of the full committee since the outbreak.

. . . As a matter of fact, on the outbreak of war the Cabinet was in almost daily session for many weeks. Many points that in time of peace would have come before the Committee of Imperial Defence were decided at once by the Cabinet, which inevitably superseded the functions of the Committee. . . .

Gradually, however, as the war progressed the machinery of the Committee was again invoked, and Sub-Committees have from time to time been appointed to deal with a considerable number of questions. . . .

The Prime Minister thinks it very probable that questions will be arising in the near future on which it will be desirable to call together the full Committee of Imperial Defence. In the meantime he has instructed me to keep you in touch with the work that is going on here, so that you may take part in any Sub-Committee in which you consider yourself to be specially interested. . . .

Misunderstanding of the situation may have been encouraged by the fact that certain meetings of sub-committees—presumably those presided over by the Prime Minister—were labelled and numbered as meetings of the committee. This was the case with the "130th meeting", the one which had provoked Borden's inquiry, on January 14, 1915; Asquith presided, but the minutes were headed "(Trade Co-ordination Sub-Committee)". There was a meeting (the 131st) of the full committee on January 27, 1915 (it is possible that Borden's question had something to do with its being held) and Perley was invited to attend. There was an important discussion on British manpower, in the course of which Lord Kitchener said, "We could not allow that the limit of recruiting had been reached until we were beyond 3,000,000."[46] Perley's comment was, "there was nothing of special interest to us in Canada";[47] had he known what lay ahead in Canada, he might have found it more interesting.

There was a 132nd meeting of the committee on February 23, 1915, which Perley did not attend. This, however, was the committee's last meeting until 1920.[48] Sub-committees did continue to meet. Perley had suggested to Hankey that it would be useful if he could attend meetings of sub-committees not entirely concerned with affairs in the British Isles; he would, he said, have been interested in the meeting of January 14 dealing with trade restrictions, etc.[49] This suggestion was acted on; Perley's name is subsequently found among the members of a sub-committee on the War Trade Department and another on the transfer of enemy vessels in neutral ports to Allied or neutral flags.[50]

The fact is that, contrary to Hankey's apparent expectation, the cabinet in its various forms wholly "superseded" the Committee of Imperial Defence for the duration of the war; indeed, it absorbed the committee's secretariat (including Hankey himself) and adopted its procedures. From the Canadian point of view, this simply meant that the one institution that had offered some limited possibility of being a link with the imperial policy-forming machinery had vanished: this in the midst of a war in which Canada was making unprecedented sacrifices for the Empire's cause. The gap would not be filled for two years after the committee's last meeting. For Sir Robert Borden and his colleagues they were unsatisfactory years.

One moderately interesting result emerged from the discussions in January 1915. Under the terms of the resolution passed by the Imperial Conference of 1902 (above, page 76) a conference would normally have taken place in 1915. There were, however, strong arguments against a wartime conference, notably the pressure of work to which ministers in all the Empire countries were subject; and Borden was inclined to accept these,[51] at least in the first instance. The one dissentient among the Dominions was Australia. On January 21 Lewis Harcourt asked the Governor General of Canada whether he might state in the House of

Commons that the Canadian ministers agreed that a normal conference was undesirable during hostilities. He added:

> Will you inform your Prime Minister at the same time that it is the intention of His Majesty's Government to consult him most fully, and if possible personally, when the time to discuss possible terms of peace arrives.

The Canadian government approved of the proposed statement.[52] Borden evidently was pleased by the commitment about peacemaking[53] (which Harcourt repeated publicly with respect to all the Dominions in the House of Commons on April 14, 1915). But this was a matter for the future, perhaps the distant future; in the meantime the war went on, with the Dominions having no share in the planning of it and little information. It is true that Perley reported to Borden on January 22 that Asquith had sent Hankey to assure him "that I should be kept informed regarding any really important matters". A "special expert committee" was considering whether new tactics might "change the present position which has lately become apparently very close to a deadlock"; and Hankey had told Perley that "if any new plan of campaign should be favoured he will advise me in order that I may communicate with you & let you know".[54] But no further communication along these lines seems to have taken place.

Borden was not alone in his worries about Canada's relation to British policy. At the end of January he received a letter from C. H. Cahan, an active Conservative and later a cabinet minister, who had just returned from England. He reported that there had been much discussion of Borden's December statement "on the necessity of Canada having representation in Imperial and International affairs":

> Liberal politicians seemed disposed to believe that the present Liberal Government would never consent that the self-governing Colonies should share in the control of foreign policies in the making of war and peace, etc., and they apparently look forward to a time when Canada and Australia will become practically independent of the control of the British Parliament and of the British Executive.
>
> To me their attitude was a very disappointing one, and I am sure that you will have to state your case again and again, with even greater emphasis, before you make any appreciable impression upon the ruling classes in England, who appear to be very insular in spirit and quite disinclined to devote time and consideration to the question of more efficient Imperial organization,

except in so far as such an organization may assure larger contributions of men and money to meet the military and naval necessities of the British Government.

Borden passed the letter on to Perley, whose comment was that there was "a good deal of truth" in it, "but I think he puts it rather too strongly". Perley thought the English Liberals more interested in the question than Cahan allowed, though he did not expect action until after the war.[55]

The questions of a possible Imperial Conference and a possible visit to England by Borden were inevitably related. Borden raised the matter of a visit as early as October 1914. Sir Richard McBride of British Columbia urged him to go and proposed to go with him. Borden cabled Perley,

> ... McBrides idea seems largely based on spectacular effect. I would be glad to have your views. Am not specially impressed by McBrides suggestion and in any case would not go unless visit were desired by Imperial Government.

Perley replied that he had consulted Harcourt, and Harcourt had consulted Asquith:

> They think time inopportune no chance spectacular effect papers full of war news everyone exceedingly busy working at full pressure they would be pleased see you but know of nothing specially requiring attention personally agree with them although would enjoy have you here as find work pretty complicated and Departments difficult to get information from.[56]

McBride went alone. Perley heard from him that his idea of "spectacular effect" meant effect in Canada with an eye to a possible election. Perley was now glad to hear that Borden and White, the Minister of Finance, might come over. Such a visit, he thought, would do nothing but good. For the time being the idea was dropped; but on January 19, 1915 Borden, telling Perley that he could safely arrange to remain in London for the next eight months at least, "and doubtless during continuance of war", added, "Hope to visit London shortly after session."[57]

In May 1915 Asquith found himself forced to transform his Liberal government into a coalition, and the Unionist leader Bonar Law became Colonial Secretary. Borden, who had had contacts with Law during his visit to England in 1912,[58] evidently hoped that his advent in this capacity would have important results. He wrote to Law on May 26, "We rejoice that in the Cabinet changes announced here this morning, your name has been associated with a post which offers such unbounded opportunities for usefulness not only in the war itself but in all that the war shall bring forth. Assuredly the seed has been sown for a great harvest."[59] This letter evidently crossed one from Law telling Borden that Asquith and himself would be greatly pleased if he could visit England, "simply in order that you might be as well acquainted as we are ourselves with everything that is going on in connection with the war."[60] But before the visit took place there was a slight tiff. Andrew Fisher, the Australian Prime Minister, still favoured an "informal" conference of all the Dominions, and Borden was now inclined to agree. But when he asked Perley about it the confidential reply from the Colonial Secretary was that it would be better for the premiers* to come separately, "but if one of others chanced to be here at same time as you it would be all right". If all came together, records would have to be kept "and it would have all the disadvantage of formal conference at this time". Borden snapped back angrily to Perley, "In my apprehension answer is unsatisfactory and reasons assigned trivial." In another interview with Perley Law was rather more conciliatory and emphasized that he was "very anxious" for a visit from Borden. The latter cabled the premiers of the other Dominions telling them he expected to be in London early in July and inquiring whether they contemplated a visit there. At the moment none of them did.[61]

Borden arrived in England on July 9, 1915 and sailed for Canada again on August 25. In the meantime he visited the Canadian force in France and saw great numbers of wounded Canadians in hospitals there and in England, an experience which certainly had its due effect upon him. He conferred with Perley and other Canadian officers and officials. On July 13 he had an audience with the King, who spoke of constitutional relations and, Borden recorded in his diary, "Says we shd have voice." On the following day he attended a meeting of the British cabinet "& sat next to Asquith who spoke of my presence as a new precedent but said it was a day for making new precedents".[62] He later recalled in his memoirs that Asquith reminded him of the tradition which strictly forbade the taking of notes; and that the chief subject of the discussion was "the question of making cotton contraband".[63]

* A word still used at this period for the prime ministers of Britain and the Dominions.

Borden also had numerous private conversations with members of the British government. These on the whole he found unsatisfactory; hard information on the British war effort seemed difficult to come by. There was something of a crisis just before Borden's departure for home. Two quotations from his all-too-slight diary give some indications of it. The first is of August 21:

... to B. Laws at Margate.... Discussed situation with Law Churchill & Smith.* All admit situation is grave. Asked them when munitions will be ample. Churchill says middle of next year. Law about 5 months. Told them I must have definite information....

The entry for August 24 reads in part:

... At 12.30 to B. Law & confce with him until 1.45 Then to lunch with him & Lloyd George [Minister of Munitions] who deld statement of munitions condition. Damning indictment of departmental negligence....

According to Borden's later account,† he had told Law that unless he got precise information he would "return to Canada with no definite intention of urging my fellow countrymen to continue in the war work they have already begun or with the intensive preparation which I am sure they are ready to undertake"; Law then asked Lloyd George, who had been ill in the country, to come to London and give Borden the information he required.[64]

Borden returned to Ottawa unimpressed by the British government's approach to the war but doubtless pleased with Lloyd George's outspokenness and consideration. Nothing had been accomplished, however, towards setting up arrangements for systematic consultation or passing of information; and as time passed the Canadian Prime Minister's sense

* Churchill was Chancellor of the Duchy of Lancaster in the coalition government; F. E. Smith (later Lord Birkenhead) was Solicitor General and not yet of the cabinet.

† The sources for this episode are unsatisfactory. Borden in his memoirs quotes from what he says is a contemporary memorandum of his conversations during his visit to England. This memorandum is not now to be found among his papers. In the papers, however, is a letter to Lord Beaverbrook, dated 1928, which gives an account similar to that in the quotations given in the memoirs though it is not word for word the same. It would seem that the contemporary memorandum did once exist but has been lost or mislaid.

of frustration merely deepened. The Canadian field force grew; the casualty lists lengthened; but the constitutional situation remained static. On October 30, 1915 a Canadian order-in-council increased the authorized force to be raised (including the men already enlisted) to 250,000; it had formerly been 150,000. On the same day Borden telegraphed Perley:

Please inform Bonar Law that we would appreciate fuller and more exact information from time to time respecting conduct of war and proposed military operations as to which little or no information vouchsafed. We thoroughly realize necessity central control of Empire's armies but Governments of Overseas Dominions have large responsibilities to their people for conduct of war and we deem ourselves entitled to fuller information and to consultation respecting general policy in war operations. The great difficulty of obtaining information during my recent visit to London seemed partially occasioned by lack proper co-ordination between several Departments responsible for conduct war. Perhaps new Council or Committee* can arrange for information and consultation suggested.[65]

Perley passed this to the Colonial Secretary in a letter that was merely a polite paraphrase of the cable. Law replied the same day. Beginning by expressing appreciation for the increase of troops, he proceeded:

We fully realise I need not say the great part which your Government is playing in this war and as Sir Robert Borden found when he was here we were only too delighted to put him into possession of all the information which was available to the Cabinet. It is of course much more difficult to keep him in touch now but it is our desire to give him the fullest information and if there is any way which occurs to him or to yourself in which this can be done I shall be delighted to carry it out.

As regards the question of consultation, here again I fully recognise the right of the Canadian Government to have some share of the control in a war in which Canada is playing so big a part. I am, however, not able to see any way in which this could be practically done. I wish, therefore, that you would communicate my view to Sir Robert Borden telling him how gladly we would do it if it is practicable and at the same time I should like you to repeat to him what I said to you—that if no scheme is practicable then it is very undesirable that the question should be raised.[66]

* This was the War Committee, composed in the first instance of Asquith, Balfour, Kitchener, Grey, and Lloyd George. Law and McKenna were shortly added to it.

Forwarding this to Borden, Perley reported on the interview with Law during which he had given him the letter containing Borden's complaint. Perley's own view, he told Borden, was that it should be possible to provide Canada with better and more frequent information; but the question of consultation was "much more difficult":

I had thought that it might be possible to arrange for you or one of the other Dominion Prime Ministers to be put on the War Council and be here most of the time for that purpose in order to represent all the Dominions. Mr. Bonar Law, however, thinks that a plan of that kind could not be put into force as the various Dominions would not be able to agree on a choice, and he seems to think that all the Dominions except the one whose Prime Minister was selected for the War Council would prefer to leave things as they are.[67]

In this last matter Law was certainly right; but his letter, admitting that Borden had a case and going on to say that nothing could be done, was most unfortunate. Borden says nothing about it in his diary, but it seems likely that it made him angrier than any other episode of the war. He appears to have contained his anger until the end of the year. Then two things happened.

First, the authorized Canadian force was doubled. This seems to have been done strictly on Borden's personal initiative. His diary states on December 30,

White, Hughes and Reid* came & I propounded to them proposal that force shd. be increased on 1st. Jany to 500000. They agreed. . . .

The increase was announced in Borden's New Year address to the Canadian people, without any formal action having been taken on it by the cabinet. Only on January 12, 1916 did an order-in-council formally authorize the Minister of Militia and Defence "to raise, equip and send overseas . . . officers and men not exceeding five hundred thousand, including those who have already been raised and equipped . . . and including also those who have been, or may hereafter be raised for garrison and guard duty in Canada."[68] It was only two and a half months since the force had been increased to 250,000.

It seems likely that this was a *beau geste* intended to impress the British government. It was, in fact, a wartime equivalent to the dramatic offer

* Ministers respectively of Finance, Militia and Defence, and Customs.

of the three dreadnoughts in 1912. It is also perhaps not irrelevant that Borden was suffering agony with lumbago, as his diary shows, when he "propounded" his plan to his three colleagues on December 30. It might be argued that to expand the country's military effort in this manner merely to add weight to the demand for a voice in foreign and military policy (if this was actually the case) was an irresponsible act contributing to the later conscription crisis. It is questionable, however, whether this gesture of fixing a new upper limit of strength actually had any practical effect on the size of the army. The force continued to increase, as it had so far, in response to the demands of the war. The final grand total of appointments and enlistments was 619,636, including conscripts; some 425,000 went overseas. The Canadian Expeditionary Force at home and abroad reached its actual peak strength (388,038 all ranks) in July 1918.[69] By that time there had, of course, been great numbers of casualties and also great numbers of discharges in Canada for various reasons.[70]

The second action which Borden took was to write a celebrated letter. On January 4, still suffering pain ("Neuritis a very troublesome Companion," he confided to the diary) he finally sent Perley a rejoinder to Bonar Law's communication of November 3, which no doubt he had thought about a good deal in the intervening weeks:

> . . . Mr. Bonar Law's letter is not especially illuminating and leaves the matter precisely where it was before my letter was sent.
>
> During the past four months since my return from Great Britain, the Canadian Government (except for an occasional telegram from you or Sir Max Aitken)* have had just what information could be gleaned from the daily press and no more. As to consultation, plans of campaign have been made and unmade, measures adopted and apparently abandoned and generally speaking steps of the most important and even vital character have been taken, postponed or rejected without the slightest consultation with the authorities of this Dominion.
>
> It can hardly be expected that we shall put 400,000 or 500,000 men in the field and willingly accept the position of having no more voice and receiving no more consideration than if we were toy automata. Any person cherishing such an expectation harbours an unfortunate and even dangerous delusion. Is this war being waged by the United Kingdom alone or is it a war waged by the whole Empire? If I am correct in supposing that the second hypothesis must be accepted then why do the statesmen of the British Isles arrogate to them-

* Later Lord Beaverbrook; at this time "General Representative for Canada at the Front".

selves solely the methods by which it shall be carried on in the various spheres of warlike activity and the steps which shall be taken to assure victory and a lasting peace?

It is for them to suggest the method and not for us. If there is no available method and if we are expected to continue in the role of automata the whole situation must be reconsidered.

Procrastination, indecision, inertia, doubt, hesitation and many other undesirable qualities have made themselves entirely too conspicuous in this war. During my recent visit to England a very prominent Cabinet Minister* in speaking of the officers of another Department said that he could not call them traitors but he asserted that they could not have acted differently if they had been traitors. They are still doing duty and five months have elapsed. Another very able Cabinet Minister spoke of the shortage of guns, rifles, munitions, etc., but declared that the chief shortage was of brains.[71]

Two things are particularly worth noting about this letter to Perley. It is evident that on further thought Borden came to the conclusion that it was too strongly worded. Eight days after sending it he cabled Perley, "Respecting my letter of 4th instant . . . please take no further steps at present."[72] However, this does not destroy the letter's value as a reflection of Borden's views. Secondly, it is interesting to observe his insistence that it was the business of the British government to produce the machinery of consultation. Borden himself had nothing to suggest. He had always taken the same line: we must have a "voice"—but he never suggested a concrete expedient. There is something faintly comic about his anger when he found that Bonar Law was as destitute of ideas as he was himself. The two eminent statesmen stood wringing their hands at each other across the Atlantic. Nearly a year would pass before the British government took the initiative that Borden had so long awaited.

In the meantime, however, Law made a characteristically half-hearted attempt. Whether it was a belated result of the discussion with Perley in November, or whether Perley, in spite of Borden's cable, had given the Colonial Secretary a hint that Borden was angry and something should be done, does not appear. Borden in his memoirs attributes the whole thing to his letter of January 4, which he prints with pride; he makes no mention of the cable cancelling it, having doubtless forgotten it. At any rate, on February 11, 1916 Law wrote a hand-written confidential letter to Borden:

* The account in Borden's *Memoirs* makes it evident that this was Lloyd George.

It has been difficult to find anything specially interesting to communicate to you as no special changes have taken place. I feel however very strongly that you ought to be kept personally more in touch with what has been going on & I have collected a number of the most important documents which have been circulated to the War Council [War Committee] & with the approval of the Prime Minister send them on to you. They are as you realize very secret & I shall be much obliged if you will treat them *as for yourself alone* & burn them after you have examined them. I shall continue to set aside the most important ones & forward them to you later. . . . I think the whole machine of the Govt is working a little better. I do not however see any sign of an early end. . . .[73]

This letter did not go at once. On February 23 Law added a postscript:

After writing the above I became anxious as to the possibility of the documents falling into enemy hands & made enquiry at the Foreign Office as to what they considered would be a safe way of transmitting them. They told me in effect that no method would be regarded by them as safe which is possible at present. I had therefore reluctantly to abandon the idea of sending them but Sir George Perley has informed me that Mr. Newcome* is leaving tomorrow morning & I am going to take the responsibility of sending them by him. Forgive me adding once more that these documents are for yourself alone.

That the British government had no secure means of sending secret documents from London to Ottawa in 1916, and was unable to improvise any, is itself revealing. (Did nobody think of sending them by diplomatic bag to the Washington embassy, and thence by courier on the overnight train to Ottawa?) The papers sent for Borden's perusal were apparently, with one exception, productions of the Committee of Imperial Defence; they dealt with such topics as the supply of arms to Russia and co-ordination of the Allies. There was also a "paper by the Genl. Staff on the Future Conduct of the war".[74]

On July 6, 1916 Law took advantage of a visit to Canada by Perley himself to send Borden a further budget of secret papers, including five General Staff appreciations.[75] It appears that papers were sent to Borden in this manner only on these two occasions.

THE CONTROL OF CANADIAN FORCES OVERSEAS

The story of the evolution of national control of the Canadian forces overseas during the First World War cannot be told in detail here, but

* Presumably E. L. Newcombe, Deputy Minister of Justice, Canada.

something must be said about it, and that something must go beyond 1916. Some account of the growth of the force, and of the early problems of command, has already been given.

There were no effective precedents to guide a Canadian government which found itself maintaining a large military force in action abroad. As we have seen, it was thought necessary to draw the senior field commander from the British Army in the first instance. And it took a long time to develop a system of overseas administration that combined a proper degree of military efficiency with a decent regard for Canada's established and steadily expanding autonomy.

So far as the force in France was concerned, the situation was comparatively simple. Its business was fighting the enemy, and it fought under the British Commander-in-Chief. His operational control was never questioned; but attention was paid to the views of the Canadian Corps Commander and his political superiors when they chose to assert themselves on such matters, as they did in a few cases late in the war. There was a notable example in the spring of 1918, when it appeared that as a result of the desperate emergency caused by the German March offensive the Canadian Corps was in danger of being broken up, its individual divisions being used under various British corps headquarters to plug gaps in the line. In a letter to Sir Douglas Haig's Chief of the General Staff, Sir Arthur Currie made a reasoned protest which stands as a classic statement of the Canadian position in such matters:

> From the very nature and constitution of the organization it is impossible for the same liaison to exist in a British Corps as exists in the Canadian Corps. My Staff and myself cannot do as well with a British Corps* in this battle as we can with the Canadian Corps, nor can any other Corps Staff do as well with the Canadian Divisions as my own.
>
> I know that necessity knows no law and that the Chief [Haig] will do what he thinks best, yet for the sake of the victory we must win, get us together as soon as you can.

A copy of this letter went to the Minister of Overseas Military Forces of Canada, who took the matter up with the British Secretary of State for War. The latter in turn pursued it with Haig. A little later a strong cable from Borden in Canada warned against any proposal to break up the Corps as likely to have "the most unfortunate effect upon public opinion".

* What he means is a corps made up of British divisions.

The protest was successful, but it was greatly resented by Haig. He felt that he had military grounds for his resentment, and so he had; but the Canadians were convinced that they, too, had a strong military argument apart from the "political" one, for it was as a national force fighting concentrated under their own commanders that they would exert the most effective pressure on the enemy. It is interesting that the British political authorities felt that they had no choice but to defer to the Dominions' views in such matters when strongly expressed. Lord Derby, the Secretary of State for War, had written to Haig about the "colonial Forces" in November 1917: "I am afraid, for various reasons, we must look upon them in the light in which they wish to be looked upon rather than the light in which we should wish to do so. They look upon themselves, not as part and parcel of the English [*sic*] Army but as allies beside us. . . ." The letter is powerful evidence of the extraordinary transformation the war was working upon the British Empire.[76]

In general, however, it was in the fields of organization and administration rather than in operations that Canadian military autonomy was asserted, and it was not until 1918 that the matter was reduced to a definite formula. At that time (when the Canadians had been fighting in France for three years and were universally recognized as a very important part of the British forces there) the British military authorities agreed to a plan by which Canadian interests would be represented at Sir Douglas Haig's headquarters by a "Canadian Section, GHQ". At the same time the division of responsibility between British and Dominion commands was defined. The arrangement was thus summarized:

> Broadly, the statement made by Canada of her position, in which the Imperial Government concurred, was that for matters of military operations the Canadian forces in the Field had been placed by the Canadian Government under the Commander-in-Chief, British Armies in France; in matters of organisation and administration, the Canadian Government still retained full responsibility in respect to its own forces.
>
> . . . Important matters, such as the allotment of reinforcements in emergencies, War Establishments, the appointment of General Officers, and those other matters which from their relation to military operations should properly receive the consideration of General Headquarters, would still be made the subject of conference between the Canadian Authorities and General Headquarters. . . .
>
> *Status.*—The Canadian Section at General Headquarters is a branch of the Ministry, Overseas Military Forces of Canada, and is directly responsible to the Minister. . . .

This arrangement was not arrived at without a good deal of discussion, and the Canadians found the British GHQ in the field more disposed to make difficulties than the War Office. GHQ undoubtedly feared that there would be interference with its operational control. The Canadian Corps Commander for his part thought that he was the best person to handle relations with GHQ so far as his own command was concerned. The Canadian Section concerned itself mainly with those Canadian units in France that were not part of the Corps.[77]

In 1917 a Canadian had taken command of the Canadian Corps, when Sir Julian Byng, an excellent soldier who had been popular with his Canadian troops, was promoted to command an army. The situation was now quite different from that in 1914; there were plenty of Canadian officers available who had learned the business of command in the best and hardest school. Sir George Perley cabled Borden (June 9, 1917), "Intend insisting on appointment Canadian." The British authorities did not demur, and the choice fell on Sir Arthur Currie, then commanding the 1st Canadian Division.[78] Currie was a prewar militia officer, in civil life a real-estate agent in Victoria, B.C., who at the moment when war broke out was involved in a serious money scandal the details of which have never been published. This made him unlikely material for a national hero. Such a hero he never became, but he was an admirable Corps Commander whose country should remember him with gratitude. Under his command in 1917–18 the Canadian Corps continued to be a pillar of the British effort in France, and Canadian national spirit worked more and more strongly within it.[79]

Even after a Canadian became Corps Commander, British officers continued to do important work in the Corps. The arrangements made in 1911 (above, page 142) had not yet produced in the Canadian Permanent Force an adequate supply of staff officers having the training necessary to enable them to assist and advise commanders and draft operation and administrative orders. In the Canadian Corps all senior General Staff* appointments, and some less senior, were held by British regulars, products in most cases of the Camberley Staff College and, it was generally agreed, highly competent professionals. In January 1917 Major-General Sir Richard Turner, the senior officer at the Canadian headquarters in London, launched what might be called today a campaign to "Cana-

* The General Staff, as distinct from the administrative branches, was concerned primarily with operations, intelligence and training. By the summer of 1917 virtually all administrative staff officers in the Corps were Canadians.

dianize" the Corps staffs; but even he considered it proper that qualified "Imperial" officers should still hold the most important appointments—the senior General Staff jobs at each division and at Corps headquarters. The request for increased Canadian staff representation met no opposition either in the Imperial War Cabinet when Sir Robert Borden raised it there on May 2, 1917, or from Sir Douglas Haig. The process went further than Turner had suggested; by the end of the fighting three of the four Canadian divisions in the field had Canadians as their senior General Staff Officers (GSOS1). Yet for all Currie's robust Canadianism, the three senior staff appointments at his Corps headquarters were held by British officers until the armistice. In his final report Currie thanks only one individual by name—Brigadier-General N. W. Webber, his Brigadier-General, General Staff, a British regular. The evidence is clear that the British staff officers made a great contribution to the Corps' efficiency, and Canadians who served with them remembered them afterwards with respect and gratitude.[80]

The problem of Canadian military organization in England was harder, thanks largely to the administrative incapacity of the eccentric and egotistical Sam Hughes. He controlled the growing force in Britain by a variety of expedients which had the effect of multiplying authorities until both the Corps Commander in France and the War Office were at a loss whom to deal with. In October 1916 Borden finally took remedial action. An order-in-council set up a Ministry of Overseas Military Forces of Canada, located in London; and Sir George Perley was appointed Minister, while still continuing as Acting High Commissioner.[81] This led to a crisis with Hughes which ended in Borden calling for his resignation; and A. E. (later Sir Edward) Kemp became Minister of Militia and Defence. The direction of Canadian military affairs overseas was now centralized under the new ministry, and the evils of divided command were ended. The advent of a more businesslike organization certainly made it easier to negotiate with the British authorities on the question of the status of the Canadian forces in France and Britain.[82]

A little may be said on the direction of Canada's small naval force. We have seen (above, page 175) that the two old cruisers were transferred to Admiralty control (as permitted by the Naval Service Act) at the outbreak of war. In 1916–18, as the submarine menace grew, a considerable patrol organization of small vessels was built up on the east coast, at the urging of the Admiralty and with its assistance. A Canadian Captain of Patrols was in charge. It does not appear that this force was ever placed formally at Admiralty "disposal", but it was certainly directed in accordance with Admiralty policy. The Director of the Naval Service in Ottawa wrote in 1917, "Knowing full well we have not a proper organization, we have most warmly appreciated and acted on the advice of the Admiralty on every occasion."[83]

More surprising than the dependence of the tiny navy is the absence of an independent air service in a war in which Canadians did so much in the air. (An RAF staff officer wrote in June 1918, "Thirty-five per cent of our total strength in pilots is Canadian.")[84] The creation of a Canadian service was often suggested but never accepted by the government. Early in 1917 a branch of the Royal Flying Corps was established in the Dominion. It proceeded to recruit Canadians as flying cadets and mechanics, and the Imperial Munitions Board organized a company known as Canadian Aeroplanes Limited to manufacture the aircraft for them to train on. This large military organization, which graduated 3,272 aircrew, and was training many more at the armistice, was a sort of state within a state in Canada; it was entirely administered by the Royal Flying Corps, and afterwards the Royal Air Force, and the Canadian government had nothing to do with it. In 1917–18, thanks presumably to tact on all sides and a general overmastering interest in winning the war, this situation caused no serious problems in Canada. But as the Second World War approached, the memory of it was to be responsible for some rather painful misunderstandings.[85]

THINKING ABOUT THE EMPIRE

In September 1915 Sir Robert Borden received an offer from an eminent Canadian who was prepared to make a study of the whole vexed question of imperial relations. Z. A. Lash was a wealthy corporation lawyer, a former Liberal who was one of the "Toronto eighteen" who had done so much to defeat Laurier and reciprocity in 1911 (above, page 147). He was much interested in constitutional matters. Apparently Borden did not take up the offer at first; perhaps he did not even acknowledge it. But at the moment early in 1916 when he was so angry with Bonar Law's failure to make an effort to solve the riddle of consultation, he wrote Lash a revealing letter:

> I would indeed be glad to have you make a study of the whole situation. The immense difficulty in creating a Parliament for the whole Empire is only too apparent; and you have properly dwelt upon the feeling which would be aroused by a proposal to surrender to such a Parliament a portion of the

power of taxation now exclusively possessed by the Federal and Provincial Legislatures.

However, such surrender would not be greater than that made by the American Colonies to Congress or by the Canadian Provinces to our Federal Parliament. Moreover the cable keeps all the self-governing Dominions in constant touch with the British Isles; and even on the basis of the time occupied in actual travel I suppose that Australia or South Africa is as near to England as New Hampshire was to Virginia in the last quarter of the eighteenth century.

I have a perfectly open mind on the question. Lord Haldane about fifteen years ago advocated the Privy Council as a means of affording more thorough co-operation and giving to the various Dominions their proper voice in the Empire's Councils. Lord Esher has suggested that the Foreign Office be put into commission, or rather that it be assisted by a Council corresponding in some measure to the India Council. This is not the Council in India but a body in London which assists and advises the Secretary of State for India in respect of Indian affairs.

Borden went on to say that he would have given more consideration to the subject had it been for his "indisposition during the autumn and the early part of the present month".[86]

This is further evidence of the fact that Borden at this time had no specific plan for giving the Dominions a "voice" in imperial policy. He was even, apparently, prepared to play with the idea of surrendering some degree of taxing power to a central imperial authority, though one is loath to take this too seriously. He was waiting for someone else to produce a formula.

Lash went actively to work. What he produced seems to have had little effect on history, so there is no point in describing it in detail. However, by February 1916 he had worked out a first draft of an untitled paper on imperial organization.[87] It was a plan for an Imperial Council with "plenary Executive and Legislative powers". The numbers of representatives to come from the British Isles and the various Dominions were left blank; these representatives were to be elected or appointed as the parliaments of the countries concerned should decide. The King by and with the advice of this council was to make laws respecting declaration of war, making of peace, military forces of the Empire, Empire finance, etc. Lash subsequently gave a copy of this paper to Lionel Curtis, the leader of the Round Table group, who had been in Canada.[88] Later in 1916 Lash wrote another paper, entitled "The Dominions and the Foreign Affairs of the

British Empire",[89] which argued for the adoption of the plan put forward in his February memorandum, and took issue with the scheme for a central authority presented by Curtis in his book *The Problem of the Commonwealth*.*

Marginal notes on Borden's copy of Lash's first paper suggest that Borden had passed it to Loring Christie for comment, and that Christie was not impressed (Christie, it is to be feared, had little respect for any intellect but his own). A characteristic note is, "Rot. How about India? He shirks it." Borden seems to have had little interest in Lash's production, and there is no evidence that he thanked him for it (thanking people was not an art that Sir Robert cultivated to the best advantage). When Lash inquired whether it would be a good idea to publish his second paper, Borden said it was up to him; he saw no objection. The paper was duly published in 1917 under the title *Defence and Foreign Affairs*.[91]

Lash was one of many people who brought forward abortive schemes for the reform of the British Empire. But the time was now not far distant when the British government itself, under the impulsion of the continuing war, would finally produce a plan for consultation that would have large and important consequences.

* It is interesting that Curtis's highly centralized plan, involving the sort of surrender of the taxing power that Borden seems to have looked at at least briefly, led to a considerable breach with the Canadian Round Tablers, who were not prepared to accept such an idea.[90] Even a Canadian Round Tabler was a nationalist when the chips were down.

CHAPTER EIGHT

COMMONWEALTH AND ANGLO-SAXON ALLIANCE, 1917-1918

SACRIFICE AND ACHIEVEMENT

The years 1917 and 1918 were grim and bloody; but they ended in the triumph of the Allied arms, and they witnessed political developments which contemporary observers thought heralded a new and better age for the British Empire and for the world at large. They seemed at the time, and still seem in retrospect, years of extraordinary significance in the history of Canada.

The apparently endless battles on the Western Front went on, and the casualty lists lengthened. The triumph of Vimy Ridge in April 1917 was succeeded by the muddy horror of Passchendaele in October and November. The great German offensive of March 1918 seemed to threaten the Allies with defeat even at that late hour. Only with the Germans' "black day" at Amiens in August did the tide turn decisively; and in the final Hundred Days from then until the German surrender on November 11 the Canadian Corps under Sir Arthur Currie continued to play a leading part and to pay the heavy price of victory.

While soldiers from the Dominions won victories in France, Dominion statesmen were in council with British statesmen in London. In 1917 the convocation of the Imperial War Cabinet and Imperial War Conference transformed the imperial scene and began the transition from Empire to Commonwealth. Sir Robert Borden found himself in a congenial atmosphere; it seemed that the Dominions had at last gained the voice for which he had long contended. In 1917, also, the United States entered the war, and Canada found herself an ally of the country that had once been a traditional and potential enemy. The result was a considerable military and economic rapprochement, one part of which was the appearance for the first time of a Canadian mission in Washington. The third and fourth years of what contemporaries called the Great War were a vital and exciting period in the history of Canadian nationality and Canadian autonomy.

IMPERIAL COUNCILS OF WAR, 1917–1918

In December 1916 the Asquith government in Britain fell, under pressure from David Lloyd George, who now became Prime Minister and leader of a new coalition. His accession, it has been said, "was more than a change of government. It was a revolution, British-style."[1] Lloyd George brought to his task a dynamism, notably lacking under Asquith, which was to be a major factor in winning the war. Power was now concentrated in a new War Cabinet of five men, served by a secretariat headed by Maurice Hankey which used the businesslike methods developed in the Committee of Imperial Defence. The new body had scarcely been installed when Lloyd George took action in the imperial sphere.

The new Colonial Secretary (who did not sit in the War Cabinet) was Walter Long. On December 14 (one week after Lloyd George kissed hands as Prime Minister) Long sent the Dominions a cable assuring them that his own absence from the War Cabinet would not affect them adversely and that the Prime Minister would make a declaration of policy when he recovered from a temporary illness. He also informed them that since the British government felt that fuller information should be given them than hitherto he proposed to send a weekly letter "for the personal and confidential information" in each case of the Governor General and the Prime Minister.[2] In fact, however, Lloyd George had already told Long on December 12 that something more than this was needed:

> I propose to say something about the Empire in my speech on Thursday. The more I think about it, the more I am convinced that we should take the Dominions into our counsel in a much larger measure than we have hitherto done in our prosecution of the War. They have made enormous sacrifices, but we have held no conference with them as to either the objects of the War or the methods of carrying it out. They hardly feel that they have been consulted. As we must receive even more substantial support from them before we can hope to pull through, it is important that they should feel that they have a share in our councils as well as in our burdens. We want more men from them. We can hardly ask them to make another great recruiting effort unless

it is accompanied by an invitation to come over to discuss the situation with us.[3]

On December 19 the new Prime Minister made a long general statement of policy to the House of Commons. It included a brief but important reference to the Dominions:

Ministers have repeatedly acknowledged the splendid assistance which the Dominions have given, of their own free will, to the old country in its championship of the cause of humanity. . . . The new Administration are as full of gratitude as the old for the superb valour which our kinsmen have shown in so many stricken fields, but that is not why I introduce the subject now. I introduce the subject now because I want to say that we feel the time has come when the Dominions ought to be more formally consulted as to the progress and course of the War, as to the steps that ought to be taken to secure victory, and as to the best methods of garnering in the fruits of their efforts as well as of our own. We propose, therefore, at an early date to summon an Imperial Conference, to place the whole position before the Dominions, and to take counsel with them as to what further action they and we can take together in order to achieve an early and complete triumph for the ideals they and we have so superbly fought for.

On December 20 the Colonial Secretary asked the Dominion governments for their views as to the date of the proposed conference. On the 25th he cabled further details:

I wish to explain that what is contemplated . . . is not a session of the ordinary Imperial Conference but a special War Conference of the Empire. H. M. Government therefore invite your Prime Minister to attend a series of special and continuous meetings of the War Cabinet in order to consider urgent questions affecting prosecution of the war, the possible conditions on which in agreement with our Allies we could assent to its termination, and the problems which will then immediately arise.

Your Prime Minister, for the purpose of these meetings would be a member of the War Cabinet.

It was hoped that the meeting could begin not later than the end of February. While the presence of the Prime Ministers themselves was "earnestly desired", any Prime Minister who found it impossible to come would, London hoped, name a substitute.[4] On January 1, 1917 another telegram indicated that the presence of ministers additional to the Prime

Minister would be welcome, "though the Prime Minister alone of course will be a member of War Cabinet". Furthermore, if Dominion governments wished to discuss "other questions of common interest not directly affecting the conduct of the war", or less suitable for the War Cabinet, "His Majesty's Government are prepared to arrange facilities for conferring on any other questions that await decision between Dominions and Imperial Government, although it may not be possible for the Prime Minister to preside".[5] Lloyd George's original vague conception was gradually developing.

All the known circumstances suggest that this striking initiative was Lloyd George's own idea. His motives are a matter of conjecture. It has been suggested[6] that he hoped to use the overseas politicians as a makeweight against the British generals, whom he disliked and distrusted. This he certainly sought to do in 1918; but there is no evidence that the idea was important in his calculations in the beginning. It is quite possible that he remembered his discussion with Borden in 1915 (above, page 189). His letter to Long probably tells the story adequately: "We want more men from them." He was a tough-minded pragmatist.

Nevertheless, after more than half a century, his action appears as perhaps the most uniquely imaginative in the modern history of the British community. The contrast with Bonar Law's hand-wringing when faced with Borden's importunity needs no comment. In fact, Law—a member of the new War Cabinet—had no use for the initiative Lloyd George had now taken, and neither had Maurice Hankey. The latter wrote in his diary, "As a matter of fact they have not a notion what they are to discuss, and as Bonar Law said, 'When they are here, you will wish to goodness you could get rid of them.' "[7] By comparison with these men, Lloyd George was a poet of politics. No doubt his ideas about the coming imperial meeting were ill-defined; but the step he took in December 1916 was a very great turning-point in imperial history. Certainly it seemed so to Sir Robert Borden. Two and a half years later Borden, who was not a man who distributed bouquets without good reason, wrote to Lloyd George when about to take leave of the Paris Peace Conference:

I hope you will permit me before my departure for Canada to express on behalf of my colleagues and myself, our profound appreciation of the broad outlook and remarkable foresight which have always characterised your attitude in respect of the British Dominions. On all questions of importance we have always had your strong sympathy and powerful support. During the

> past six months some notable pages have been written in the constitutional development of our Empire. That development began in December 1916 when you summoned Dominion Ministers to sit for the first time in a great Council of the Empire on terms of perfect equality with the Ministers of the United Kingdom. In recalling these great events, the vast significance of which has sometimes escaped us in the turmoil of war through which we have passed, you of all men have the best, and indeed the only right to say, "Quarum magna pars fui".

Borden's Latin was a trifle shaky, but his sentiment was clear, and its sincerity seems obvious. His associate Christie felt the same way: "I shall always pin large roses on Lloyd George as the first Prime Minister who ever saw the British Commonwealth."[8]

The Canadian government seems to have had little doubt about the desirability of accepting the invitation. Borden's diary recorded on December 26, 1916, "Council at four. Decided I must go to London. . . ." Parliament was summoned for January 18 in order that business should advance as far as possible before the Prime Minister's departure. Speaking in the Commons on January 22, Sir Wilfrid Laurier, while expressing some constitutional doubts, announced that he would agree to an adjournment to facilitate Borden's attendance at the London meeting. The Prime Minister sailed on February 15, accompanied by two of his least important cabinet colleagues, J. D. Hazen, Minister of Marine and Fisheries and of the Naval Service, and Robert Rogers, Minister of Public Works, whose chief qualification for the mission seems to have been that they wanted to go. The Minister of Finance, Sir Thomas White, did not care to make another journey to England at this time.[9] The invaluable Loring Christie went with his chief.

When the "Imperial War Cabinet" met for the first time in London on March 2, 1917, there was an important gap at the table. W. M. Hughes, the aggressive Prime Minister of Australia, had visited England in 1916. Like Borden in 1915, he was invited to the cabinet (though not, he complained, regularly) and, again like Borden, he found the general situation concerning the Dominions unsatisfactory. But he was a louder man than Borden. As Lloyd George remarked, the consultations between Hughes and Asquith "were not agreeable to either". Now Australia was in political turmoil; and it was not represented in the Imperial War Cabinet until the cabinet's second series of sessions in 1918.[10] New Zealand, with a coalition government, had to have two representatives, Massey and Ward.

South Africa's Prime Minister, Botha, did not come, but was represented by the Minister of Defence, Lieutenant-General J. C. Smuts. India, which was not a self-governing unit of the Empire, was to have representation of a sort: the Secretary of State for India and three assistants ("assessors") appointed by the (British) government of India; two of the three had brown faces. Sir E. P. Morris, Prime Minister of Newfoundland, was also a member of the new "Cabinet". As for Canada, it was resolved, probably because of the New Zealand situation, that she should have two members, Borden and Sir George Perley, Minister of Overseas Military Forces and still Acting High Commissioner. Rogers and Hazen were among those "also present", as the minutes put it.[11] The United Kingdom was represented by the members of the British War Cabinet, which continued to exist and meet as a separate body. The Dominion ministers were not members of it except when they attended by invitation, as Borden did on March 6.[12] The Colonial Secretary, Walter Long, though not a member of the British War Cabinet, was ex officio a member of the imperial body. Lloyd George, of course, presided over both cabinets.

As forecast in the British cable of January 1, an Imperial War Conference met concurrently with the Imperial War Cabinet, though on alternate days, to discuss matters of imperial concern not directly connected with the war. It met at the Colonial Office under the chairmanship of the Colonial Secretary.[13]

In one notable respect these gatherings in London differed from the Imperial Conferences of the past. The arrangements for them, including membership, were made by decision of the British government, whereas the procedures of Imperial Conferences had been decided by vote of the members. The inclusion of Indian representatives, for instance, was contrary to a decision of the conference of 1907. However, the Imperial War Conference passed a resolution recording its view that that decision should be modified to permit India to be fully represented at future Imperial Conferences.[14] India, like the self-governing Dominions, was making great sacrifices for the common cause.

Sir Maurice Hankey, who was secretary of both War Cabinets, was apparently responsible for the designation "Imperial War Cabinet". L. S. Amery, an assistant secretary, had, he claims, suggested the association of the Dominion representatives whom Lloyd George was inviting to come over with the British War Cabinet.[15] These men, and apparently Lloyd George himself, evidently hoped that the Imperial War Cabinet would be a genuine central imperial executive, a body capable of making decisions and carrying them out. The British Prime Minister could hardly have been more definite on this point than he was in his opening remarks to the first meeting:

> Perhaps you will permit me, on behalf of the British Government, to give the representatives of the great Dominions and of the Indian Empire welcome to the first Imperial Cabinet ever held in the British Empire. I need not dwell upon the essential distinction between this gathering and any other Imperial gathering we have ever held of representatives of the Empire. Previous gatherings were very properly characterised as Conferences, but this is a Cabinet in the real sense of the term, with power to take decisions and to give effect to them. . . .[16]

Nevertheless, it soon became apparent that the Dominion representatives took a different view of the gathering. Lloyd George's interpretation was not challenged at the council board (perhaps it might have been if Hughes had been there) but within a fortnight Borden, speaking to the Empire Parliamentary Association, presented a somewhat different one:

> For the first time in the Empire's history there are sitting in London two Cabinets, both properly constituted and both exercising well-defined powers. Over each of them the Prime Minister of the United Kingdom presides. One of them is designated as the "War Cabinet", which chiefly devotes itself to such questions touching the prosecution of the war as primarily concern the United Kingdom. The other is designated as the "Imperial War Cabinet", which has a wider purpose, jurisdiction and personnel. To its deliberations have been summoned representatives of all the Empire's self-governing Dominions. We meet there on terms of equality under the presidency of the First Minister of the United Kingdom; we meet there as equals, he is *primus inter pares*. Ministers from six nations sit around the Council Board, all of them responsible to their respective Parliaments and to the people of the countries which they represent. Each nation has its voice upon questions of common concern and highest importance as the deliberations proceed; each preserves unimpaired its perfect autonomy, its self-government, and the responsibility of its Ministers to their own electorate. For many years the thought of statesmen and students in every part of the Empire has centred around the question of future constitutional relations; it may be that now, as in the past, the necessity imposed by great events has given the answer.*

* The *Report* of the War Cabinet for 1917 gives the date of this address as April 3. Borden in his *Memoirs* gives it as April 2, a date which is supported by his contemporary diary.

The following year, when in England for the second series of Imperial War Cabinet meetings, Borden, speaking again to the same association,[17] made his point still more distinctly:

... It has been said that the term "Imperial War Cabinet" is a misnomer. The word "Cabinet" is unknown to the law. The meaning of "Cabinet" has developed from time to time. For my part I see no incongruity whatever in applying the term "Cabinet" to the association of Prime Ministers and other Ministers who meet around a common council board to debate and to determine the various needs of the Empire. If I should attempt to describe it, I should say it is a Cabinet of Governments. Every Prime Minister who sits around that board is responsible to his own Parliament and to his own people; the conclusion of the War Cabinet can only be carried out by the Parliaments of the different nations of our Imperial Commonwealth. Thus, each Dominion, each nation, retains its perfect autonomy. I venture to believe, and I thus expressed myself last year, that in this may be found the genesis of a development in the constitutional relations of the Empire, which will form the basis of its unity in the years to come.

Borden, it is pretty evident, considered that the Imperial War Cabinet system was probably the institutional answer to the problem which he had long been considering, but which he had regarded as one for the British authorities to solve: the problem of providing Canada with an adequate voice in the determination of imperial policy. But he was unwilling to interpret this system in terms that detracted from Canadian autonomy.

Lloyd George, with his usual sure instinct, was quick to sense that the remarks with which he had welcomed the overseas premiers were not realistic. When on May 17, 1917 he spoke in the British House of Commons about the Imperial War Cabinet, whose first series of sessions had lately concluded, he used rather different terms. The essence of the new institution, he said, was "that the responsible heads of the Governments of the Empire, with those Ministers who are specially entrusted with the conduct of Imperial Policy should meet together at regular intervals to confer about foreign policy and matters connected therewith, and come to decisions in regard to them which, subject to the control of their own Parliaments, they will then severally execute. By this means they will be able to obtain full information about all aspects of Imperial affairs, and to determine by consultation together the policy of the Empire in its most vital aspects, without infringing in any degree the autonomy which its parts at present enjoy." Lloyd George explained further that at the last session (on May 2) he had proposed on behalf of the British government "that meetings of an Imperial Cabinet should be annually, or at any intermediate time when matters of urgent Imperial concern require to be settled, and that the Imperial Cabinet should consist of the Prime Minister of the United Kingdom and such of his colleagues as deal specially with Imperial affairs, of the Prime Minister of each of the Dominions, or some specially accredited alternate possessed of equal authority, and of a representative of the Indian people to be appointed by the Government of India." This proposal had been cordially approved and, Lloyd George added, "we hope that the holding of an annual Imperial Cabinet to discuss foreign affairs and other aspects of Imperial policy will become an accepted convention of the British Constitution."[18]

In the meeting on May 2 Sir Robert Borden had strongly supported Lloyd George's proposal, largely on the ground that it gave scope to the Dominions' rapidly developing sense of nationality:

> He considered the step of summoning an Imperial War Cabinet had been a very remarkable one, which had met the national consciousness of the Overseas Dominions in a way in which it had never been met before. Speaking for Canada, he wished to lay stress on the tremendous power with which the sense of nationhood had developed there in the last three years, and he was confident that it would be most unfortunate if the step in advance now taken were not repeated. The Prime Minister's view of the constitution of future Imperial Cabinets corresponded very much with what had been in his own mind. . . . He considered that the step taken had been a very remarkable advance, and one which would be looked upon as such in future years if it became a convention of our Constitution, a Constitution founded on usage. He heartily welcomed it.

The only Dominion representative to express any reservations about Lloyd George's suggestion was Smuts, who said that it seemed to him "tentatively to be the best solution".[19]

What actually went on in these London meetings that commended them so strongly to the men from overseas? The minutes kept by Hankey and his staff enable us to eavesdrop on what happened around the table.

The meetings, of course, gave the British government an opportunity to state and explain to the Dominions the nature of the further assistance it needed from them for the prosecution of the war. In the light of Lloyd George's letter to Long (above, page 203), it is not surprising that in his initial statement to the Imperial War Cabinet he emphasized the overpowering importance of manpower: "The first thing we must get is this: we must get more men."[20] This was to be the chief message that Borden took home to Canada.

It was a grim message, but the Dominion politicians doubtless appreciated it for its frankness. They appreciated, too, the fact that in the Imperial War Cabinet they were getting genuine information about the course of the war. The Empire's war effort was certainly being directed in a different body—the British War Cabinet; but the First Sea Lord and the Director of Military Operations at the War Office attended the Imperial War Cabinet regularly and reported on events. When special questions arose there were special reports; thus when there was a flurry of anxiety over the heavy casualties being suffered by the Royal Flying Corps, Lieutenant-General Sir David Henderson, Director-General of Military Aeronautics, came to the Imperial Cabinet and made a detailed statement supported by statistics.[21] All this was a change from the conditions of 1915 and 1916.

The minutes record many specific decisions made by the Imperial War Cabinet. A large proportion of these relate to its own procedures. Some, however, dealt with questions of military and foreign policy. The Imperial War Cabinet gave considerable attention to German attacks on hospital ships, and on April 12, 1917 it agreed that reprisals should be undertaken:

> Having regard to the public announcement that reprisals should be taken, and to the impossibility of protecting our hospital ships in any other way, the Imperial War Cabinet were agreed that reprisals in some form or another would now have to be taken. In view of the conclusions of the Committee which had been enquiring into the question, that the only practicable form of reprisals, and the one that had proved most effective in the past, was the aerial bombardment of an open German town, the Imperial War Cabinet, though most reluctant to embark upon a policy which might involve the killing of women and children, were agreed that there was no other alternative. It was explained that the bombardment which would shortly take place would be definitely announced as a reprisal for the sinking of the hospital ship "Asturias". The Imperial War Cabinet decided that —
>
> This measure of reprisal should be followed by a carefully prepared statement of justification by the Admiralty, explaining that no further reprisals would be taken as soon as the Germans ceased their attacks upon our hospital ships.[22]

It will be noted that in this case the Imperial War Cabinet was pursuing decisions already taken elsewhere—actually, by the British War Cabinet.[23] The committee referred to had not been appointed by the Imperial War Cabinet.

The confused situation in Greece, and the disagreements with France over policy there, supplied another topic for discussion in the Imperial War Cabinet. We find it deciding on April 13, 1917 that,

A strongly worded telegram should be sent by the Secretary of State for Foreign Affairs, on behalf of the Imperial War Cabinet, to the French Government, urging that the advance against the Bulgarians on the Salonica Front should be carried out without delay.

The Imperial War Cabinet also instructed Lord Robert Cecil [Minister of Blockade] to telegraph to the French Government that no steps should be taken as regards Greece until the Italian Government had been consulted.[24]

The minutes do not suggest that these initiatives owed much to the Dominion representatives. It would probably be fair to say that the British government was choosing at this point to conduct some aspects of foreign policy through the Imperial War Cabinet.

The Imperial War Cabinet also devoted some time to considering the future terms of peace. On April 12, 1917 it set up two sub-committees on the question, one under Lord Curzon (Lord President of the Council) to consider "territorial *desiderata*", the other under Lord Milner (a member of the British War Cabinet without portfolio) to consider "economic and other non-territorial *desiderata*". The reports of these committees were discussed at some length on April 26 and May 1. Borden's chief contribution was to emphasize the importance of discussion with the Empire's allies and particularly with the United States: "He considered that the United States and the British Empire in agreement could do more than anything else to maintain the peace of the world."[25] The final decision was highly general:

The Imperial War Cabinet considers that the policy of the Empire should have the following ends in view:

a) The re-establishment of liberty and public right in Europe and on the high seas, the settlement of the political boundaries of Europe in accordance with the wishes of its peoples, and the liberation of the oppressed nationalities of the Turkish Empire from the Turkish yoke.

b) The security and integrity of the British Empire and of the nations of which it is composed.

c) The framing of measures for the preservation of lasting peace in concert with our Allies.[26]

All the discussions that have been mentioned took place during the sessions of 1917. In 1918 the Imperial War Cabinet was to take a considerably more active interest in the direction of the war.

On one other matter—the "constitution of the Empire"—the sessions of 1917 had important results.

These found their chief expression in Resolution IX of the Imperial War Conference, passed on April 16, 1917. The text of the resolution may as well be given at once:

The Imperial War Conference are of opinion that the readjustment of the constitutional relations of the component parts of the Empire is too important and intricate a subject to be dealt with during the War, and that it should form the subject of a special Imperial Conference to be summoned as soon as possible after the cessation of hostilities.

They deem it their duty, however, to place on record their view that any such readjustment, while thoroughly preserving all existing powers of self-government and complete control of domestic affairs, should be based upon a full recognition of the Dominions as autonomous nations of an Imperial Commonwealth, and of India as an important portion of the same, should recognize the right of the Dominions and India to an adequate voice in foreign policy and in foreign relations, and should provide effective arrangements for continuous consultation in all important matters of common Imperial concern, and for such necessary concerted action, founded on consultation, as the several Governments may determine.[27]

Thus while formal consideration of the constitution of the Empire (and the use of the new word "Commonwealth" is one of the notable features of the resolution)* is postponed until after the war, certain fundamental

* The word seems to have been first applied to the Empire by Lord Rosebery in 1884. More recently it had been given some currency, one might say, by Lionel Curtis (above, page 201). Although Borden used the words "a new and greater Imperial Commonwealth" in his speech to the Empire Parliamentary Association on April 2, the phrase does not occur in his first draft of the resolution; it may have been contributed by Smuts. "Commonwealth" was hardly a favourite Canadian word. Even Mackenzie King, as late as 1923, wrote in his diary, "I confess I dislike the word Commonwealth—it seems an affectation. Empire is losing some of the distaste it had. It seems about the only word to serve the purpose."[28]

principles are firmly stated in the meantime. In particular, the status of the Dominions as autonomous nations is proclaimed, as are their right to a voice in foreign policy and the desirability of a common imperial policy based on consultation.

The history of this celebrated resolution illustrates the extent to which Sir Robert Borden's contributions to the imperial discussions in London in 1917–18 have been underrated. Historians have accorded General Smuts far more credit and consideration. Smuts was a striking figure; on the one hand his undoubted intellectual distinction, and on the other his romantic appeal as the Boer general of the war of 1899–1902 who became a pillar of the British community, served to compel attention. In Britain he has been regarded, in fact, as a sort of honorary Englishman; his statue stands in Westminster near the Houses of Parliament. (You will look in vain for any effigy of Borden or Mackenzie King in those purlieus.) He has regularly been described as the author of Resolution IX. His biographer began by saying that Smuts "drafted and carried through" the resolution, and finally convinced himself that he moved it.[29] Borden, while stating that he himself moved the resolution, added incorrectly that Smuts seconded it.[30]

The recorded facts are that in the Imperial War Conference on April 16, 1917 Resolution IX was moved by Borden, seconded by W. F. Massey, and supported by Smuts.[31] All these and others had had parts in shaping it, but it is now possible to say with considerable confidence that it was Borden's conception (unless it was Christie's!), that Borden (or Christie?) made the first draft of it, and that it was Borden who "carried through" the project to its final approval. The evidence consists mainly of a file of successive drafts of the resolution, in the handwriting of the various principals in the discussion, which was evidently preserved and annotated by Loring Christie and remained in the records of the Canadian Department of External Affairs.[32] This file makes it possible to reconstruct the discussions of March and April 1917.[33]

It is unnecessary to do this in detail here, but an outline can be given. The first draft in the file, marked "Borden", consists of just one long sentence:

While the Imperial War Conference are of opinion that the readjustment of the constitutional relations of the component parts of the Empire is too important and intricate a matter to be dealt with during the war and should form the subject of a special Imperial Conference after the war (*in which* *all recognized political parties should be represented if possible)** they place on record their view that any such adjustment should be based upon a full recognition of the status of the Dominions as nations of the Empire, should declare and establish their right to an adequate voice in foreign policy and in foreign relations, and should include necessary arrangements for continuous consultation in regard to all important matters of common concern such as defence and for concerted action therein when necessary.

Like other drafts in the file, this one is undated. It evidently formed a basis for discussion in a committee consisting of Borden, Massey, and Smuts. Borden's diary indicates that this group first met on March 19, when also Borden first met Smuts, who impressed him as "a strong & straightforward man". On the 21st, at the initial meeting of the Imperial War Conference, the three men were formally constituted a committee "to prepare agenda".[34] On the 22nd, Borden recorded, they had an hour's discussion "as to agenda and as to resolutions to be moved respecting constl. relations":

I insisted on a clause declaring our right to an adequate voice in foreign policy. Smuts fears this may involve responsibility for financial aid in defence &c.[35]

This account of Smuts' attitude is supported by a draft by Smuts included in the file. It is evident that the South African was very conscious of the importance of giving no ammunition to the Nationalist opposition in his country.

On March 27, with these difficulties with Smuts not fully resolved, Borden consulted the Colonial Secretary. Long evidently preferred Borden's version and that evening the three-man committee reached agreement.[36] Probably the same day Long wrote to Lloyd George describing the situation as he knew it:

Massey is very Imperialistic and determined to force the issue. Ward ditto; – Borden is very anxious for progress, says "My people expect it" "they will be very disappointed" etc. At the same time we know Laurier is watching, that an Election must take place before very long, that he has the French Canadians against him, and that if he makes any slip Laurier will use it against him—but I am sure he is ready to be *led* on.

Smuts is of course in a difficult position, he would face the music I feel

* The italicized words are struck out in the original.

confident if he had only himself to consider, but Botha and his Government are very much afraid of both questions* and Borden does not help so Smuts is all for putting off "till after the War". To meet his views and carry him along Borden toned down his Resolution—Borden talked this all over with me very fully and confidentially. . . .[37]

Although Long spoke of a coming meeting which was to consider the matter, the records of the British War Cabinet contain no reference to the resolution.[38] On March 28 Borden gave notice of his motion. There was further modification of the draft in various details. When it came before the conference formally on April 16 Sir S. P. Sinha, one of the Indian "assessors", asked that India should be brought within its scope (something that none of the Dominion representatives seems to have thought of) and Borden accepted his amendment.[39]

The passage of Resolution IX marks an advance of some note in imperial constitutional development. The new status for the Dominions which it recognized had been won by their soldiers on the battlefield, but the initiative towards obtaining the recognition had been largely Borden's. Quite apart from the evidence for his primacy in the matter which we have noted, his mark is clear upon the resolution, in particular, in the phrase "an adequate voice in foreign policy and foreign relations", which echoed declarations made by Sir Robert on many occasions since 1910. No doubt it was a satisfaction to him to see his conceptions formally written into a statement of imperial constitutional principles; though, characteristically, he said little of this in his diary. The satisfaction might have been dimmed had he been able to see into the future. Canadian policy was not to continue to follow the line he had mapped for it. "Status", yes; "closer union", no.

On May 18, 1917 Borden laid before the Canadian Parliament the record of the Imperial War Cabinet and the Imperial War Conference so far, emphasizing Resolution IX and the proposal to hold annual meetings. (He presented the latter as an "offer" of the British government rather than as a decision of the Imperial War Cabinet—and indeed there had been no formal resolution.) He spoke of the new arrangements in a tone of warm approval, while cautiously refusing to "prophesy" what form the

* That is, "closer union and Imperial preference". The Conference passed a separate resolution on the latter question.

constitution of the Empire might finally take. He went on to speak firmly on the question of Dominion autonomy:

> But this at least may be said of Mr. Lloyd George's proposal: it does not sacrifice in the slightest degree the autonomy of the power of self-government which is possessed by each of the dominions. The ministers from overseas go there as the heads of their governments. They are responsible to their own parliaments; as the Prime Minister of the United Kingdom goes there responsible to his parliament.
>
> ... There is, on the other hand, opportunity for consultation, co-operation and united action, which I venture to think will prove of great advantage to the Empire as a whole.

Sir Wilfrid Laurier commented the same day. Not surprisingly, his enthusiasm for these innovations identified with Borden's government was distinctly restrained; but his chief criticism was of nomenclature. Bonar Law had been reported as saying that the Imperial War Cabinet was at once executive and consultative. This, said Laurier, was unacceptable doctrine. The Imperial War Cabinet had no executive power; it could simply report to the Crown in Parliament in the various countries of the Empire, and the various parliaments could accept or reject its conclusions. It was clearly the use of the word cabinet that Sir Wilfrid objected to, though he did not precisely say so. "I do not object to it as a consultative body. But I object to terms being used which, in their very nature, cannot accord with the rules of parliamentary government. . . . But if I am told that there is a body which is to be known by the name of the Imperial Council, I am not disposed to quarrel with the name. I do not object to there being consultations, quite the contrary. My right hon. friend has stated that this body—so named, and misnamed—is to meet once every year. As to this, I have no objection whatever." It appeared that the two sides of the House were agreed on essentials.

THE YEAR OF UNEXPECTED VICTORY

When Borden returned to England for the second series of Imperial War Cabinet sessions in June 1918, it was as the leader of a new administration. Four days after landing in Canada in May 1917 he had announced to Parliament the government's intention of introducing a measure authorizing compulsory service. His colleagues from Quebec had no illusions about the consequences:

Patenaude* and Blondin said they are prepared to stand by us but that it will kill them politically and the party for 25 years.[40]

After a bitter fight the Military Service Act received the royal assent on August 29. The Liberal party had split on the issue. An amendment by Sir Wilfrid Laurier providing for a referendum was defeated.

In May Borden had approached Laurier with a proposal for a coalition government, but after a fortnight the negotiations foundered on the rock of conscription. In October, however, Borden formed a Union government without Laurier, composed of fifteen Conservatives, nine conscriptionist Liberals, and one Labour representative. On December 17 there was a general election. The campaign was fierce and violent. The general result was that the Unionist party won a decisive victory, taking 153 seats to the Laurier Liberals' 82. But in the province of Quebec Borden got only 3 seats against Laurier's 62. Borden's two French-Canadian ministers were defeated. Quebec was politically isolated, and French Canada found itself represented in the cabinet only by a senator.[41] The conscription crisis of 1917-18 left on the public life of Canada a deep mark, which would affect the external policies of the next generation.

The change of ministry brought with it a change in Canadian representation in London. Sir George Perley had disliked his position as *Acting* High Commissioner combined with a seat in the cabinet, and underrated the advantages he obtained from the arrangement. As early as the first month of the war he had urged Borden to make the high commissionership itself a cabinet portfolio, something Borden was not prepared to do. On the advent of the Union government, Perley was at last appointed High Commissioner, but ceased to be a minister, being succeeded as Minister of Overseas Military Forces by Sir Edward Kemp, formerly Minister of Militia and Defence.[42] After the first sessions of the Imperial War Cabinet ended in May 1917, direct Canadian contact with the British War Cabinet lapsed, and as Leo Amery pointed out, there was no consultation concerning the serious military decisions that had to be taken that summer:

The British Government was confronted with the very difficult responsibility of sanctioning, and afterwards continuing to sanction, the offensive in Flanders.† It had to shoulder that responsibility alone. Consultation by cable

* Patenaude subsequently lost his nerve and resigned.

† This was the offensive that ended in what is usually called the Battle of Passchendaele.

on decisions of that character is practically impossible and was rightly not attempted.[43]

In fact, there had been no strategic discussions of the sort suggested here during the Imperial War Cabinet's 1917 meetings. But they could hardly have been avoided if that body had continued to meet through the summer.

When in November 1917 the Canadian government raised the question of Dominion representation at an Inter-Allied Conference then proposed, the British took the opportunity to inquire what would, from the Canadian viewpoint, be the best date for another session of the Imperial War Cabinet and Imperial War Conference, and simultaneously suggested that any visiting Canadian ministers would be welcomed to the British cabinet, "not of course as members of War Cabinet but for consultation". Borden replied that he would be glad to have Kemp invited to the War Cabinet, and Kemp attended meetings on January 3 and 4, 1918. Perley seized the opportunity to revive the suggestion that the High Commissioner should be a member of the Canadian cabinet and should represent Canada at meetings of the British War Cabinet.[44] But Perley's days of attending War Cabinets were over.

Borden explained that he could not expect to visit England until after the coming parliamentary session ended, in the middle of May or at the beginning of June. In fact he sailed from New York on May 27. He was accompanied by three of his colleagues: N. W. Rowell, President of the Privy Council; Arthur Meighen, Minister of the Interior; and J. A. Calder, Minister of Immigration and Colonization. These were later relieved by Major-General S. C. Mewburn, Minister of Militia and Defence, and C. C. Ballantyne, Minister of Marine and Fisheries and of the Naval Service. Kemp also attended. For the 1918 sessions all the Dominion ministers were considered members of the Imperial War Cabinet.[45]

The second series of sessions began on June 11 and ended on August 2. The atmosphere was one of crisis; the Allies, as Lloyd George put it, were passing through a "rather dark tunnel". The Bolshevik Revolution had put the Russian ally out of the war; on the other hand, the new ally, the United States, had been disappointingly slow in placing forces in the field. And the German offensive in the west beginning on March 21 had been a great military disaster for the Allies. The British Prime Minister did not mince words in describing the situation to the first Imperial War Cabinet meeting on June 11; there would be, he said, "a very critical time during the next six weeks or couple of months", until large American aid could arrive.[46] Nor did Sir Robert Borden mince words at the second meeting two days later. Obviously shaken by Lloyd George's exposition, he had consulted Sir Arthur Currie, who was in England, and, he told the Imperial War Cabinet, "ordered him to tell me the truth so far as he understood it with respect to the occurrences of the past few months." The Corps Commander, clearly still bitter from the experience of Passchendaele, had some hard things to say about the practices of the British Army, and Borden passed them on:

> There was lack of preparation and of foresight. There was also lack of proper intelligence. Three days before the offensive of the 21st March a tip was given by the British Intelligence service to the Canadian Army Corps that there would be no offensive at all. . . .
>
> I am informed that there has been conspicuous failure to remove incompetent officers. . . . Is it or is it not the case that men of great ability who have gone into the army during this war have been systematically held down to positions no higher than Brigadier-Generals? If that is the case, I say with all respect, that it amounts to scrapping the brains of the nation in the greatest struggle of history. . . .
>
> . . . The future of this war in more senses than one depends upon our earnestness. We came over to fight in earnest; and Canada will fight it out to the end. But earnestness must be expressed in organisation, foresight, preparation. Let the past bury its dead, but for God's sake let us get down to earnest endeavour and hold this line until the Americans can come in and help us to sustain it till the end.[47]

This was perhaps the plainest speaking ever heard in the Imperial War Cabinet. Borden's remarks were certainly not objectionable to Lloyd George. They might have been even more welcome had the Canadian Prime Minister attacked Sir Douglas Haig; but Currie evidently had not criticized the Commander-in-Chief. Later the same day Lloyd George had an interview with Borden and Currie. He told Hankey that he had "ascertained that Smuts had prompted Borden".[48] This does not seem to have been strictly true. Smuts was now a member of the British War Cabinet, an interesting constitutional situation since he was a member of neither house of the British Parliament. Borden had in fact taken Currie to see Smuts, and he records that he thought the South African "virtually promised to support me". Smuts, however, remained silent on June 13.[49]

Borden's strictures went unanswered by the British military authorities. He recalled later that Sir Henry Wilson, the Chief of the Imperial General Staff, left the room when he began to speak, but that Lloyd George sent for him when it became evident that Borden was criticizing the British command. (The minutes note his arrival as Borden began his criticisms, but say nothing of the earlier departure.) According to Borden, Lord Milner, the Secretary of State for War, who was sitting beside Sir Robert, whispered to him that what he had said would be answered. But it never was, then or later.[50]

The political authorities could not be so cavalier, especially as Massey of New Zealand had associated himself with Borden's position. "There is something wrong somewhere," he said, "and we have got to find it."[51] Lloyd George asked Hankey's advice as to how to meet the situation. The secretary suggested that action must await the arrival of Hughes from Australia, which was not to be unrepresented this year as it had been in 1917; and "the best method would be to deal with it in a Committee of Prime Ministers only".[52] Lloyd George adopted this suggestion. On June 14 he told the Imperial War Cabinet that the issues raised by Borden "could not be left where they were", but that Australia's views must first be heard. Hughes attended his first Imperial Cabinet meeting on June 18. On June 20 he spoke in terms similar to Borden's: "He wished to feel sure that the sacrifices that were being made were not wasted for want of proper leadership and strategy." Lloyd George then put forward Hankey's formula:

> He suggested that the whole issue should be relegated for preliminary discussion to a Committee consisting of the Prime Ministers, including General Smuts, as General Botha's representative, and the Secretary of State for War, with the Chief of the Imperial General Staff if his presence was required, and that this Committee should meet without delay. Any conclusions which the Committee might come to should then come back to the Imperial War Cabinet for discussion.

This was agreed to.[53]

Borden had started something, something that would have gone a good deal further than it did if the war had not ended so soon. The Committee of Prime Ministers dealt with matters not included in its official terms of reference just quoted (which were, in fact, decidedly vague), and may be said to have come closer to being a real cabinet than the Imperial War Cabinet itself. Hankey's description of the situation is worth quoting:

> These meetings of Prime Ministers rather tended to overshadow the Imperial War Cabinet, although both bodies were meeting regularly. Nominally and constitutionally the Prime Ministers were merely a sub-committee of the Imperial War Cabinet appointed to consider and report upon recent failures on the Western Front and the conduct of the war by the High Command. In fact, however, force of circumstances compelled them, every time they met, to take decisions on current matters that would brook no delay, and the specific investigations for which they were appointed proceeded somewhat slowly. . . . The Imperial War Cabinet was supposed to deal with the wider conduct of the war; the British War Cabinet with the British war effort; and the Prime Ministers with the reference already described. Inevitably, however, with events moving fast there was a good deal of overlap, but the threatened confusion was mitigated by the fact that Lloyd George presided at all the meetings, that the Empire Prime Ministers were members of the Imperial War Cabinet as well as of the Committee of Prime Ministers; and that the secretary was the same for all these meetings.[54]

One detail has interest. Lloyd George told Hankey that he did not want minutes of the Prime Ministers' meetings circulated; he was afraid (so he said) that they would "talk for the Minutes, instead of what they really think". But he wanted a record, which Hankey called "Secretary's Notes". Hankey wrote, "I am sending copies of them to Smuts, Milner, and CIGS to check."[55] The distinction between the members of the British War Cabinet and the Dominion Prime Ministers is evident. Hankey knew who his bosses were.

The Prime Ministers had their first meeting on June 21. The chief business was a decision as to whether or not to transfer certain forces from Palestine to France. Hughes, however, made "a fiery statement demanding a greater voice in the war", to which Borden rejoined that "if he had no voice it was because he neglected to attend the Imperial War Cabinet last year."[56]

In the course of the summer the Prime Ministers attacked the task originally committed to them, not only reviewing the past but also turning their eyes to war policy for the future. Borden left for Canada in mid-August, and it was desirable that a report should be prepared before his departure. As with so many cabinet papers, the drafting fell to Hankey. The first to see his draft were members of the British War Cabinet. With their comments incorporated, it was circulated to the Dominion Prime Ministers and discussed by them at a meeting on the morning of August 16. Borden left London the same day. Hankey recorded that the report was approved by all the Prime Ministers save Hughes, from whom he got an "enigmatic letter" on the subject. "The result was that I could never get Lloyd George to sign it, or to allow me to circulate it. . . ." It remained an unsigned draft.[57]

That the Prime Ministers of the Dominions should have been engaged in 1918 in considering the future conduct of the war was a remarkable fact, and the draft report[58] was itself a somewhat remarkable document. It more than once referred in critical terms to the Flanders offensive of 1917. With respect to the reverses in the spring of 1918, it drew the conclusion that "too much importance cannot be attached to the selection of the very best men for the Higher Commands and Staff of the Army", and specifically made the point that Borden had dwelt upon, that the higher posts should be open to "civilian soldiers, who not only now form the bulk of the Army, but include the best intelligence of the nation". It emphasized that ultimate control should rest with the civil government, which, "as trustee of the nation, has the right and duty of assuring itself that military operations are not undertaken involving casualties out of proportion to their probable effect on the final result of the War". It proceeded:

> It follows that the Head of the Government should keep himself informed beforehand, through the Chief of the Imperial General Staff, of any major operation to be undertaken in any theatre of war, and should use his discretion in consulting his colleagues of the Imperial War Cabinet on the subject.

The British manpower situation was serious, and the Empire's allies should be informed that it was no longer possible to maintain the British field army at its existing strength and also to keep up the present scale of industrial production. A situation should not be allowed to develop by which by the end of 1919 the British Army would be so shattered "as to have become an inconsiderable factor in the military situation". Therefore the army on the Western Front should be gradually reduced "to such size as the Government are satisfied that they can maintain at full strength throughout 1919": the figure suggested was about thirty-six divisions, including Dominion forces.

Nobody had suggested to the Committee of Prime Ministers that victory was likely to be attainable in 1918. The Committee recommended a cautious policy during the rest of that year, husbanding resources for a later decisive effort. The report indeed accepted the possibility that such an effort on the Western Front would have to be postponed until 1920. The Allied force in Italy should be strengthened and any opportunity for eliminating Austria, Bulgaria or Turkey from the war should be seized. The "re-creation" in some manner of the Eastern Front, forcing the Germans to send forces back there, would be a most important development. And there was a bloodthirsty note, foreshadowing the unpleasant shape of the distant future:

> The Committee attach importance to the intensification of aerial warfare, particularly so far as this can be directed to the bombing of German towns, by which means alone it appears at present practicable to force the German people to experience the worst hardships of modern warfare, and to realise what the future has in store for them if the War is continued.

This pessimistic paper was being overtaken by events even before the Prime Ministers discussed it on August 16. That they could have thought in terms of the war continuing into 1920 is evidence of the gulf that had developed, in terms of information and confidence, between the government in London and GHQ in France. To bridge this gulf, we have noted, was one of the objects of the paper. As it was, the great Allied attack east of Amiens on August 8, spearheaded by the Canadians and the Australians, was the beginning of the end.* This victory put a stop to the talk, of which some had been heard in the Committee of Prime Ministers, of a change in the command of the British forces in France. On November 11, with their allies fallen away from them, their Emperor in flight and their armies decisively defeated in the field, the Germans surrendered.

Long afterwards Sir Robert Borden read with indignation published portions of Sir Henry Wilson's diaries which suggested that the overseas representatives in the Imperial War Cabinet were faint-hearted. Wilson himself, said Borden, was the most faint-hearted of all; he considered July 1, 1919 the earliest possible date for a decisive attack on the Western Front.[60] The minutes of the Imperial War Cabinet, however, suggest that there was one overseas minister who had doubts about persisting with

* It is interesting that Hankey notes that on August 1 Borden told the Prime Ministers in strict confidence that he had heard that the Canadian Corps was being moved with a view to a coming offensive.[59] The implied assumption is that Currie was keeping his Prime Minister informed of military events.

the war until a clear-cut victory was won. This was Smuts. At one of the earliest meetings of the Imperial Cabinet, on March 23, 1917, a discussion took place on Smuts' initiative on the possibility of securing peace that year, "even if that meant some modification of the maximum demands which we had publicly defined". And on August 14, 1918 he told the Imperial War Cabinet that he was "very much against fighting to the absolute end, because I think that, although the end will be fatal to the enemy, it may possibly be fatal to us too".[61] Modern opinion may see much good sense in this attitude, but it did not commend itself to the majority then, and certainly not to Borden. The Canadian Prime Minister's view had been expressed on June 13: "Canada will fight it out to the end."[62]

The Imperial War Cabinet sessions of 1918 witnessed a further discussion on constitutional relations, in which W. M. Hughes took a leading part. It began in the Imperial War Conference, which invited the Imperial War Cabinet to give consideration to the creation of "suitable machinery" for a change in administrative arrangements and channels of communication to bring the represented governments "more directly in touch with each other". Launching the Cabinet discussion on July 23 Hughes said it was generally agreed that "the time had come when the self-governing Dominions should be in direct touch with the Prime Minister of the United Kingdom". While the Imperial War Cabinet was in session, there was such contact; but when they separated they would have to "meander again through the indirect channels of the Colonial Office". There should be direct touch with the British Prime Minister; "a formal but real recognition of the fact that the Dominions were participants in the councils of the Empire on a footing of equality". Borden supported Hughes. He had, he said, "not a word of criticism against the attitude of the Colonial Office", but the change suggested was logical:

He pointed out that the Dominions had come into the war voluntarily, as free nations of the Empire, because they believed it to be their duty. But the British Government could not call upon Canada to come into another war with regard to the causes of which she had had no voice. Canada was a nation of 8,000,000, twice as large as the United States when they became independent, and they must have a voice in foreign affairs. Unless she could have that voice in the foreign relations of the Empire as a whole, she would before long have an independent voice in her own foreign affairs outside the Empire. At present the Imperial War Cabinet met for only two months in the year. It was essential that there should be means of constant consultation. . . .

General Smuts was inclined to shelve the whole question of machinery until after the war. The Foreign Secretary, A. J. Balfour,

pointed out that the real crux of the problem lay in how secure unity of control to equal States over a single foreign policy . . . it was not possible to have more than one Foreign Office or one foreign policy at a time. That was the problem the solution of which was most difficult to find. . . . If the united strength of the Empire was to be put forward for any external purpose, the Dominions would have to exercise a share in the control of a single Foreign Office.

Sir Robert Borden remarked that unless the Dominions shared in the direction of foreign policy they could not share in the responsibility which it entailed.

The discussion continued on July 25. On that day N. W. Rowell raised specifically the question of the position of Governors General. "He suggested that the status of the Governors-General had largely changed as a matter of practice, and urged that the change should now be frankly recognised, and that the Governors-General should no longer act as a channel of communication with the Colonial Office, but should be confined to their position as representatives of the Sovereign." The discussion ranged over permanent arrangements for the future as well as immediate expedients, and Borden was moved to an interesting declaration. Hughes had said that Australia would have nothing to do with any Committee to discuss "a scheme of Imperial Federation" or anything of the sort: "He thought that the view of the Australian people would be that, if Australian representatives were sent to a Council of Empire, they would be entangled and doubly committed if a war broke out, and that the last state would, in fact be worse than the first."

Sir Robert Borden admitted that a similar view was also held in certain sections in Canada. Sir W. Laurier had always taken up that attitude. He himself had disagreed. He would himself sooner go out of the Empire altogether than adopt this attitude. If he stayed in the Empire it was on condition that he had a voice in the conduct of its affairs.

The matter was again discussed on July 30. Borden then informed the Imperial War Cabinet that, in the meantime, the Dominion Prime Ministers had met separately to discuss a formula put forward by Lloyd George, which had included "an informal Committee to investigate the machinery for carrying on the business of the Empire after the war"—the suggestion that had aroused Hughes. While agreeing with the British Prime Minister's other proposals, they were not prepared to agree with this one. It was at once dropped, and the Imperial War Cabinet's decision made at this meeting was as follows:

I (1) The Prime Ministers of the Dominions, as members of the Imperial War Cabinet, have the right of direct communication with the Prime Minister of the United Kingdom, and *vice versa.*

2) Such communications should be confined to questions of Cabinet importance. The Prime Ministers themselves are the judges of such questions.

3) Telegraphic communications between the Prime Ministers should, as a rule, be conducted through the Colonial Office machinery, but this will not exclude the adoption of more direct means of communication in exceptional circumstances.

II In order to secure continuity in the work of the Imperial War Cabinet and a permanent means of consultation during the war on the more important questions of common interest, the Prime Minister of each Dominion has the right to nominate a Cabinet Minister either as a resident or visitor in London to represent him at meetings of the Imperial War Cabinet to be held regularly between the plenary Sessions.[63]

This was the furthest point reached in imperial constitutional development during the war. In mid-August 1918, as we have seen, Borden left for Canada. During his absence four meetings took place denominated "War Cabinet (With Prime Ministers of Dominions)" and given numbers in the Imperial War Cabinet as well as in the British War Cabinet series.[64] No Canadian representative attended. When Borden returned to the Imperial War Cabinet table on November 20 Germany had surrendered, and the task now was to discuss the procedures for making peace.

WASHINGTON: A MILDER CLIMATE

For more than two and a half years, while Britain and Canada fought for their lives against Germany, the United States was neutral. Then, on April 6, 1917, the American Congress voted the republic into the war, and for the first time Canada and the United States found themselves allies. These simple facts dictated the pattern of Canadian-American relations during the years 1914–18.

To anyone well acquainted with the history of the United States, or, it may be added, with the ethnic make-up of the country, it could hardly be a matter of surprise that there was a strong thrust towards avoidance of involvement in Europe's war. But Canadians, though fond of asserting that they understood the United States much better than Englishmen could, in general knew little American history; and increasingly, particularly after Canadian casualty lists began to grow, emotional hostility against American neutralism developed among the Canadian public. At the same time another old Canadian political superstition made itself felt: the "linch-pin" theory—the idea that Canada's special destiny is to serve as interpreter between Great Britain and the United States. This idea both Sir Robert Borden and his adviser Loring Christie cherished; and Sir Robert sought to turn the theory into practice by various speeches which he made in the United States during its period of neutrality. Thus he spoke to the New England Society in New York City on December 22, 1915, and to the Pilgrims' Society there the following day. On November 18, 1916 he was again speaking in New York, to the Lawyers' Club. This speech, largely based on a draft by Christie, argued that the Allies were fighting for the rule of law between nations; it looked forward to "a world tribunal backed when necessary by world-wide force for the restraining of an outlaw nation". Such addresses perhaps had little influence on the American situation. Borden's audiences were undoubtedly composed mainly of Americans who were already whole-heartedly devoted to the Allied cause; those who were pro-German or supporters of neutrality were elsewhere.[65]

In some respects ancient history was repeating itself. The United States was again contending, in its own behalf, for the protection of neutral rights at sea—the old and dangerous question that had helped to bring on the War of 1812. The most potentially perilous period of the war in this respect, from the British point of view, was the earliest months, when the developing British blockade of Germany threatened serious interference with American trade, and there was little German action of which Americans could complain. The danger passed, thanks largely to the tact and good sense of Sir Edward Grey, the British Foreign Secretary, and to his then unassailable prestige in Britain. When the Germans began to use the submarine weapon against merchant shipping things changed. Particularly after the *Lusitania* was sunk (May 7, 1915), taking 128

American citizens to their deaths, the United States became involved in a bitter diplomatic battle with Germany.[66]

Simultaneously, however, contention went on with Britain over her interference with neutral trade. The British felt, as they had in Napoleon's day, that they were fighting freedom's battle, and that the Americans should be helping them instead of trying to strike sea power, their best weapon, from their hands. Woodrow Wilson's government found it only too easy to appear over-righteous, as when it made representations against the arming of British merchant ships. "Any armament . . . on a merchant vessel," wrote Robert Lansing, the Secretary of State, "would seem to have the character of an offensive armament."[67] In September 1916, with the President in possession of drastic powers of retaliation against Britain provided by Congress, both the British Ambassador in Washington and the Colonial Secretary suggested that Canada should use her influence in the American capital to prevent these powers being used. The Ambassador (Sir Cecil Spring-Rice) said that the next two months, the period of the presidential election campaign, were a dangerous time: "It might perhaps be useful, considering the very friendly feelings here towards Canada, if a private warning came from your govt."[68] The Canadian cabinet considered the question on September 21 and, Borden recorded, "We all thought such course unwise."[69] The Prime Minister wrote to Spring-Rice that, in the improbable event of the President's powers really being exercised, "we are unable to believe that consideration of relations with the Dominion would deter those responsible for so serious a course." He added a bit of political wisdom: if political conditions should actually produce the apprehended disaster, "is it not probable that any communication from this Government might be put to a most unfortunate and detrimental use in the heat of an election campaign which will daily grow in intensity?"[70] If the linch-pin functioned at this crisis, it was in a purely negative manner: a procedure, one reflects, which Mackenzie King, a later Prime Minister, would have thoroughly approved. The retaliation never took place.

Relations with the British Empire were not at first improved by Wilson's narrow victory in the election in November, for he set to work at once to bring the combatants to a negotiated peace—a "peace without victory".* Unfortunately his timing was bad; his proposal made on De-

* This phrase, bitterly resented in British quarters, and criticized by many Americans, was used by Wilson in a famous speech of January 22, 1917.

cember 18 followed by less than a week a German invitation to negotiate.[71] Relations were now at their lowest point; on December 23 the Chief of the Imperial General Staff (General Sir William Robertson) actually asked whether a confidential warning of possible serious trouble with the United States should not be sent to Canada. The British War Cabinet wisely decided that this was not necessary.[72] This was the dark hour before the dawn. At the end of January 1917 the Germans announced unrestricted submarine warfare against all merchant vessels in zones surrounding the British Isles and in the Mediterranean. They completed their own destruction by proceeding to sink American ships. The result was Wilson's recommendation to Congress to declare war.

Virtually simultaneously with the American entrance into the war, proposals began to be heard for the representation of Canada in Washington. Within a week, Borden, then in England, had arranged for two Canadian ministers, White and Foster, to be appointed to a delegation which the Foreign Secretary, A. J. Balfour, was to lead on a special mission to the United States. At the same time the Colonial Secretary agreed that there should be a Canadian on the staff of the Washington embassy. This appointment was never made, however, partly perhaps because of hostility in both the embassy and the Governor-General's office. In October 1917, faced with the need for finding a job for his colleague J. D. Hazen when the ministry was reorganized, Borden proposed to send him to Washington as "high commissioner" with a largely independent position: "In matters that may concern the whole Empire he will of course consult with the Embassy but in matters solely touching our own affairs he would communicate direct with the United States Government and its various commissions."[73] Walter Long fought against this, seeking to make Hazen in effect the attaché on the embassy staff agreed to earlier. Borden would not accept any such status; but the whole project collapsed after a report from Spring-Rice on the expense of an establishment in Washington. Hazen subsided into the office of Chief Justice of New Brunswick.[74]

The next proposal for representation had a solid economic basis. The Canadian industrial war effort—directed now by the Imperial Munitions Board, an agency of the British government though headed by an eminent Canadian financier, J. A. (later Sir Joseph) Flavelle—had grown to large proportions and was dependent in great part on materials imported from the United States. The Board itself had an office in the United States, but by the beginning of 1918 Borden was becoming convinced that efficient economic co-operation required official representation and that the necessary facilities were not available through the British Embassy. He may perhaps have been influenced by a strong representation (January 14, 1918) from the Montreal Harbour Commission, which argued "the necessity and urgency of having a Canadian Representative in the United States, so that Canadian interests may be looked after"; the export business of Montreal harbour had been dropping, trade being diverted to American ports due to "American Financing of Business".[75] On January 19 Borden consulted Lloyd Harris, the Imperial Munitions Board representative in the United States, who subsequently wrote to him, "I would think that the proper course for Canada to pursue at present would be to appoint a Canadian War Mission for the purpose of looking after Canadian interests and needs, and also in securing favourable consideration from the United States Government in their dealings with Canada at the present time on all trade matters. . . ."[76] He reported that Flavelle would be glad "to have the work of both offices under the control of myself and associates" if the government so desired.

The Canadian War Mission, with Lloyd Harris as chairman, was set up without consultation with London, though Christie was sent off to Washington to discuss the matter with the British Embassy. The latter had no serious objections; it did make the suggestion that the chairman might be "under" the ambassador, but this was not adopted. On February 2 the order-in-council setting up the War Mission was approved. It did not contend for diplomatic status for the chairman, noting that the negotiations the Mission would conduct were "not diplomatic in their nature but rather are largely of a business and commercial character requiring different, more direct and prompt treatment". It provided further,

> The Chairman will keep His Majesty's High Commissioner and Special Ambassador at Washington generally informed of the main lines of his action and will request the Ambassador's advice or assistance whenever these may be required.[77]

The thing having been done, the Governor General sent a copy of the minute of council to the Colonial Office. With it went a word of reassurance from Borden:

> My Prime Minister . . . points out that . . . it is not intended that any steps should be taken which could be construed as being in any way incompatible with the unity of the British Commonwealth in its relations with a foreign state.[78]

This undoubtedly was a simple statement of the truth as Borden saw it. Nevertheless an official of the Foreign Office in London remarked in a minute that the Canadian order-in-council gave the chairman of the Mission "powers and status inconsistent with the continuance of the old relations between Canada and H. M. Ambassador and FO". He added gloomily, "No doubt inevitable."[79]

During the remaining months of the war the Canadian War Mission seems to have fully justified its creation. Only a month after it was set up it played a part in a negotiation of vast importance. Canada was faced with a desperate balance-of-payments problem vis-à-vis the United States, the anticipated deficit in the coming fiscal year being some $500 million. Sir Robert Borden, accompanied by several advisers, went to Washington to seek a solution. They arrived there on February 25, 1918. The next day was devoted to discussions with Canadian and British officials. Harris had found Americans unwilling to use Canadian manufacturing facilities, the expedient best fitted to resolve the difficulties. Borden was urged to make a strong appeal to the President. At the White House on February 27 Borden found Woodrow Wilson very cordial. The Prime Minister explained the Canadian problem; and the President "agreed that Canadian facilities should be used" and asked Borden to see William G. McAdoo, Secretary of the Treasury, and Bernard M. Baruch, Chairman of the War Industries Board. No doubt the President communicated with both men; and Borden found them both anxious to assist. Returning to Ottawa, he reported to the Governor General that McAdoo's attitude made him confident that the difficulties would be "worked out satisfactorily".[80]

They were. Two and a half months later Lloyd Harris wrote to Borden about the work of his Mission:[81]

> For your own information, I thought it would be interesting to you to know that up to May 1st, 1918, we have secured allocations of contracts for Canada for munitions and aeroplanes, amounting to approximately $70,000,000 and during the month of May to date, we have secured allocations amounting to over $30,000,000 so that munitions contracts alone will exceed $100,000,000.
>
> The relationship we now have with the Ordnance Department is such that they are willing to give us as much business as we can properly handle.
>
> I am just completing arrangements with the Quartermaster-General's Department, and think we will establish the same kind of relationship with them, as we have with the Ordnance Department. . . .

There were other large possibilities, including shipbuilding. It was clear that the solution of the balance-of-payments problem was in sight. Borden's conference with the President had produced enormous dividends.

Twenty-three years later it all happened over again.

The generous response to Borden's request for economic assistance was the most striking example of Canadian-American co-operation in the First World War. There was also co-operation in the purely military sphere, and there would doubtless have been more had the war lasted longer. Seven American vessels served in the Atlantic Coast Patrol, organized by the Royal Canadian Navy to protect Canadian waters against the submarine menace. The United States Navy gave active help also in organizing the Royal Canadian Naval Air Service, with flying-boat stations at Dartmouth and Sydney, Nova Scotia, to serve the same purpose, safeguarding U.S. troops sailing from Canadian ports. This force in fact was "only nominally Canadian". The large and successful training organization set up in Canada by the Royal Flying Corps (above, page 199) did not teach Canadians only; it trained also the personnel for more than ten squadrons of the American air service, while arranging furthermore for Canadians to be trained in Texas.[82]

To many people in both Britain and Canada, and to some also in the United States, the horrors of the First World War seemed in some degree redeemed by the fact that the two halves of the English-speaking world had been brought together to fight in a common cause. Back in 1898, in the days of the flood-tide of imperialism, Joseph Chamberlain had said that "even war itself would be cheaply purchased, if, in a great and noble cause, the Stars and Stripes and the Union Jack should wave together over an Anglo-Saxon alliance."[83] (Chamberlain more than hinted that the alliance might suitably be triple, with Germany included, and that the enemy might be Russia. This was not the way things happened.) Canadians, an unmilitary people except when forced to it by the stress of a great emergency, were less likely than most, perhaps, to make excuses for war; but they were particularly susceptible to the charms of an Anglo-Saxon alliance. Now that alliance had, after a fashion, come to pass; and Canadians undoubtedly were delighted. The two nations that filled their horizon—the mother country and the great neighbour—were partners as they had never been before, and Canadian problems were correspondingly simplified and Canadian hearts lightened and lifted. For a moment at least, the old hostilities that had always clouded the relations of Canada and the United States were alleviated; and they would never be as powerful again as they had been before 1917.

Nevertheless, the rapprochement of 1917–18 was only partial and in many ways temporary. Among the reasons for this one may cite the fact that many generations of enmity and suspicion are not quickly dispelled. But the fact must also be faced that the very strong anti-American feeling which we have noted as growing in Canada during the years of American neutrality continued to affect the popular mind even after the American intervention.[84] People remembered the long cold years when Canadians were shedding their blood in Flanders and the United States was maintaining what seemed to them a callous and pharisaical neutralism, which Americans garnished with such phrases as "too proud to fight". In the school year 1918-19 the writer was in the top form of the Normal Model School in Toronto. One of our academic exercises was known as "oral composition". A classmate of mine took as his topic "The United States in the War". My recollection is that it was a pretty scarifying presentation, and that it was universally acclaimed. I remember specifically one point, the story with which the boy ended. It concerned General Pershing in Paris. The general, it seems, called a taxi, and it did not arrive quite on time. When it did arrive, Pershing protested to the driver, who was a female: "My good woman, you're three minutes late." And the lady replied, "My good man, you're three years late." We twelve-year-olds thought that a sparkling piece of repartee; and I am sure that in this we were fairly representative Canadians of that day.

It is certain, at any rate, that in terms of public feeling the First World War was not a great turning-point in the relations of Canada and the United States. In English Canada (and it is of English Canada I am primarily speaking here) wartime emotions strengthened the bond with Britain rather than the friendship with the republic. Had Woodrow Wilson combined with the ideals that made him a natural leader of international liberalism the political tact and affability of a later American war president, many things—including relations with Canada—might have been different. Unfortunately, he had considerable capacity for arousing hostility at home and abroad.

But seen in retrospect the war was an important turning-point in the development of the Canadian-American economic relationship. It probably did a good deal to make Americans think of Britain and Canada more as sister democracies and less as politically backward communities ruled by a close relative of George III. So far as Canadians were concerned, the war left the British connection—developing as it was in a manner calculated to flatter Canadian national feeling—still the dominant fact in Canada's external relations; and the state of Anglo-American affairs in the years after 1919 did not make for a warm Canadian-American situation. On balance, there was probably better feeling than there had been before 1914. But anything like a real union of hearts had to wait for Adolf Hitler and Franklin D. Roosevelt.

THE WAR AND THE NATION

Whatever the effect of the war upon the Canadian-American relationship, there is little doubt about its effect upon Canadian nationality. The tremendous effort and the tragic losses of 1914-18 did not wholly transform Canada and the Canadians; but they certainly left them rather different from what they had been before.

As in so many other matters, one can scarcely speak intelligently about the impact of the war on "Canada". What one must look at is the *regions* of Canada; and there is no better piece of evidence than the statistics of voluntary enlistment in the regions during the four years of war. Here are the best figures available, as given to Parliament in 1919:

	*Estimated Population 1916**	*Voluntary Enlistments†*	*Percentage*
Nova Scotia and Prince Edward Island‡	597,000	24,456	4.0
New Brunswick	368,000	18,935	5.1
Quebec	2,154,000	52,993	2.4
Ontario	2,713,000	205,808	7.5
Manitoba	554,000	54,756	9.8
Saskatchewan	648,000	27,044	4.1
Alberta	496,000	36,013	7.4
British Columbia	456,000	43,652	9.5
Yukon	7,000	2,327	33.0

* *Canada Year Book*, 1938, p. xxxi.

† Canadian Sessional Paper No. 264, 1919 (PAC, RG 14, D2, vol. 52).

‡ The fact that Nova Scotia and Prince Edward Island are bracketed together suggests the possibility that these statistics are based not on provinces but on Military Districts (these two provinces together constituted Military District No. 6). If this were the case, it would involve the figures for four thinly-populated counties in western Quebec, which were part of Military District No. 3 (headquarters, Kingston) being added to Ontario and lost to Quebec; and the figures

These figures, relatively crude and unscientific though they are, have value as a general index of attitudes: of the degree of commitment of some regions to the war, and of others' relative indifference or hostility. These statistics of response to the greatest international crisis Canada had ever confronted seem also to have some general significance as reflecting the isolationist predilections of some regions, and the existence in others of important ties of mind and heart with parts of the outside world. The dominating feature of the table is, of course, the low figures for the province of Quebec, which document most dramatically the traditional isolationism of French Canada. When one remembers the considerable English-speaking minority in Quebec, which certainly provided a material proportion of the enlistments, the contrast with other parts of the country becomes still more striking. The figures for Saskatchewan, the central prairie province and at that time the most populous of the three, are very low; its evident high degree of indifference to the war may perhaps be attributed to its large Central and Eastern European population (in 1911 there were 110,279 people of actual German or Austro-Hungarian origin in Saskatchewan,[85] most of them recent arrivals) and its predominantly rural and agricultural character. Hostility to military service, particularly of the compulsory sort, was a rural as well as a French-Canadian characteristic.

The contrast between Saskatchewan and the other prairie provinces is marked, especially in the case of Manitoba where (if we disregard the extraordinary performance of the Yukon Territory) enlistments were the highest of all. Here we see, perhaps, the results of older settlement than in Saskatchewan, of the fact that many of the settlers came from Ontario, and of the presence of a large urban centre, Winnipeg. Somewhat similar forces—barring the date of settlement—were at work in Alberta. In British Columbia the very high enlistment figures are probably related to the British origins of a large proportion of the population (some 64 per cent in 1911); urbanization was also well advanced here. In the old-settled Maritime provinces the low enlistment rates present something of a puzzle, in the light of the fact that their population was overwhelmingly

---

for the Lakehead district of Ontario, which was part of Military District No. 10 (headquarters, Winnipeg) being lost to Ontario and added to Manitoba. However, it is not certain that this is the case; for British Columbia and the Yukon together constituted Military District No. 11, and the figures for these two communities are given separately in the return.

of British origin (about 76 per cent in the case of Nova Scotia).[86] Two explanations suggest themselves: the absence of large cities (Halifax had only 46,619 people in 1911),[87] and the fact that only a few of the teeming immigrants of the prewar years went to the Maritimes.* We must recall that about *half* of all the voluntary enlistments in Canada came from the British-born.[89] A considerable factor in the geographical distribution of those enlistments, then, must have been the location of the prewar immigrants from the British Isles, and it seems evident that they went in large numbers to Ontario and the western provinces.

Ontario, with its large population, produced roughly half of all the country's voluntary recruits; in percentage terms, however, it was somewhat below the highest provinces. Perhaps it is relevant here that the 1911 census, which credited Ontario with 1,927,099 people whose origin was British,† also recorded the presence in the province of 202,442 of French origin. And there were 192,320 of German origin, in a great many cases certainly remote. Communities including many German Canadians were naturally less enthusiastic for the war than others, and one of the painful stories of the time in Ontario is the divisions in the city of Berlin, which in 1916, after much controversy, changed its name to Kitchener.[90] But it is pretty clear that the chief factor that brought Ontarians flocking to the colours was the province's predominantly British origins and traditions, helped by the extent to which it had become urbanized. It was the urban Canadian, in the main, who had most awareness of the outside world; it was the Canadian of British origin who was most disposed to cross the seas to fight what were thought of as the Empire's battles; and it was the Canadian who had been born in the British Isles who was first at the recruiting-station.

In 1900 Sir Wilfrid Laurier had made a famous speech in Parliament about the little body of Canadians who were then fighting in South Africa. When the news of their successes came, he said, "is there a man whose bosom did not swell with pride, the noblest of all pride, the pride

* Of 382,841 immigrants (British and other) in the fiscal year 1912–13, only 14,440 reported their destination as the Maritime provinces; 119,178 went to Ontario and 57,104 to Quebec.[88]

† Note that Canadian records made no provision for recording United States immigrants (who were numerous at this period, particularly in the West) as such. An American, however long his family had been in North America, would be set down as of (perhaps) English or German origin as he might declare.

of pure patriotism, the pride of the consciousness of our rising strength, the pride of the consciousness that that day the fact had been revealed to the world that a new power had arisen in the west?"[91] These inflated phrases look absurd in the context of the Battle of Paardeberg, where a single Canadian battalion gave a good account of itself. In the context of Second Ypres and Vimy Ridge and a death-roll of 60,000 they might still seem a trifle inflated, but they would not be absurd. The war had some lamentable results in Canada apart from its cost in blood; by far the worst of them was the divisive effect of the experience upon the relations between English and French. But it left behind it a national legend, the stuff of which nations are made. The creation of the Canadian Corps was the greatest thing Canada had ever done.

In the spring of 1919 Mackenzie King, who would be elected leader of the Liberal party that August, made a trip overseas. He visited the battlefields; and he met Sir Arthur Currie, and made a careful record of his interview with him.[92] The general told him, "The Canadians are going back to Canada with feelings for England and affection for her; but with a feeling also that they are just as good as any men they have found on this side. I have been up against the real situation in many ways, and at no single point have I ever found superior organization or efficiency or capacity." All the battles the Canadians had fought "had been decisive battles". "They had never lost a gun, which was a record that no other army had."* King, the most totally unmilitary of men, was impressed. He cannot have failed to sense that the attitude Currie typified and described, however exaggerated it might be, was to do much to shape the Canadian future.

Not everything happens at once. A self-governing colony evolving into a nation under the impulsion of a world crisis is bound to leave loose ends. The facts of Canadian munition production being directed by an agency of the British government, and of the Canadian air effort (including

* So far as the Canadian Corps was concerned, this seems to have been true. The Royal Canadian Horse Artillery Brigade, not operating as part of the Corps, lost a gun on March 21, 1918. It had been taken into the front line, and when the area was abandoned to the enemy the gun had to be abandoned too, though the breech-block was removed.[93] Had the Canadian Corps been in the path of the German offensive that began that day, it is conceivable that it might have lost some guns like other people. Currie, however, would certainly not have admitted this.

training in Canada) being entirely controlled by the British air services, were colonial survivals by no means surprising in the circumstances. The dynamic aspects of the situation were represented by Sir Robert Borden in the Imperial War Cabinet and the Canadian Corps on the fields of France.

Sir Robert himself never had any doubt as to who deserved the chief credit for the transformation of Empire into Commonwealth. In 1933 the death of John S. Ewart, the acid ultra-nationalist writer on constitutional themes, who had pioneered many causes that had now triumphed, led him to make a private comment:

> Some rather foolish things have been said and written as to the influence of his propaganda in the development of constitutional relations through which Canada and other Dominions have entered the portal of full nationhood. That development was due to the valour, the endurance and the achievement of the Canadian Army in France and Belgium which inspired our people with an impelling sense of nationhood never before experienced. When the Dominions, with Canada in the lead, insisted upon recognition at the Peace Conference, at the beginning of 1919, and when Clemenceau learned that these Dominions had put a million men in the field or in training, he said that this record was enough for him, and so Canada and the other Dominions at that Conference entered into the Society of Nations to take their place in the concert of the League.[94]

CHAPTER NINE

THE PEACE AND THE LEAGUE

THE BRITISH EMPIRE DELEGATION AND THE PEACE CONFERENCE

In 1918 there was no doubt that the British Dominions would have to be consulted about the terms of peace. The British government had committed itself to this in principle as early as 1915 (above, page 186). But this commitment was strictly British, applicable only to consultation within the Empire. What the other great Allied powers might say about the admission of the Dominions to an international peace conference remained to be seen. It was for London to persuade them, if it could and would.

So far as the British family discussion was concerned, the forum was ready to hand, in the Imperial War Cabinet. W. M. Hughes of Australia was still in England. Lloyd George communicated with the other Dominion Prime Ministers on October 27. The telegram to Borden ran:

> I think that you ought to be prepared to start without delay for Europe, if the Germans accept the terms of the armistice which we shall propose after our meeting at Versailles this week, as the Peace Conference will in that event probably open within a few weeks, and this will have to be preceded by Inter-Allied Conferences of at least equal importance. It is I think very important that you should be here in order to participate in the deliberations which will determine the line to be taken at these conferences by the British Delegates.[1]

Borden immediately replied that he was preparing to start. A day later he sent Lloyd George another cable defining the Canadian position:[2]

SECRET. PRIVATE. PERSONAL. There is need of serious consideration as to representation of the Dominions in the peace negotiations. The press and people of this country take it for granted that Canada will be represented at the Peace Conference. I appreciate possible difficulties as to representation of the Dominions but I hope you will keep in mind that certainly a very unfortunate impression would be created and possibly a dangerous feeling might be aroused if these difficulties are not overcome by some solution which will meet the national spirit of the Canadian people. We discussed the subject today in Council and I found among my colleagues a striking insistence which doubtless is indicative of the general opinion entertained in this country. In a word they feel that new conditions must be met by new precedents. I should be glad to have your views.

Perhaps the phrase "new precedents" was a calculated reminiscence of Asquith's words in the cabinet on July 14, 1915 (above, page 188). Lloyd George answered that he fully understood the importance of the question and that he was more than ever impressed with the desirability of Borden's coming to Europe at once, since such problems could not be solved by correspondence. Borden arranged to sail on November 10. With him went Sir George Foster, the Minister of Trade and Commerce, and Arthur L. Sifton (an older brother of Sir Clifford), the Minister of Customs. C. J. Doherty, the Minister of Justice, joined them later. In the entourage were Christie and Lieutenant-Colonel O. M. Biggar, the Judge Advocate General. Before their ship was well out to sea the wireless brought the news that Germany had signed the armistice.[3]

The conditions of the armistice were primarily designed to make it impossible for Germany to renew the war. They were hard: not only the evacuation of occupied territory, but the occupation by the Allies of German territory up to the Rhine and bridgeheads beyond; and the surrender of the effective part of the German fleet, including all submarines, and of 5,000 guns, 300,000 machine-guns, and 2,000 aircraft.[4] Britain had not consulted the Dominions about these conditions; indeed, it is not clear how, in the pressing circumstances of the time, she could have contrived, without incurring serious difficulties with her allies, to consult governments in Ottawa, St. John's, Melbourne, Pretoria, and Wellington. But W. M. Hughes, angered no doubt because he was in England and yet had been given no chance to express an opinion,* chose to consider that

* He heard of the terms at one of the interim meetings of the Imperial War Cabinet, on November 5.

the British had broken their commitment on consultation concerning conditions of peace, and boiled over in public before the armistice was signed. Subsequently he reported to Lloyd George that the Australian cabinet were "surprised and indignant" at this "painful and serious breach of faith".[5] It was clear that the Dominions were going to insist on being heard.

The Imperial War Cabinet settled down to business again on November 20, with Borden and Hughes both present, as were also Foster and Smuts (the latter as Minister of Defence for South Africa). W. F. Lloyd (Prime Minister of Newfoundland) attended beginning on December 3, and General Louis Botha (Prime Minister of South Africa) first attended on December 18, on which date also the Maharaja of Bikaner and Sir S. P. (shortly Lord) Sinha appeared representing India.[6] The only reference to the question of representation during the first meeting was a report by Lloyd George that M. Clemenceau, Prime Minister of France, had made the "informal suggestion" that there should be five representatives of "each of the Allied countries" at the peace conference. The British Prime Minister remarked that "It was undoubtedly necessary that there must be permanent delegates, but it appeared desirable that other representatives should be present in order to discuss problems which particularly affected them."[7] The phrasing suggests that at this stage he may have been thinking of "permanent" representatives from the United Kingdom, with the Dominions appearing only when their own special interests were to be discussed.

There was some discussion of peace-conference procedures at another Imperial War Cabinet meeting on November 26.[8] Sir Robert Borden stated the principle, from which there was no dissent, that "The attitude of the British Empire on all important questions ought to be determined by discussion in the [Imperial] War Cabinet, so far as there is any room for debate. Then should follow a discussion between the representatives of the important Allied nations. . . ."

Only at its last meeting, on December 31, 1918, did the Imperial War Cabinet seriously get down to discussing the representation of the Dominions at the peace conference. By that time there had been considerable discussion elsewhere. On December 4 Borden's colleagues in Ottawa, who obviously felt that this was a question on which Canadians would have strong views, urged that "provision should be made for special representation" of the Commonwealth nations at the conference, "even though it may be necessary that in any final decisions reached they should speak with one voice; that if this is not possible then you [Borden] should form one of whatever delegation represents British Commonwealth".[9] It is clear that the British Ministers' idea now was that there should be a permanent delegation of five: four from the United Kingdom, and Borden to represent the Dominions and India. Borden, though doubtless flattered, seems to have had some doubts about this scheme, which was very unlikely to commend itself to the other Dominions. Hughes in fact evidently scuppered it, taking the line that if there was to be any Dominion representation Hughes himself would have to be appointed.[10] On December 2 British, French and Italian representatives, meeting in London, agreed on the following formula:

> That there should be five delegates at the Inter-Allied Conference of each of the great Allied and Associated Powers, namely: France, Great Britain, Italy, Japan, United States of America.
>
> Representatives of the British Dominions and India* should attend as additional members of the British delegation when questions directly affecting them are under consideration.[11]

When the Allied visitors met with the Imperial War Cabinet next day Hughes showed doubts as to the formula's adequacy.[12]

The Imperial War Cabinet, when it met on December 31 to deal with the question, had before it a telegram from the British Ambassador in Paris presenting the French government's views. It suggested that the great Allied powers should have five representatives each; the "smaller Allied Powers", three each; new states recognized as allies, two each; states in course of formation, one each; neutral states, one each. There was no reference to the British Dominions, and those present at the Imperial War Cabinet clearly (and undoubtedly rightly) were of the opinion that the French did not propose to class them among the "smaller Allied Powers". Lord Robert Cecil, the Assistant Secretary of State for Foreign Affairs, said that it was intended to reply accepting the French suggestions generally, but adding, "We assume, of course, that arrangements come to in recent Inter-Allied conversations in London with regard to representation of British Dominions hold good."

These proposals were attacked by both Hughes and Borden in strong terms. Hughes said that under the French proposals "the Dominions

* The formula was amended to include India at the meeting with the Imperial War Cabinet on December 3, on the initiative of Lloyd George.

would not be accorded representation equivalent to, say, Sweden. . . . Australia had put and kept more men in the field than Belgium, and deserved as much representation at the Conference." Lloyd George argued that under the proposals of December 2 the Dominions and India would be at least as well off as the smaller Allied powers, which were to have no right of representation at all meetings, but only when questions concerning them were being discussed. Moreover, it had always been intended that one of the five British delegates should be a representative of the Dominions and India. Borden then spoke, and for once—if we accept the minutes as accurate—he was more forthright than Hughes:

> . . . It would be regarded as intolerable in Canada that Portugal should have a representation in the Peace Conference which was denied to that Dominion. Canada had lost more men killed in France than Portugal had put into the field. If the French proposals were adopted as put forward in Lord Derby's telegram, the result upon public opinion in Canada would be such as he did not care to suggest, or even contemplate. The status of the Dominions was not well understood by foreign Powers, and it would be not only proper, but necessary, for the British Government to set it forth fully. . . . Each Dominion should have as ample a representation as Belgium or Portugal. There was no question on which the people of Canada were more insistent than their claim to representation at the Peace Conference which would settle the issues of a war in which they had taken so notable a part. He hoped that the Cabinet would appreciate, although it was almost impossible for them fully to appreciate, the strong feeling in Canada on this subject. To provide that Canada should be called in only when her special interests were in question would be regarded as little better than a mockery. It would be most unfortunate from the point of view of the Dominions that the British delegation should be selected entirely from the British Isles. That delegation had authority to represent not only the British Isles, but the whole Empire. He, therefore, strongly urged that the delegation representing the British Empire should be in part selected from a panel,* upon which each Prime Minister from the Dominions should have a place, and that one or more of those Prime Ministers should be called from time to time, as occasion might require, to sit in the delegation representing the whole Empire at the Conference.

Opposition, so far as there had been any, now collapsed, except that Lloyd George pointed out how unwise it would be to ask for five delegates

* The panel system seems to have been first suggested by General Smuts, as a means of filling the fifth position on the British delegation.

from Britain and three from each Dominion and India—a total of twenty-three, which would certainly have aroused hostility among the Allies. The decision of the Imperial Cabinet was:

a) Representatives of the British Dominions and India ought to be present at the opening session and at any other session of the Peace Conference or the Allied Preliminary Conference (should it be held) at which Belgium and other smaller Allied States were represented.
b) The British Dominions and India should in all respects have the same powers as, and be on an equal footing at the Conference with, Belgium and other smaller Allied States.
c) Lord Robert Cecil should re-cast the telegram to Paris on these principles.
d) The Prime Ministers of the Dominions and the representatives of India should be placed on a panel from which part of the *personnel* of the British delegation could be filled, according to the subject for discussion.[13]

The ultimate result of this recommendation was that the Dominions and India had dual representation at the conference: separately, as powers in their own right; and collectively as members of a British Empire Delegation. Hughes' biographer reads the record as indicating that Hughes was responsible for the separate representation and that Borden would have been happy with representation merely through the panel system.[14] He may be right, but the minutes of the meeting of December 31 are hardly conclusive. And we must not overlook the fact that Borden cabled his colleagues in Ottawa after that meeting,

... My proposal which I consider the most satisfactory solution that is practicable and which was accepted by the Cabinet is as follows:

First, Canada and the other Dominions shall each have the same representation as Belgium and other small allied nations at the Peace Conference.

Second, as it is proposed to admit representatives of Belgium and other small allied nations only when their special interests are under consideration, I urged that some of the representatives of British Empire should be drawn from a panel on which each Dominion Prime Minister shall have a place. . . .[15]

The scene now shifts to Paris. Early in January 1919 the Imperial War Cabinet moved to the French capital under a new name: the British Empire Delegation to the Peace Conference. There were still battles to be fought over the representation of the Dominions.

It at once became apparent that there was to be no conference in the sense of a discussion of terms between victors and vanquished. The victors were to settle the terms among themselves and present them to the losers. It likewise became evident that the minor Allies were to have very little part in the proceedings. The great powers kept the business in their own hands; the essential decisions were made by the Council of Ten (the Prime Ministers or other first delegates and Foreign Secretaries of Britain, the United States, France, Italy, and Japan), a continuation of the Supreme War Council set up late in 1917 to co-ordinate the Allied effort. Subsequently, power was further centralized in a Council of Four, representing the great Allies minus Japan. Plenary sessions, at which the minor powers appeared, were few and were not much more than formalities.[16]

On January 12 there was "a conversation" between representatives of the five great Allies (it was in fact a meeting of what came to be called the Council of Ten). It was agreed that these five powers should each have five representatives, as proposed by France; the representation of the smaller Allies was reduced to two each. The question of Dominion representation was then raised, and this produced, in Lloyd George's later words, "a very severe contest" with the representatives of the United States, President Wilson and Secretary of State Lansing. A report to the Canadian cabinet, which must have been based on information from Lloyd George, runs in part, "Secretary Lansing was somewhat arrogant not to say offensive and desired to know why Canada should be concerned in the settlement of European affairs. Mr. Lloyd George replied that they believed themselves to have that right because some hundreds of thousands from the Dominions had died for the vindication of public right in Europe and that Canada as well as Australia had lost more men than the United States in this war." Clemenceau showed himself sympathetic to the Dominions' case but, Lloyd George reported, "was considerably astonished" when he heard that the British were asking for two representatives each for the Dominions and for India. "The most forcible argument used by President Wilson was that the British Dominions were not on the same footing as Belgium or Serbia, as these last stood alone, whereas the case for any British Dominion would be backed by five delegates of one of the most powerful members of the alliance." The President finally agreed that the Dominions and India might have one representative each. Lloyd George was not prepared to accept this without consulting the parties concerned.[17]

When Borden heard this story he arranged for a meeting of the Dominions' ministers, who, a Canadian record says, "agreed that they should stand together and insist upon representation equal to that of the smaller Allied nations. It was considered that this was a real test of their status as autonomous nations of the British Commonwealth."[18] Thereafter the British Empire Delegation held its first formal meeting and discussed the question. Borden, Hughes, and Botha all objected to Wilson's proposal. Borden's version is that the other Dominion representatives supported him up to a point and then "weakened"; finally he accepted the Wilson formula "but said I could not be responsible for the consequences". From the official minutes it emerges that the British ministers had serious doubts about the wisdom of insisting upon the larger representation. A. J. Balfour put it pointedly:

... He quite understood the strong sense of nationhood in the various fractions of the British Empire. This phenomenon was natural, and it would be foolish to deplore it. But the problem we had to solve was that of reconciling this intense patriotism with the sense of Imperial unity. If each time we met other nations in conference we said that the British Empire must be represented as a whole, and also separately, then *vis-à-vis* with the rest of the world we should be asking for too much. This was clearly the feeling of President Wilson. He was quite friendly, but he felt that he could not disguise this difficulty.

The delegation accepted the idea of a single representative each for the Dominions and India, on the understanding that they would in addition be entitled to representation through the panel system.[19]

Nevertheless, most of the Dominions got their two representatives, for what they were worth. At a further meeting of the Council of Ten the same afternoon Lloyd George returned to the subject and reported the Dominion premiers' disappointment. President Wilson had perhaps given the matter further thought. At any rate, he now said that he "wished to remove any impression that he personally had any objection to the British Dominions being separately represented. He fully admitted that their claims were great. He had merely been guided by the desire to remove any cause of jealousy by the other smaller States." Lloyd George seized the opportunity to "quote a remark made to him that day by Sir Robert Borden":

He had pointed out that, if he returned to Canada and confessed that Canada was getting merely half the number of representatives that had been allotted to Serbia or Roumania or Belgium, there would be a feeling that they were being badly treated, especially when it was known that the Canadian losses during the war had been greater than those of Belgium. Nevertheless, if it were thought that a greater representation of the Dominions would create a bad feeling outside, he did not wish to press the question.

Wilson now inquired "whether Mr. Lloyd George would feel satisfied to give Canada two representatives, South Africa two representatives, Australia two representatives, and New Zealand one representative". Lloyd George agreed that this would be fair, but was not prepared to make the proposal himself. Wilson then said that he would himself submit it, and proceeded to suggest two representatives for India—one for British India, one for the Native States. This was agreed. As for Newfoundland, the Ten decided that it would not be given separate representation, but would be eligible for the British panel.[20]

These decisions were much resented by New Zealand (whose representatives, W. F. Massey, Prime Minister, and Sir Joseph Ward, first attended a meeting of the British Empire Delegation on January 23) and by Newfoundland. Massey complained that New Zealand was placed in the same class with "Cuba, Honduras, Guatemala, Hayti, &c."; Ward threatened to go home. With respect to Newfoundland, Lloyd George explained that, "having regard to its size, a good deal of comment would be provoked in the United States if separate representation were accorded". It would, he thought, be very difficult to re-open the question; and the decisions were allowed to stand.[21] One other matter had vexed the Dominions. In spite of the general rule that small Allied powers were to get two representatives, on Wilson's initiative Brazil was allotted three by the Ten on January 13, the argument being used that this would help to diminish the German influence existing in the country.[22] Then, on January 17, the Ten, moved by sentiment for two small countries which had suffered greatly, likewise allotted three each to Belgium and Serbia, over the opposition of Lloyd George. This came as a surprise to the Dominion delegations, and Borden and his Canadian colleagues made a written protest which was circulated to the British Empire Delegation. With three of the "smaller Allied powers" now having three representatives, they wrote, "It is hardly to be anticipated that Canadians will consider that their country is suitably recognized by being placed on an equality with Siam and Hedjaz."[23] They probably expected no action, and none was taken.

On January 18 a "plenary session" of the "Preliminary Peace Conference" (i.e., the Allied and Associated Powers and those that had broken diplomatic relations with the enemy powers) was informed of the "Rules of the Conference" as decided by the Council of Ten, including the arrangements for representation.[24] These rules, as already indicated, were not in fact followed. At a meeting of the British Empire Delegation on January 23, and again at a plenary session of the conference on January 25,[25] Sir Robert Borden pointed out that they provided for conferences on two levels: one, composed of five representatives each from the five great Allied nations; the other including as well the representatives of other powers. These rules were not being followed; instead, "conversations were going on between two representatives only from each of the Allied Great Powers". If this continued, the panel system and the Dominion representation provided under it would be inoperative. It did continue, with the result which Borden had stated. Nevertheless, although the Dominions seldom had direct access to the Council of Ten or the Council of Four, certain matters of secondary importance were settled by five-power meetings (the "Council of Five") in which a Dominion statesman sat for the British Empire. Thus on April 15 there was such a meeting at which the Empire was represented by Borden assisted by Lord Hardinge of the British Foreign Office. It discussed such questions as defraying the cost of the Allied Army of Occupation in the Rhineland; the opium traffic; the future status of Belgium; and minor amendments to the military peace terms as drafted.[26]

After all that has been said, it is hardly necessary to state that the Conference of Paris was in many respects a gigantic sham. Nothing was settled by voting; everything was settled by consensus between the great Allied powers. The complicated apparatus of representation on which so much time and ink had been spent was meaningless; if Belgium had more influence than Portugal it was not because one had three representatives and the other two. Neither had much influence. But if no one else profited by the system of representation, the British Dominions did. It established them pretty effectively, for the first time, as "international persons" in their own right. Canada might complain that she was placed on an equality with Siam, New Zealand that it was classed with Cuba; but there were advantages even to this, for, unimportant as Siam and Cuba might be, no one denied that they were sovereign states. There were uncertainties in many minds, including Canadian ones, as to precisely what the status of these late self-governing colonies now was; but it was evident that it had changed, and that it had risen.

It was clear to contemporaries, and is even clearer today, that Canada and the other Dominions were singularly fortunate at Paris. They got the best of both worlds, combining the status of small independent countries with the solid advantages of association with a great power—called in the language of the Conference the British Empire. Loring Christie, than whom there was no more acute observer in the conference chambers and antechambers (he acted as an assistant secretary of the British Empire Delegation, and was close to Borden in his various conference activities), in an account written later the same year described the Dominion position as follows:

> In the result . . . the Dominions secured a peculiarly effective position.
>
> a) At the Plenary Sessions there were sometimes three Canadian Plenipotentiary Delegates—two representing Canada and one representing the British Empire.
>
> b) At all times throughout the Conference, the Dominion Delegates were at the heart of the machine and had access to all papers recording the proceedings of the Conference. This enabled them effectively to watch and check the proceedings in the interest of their respective Dominions, and placed them in a position distinctly more advantageous than that of the smaller Powers, who did not receive the confidential papers of the Conference such as the minutes of the Council of Ten and the Council of Five.
>
> c) Dominion Ministers were nominated to and acted for the British Empire on the principal Inter-Allied Commissions of the Peace Conference, which were appointed by the Conference from time to time to consider and report upon special aspects of the conditions of peace. . . .
>
> d) All the Dominion Prime Ministers took part in the Council of Ten when the disposition of the German Colonies was being discussed and decided.
>
> e) The Prime Minister of Canada on several occasions attended as the British Empire representative on the Council of Five. He also attended the Council of Four on several occasions to put forward the British Empire case in respect of the clauses on economic questions, on the international control of ports, waterways and railways, and on submarine cables.
>
> f) It is especially significant of the new status that during his last month in Paris, the Prime Minister of Canada regularly acted as chairman of the meetings of the British Empire Delegation . . . whenever the Prime Minister of the United Kingdom was unable to attend.[27]

Something further may be said of Canadian participation in commissions and committees connected with the conference.[28] Canadians had membership in a number of committees on special subjects set up by the

British Empire Delegation. As for Inter-Allied Commissions, Sir Robert Borden found himself vice-president of the Commission on the Greek Question, and spent a good deal of time studying the boundaries of Greece; Sir Eyre Crowe later claimed that his performance was undistinguished, but it seems at least to have been conscientious.[29] Borden was asked by Lloyd George to be the British delegate to a Commission on the Russian Question, apparently after other people had declined or turned out to be unavailable. He accepted (to the alarm of some of his colleagues in Ottawa). This would have involved attending a conference of the various parties fighting for control in post-revolutionary Russia which it was proposed to hold at Prinkipo (Prince's) Island in the Sea of Marmora. But the conference (which Borden himself had in fact suggested in the British Empire Delegation) never took place.[30]

Sir George Foster was vice-president of the Inter-Allied Economic Commission and was a member of the British Empire panel of the Supreme Economic Council; Sifton and Doherty were alternates on this panel. Sifton was vice-president of the Inter-Allied Commission on the International Regime of Ports, Waterways and Railways. These were the major appointments, disregarding sub-committees.[31]

From what has already been said it emerges clearly that what Canada and the other Dominions were primarily interested in at Paris was their own status in the Empire and the world. They were in a position to do something about their status, and they pursued this object with determination and considerable success. The circumstances of the conference did not encourage them to devote themselves with equal determination to the task of making a better world for future generations of mankind at large, which supposedly was the concern that had brought the representatives of so many nations to the French capital. The great Allied powers appeared to think themselves quite capable of looking after all that; no help was wanted.

Nevertheless, some contribution was made. Part of it was made through the commissions and committees, exemplified in Borden's labours on the boundaries of Greece, which helped to produce a settlement that has stood to the present day. More of it was made through the British Empire Delegation.

As Christie said, and as many other people have said since, membership in the delegation gave the Dominions extraordinary advantages. For one thing, it gave them information; through the United Kingdom representatives and the papers they received, they knew what was going on in the inner circle of the conference. And the meetings of the delegation gave the Dominion people a chance to express their views on events to men who sat in the inner circle. In this way they were accorded a degree—if only a degree—of influence unknown to the representatives of small Allied powers outside the British family.

How much influence did Canada exercise, through the available channels, on the settlement with Germany? The answer must be, very little. Borden commented rather adversely on the British proposals for a trial of the Kaiser, but on a point of procedure rather than of principle.[32] The matter on which Canada's voice was chiefly heard was that of reparations and indemnities to be exacted from Germany. Here the argument was based on economic logic. Sir George Foster pointed out that it was proposed to deprive Germany of her gold, her ships, and other economic assets, and that it was nevertheless being argued that Germany should be made to pay £24,000 million and that she could pay £1,250 million per year as interest on that sum. He was not prepared to dispute the now rather astonishing proposition that the enemy powers should be made to pay the whole cost of the war; but he saw no grounds for believing that Germany could actually pay such sums as these.[33] When the cabinet in Ottawa proposed to make the damage caused by the Halifax explosion of December 1917 the basis of a claim against Germany, Borden refused to hear of it, arguing that it would merely encourage the French, Italians, and Belgians in the vastly inflated claims which they were making ("Italy even claims indemnity for increased cost of living").[34]

In later years, when arguing the value of the British Empire Delegation at Paris, Lloyd George liked to recall[35] its meetings on June 1 and 2, 1919. On May 7 the enormous draft treaty, assembled from the meeting-rooms of many commissions and committees, was presented to the German delegates. On May 29 the Germans made their written reply, complaining of the terms' harshness and making counter-proposals. Lloyd George called several of his cabinet colleagues from London and assembled the British Empire Delegation to consider the situation: should concessions be made, or not?[36]

The discussion lasted the better part of two days, and there was a decided consensus in favour of concessions.[37] General Smuts "led off with a severe criticism of the Treaty" and seems to a large extent to have set the tone of the meeting. The other South African, Botha, made a point of powerful general appeal. It was just seventeen years, he recalled, since he and Lord Milner (who was also present in Paris) had put their signatures to the Treaty of Vereeniging which ended the South African War. "On that occasion it was moderation which had saved South Africa for the British Empire, and he hoped on this occasion that it would be moderation which would save the world." Smuts' comments are closely related to the final decisions, which may be summarized as follows. The delegation resolved that Lloyd George should press for concessions to the enemy in four respects: a modification of the clauses dealing with the eastern frontiers; holding out to Germany some promise of entrance to the League of Nations at an earlier date than the draft would allow; modification of the clauses concerning the army of occupation, in the direction of reducing its strength and making the period of occupation as short as possible; modification of the reparation clauses in the direction of fixing the liability of the Germans at a definite amount.

Sir Robert Borden had left Paris on May 14. His colleagues in Ottawa had long been pressing him to return to look after his political obligations, and now, in spite of urgings from Lloyd George in the opposite direction, he could resist them no longer. Accordingly it fell to Sir George Foster to speak for Canada in these important meetings. The Prime Minister, had he been present, might have been more assertive, but Foster expressed firm opinions, agreeing with the consensus on all four points except the question of the army of occupation, which he did not mention. In part he spoke as follows:

> As to reparations and the Economic terms—it was impossible to undertake to carry out a system of administration by a foreign Power in a country containing 60,000,000 inhabitants for a long period of years. No people would stand it. The very men who now were pressing their leaders to demand the whole costs of the war and occupation till it was obtained would be the men who in six or twelve months would denounce the Governments because they had not carried out reparation in a practical way. It was impossible for an individual to get credit if his liabilities were indefinite. The case of a nation was the same, especially when the determination of the liability rested on the will of a foreign Commission.
>
> He would make the sum as moderate as possible, in view of Germany's capacity to pay, with the idea of getting the Peace signed. . . .
>
> He had never heard a good reason given for the exclusion of Germany from the League of Nations. If Germany were admitted to the League of Nations, the solution of many of these problems would be greatly assisted.

Struggling to gain Allied assent to the British propositions, Lloyd George found himself in serious difficulties with both the United States and, still more, France. In the end, however, some limited concessions were obtained on all four points of the British submission; though on the question of Germany's admission to the League all that could be gained was an expression of readiness to consider the matter "in the early future". Critics, of course, have had no difficulty in pointing out that the British proposed no concessions on matters of primary importance to themselves. There was no suggestion of permitting the German navy to revive; and the Australasian Dominions and South Africa had no idea of allowing the return of the German colonies which they had conquered. All the great Allied powers share the blame for the defects of the settlement; nevertheless the performance of the British Empire Delegation in the final stages of the negotiation did some credit to its members' hearts and heads.

It was doubtful whether the Germans would sign the modified treaty. They finally did so under the threat of the Allied forces resuming their advance into Germany. On June 28, 1919, in the Hall of Mirrors at Versailles, where the German Empire had been proclaimed in 1871, the Emperors' republican successors signed the humiliating peace.

Borden had taken steps in March to provide for what he considered a satisfactory procedure for the signing of the treaty by the Dominions, obtaining the consent of all the Dominion Prime Ministers to a memorandum which was sent to the secretariat of the British Empire Delegation. This ran in part,

> b) The recital in the Preamble of the names of the Plenipotentiaries appointed by the High Contracting Parties for the purpose of concluding the Treaty would include the names of the Dominion Plenipotentiaries immediately after the names of the Plenipotentiaries appointed by the United Kingdom. Under the general heading "The British Empire" the sub-headings "The United Kingdom", "The Dominion of Canada", "The Commonwealth of Australia", "The Union of South Africa", etc., would be used as headings to distinguish the various Plenipotentiaries.
>
> c) It would then follow that the Dominion Plenipotentiaries would sign according to the same scheme.[38]

These suggestions were followed, with one not wholly insignificant exception. The British delegates were not described in the treaty as representing the United Kingdom. In the list in the preamble of the High

Contracting Parties and their representatives, the names of Lloyd George and his four British colleagues directly followed the recital of the King's titles ("His Majesty the King of the United Kingdom of Great Britain and Ireland and of the British Dominions Beyond the Seas, Emperor of India, by . . ."); then came

And
for the Dominion of Canada, by:
The Honourable Charles Joseph Doherty,
Minister of Justice;
The Honourable Arthur Lewis Sifton,
Minister of Customs;

followed by the other Dominion representatives in the same manner.[39] It could thus have been argued that the five British ministers represented in themselves the King and the British Empire, and that the attendance of the Dominion and Indian delegates was incidental and unnecessary. This point seems not to have been discussed in any meeting of the British Empire Delegation.

Formal authority to sign the treaty took the form of the customary "full powers" signed by the King. These were issued to all the Canadian delegates who might be required to sign, on the authority of a Canadian order-in-council moving the King to take such action, which was forwarded through the Colonial Secretary.[40]

Sir William Orpen's well-known painting of the signing of the German treaty is an example of artistic licence combined with a strong dash of politics. The two Germans signing in the foreground are comic-strip caricatures. The scene is dominated by the twelve statesmen seated behind the table; and only two of them are not from the two great English-speaking powers. Even Orlando of Italy, a member of the Council of Four, is relegated to the background. The onlooker finds himself wondering whether perhaps the Marquis Saionji got to the table by virtue of the Anglo-Japanese Alliance. As for Georges Clemenceau, even the most English of artists could hardly leave *him* out. The five British and the five United States delegates are all carefully delineated. Tough little Serbia and gallant little Belgium are honoured by inclusion. At Lloyd George's shoulder, Maurice Hankey is about his business. The Maharaja of Bikaner in his turban reminds one that Britain still holds the gorgeous East in fee, even if perhaps a little less securely than before. And on the flanks statesmen of three British Dominions may be observed to lurk.

Suitably enough, Botha looks pensive and Hughes rather combative. Canada is represented by the long solemn features and picturesque white beard of Sir George Foster, who wasn't there.

It is a pity that Borden was unable to sign the treaty, for—although he was not mentioned in the early volumes of Harold Temperley's *History* of the conference, and resented it—he was a figure of some degree of importance at Paris, particularly within the British Empire Delegation. More than any other individual, he was responsible for the new position which the Dominions consolidated there. When leaving the conference he sent his Canadian colleagues who were remaining a memorandum summarizing the progress that had been made, and remarking, "In all this insistence upon due recognition of the nationhood of the Dominions, Canada has led the way; and in most cases her representatives have made the fight without active assistance from, although with the passive support of, the other Dominions."[41] If this was an exaggeration, it was not a very great one, and there is a good deal of evidence to support Borden's statement. Since he could no longer lead the Canadian delegation, Foster naturally succeeded him as the next senior; but Foster was shortly called home when his wife fell ill, and Sifton, who had left for Canada with Borden, returned to take his place.[42] As already noted, Doherty and Sifton signed the Treaty of Versailles for Canada, setting their names down immediately following those of the five British ministers.[43]

Two other treaties were signed, less ostentatiously, on the same day as the Treaty of Versailles. On May 5 Lloyd George had told the British Empire Delegation that the French were dissatisfied with the security provided by the treaty's clauses concerning the army of occupation, and he had found it necessary to undertake to recommend to Parliament an undertaking by Britain to come to France's aid if she were wantonly attacked by Germany. President Wilson had agreed to a similar guarantee, which would of course have to be ratified by the United States Senate. Sir Robert Borden remarked that he feared that Canadians "would be reluctant to accept such a commitment". He at once telegraphed asking for the comments of his colleagues in Ottawa, writing, "Australia and New Zealand have signified their willingness. Canada and South Africa have reserved answer."[44] No immediate reply seems to have come, but on the same day on which Borden made his verbal comment the British Prime Minister wrote Clemenceau formally advising him of his intention to propose the guarantee; he added that the Dominions would not be bound by the treaty until it had been ratified by their Parliaments.[45]

Article v of the Anglo-French treaty signed on June 28, 1919 accordingly ran: "The present Treaty shall impose no obligation upon any of the Dominions of the British Empire unless and until it is approved by the Parliament of the Dominion concerned." Article II provided that the treaty would come into force only when the Franco-American treaty in similar terms, signed on the same day, had been ratified.[46] The whole tripartite security arrangement accordingly collapsed when the United States Senate, as many people had feared from the beginning, declined to consider the treaty with France; it never came out of the Foreign Relations Committee.[47] Borden, overcoming his doubts, momentarily at least, cabled Botha, who had asked what he proposed to do, that he intended to lay the Anglo-French treaty before the Canadian Parliament for approval. He gave his reasons:

First. It is a necessary complement of the Peace Treaty, which could not have been consummated without it. Second. It does not materially extend obligations under League of Nations Covenant, although it may demand prompter action. Third. Its moral influence will be a strong safeguard against further German aggression. Fourth. That moral influence would be lessened if the Empire did not maintain a united front. Fifth. Its effects in bringing about closer co-operation and indeed a virtual alliance between the British Empire and the United States. Sixth. The unfortunate effect upon United States Congress if Canada should refuse to ratify.

Two days later Borden showed signs of wavering. He now told Botha that the treaty would probably not go before Parliament until the regular session commencing about February 1920: "It is thought desirable that our people should be afforded ample time for consideration of that Treaty and the responsibilities which it involves." It never did go before Parliament. The United States Senate relieved the Canadian government of the need for making a final decision upon it.[48] But the treaty's provision for Dominion concurrence—an echo of the prewar practice in commercial treaties (above, page 48)—was to be remembered in Canada as an important precedent.

The treaty with Germany was only part of the postwar settlement. There were also the Treaty of Saint-Germain-en-Laye (signed September 10, 1919) with Austria; the Treaty of Neuilly (November 27, 1919) with Bulgaria; the Treaty of Trianon (June 4, 1920) with Hungary; and the Treaty of Sèvres (August 10, 1920) with Turkey. All of these were signed on behalf of Canada, all by Sir George Perley, the High Commissioner in London, except the Austrian treaty which was signed by Sir Edward Kemp. It is clear, as Mr. Glazebrook says, that "on the whole Canadians concerned themselves little, either in Paris or Ottawa, with anything other than the German treaty". The nearest thing to an exception was the treaty with Turkey, the only one of these subsidiary treaties that was to have later importance in Canada. Though no correspondence on the subject has been found, it would seem that there may have been an arrangement with London, late in 1919, that Canada did not desire to be represented during the Turkish negotiations, but that the Canadian government would be kept informed of their progress and would arrange for a Canadian representative to sign the treaty. In fact, as the negotiations proceeded early in 1920, very little information about them reached Ottawa. The Canadian government complained more than once, but it was only after Loring Christie raised the question with the Colonial Secretary, Lord Milner, during a visit to London in the spring that the situation improved. It is interesting that Canada made representations on two matters concerning the treaty, both under pressure from interested groups in the Dominion. Humanitarians had called attention to the desirability of protecting the long-persecuted Armenians; and the Canadian Jewish Congress had urged the government to press the British authorities to accept a mandate for Palestine, in the expectation that they would implement the Balfour Declaration (November 1917) that the British government favoured the establishment in Palestine of a national home for the Jewish people. Ottawa said a word for the Armenians, and also cabled London, "Canadian Government shares hope that His Majesty's Government may be appointed mandatory for Palestine." Thus the Canadian government took the responsibility of urging the United Kingdom to undertake this thankless task, and by implication associated itself with the fateful policy of establishing a Jewish national home in the Middle East.[49]

THE LEAGUE OF NATIONS

The creation of the League of Nations is part of the story of the Treaty of Versailles. The Covenant (or constitution) of the League was a portion of that treaty, and of the other treaties with enemy states. As a matter of convenience, however, the origins of the League, and the Canadian connection with them, are here treated separately.

It was inevitable that people living through the dreadful events of 1914–18 should think of some future Parliament of Man that would make a repetition of such happenings impossible. One remembers Sir Robert Borden's New York speech of 1916 about a "world tribunal" to restrain outlaw nations (above, page 228). He was one of many. Idealists, particularly in the English-speaking countries, were big with schemes of international organization. Britain, which had its full quota of idealists and was also close to the firing-line, had both a "League of Nations Society" and a "League of Free Nations Association", which sensibly amalgamated to form the League of Nations Union. In the United States respectable people founded a "League to Enforce Peace", which had among its early supporters two men who, in the light of later events, seem strange bedfellows: President Wilson and Henry Cabot Lodge. There seems as yet to have been no such association in Canada, but there were plenty of people devoted to the cause of peace; very frequently at the time such people pointed to the pacific relationship between Canada and the United States as a lesson to the nations.[50]

The development of the concept of the League of Nations cannot be even outlined here. But by January 1918 both Wilson and Lloyd George had proclaimed the establishment of a League as among their countries' war aims. Lloyd George spoke of "the creation of some international organization to limit the burden of armaments and diminish the danger of war" (January 5, 1918); and Wilson, in his famous Fourteen Points speech to Congress (January 8, 1918) made as the last point the necessity of a League:

> A general association of nations must be formed under specific covenants for the purpose of affording mutual guarantees of political independence and territorial integrity to great and small States alike.[51]

The British Foreign Office put Sir Walter (afterwards Lord) Phillimore and a committee to work on the project, and their report was briefly referred to in the Imperial War Cabinet in August. Sir Robert Borden took the occasion to make a very general remark:

> Even if I thought the proposal for a League of Nations absolutely impracticable, and that statesmen a hundred years hence would laugh at it as a vain attempt to accomplish the impossible, nevertheless, I would support the movement because of its supreme purpose and because it might succeed. I think we ought to do our utmost to support it.[52]

The Phillimore paper was "the first formulation of League of Nations suggestions in a definite text under Governmental direction", and much of it survived, in one form or another, in the final Covenant of the League. Wilson's aide the celebrated Colonel E. M. House made considerable use of it in preparing the first United States draft plan for a League of Nations for the President.[53]

Two Commonwealth political idealists made vital contributions to the idea and the constitution of the League. Lord Robert Cecil told the Imperial War Cabinet on August 13, 1918 that he was "very violently in favour of this scheme", and he gave his best to it. In a paper circulated to the British War Cabinet on October 5 he emphasized the point that it was vital that the new organization should be created by the treaty ending the war:

> The great force on which we must rely is the hatred of the cruelty and waste of war which now exists. As soon as the war is over the process of oblivion will set in. . . . The chauvinists who believe that all foreigners are barbarians, the bureaucrats who think that whatever is, is right, the militarists who regard perpetual peace as an enervating evil, will combine with the disciples of the late Lord Melbourne to say "Can't you let it alone". It is only therefore, while the recollection of all we have been through is burningly fresh that we can hope to overcome the inevitable opposition and establish at least the beginning of a new and better organization of the nations of the world.[54]

The other great Commonwealth contributor was Jan Smuts. In December 1918 he produced a paper called in its published form *The League of Nations: A Practical Suggestion*.[55] This made specific recommendations for a constitution for a League. It also sounded a clear call for immediate and lofty action. "The psychological and moral conditions are ripe for a great change. The moment has come for one of the great creative acts of history." It ended with the famous passage announcing that "mankind is once more on the move. . . . The tents have been struck, and the great caravan of humanity is once more on the march."

Just at this moment, on December 13, 1918, President Wilson landed in Europe, the first American president to leave the United States while in office, hailed by millions as a saviour and as mankind's best hope, and determined to found the new international order for which so many voices were calling. He was as convinced as Cecil or Smuts that the Peace Conference must create the League of Nations, and must give that creation its best priority.[56]

The Council of Ten decided, and the decision was ratified by a plenary session of the conference, to set up a committee or commission "to work out the details of the constitution and functions of the League". President Wilson himself was its chairman. Each of the five great powers was to appoint two members. Smuts and Cecil were the obvious British representatives, and on January 23, 1919 the British Empire Delegation, without discussion, "agreed to confirm the designation by the [British] Prime Minister" of these two. Canada was thus denied any direct share in one of the few conference activities in which the Canadian ministers felt their country had a special interest. Subsequently first five, and then four more smaller powers were added to the committee. Borden now complained to Lloyd George, expressing the hope that Canada could be given the same consideration. Doherty, the Canadian Minister of Justice, had, Borden said, devoted much study to this question. Lloyd George, through his secretary, replied that he felt things had gone too far for additional representation to be arranged. If Borden disagreed, he suggested that he raise the matter in the British Empire Delegation. Borden evidently did not think it worth while to do so. Doherty had to content himself with serving on the delegation's committee on the position of the Dominions and India in the League, which, as he complained, was a much less important body.[57]

It would be pleasant to be able to record the opinion that the world is the poorer for Doherty's absence from the main committee. Unfortunately the evidence appears to be against any such proposition, even though Doherty seems to have had a fair conceit of himself as a constitutional thinker. He did in fact produce a document on the proposals for the League as they stood late in January 1919.[58] It is notably wordy and its content is unimpressive. The main point it attempts to make is that the "popular house" of the League should represent, not governments, but peoples: the representatives should be "elected . . . by popular vote". The suggestion does not seem to have been seriously discussed, and after more than half a century it still seems totally unpractical.

The Canadian voice spoke to somewhat better effect at a later stage. On February 14 the draft Covenant prepared by the League Commission was presented to a plenary session of the conference for information and comment, and the Canadians made the most of the opportunity, such as it was. Borden asked his colleagues and staff to produce observations, and went to work himself.[59]

The drafters had worked hard, and the Covenant already presented an appearance not unlike the final form which was to be familiar to the next generation.[60] The League's organs were to be a Body of Delegates (later called the Assembly) representing all the members; an Executive Council (called finally simply the Council) representing the five great Allied powers and four other powers selected by the Body of Delegates; and a Secretariat. The action to be taken in the event of a threat to peace was detailed in a series of articles the first of which was already denominated Article 10:

> The High Contracting Parties undertake to respect and preserve as against external aggression the territorial integrity and existing political independence of all States members of the League. In case of any such aggression or in case of any threat or danger of such aggression the Executive Council shall advise upon the means by which this obligation shall be fulfilled.

This article became the chief target of the Canadian criticism; a criticism which was to continue for years to come.

At an earlier stage Doherty had complained to Cecil that a draft Cecil had prepared[61] left the Dominions' status in the League very doubtful.[62] The objectionable passage did not recur in the draft of February 14, which indeed did not define who were to be members of the League. However, since it provided for the inclusion of self-governing Dominions and colonies among the countries not signing the treaty which might be admitted later, Doherty now assumed that Dominions which were original subscribers to the Covenant would be full members of the League.[63] In the "very prolix" paper which he prepared for Borden he addressed himself primarily to Article 10. "This Article," he wrote, "is open, in my judgment, to the very gravest objections, both generally, and from the point of view of countries in the condition and stage of development of Canada in particular." Canada was unlikely to profit by the article, "having actually no disputed or disputable territory with but one [*sic*] Continental Neighbour at whose hands there is no ground to apprehend aggression upon her territory and whose every interest as well as declared and settled policy is to protect her from territorial aggression on the part of others." The Canadian people were likely to resent it:

> The war from which they have just emerged they went into willingly impelled thereto by many and varying motives—not least among them the call of the blood that appealed to so many to make common cause with their British Brothers—And yet throughout that war there existed—growing with the war itself—very wide-spread feeling that while it had been and was true that

> when "England was at war Canada was at war" that [*sic*] it was a situation that called for modification. That feeling while it grew with the war will not die with it. It will remain with us sturdier and stronger than ever. A way must be found said and says Canadian Public Opinion whereby Canada shall have, if not complete, at all events a very large measure of control over the events that in the future might lead her into war.
>
> If this be her view when it is a question merely of being involved in wars because they are England's wars, what will be her attitude to a convention so easily susceptible of the interpretation that France's Wars, Italy's Wars are in the future to be hers wherever and whenever such a war is initiated by territorial aggression? What reception will she give to those who have bound her or seek to bind her to such a convention?

Doherty concluded his paper by stating once more his conviction that the League would fail if it did not find machinery "whereby the voice of the peoples may make itself heard and its influence felt". Borden had no use for this idea, and he did not put it forward on behalf of the Canadian delegation. Clearly, however, he agreed with the views of the Minister of Justice on Article 10. Badly as Doherty expressed himself, he was probably accurate in his interpretation of Canadian public opinion, and the Prime Minister made a strong attack on Article 10 in his own paper.

Apart from Doherty, Borden sought advice from Lord Bryce, from Christie, and from N. W. Rowell, President of the Council in Ottawa. Rowell's comments were made too late to affect Borden's memorandum. He thought Article 10 "open to grave question"; but he expressed warm general approval of the idea of a League and gave assurances that it commanded wide support in Canada. Bryce commented on lax draftsmanship but likewise had no doubt of the commanding merits of the plan. Christie had given Borden a summary of available information on the League project earlier; now he probably contributed chiefly precision and clarity of language.[64] The precise manner in which the Canadian memorandum dated March 13 was produced remains obscure; but a copy of it exists with Christie's careful marginal suggestions on points of detail. It seems likely that it was the product mainly of Christie's drafting skill and of the Prime Minister's solid common sense.

The paper[65] was long but not long-winded; it was crisp and businesslike. It dealt with the draft Covenant article by article, in many cases suggesting amendments which were often primarily improvements in wording, frequently simply the elimination of unnecessary words. Its effectiveness in this respect can be illustrated by Article 1 of the draft:

DRAFT OF 14 FEB.	CANADIAN AMENDMENT	FINAL VERSION
The action of the High Contracting Parties under the terms of this Covenant shall be effected through the instrumentality of meetings of a Body of Delegates representing the High Contracting Parties, of meetings at more frequent intervals of an Executive Council, and of a permanent international Secretariat to be established at the Seat of the League.	The action of the High Contracting Parties under this Covenant shall be effected through the instrumentality of a Body of Delegates, of a Council, and of a permanent Secretariat.	*(Article 2)* The action of the League under this Covenant shall be effected through the instrumentality of an Assembly and of a Council, with a permanent Secretariat.

In the case of Article 10 the memorandum said, "It is submitted that this Article should be struck out or materially amended." The argument that followed was brief and rather legalistic, avoiding Doherty's emotional approach and references to public opinion. It was suggested that the article was inconsistent with those following (12 to 17) providing in detail for action by the League in certain emergencies. This was the only case where the Canadians recommended total deletion of an article. Their paper ended with some "general observations" of which two may be noted: in view of criticisms "in certain quarters", provision should be made for the peaceful withdrawal of states from the League (this was presumably to meet objections being heard in the United States); and it was assumed "that the Dominions of the British Empire are entitled to become Signatories to the Covenant".

This, the most important paper produced by the Canadian delegation at Paris, had little effect. It was circulated to the British Empire Delegation,* and Borden sent a copy personally to President Wilson, emphasizing that he desired to be helpful and not critical in approaching "this supremely important document upon which the future of humanity so greatly depends". He added "a word of earnest and intense appreciation" for the great part which Wilson had played.[66] It appears that Wilson never acknowledged this letter.

The British Empire Delegation never met to discuss the memorandum (or a parallel one by Hughes) as such. However, on March 28 Lord Robert Cecil wrote Borden thanking him for the paper and reporting what the

* *Documents on Canadian External Relations*, Vol. 2, is mistaken in indicating (page 73) that it was submitted to a plenary session of the Peace Conference.

League Commission had done since it was received.[67] (Although Cecil did not say so, and the minutes do not mention it, it appears that the paper had finally been circulated, along with that by Hughes, to the commission on March 26.)[68] On a fair number of points Cecil reported that amendments had been made along the lines of Borden's suggestions. (One was the wording of Article 1, and one wonders whether this was perhaps arranged to give the Canadian the feeling that he and his colleagues had accomplished something.) On many others, it had not been practicable to do so. With respect to Article 10, Cecil observed, "I am not quite happy about this Article, but I was unable to persuade my colleagues on the Commission to agree to its alteration." The withdrawal clause had been added, and Cecil assured Borden that the Dominions were entitled to become signatories.

On April 21 the British Empire Delegation, with Borden in the chair in the absence of Lloyd George, discussed the League Covenant, the commission having now completed its work. The discussion arose out of the question of the status of the former German colonies under the treaty, and Cecil went on to discuss the revised Covenant generally. Arthur Sifton raised the question of Article 4, which provided that the Council should consist of representatives of the five great Allied powers, "together with Representatives of four other States which are Members of the League".[69] This would mean that the Dominions (since, as Hughes remarked, it would be argued that the Dominions could not be regarded as States "other" than the British Empire) were not eligible for election to the Council. Sifton suggested that the words "States which are" should be deleted. Cecil replied that it had in fact been intended to substitute "Member of the League" for "State" throughout the document; the delegation agreed that this ought to be done, and it was done except at certain points.

Borden brought up Article 10. Cecil said that an attempt had been made to alter it, but no generally acceptable formula had been found and the commission had "been obliged to return to the original form". He pointed out that Article 10 was in effect qualified by Article 19,* pro-

* Article 19 of the final Covenant was originally proposed by the British members of the commission on February 11. Cecil raised the question of Article 10 (and read Borden's criticism of it) in Anglo-American conferences on March 18; he proposed amending the article by inserting after "undertake" the words "subject to the provisions of Article 24" (later 19). Wilson would not hear of it, saying that this was "the one article on which the French relied".[70]

viding for the reconsideration by members of the League of treaties that had become "inapplicable". Doherty proceeded to make a strong attack on Article 10. It amounted, he said, to saying that whatever is, is right. "The risks to which different members of the League were subject were by no means equal. In Canada, for instance, the risk of invasion was remote. . . . Nor was it just to throw the same obligation upon young, undeveloped countries as upon long-established and wealthy States. . . . Before the war there had been murmurings at the doctrine that when Britain was at war, Canada was at war. Now Canada was to be asked under this Covenant to accept even greater liabilities." Borden said that he still thought the article should be omitted; its purpose was covered by others less open to criticism. Cecil fell back upon the provisions of Article 4, which required that states not represented on the Council should be invited to send representatives to sit as members when "matters specially affecting" their interests were being considered; if Canada were asked to "embark upon a military expedition" on behalf of the League, then a Canadian representative must be invited to attend the Council, and under the League's rule of unanimity "if he disagreed there was an end of the matter". Australia and New Zealand, through the mouths of Sir Joseph Cook and W. F. Massey, refused to support Canada: Cook was clearly shocked by Doherty's comment about the principle that when Britain was at war Canada was at war. Hughes, whose own paper had said nothing about Article 10, was silent.[71]

Doubt still lingered in Canadian minds concerning the Dominions' status in the League and eligibility for election to the Council. Borden finally dispelled this when on May 6 he obtained the signatures of the three dominant figures of the conference, Clemenceau, Wilson, and Lloyd George, to a very definite document:[72]

> The question having been raised as to the meaning of Article IV of the League of Nations Covenant, we have been requested by Sir Robert Borden to state whether we concur in his view, that upon the true construction of the first and second paragraphs of that Article, representatives of the self-governing Dominions of the British Empire may be selected or named as members of the Council. We have no hesitation in expressing our entire concurrence in this view. If there were any doubt it would be entirely removed by the fact that the Articles of the Covenant are not subject to a narrow or technical construction.

At the same moment when Borden was finally settling the question of membership in the Council, he won a final success in another and more difficult contest: the controversy over the position of the Dominions in the International Labour Organization.

At an early stage in the drafting of the League Covenant it was proposed that it should include an expression of concern for fair and humane conditions of labour and a declaration of intention to set up international organizations to that end. These points were incorporated in what became Article 23 of the final Covenant, and a commission whose chairman was Samuel Gompers, president of the American Federation of Labor, was appointed to produce a plan of organization. The British Dominions were not represented on this commission, and the British minister chiefly concerned, G. N. Barnes, the Labour member of the British War Cabinet, was clearly not greatly interested in their problems. To make a long and complicated story short, in spite of Canadian protests expressed in the British Empire Delegation, the plan that had emerged by April contained the provision that "No High Contracting Party together with its Dominions and Colonies, whether self-governing or not, shall be entitled to nominate more than one member."[73] Borden had no disposition to accept this, and in any case Arthur Sifton, who was particularly watching labour developments on behalf of the Canadian delegation, kept him under pressure. Failing to get satisfaction through the British channel, Borden chose to raise the matter in a plenary session held on April 11. On that occasion Barnes moved the approval of the draft Labour Convention prepared by the commission; and Borden, in a speech of studied moderation, moved the following amendment:

> The Conference authorizes the Drafting Committee to make such amendments as may be necessary to have the Convention conform to the Covenant of the League of Nations in the character of its membership and in the method of adherence.

This was accepted by the conference.[74] The Canadians seemed to have won a victory, but it was illusory. As we have seen, the idea that decisions of plenary sessions should be binding on the conference had never been accepted, and the Drafting Committee simply chose to disregard this one.

On April 29 Borden, in accordance with a suggestion from Lloyd George, discussed the question with Henry M. Robinson, an American labour expert. He reported to the British Prime Minister afterwards:

> We discussed the question very amicably, but I found him quite immovable in his opposition to my proposal that Canada and the other Dominions should

not be barred from selection for representation on the Governing Body. He based his view upon supposed public opinion in the United States which regards the British Empire as exercising too much influence in the League of Nations and in the Labour Convention. Apparently public opinion is so ill-informed in that country as to believe that in matters affecting the peace of the world or labour conditions, the Governments of the various Dominions do not exercise a thoroughly independent judgment.

Borden went on to say that while the peace treaty must be signed and ratified, "and the Labour Convention for the time being", the Canadian Parliament might require that Canada should give notice of withdrawal from the League in order to withdraw also from the Labour Convention. "I am confident," he wrote, "that the people of Canada will not tamely submit to a dictation which declares that Liberia or Cuba, Panama or Hedjaz, Haiti or Ecuador must have a higher place in the international labor organization than can be accorded to their country which is probably the seventh industrial nation of the world, if Germany is excluded from consideration."[75]

It seems apparent that the American representatives—Gompers was presumably not responsible, for he had gone home—were being influenced by reports of the criticism of supposed British over-representation which was rife in the United States; and they clung to their position obstinately. In the British Empire Delegation on May 5 Borden argued that the action of the plenary session of April 11 was ample warrant for the change that he was requesting; but Cecil Hurst, the British member of the Drafting Committee, said that he had urged this upon his colleagues on the committee, "and when they would not agree he had asked them to put the point to their political chiefs, who might quite properly give them instructions which would bring about the desired result. The United States representative, however, had declined."[76] Borden's only recourse was to go to the summit himself, which he did, through Lloyd George, on May 6, asking the British Prime Minister to obtain the necessary decision from Clemenceau and Wilson in a conference which he was to have with them that day.[77] Out of that conference emerged the document already quoted which confirmed the Dominions' right to be elected to the League Council, and also a direction to the Labour Convention Drafting Committee to suppress the sentence in the Convention which would have limited any member and its Dominions and colonies to one member on the governing body.[78] Thus on the very eve of the presentation of the treaty to the Germans Borden clearly won his two great arguments over status.*

It may be noted that he won another, and perhaps a more doubtful, success relative to the Labour Convention. The drafters in the first instance included a statement of nine fundamental principles of labour policy on which the British Dominions had been given no chance to express opinions. The eighth of these clauses ran, "In all matters concerning their status as workers and social insurance foreign workmen lawfully admitted to any country and their families should be ensured the same treatment as the nationals of that country." This the Canadian government found objectionable because "it would conflict with provincial legislation in Saskatchewan and British Columbia which imposes restrictions on Oriental labour in certain trades and occupations". Borden took the matter up with Lloyd George, Wilson, and Clemenceau, arguing that this clause might "lead to great disorder, and possibly rebellion, on the Pacific Coast of the United States and of Canada". The upshot was that at the plenary session of April 28 Borden moved a new set of principles in which the eighth had been rendered totally innocuous:

> The standard set by law in each country with respect to the conditions of labour should have due regard to the equitable economic treatment of all workers lawfully resident therein.

This was duly passed; and unlike Borden's earlier amendment it was effective, because it had been cleared earlier with the great powers.[79]

THE TRIANGLE AT PARIS

Before taking leave of the famous Peace Conference of Paris, an episode

* He failed, however, in another matter. At this moment he again raised with Lloyd George the desirability of inserting "The United Kingdom of Great Britain and Ireland" immediately after "The British Empire" in the annex to the Covenant naming the original members (see above, page 254) Lloyd George took no action; and in the annex as printed the names of Canada, Australia, South Africa, New Zealand, and India were indented following the words "British Empire", throwing some shadow of doubt upon their separate status. The ex-Canadian James T. Shotwell claims that he was responsible for this arrangement, adopted in a great hurry as the annex was going to the printer on February 12 (*At the Paris Peace Conference* [New York, 1937], pp. 174 and 414). The date at least is clearly wrong: see *Documents on Canadian External Relations*, 2: 163.

of unique importance in Canadian history, it is worth while to glance at the conference in terms of the North Atlantic Triangle, a catch-phrase which had not yet been coined.

It is a curious but not a really surprising fact that, although thirty-two nations were entitled to take part in plenary sessions of the conference, Canada's concerns there continued to be dominated almost entirely by her relations with two of them. Like her external affairs at large, her business at Paris was mainly involved with Britain and the United States.

In the case of Britain this was inevitable. Canada and the other Dominions came to the conference as units of the British Empire, with a status within the Empire that had been enhanced enormously in recent years but with no international status, or virtually none. Loring Christie, in a paper written in March 1918, suggested that the Dominions might be considered "part-sovereign states" on the analogy of Saxony and Bavaria, which had continued to appoint diplomatic representatives after being absorbed by the German Empire.[80] But whether foreign countries would be willing to go so far in recognizing them was not certain. A controlling factor would be the attitude of Great Britain, whose Foreign Office was technically fully responsible vis-à-vis foreign nations for these newcomers on the world scene.

The position to be taken on the Dominions' claims to international status was one of the problems faced by the British government as the fighting ended, but it was not the most important one. No evidence suggests that Whitehall had developed in advance anything like a complete policy in the matter. The British ministers "played it by ear", as they and their predecessors had played so many things before, dealing with questions as they arose. Mixed feelings undoubtedly there were. Many foreigners, including Americans, saw proposals for Dominion representation in the Peace Conference and in the League as part of a Machiavellian plot for the extension of British influence. Englishmen were quite as likely to see it as a fragmentation of British power, with decentralization substituted for organized authority; at best, a vast complication of the old simple processes by which foreign policy was formed and executed.

Nevertheless, British statesmen really had very little choice. If these rising communities beyond the seas, which had sent formidable fighters by hundreds of thousands to reinforce the British armies, chose to demand the appurtenances of sovereignty, they would have to have them; there was no real possibility of resisting. And from the British point of view, it was far better that they should have them with the aid and goodwill of Britain than in spite of her. In any case, it is amply clear that the British representatives, and Lloyd George in particular, gave strong support to the Dominions' case at Paris. (Barnes, in the matter of the International Labour Organization, is perhaps the exception that proves the rule.) One recalls Lloyd George contending with the Americans on January 12, 1919:

Take Australia, for example. They had sent more men to the war than Belgium or Serbia or Roumania. They had proved the most magnificent fighters, and had, he believed, actually lost more dead than the United States of America. They said that they were entitled to separate representation. It was no good saying that the British Government represented them, because, in fact, on many questions they could not. . . .[81]

The British were the necessary intermediaries through whom Dominion aspirations achieved recognition at the Paris Conference. If Lloyd George and his colleagues had not chosen to sponsor these aspirations, they would still have been realized; but their realization would have been delayed, and there would have been much unnecessary unpleasantness. These men's decision—doubtless a largely automatic one—to do what they did is to the credit of British statesmanship: that is to say, of British common sense.

Turning to the United States, we find in the first place that the Canadian delegation, and Borden in particular, approached the conference with an evident determination to make relations with their country's neighbour one of their special cares. This emerges with particular clarity from the meeting of the Imperial War Cabinet on December 30, 1918, which was largely concerned with relations with the United States concerning the settlement. Lloyd George reported on the conversations which he and Balfour had had with President Wilson during the President's recent visit to England. He spoke of Wilson's overmastering interest in a League of Nations, his vagueness on the "Freedom of the Seas" (the second of his Fourteen Points, and the one on which the British had the firmest reservations), his inclination to give "pure reparation" priority in the matter of indemnities, his doubts about the retention by Australia and New Zealand of the German Pacific colonies which they had occupied. It was presumably this last point that set off an anti-American outburst from W. M. Hughes, which takes up an entire page of the minutes. "If the saving of civilisation had depended on the United States," he said, "it would have been in tears and chains to-day." He demanded that Lloyd

George should "resolutely insist upon such terms of peace as were necessary for the safety of the Empire, through whose sacrifices and efforts victory had been won". Lord Reading, High Commissioner and Special Ambassador to the United States, who was present, was clearly alarmed. He did not believe that Wilson and Lloyd George were divided in any significant way, and he hoped "that we should not lightly abandon the position that, consistently with the maintenance of our rights, our main object was to bring about the closest co-operation hereafter between ourselves and the United States".

Borden, without addressing himself directly to Hughes, dissociated Canada entirely from the Australian's point of view, and proclaimed a North American interpretation of imperial foreign policy; one recalling George Washington's warning to his countrymen against entangling alliances:

Sir Robert Borden said that he would regret if we entered on the Peace Conference with any feeling of antagonism towards President Wilson or the United States. He considered that the recent conversations had, on the whole, been as favourable as he had anticipated. Future good relations between ourselves and the United States were, as he said before, the best asset we could bring home from the war. With regard to the two points on which there had been a pronounced difference, namely the Pacific Islands and indemnity, there was no reason to conclude that we had yet got the President's final point of view. He agreed that with regard to these we should maintain our position strongly. He wished, however, to make clear that if the future policy of the British Empire meant working in co-operation with some European nation as against the United States, that policy could not reckon on the approval or the support of Canada. Canada's view was that as an Empire we should keep clear, as far as possible, of European complications and alliances. This feeling had been immensely strengthened by the experience of the war, into which we had been drawn by old-standing pledges and more recent understandings, of which the Dominions had not even been aware.* He was in no sense reproaching the Imperial Government with regard to the past, and admitted— in answer to a question by Mr. Lloyd George—that since the Imperial War Cabinet had been set up the Dominions had not been committed to any treaty binding upon them without their knowledge.[82]

* The reference is doubtless mainly to the secret Treaty of London (April 1915) by which Britain, France, and Russia bribed Italy to enter the war, and to the prewar "military conversations" with France (above, page 138).

The attitudes reflected in this exchange would recur in a more famous imperial meeting two years later (below, pages 340–43).

Did any thought cross the minds of the Americans in Paris that Canada might possibly be an element friendly to their country within the councils of the British Empire, a community whose representatives might make it their business to present an informed and understanding interpretation of American policy to their imperial colleagues? If it did, it might have occurred to them that representation for Canada was almost as good business for the United States as extra representation for Brazil. But there is no indication that any such idea was ever entertained and, given the current state of information about Canada among American public men, one has no right to be surprised. Is it unkind to quote a remark of Robert Lansing in the Council of Ten on January 12, 1919?

> Mr. Lansing inquired how many Dominions there were. If Newfoundland, New Zealand, Australia, South Africa and India were included, that would mean five additional representatives.[83]

The Secretary of State had only forgotten one.

To the American delegation in 1919, Canada (when they remembered it) was just one limb of the spreading British imperial tree. The British were the advocates of Canadian representation, the Americans were its only determined opponents. The French did not care much, but were not unfriendly; the Italians and Japanese do not seem to have cared at all. What Canada got she got in spite of the United States. The very resolute opposition to Canada being given full national status in the International Labour Organization is particularly striking. In justice to the United States delegates, however, it should be noted that President Wilson told Sir Robert Borden that he saw "no difficulty whatever" about Canada, but that there was difficulty about "some other Dominions and especially India". Borden replied that the Canadians "could not ask to be placed in a different position from them".[84] This would certainly have produced outcry from the other Dominions. The fact is that the Americans had to accept the whole family, including India, whose credentials were so very doubtful; and in the end Wilson, when appealed to, "overrode advice of his Labour experts"[85] and did so.

It is curious, indeed, that the Americans did not make more of the question of India, for this was the weak point of the British position. India in 1919 was by no stretch of the imagination a self-governing country; the government of India took its orders from London. The argument for including India in the Imperial War Cabinet was the great numbers of men she had given to the war. From the Cabinet she moved into the British Empire Delegation and thence into the League of Nations. But in the League, it must be admitted, the India of that day had no rightful place: "The voice of India came . . . from a dusty corridor in Whitehall."[86] To this limited extent those who claimed that Britain had packed the League were justified.

APPROVAL AND RATIFICATION

On the ratification of the Treaty of Versailles there was a brief controversy with the British government.

On July 4, 1919 the Colonial Secretary cabled Ottawa expressing the hope that the treaty might be ratified by three of the principal Allies and Germany before the end of July. Borden replied that he was "under pledge to submit the Treaty to Parliament before ratification on behalf of Canada", and since Parliament had been prorogued he could not see how ratification on behalf of the whole Empire could be accomplished so soon. To Arthur Sifton, who was still overseas, he telegraphed, "Does Great Britain expect to ratify on behalf of whole Empire? If so our attendance at Paris and our signature to the Treaty was an utterly idle formality. On the other hand if she intends to ratify without including Dominions then Great Britain will technically be at peace with Germany while the Dominions are technically at war with that country."[87]

Lord Milner shortly produced an ingenious argument.[88] Nothing in the British constitution required parliamentary consent before ratification; the King could ratify on advice of his ministers. In such a treaty as the present one, the King certainly ought to act at the instance of all his constitutional advisers, including those in the Dominions. "But inasmuch as Dominion Ministers participated in peace negotiations, and side by side with Ministers of the United Kingdom signed preliminaries of Treaty, we hold that His Majesty if he now ratified the Treaty for the whole Empire would have the same constitutional justification in doing so in respect of Dominions as he has in respect of the United Kingdom." The Canadian Prime Minister did not swallow this. He replied, ". . . it seems to us that there is considerable doubt whether under modern constitutional practice the King should ratify without first obtaining the approval of Parliament . . . we do not entirely understand the suggestion that in the case of the Dominions the signature of the Dominion plenipotentiaries is equivalent to the tendering of advice to ratify. Do you regard this as holding good in the case of the signature of United Kingdom plenipotentiaries?"[89] To this interesting question there seems to have been no answer.

The British government did in fact lay the treaty before Parliament before advising the King to ratify it, and had done so before Milner presented his argument to Borden. The measure passed by the House of Commons on July 21 did not "approve" the treaty, but authorized the action required to give effect to it. On the same day the House voted "approval" of the Anglo-French treaty of guarantee (above, page 256). On August 4 Borden cabled Milner that the Canadian Parliament had been summoned for September 1. He added, "I cannot emphasize too strongly the unfortunate results which would certainly ensue from ratification before Canadian Parliament has had an opportunity of considering Treaty."[90]

The debate at Ottawa will be discussed in the next chapter. It was not a long debate, though longer than that at Westminster which occupied less than a day of the time of the House of Commons. On September 12 an order-in-council was approved noting that the Senate and House of Commons of Canada had by resolution approved the treaty with Germany, and ordering "that His Majesty the King be humbly moved to approve, accept, confirm and ratify the said Treaty of Peace, for and in respect of the Dominion of Canada".[91] In spite of all the British government's earlier urgings, it had turned out that there was no appalling need for haste. On October 8 King George V signed the instrument of ratification. The document contained only one indication that the ratification was on behalf of the whole Empire, including Canada; the fact that it referred to "Our Great Seal" instead of the traditional form, "the Great Seal of Our United Kingdom of Great Britain and Ireland".[92]

This may be called the final formal incident of the Versailles Treaty story as it affected Canada. The story is remarkable enough. The last word in commentary can be left to Loring Christie, who wrote in the same year, in firm yet suitably cautious language, "Canada through her representatives has definitely declared herself as in some degree an international person. . . . All this is unmistakable evidence of a new position in the world definitely assumed."[93]

RUSSIA: INVOLVEMENT AND WITHDRAWAL

While the German treaty and the Covenant of the League were being worked out at Paris, a curious episode in Canadian history was drawing to a close in Russia: the Canadian participation in the Allied military intervention against the Bolsheviks.

The Communist revolution in Petrograd in November 1917 was followed in March 1918 by peace between the Communist government and Germany. Russia's withdrawal from the war was a great Allied disaster, and it is not surprising that the Allies should look hopefully at the possibility of reconstructing the Eastern Front by assisting the elements in Russia that were resisting the Bolsheviks. Nor is it surprising, in the light of the close integration of the Canadian forces with the British in France, and the still uncertain state of the war there in the early summer of 1918, that Canada should be asked to contribute to the forces being sent to Russia.

The first Canadian contribution had in fact been made at the beginning of the year.[94] Sir Edward Kemp, the Minister of Overseas Military Forces, was invited by the British authorities to provide some high-grade individuals for a force intended to organize an irregular army to operate in the Caucasus region and protect the Baku oilfields from the Turks. At this time it was still hoped that the Bolsheviks might co-operate with the Allies against Turks and Germans. Forty-one Canadian officers and non-commissioned officers—all volunteers from the Corps in France —accordingly joined "Dunsterforce"* and took part in an unusual, hazardous but fortunately almost bloodless enterprise in Persia and Trans-Caucasia.[95]

In the early summer of 1918 the real intervention in Russia began. Small Allied forces were sent to the ports of Murmansk and Archangel, the northern termini of railway lines running to Petrograd and Moscow respectively. The Archangel force was known by the code name "Elope", the Murmansk one was called "Syren". In May, when these forces were being organized, the British War Office asked Sir Edward Kemp to provide sixteen Canadian officers and NCOs for "Elope", intended to assist in raising and training local anti-Bolshevik troops; and he did so. In July the British Army Council asked for something bigger: an infantry battalion for Murmansk. Since the recent Canadian conscription crisis had

* The force was commanded by Major-General L. C. Dunsterville, famous in another connection as the "Stalky" of Kipling's *Stalky & Co.*

been largely occasioned by shortage of infantry reinforcements, the Canadian decision (concurred in by Sir Robert Borden, who was at this time in London) was to refuse this request and "hold our Forces for the Western Front".[96] However, another party of officers and NCOs, ninety-two in number, was provided for Murmansk in lieu. The last and the most important Canadian contribution to the intervention in North Russia was authorized in August, when a field brigade of artillery (two 18-pounder batteries) was organized in Britain for the Archangel force.[97] These gunners, all volunteers, were the only Canadians who saw serious fighting in Russia.*

The largest commitment of troops, however, was in another quarter. In July 1918 President Wilson, who had long been under pressure from the Allied Supreme War Council to accept and take part in intervention in Siberia through Vladivostok, agreed to the project and to United States participation. It was clear that the major part of the force would have to be Japanese. A considerable element in the President's decision was clearly a feeling of responsibility for a large Czech force, formerly serving in the Russian Imperial Army, which was trying to make its way out of Russia to join the Allies. A Czech detachment had seized Vladivostok.[98] The British, desperately short of troops, asked in effect whether Canada could furnish the "British" contingent for this new front—two infantry battalions, an artillery battery, an engineer company, and other units; a British battalion from Hong Kong would come under the Canadian commander.[99] The Canadian units would go from Canada. After consideration —complicated by the fact that the British nettled Borden by cabling Ottawa on the subject after raising it with him in London—a Canadian order-in-council of August 12 authorized mobilizing the required force, "about four thousand all ranks". Not enough volunteers came forward, and the ranks had to be filled with conscripts. The first 680 men sailed from Vancouver on October 11.[100]

Extraordinary as it now appears, an element in the decision to send Canadian troops to Siberia was calculations (if that is not too precise a word) of postwar economic advantage in that region. Mewburn, the Minister of Militia, wrote Borden on July 12, after visiting the War Office, "It has been suggested that the trade conditions in this territory,

* They were also (if my memory of a conversation many years later with their commander, Colonel C. H. L. Sharman, is accurate) the only Canadian artillerymen who ever fought guns at 66° below zero Fahrenheit.

will be a vital factor, looking to the future, and it might be advisable to have some Canadian representative accompany this force, as far as Trade and Commerce goes. This matter is for your consideration." Borden took this seriously. Intimate relations with Siberia, he wrote to Mewburn later, "will be of great advantage to Canada in the future. Other nations will make very vigorous and determined efforts to obtain a foothold and our interposition with a small military force would tend to bring Canada into favourable notice by the strongest elements in that great community." On October 21 a Canadian order-in-council set up a four-man trade commission under the Department of Trade and Commerce to function at Vladivostok, where L. D. Wilgress, formerly Trade Commissioner at Omsk, was already installed.[101]

Young Mr. Wilgress was himself a symbol of Canadian economic aspirations in Russia. A McGill graduate of 1914, he had been recommended by Professor Stephen Leacock to George E. Foster, who as Minister of Trade and Commerce was pursuing the aim of strengthening the Canadian Trade Commissioner Service and considered the best means of doing so was hiring university-trained men. Apparently Foster's interest in Siberia as a possible Canadian market was aroused in 1915 by a lecture by Mackintosh Bell, a Canadian mining engineer who had been working near Omsk. In 1916 trade commissioners were established there and at Petrograd, the incumbent at the capital being C. F. Just. The dream faded, temporarily, after the Bolshevik revolution, but the prospect of the intervention revived it. Mr. Just, back in Ottawa, campaigned actively for an economic offensive to accompany the military movement, painting a picture of "the exploitation of Siberian forests under Canadian direction and with Canadian appliances and machinery". He recommended the appointment of the trade commission to Vladivostok, and was made a member of it.[102]

The command arrangements for the Canadian force were complicated. The commander was Brigadier-General J. H. Elmsley, a successful brigade commander on the Western Front. He was promoted major-general, presumably to give him more status in international councils. The British units in Siberia (ultimately, two infantry battalions) came under his command; but since his force was the "British" contingent of the army of intervention, he was under the operational direction of the War Office in London—subject to the fact that the whole Allied force based on Vladivostok was commanded by General Otani, the Japanese commander, whose contingent was by far the largest. Moreover, the Canadian government felt obliged to maintain as close control of its own troops as possible. Another element in the situation was Major-General Alfred Knox, former British military attaché in Petrograd and now chief of the British Military Mission in Siberia. By September 12, 1918 the following formula had been agreed upon between the War Office and the Canadian military authorities:

> There will be direct communication regarding matters of Policy and Operations between the War Office and the Canadian Commander of the Force, and all orders sent to, or reports made by the Commander will be repeated to the Militia Department, Ottawa. The Canadian Government is to deal with all questions concerning the administration of the Force, and on such matters there will be direct communication between the Commander of the Force and the Militia Department, Ottawa—all such communications being repeated to the War Office. Notwithstanding the foregoing the Canadian Government has stipulated and the Imperial Government has agreed that no disposition of the Force in the Field shall be made, nor shall such Force be committed to any Military Operations without carrying the judgment of the Canadian General Officer Commanding and therefore the latter shall at all times have the right of direct communication with the Canadian Government.[103]

This arrangement was clearly based upon the agreement concerning the control of the Canadian force in France (above, page 196): military operations were the province of the British command, but the administration of the Canadian forces was a matter for Canadian authority. There was, however, a fundamental difference. In France the Canadians were a small part of the British armies. In Siberia they constituted the major part of the Empire force. In these circumstances the Canadian authorities were able to insist that their general should have in effect a power of veto in respect of the commitment of his force to operations, and should possess at all times the right of communication with and appeal to his own government.

In fact, there were no military operations at Vladivostok. A fortnight after the Canadian advance party reached there, the armistice with Germany destroyed the only generally acceptable motive for the presence of Canadian forces in Russia—the re-creation of an Eastern Front. To keep troops there now was to interfere in Russia's internal affairs, and although many Canadians disliked and feared Bolshevism few were prepared to spend money and men in opposing it. Four years of war had been more than enough.

Three days after the armistice, while Borden was on the ocean, the Acting Prime Minister, Sir Thomas White, cabled the Minister of Overseas Military Forces that the cabinet felt that public opinion would not support them in continuing to send troops to Siberia. "We are all of opinion," he wrote, "that no further troops should be sent and that Canadian forces in Siberia should, as soon as situation will permit, be returned to Canada."[104] Borden, however, on arriving in England took the line that "withdrawal from our deliberate engagement will have extremely unfortunate effect". Nevertheless, continued representations from Ottawa led him to explain the difficulties to the War Office in terms which caused the authorities there to assume that the Canadian participation would end shortly. Then Borden heard that his colleagues at home, responding to his original attitude, had decided to proceed with the Siberian expedition as first planned. He was somewhat taken aback; he cabled, on behalf of the Canadian ministers in London, "Our view is that Canada's military operations in Siberia should be reduced to a minimum and that troops should be withdrawn as soon as conditions will reasonably permit." He also observed, "Please dispose of matter without further reference to us."[105] In doing so the cabinet was troubled by the fact that there seemed to be no agreed Allied policy for the Vladivostok force, and it was evident that the Americans and the Japanese were at odds. On December 22, 1918, accordingly, the Chief of the General Staff in Ottawa told the War Office that it was Canadian policy that all Canadian troops in Siberia should return home next spring; meanwhile, he added, "Dominion Government cannot permit them to engage in military operations nor, without its express consent, to move up country."[106] This situation was very disagreeable to General Knox, and there were "heated exchanges" between him and General Elmsley.[107]

On February 17, 1919 the British Empire Delegation at Paris considered the Russian situation. The Secretary of State for War, Winston Churchill, the leading advocate of the intervention policy, had come from London to seek some decision. He admitted that "elaborate and effective" military action was out of the question, but he clearly favoured continued support of the anti-Bolshevik forces. There was a possibility of the Germans intervening. "In the ultimate result we could contemplate a predatory confederation stretching from the Rhine to Yokohama menacing the vital interests of the British Empire in India and elswhere, menacing indeed the future of the world."

However uncertain Borden had been earlier, he knew his mind now.

Canada being "the only Dominion with troops in Russia", he spoke as soon as Churchill had finished, and made it clear that Canada was finished with the idea of intervention:

> Early in the month he had received a telegram from the Minister of Militia in Ottawa concerning the great anxiety felt in Canada for the return of the Canadian troops from Siberia. He (Sir Robert Borden) had submitted this to the [British] Prime Minister on the 7th February, saying at the same time that he proposed to recall these troops early in April, and asking for the views of the Government of the United Kingdom. He had received no reply and had recently decided that the proposed recall should be carried out. The Canadian Minister of Militia had been so informed.
>
> There was much strong feeling on the subject in Canada. It was with great difficulty that he had been able, after the Armistice, to secure the agreement of his Government to go on sending troops to Siberia. The Canadian Parliament could open on the 20th of the present month, and there would undoubtedly be demands to know what purpose these troops were serving in Russia and how long it was proposed to keep them there. Canadian public opinion had not yet been convinced that it was necessary to send troops to Russia, and he was absolutely certain that public opinion would never sanction the use of the Military Service Act for the purpose of military operations in Russia. He appreciated the view-point expressed by the Secretary of State for War, but there were other considerations to be borne in mind. The telegrams and papers received on the subject invariably disclosed that the anti-Bolsheviks in Russia themselves admitted that they could not fight alone. That meant that if we should embark upon any active operations against Russia, however limited, we might inevitably be drawn into a course whose consequence it was impossible to foresee. Public opinion would certainly not sanction our embarking upon such a hazard....
>
> His conclusions on the whole were that the Russian pot would simply have to boil, that Russia would have to work out her own salvation....
>
> At all events ... even if it were necessary to face the possibility that Germany might gain a dominant position in Russia, he felt that the case had been so presented to the world, or had so presented itself, that it would be impossible to persuade the Canadian Parliament to undertake any active operations however limited, and it was, therefore, necessary for him to say to the Imperial War Cabinet that the Canadian troops would have to be withdrawn in the spring, or, at the latest, in the early summer.

Borden inquired also as to the possibility of withdrawing the Canadians in North Russia at an early date. Churchill remarked that the two British battalions put in through Vladivostok had been pushed forward to

Omsk (roughly 2,500 miles inland!) where they dammed off a vast area of Russia from the Bolsheviks; if the Canadians left Siberia, these battalions would have to withdraw. Borden showed no sign of being moved by this argument.[108]

During the next few months the Canadian share in the intervention was gradually liquidated. Some 3,800 Canadians had actually reached Vladivostok. They began to withdraw in April 1919, and the last party sailed on June 5.[109] Before the detachments in North Russia withdrew there were further appeals from Churchill. On May 1 he wrote rather emotionally to Borden asking that Canadians should be allowed to volunteer for service in this area ("Even a few hundred Canadian volunteers would be of great assistance and would make a name for themselves in this most righteous crusade").[110] Arthur Sifton saw no objections, provided the volunteers became members of the British army; he felt that the Canadian government should take no responsibility for a force "which would not be under their jurisdiction and over which they could exercise no special supervision or control". Canadian ministers were not in the market for crusades in May 1919. Borden evaded the issue by suggesting that Churchill telegraph the Acting Prime Minister in Ottawa through the Governor General. The Secretary of State for War does not seem to have done this; he presumably knew when he had been brushed off.[111] On May 18 Borden wrote Churchill, "Beyond question it is imperative that the Canadian Forces now at Archangel should be withdrawn without delay." There had been some disaffection in the Allied forces there, including what seems to have been a minor incident in the Canadian artillery. The artillery brigade embarked for England on June 11.[112] In July Churchill begged Borden not to insist on the prompt withdrawal of the small Canadian detachment at Murmansk, which he said would "lead to an immediate disaster and the destruction of British troops". The Canadian government of course acceded to this request; but all Canadians were out of North Russia by September. The campaign there had cost them twenty-four battle casualties, of which eight were fatal.[113]

This queer and on the whole distinctly unheroic incident of the Russian intervention is, however anticlimactic, not an entirely unsuitable conclusion for the tremendous drama of Canada's part in the First World War.

For one thing, the affair reflected rather strikingly the change in the Dominion's status since 1914. Although the adventure was undertaken in the first instance primarily as part of the continuing war against Germany (and Canada would probably never have got involved in it on any other basis), the decision to send a Canadian force to Siberia was consciously national, a rather different matter from the automatic involvement of 1914. A new commitment was being undertaken, and it was undertaken deliberately after consideration by the cabinet in Ottawa. It was justified, moreover, on grounds of Canadian national policy—not merely as contributing to the defeat of Germany, but also as producing economic advantage for Canada. That this idea now appears almost incredibly naïve is perhaps beside the point.

The command arrangements for the Siberian force also reflected change. For the first time a Canadian officer commanded a joint Commonwealth force. Perhaps this was not enormously important; it would have been more so had the force gone into action. It was important that the Canadian government insisted on maintaining control of the employment of its own troops and specified that they should not be sent into the interior without its previous consent. The Canadian Siberian contingent was under firmer national control than any other Canadian force that served abroad in the First World War. Four years of bloody battles had left the Dominion government more sophisticated, more confident and more assertive than it had ever been before. The Siberian affair prefigures much of the tone of Canadian policy in the years ahead.

It also gives us a glimpse of the tendencies of opinion that went far to produce that tone. Through the war with Germany the Canadian community was under great and growing strain. Tremendous sacrifices were made with little complaint. Then came the armistice, and the taut wire snapped. It is symptomatic that the government that had been quite prepared to send Canadian soldiers to Siberia as long as Germany was fighting became doubtful as early as three days after the armistice whether Canadian public opinion would support a continuance of the enterprise. The issue was, pretty clearly, a threat to the unity of Borden's coalition cabinet; three of the four ministers whom Sir Thomas White mentioned as particularly opposed to persisting with the intervention were ex-Liberals.[114] One of them, T. A. Crerar, Minister of Agriculture and regarded as the voice of the western farmer in the government, wrote White a strong letter opposing sending more troops to Siberia and demanding that those already there should be brought home. He had supported the original decision to send the force but, as he saw it, the whole situation had been transformed by the collapse of the Central Powers.[115]

On November 25, 1918 White wrote Borden, "There is an extraordinary sentiment in Canada in favour of getting all our men home and at work as soon as possible."[116] On December 7 he wrote again, "There is a good deal of feeling in labour and other quarters here against our continued participation and my personal view is that a serious political situation may arise later unless some definite statement can be made as to the return of the expedition within a reasonable time."[117] The Chief of the Canadian General Staff told the War Office, "people war-weary, nervous, irritable".[118]

As we have already seen, Borden, discussing the question in Paris, did not really attempt to weigh the merits and disadvantages of continued intervention in Russia. He simply said that the state of Canadian opinion rendered further Canadian participation impossible. The fact is that at the very outset of what was to be a twenty-year interval between two world wars, Canadians were already demonstrating the spirit of disenchantment that was to dominate those years. War-weary they certainly were; proud of what their country had done, but determined for the most part, it would seem, that so far as they could control events it should never be called upon for such sacrifices again. Like their southern neighbours, though in rather different patterns of circumstance, they were rebounding from idealism into isolation.

CHAPTER TEN

REACTION FROM THE HEROIC AGE, 1919-1920

LEADERS GO, AND COME

As that tremendous experience, "the Great War", began to recede into history, the men who had long dominated Canadian politics made way for new leaders.

Sir Wilfrid Laurier had led the Liberal party since 1887, and had been Prime Minister from 1896 to 1911. When the war ended he was almost seventy-seven, and ailing. Arrangements were made to call a national convention of the party in 1919. But before it could meet Sir Wilfrid died, on February 17. There were several candidates for his mantle. One was W. S. Fielding, who had been Minister of Finance throughout his administration. But Fielding himself was seventy, and many Liberals held against him the fact that he had been a supporter of conscription, though he never joined Borden's Union government. The Liberal caucus chose as temporary leader in the House of Commons a comparative nonentity, D. D. McKenzie, an anti-conscriptionist who had never sat in a cabinet. But the man the Liberal convention finally elected as leader was William Lyon Mackenzie King.

King, who had been Laurier's Minister of Labour from 1909 to the government's defeat in 1911, had not been in Parliament since he lost his seat in that debacle. He had, however, run unsuccessfully as a Laurier Liberal in the 1917 election, and this was an advantage to him in the contest for the leadership. His reflection recorded in his diary after hearing of Sir Wilfrid's death was, "Quebec dominates the situation in the House of Commons, the Liberals of Quebec will never take as a leader any man who 'betrayed' Sir Wilfrid at the last election."[1] In fact, it seems evident that it was primarily the almost solid support of Quebec at the convention that made him party leader.[2] These things King never forgot.

In one respect it was well for King that he had not been more directly involved in the bitter struggles of the war years. Nevertheless, his wartime activities were a political embarrassment to him, for while he never gave up his Canadian residence he spent a good part of his time in the United States, and it was easy for those who disliked him to say that he had abandoned his country in its hour of need. In fact, King was in his fortieth year when war broke out, and had had no military experience. To upbraid him for not joining the forces is absurd. What he was actually doing was acting as an industrial consultant to labour matters, usually at the behest of John D. Rockefeller, Jr. King had met Rockefeller in 1914, when the Rockefeller Foundation invited him to undertake a far-reaching study of industrial relations and problems in the United States and he produced a plan that restored peace and harmony to strike-torn Rockefeller mining properties in Colorado. The two men were friends for the rest of their lives, and King's Rockefeller connections (and his connections with other American corporations which sought his aid) gave him a unique entrée to big business circles and wealthy society in the United States. It was not difficult to argue that by keeping American mines and factories working he was making an important contribution to the Allied war effort. Nevertheless the slurs rankled, and on April 20, 1920 he delivered a carefully prepared defence of his war record in the House of Commons.[3]

In the latter part of the war King devoted much of his time and energy to writing a book on the problems of industrial relations, which appeared at the end of 1918 under the title *Industry and Humanity*.[4] It was a strange production, which most people have found close to unreadable: turgid, sentimental, grotesquely ill-organized, and illustrated by a set of charts that would have done credit to a graduate astrologer. It was hardly worthy of its author's very considerable achievements in the field of labour peace. King, however, was extremely proud of it. A few days after he finished it he reflected happily that his "humble little home" at Kingsmere near Ottawa might shortly "have a place perhaps in the world's thought".[5] Throughout the rest of his life he referred frequently to the book, citing it particularly as evidence of his liberal views on social policy. It is relevant here in another connection. King believed, and said in the book and many times later, that the problem of maintaining peace between labour and management was essentially similar to the problem of maintaining peace between nations. The basic principles in both cases were those laid down in the Industrial Disputes Investigation Act, drafted by King as Deputy Minister of Labour and passed by the Canadian Parliament in 1907.[6] The central feature of the procedure it prescribed was the "conciliation board", comprising representatives of both parties to the dispute and a neutral chairman. The key words were "investigation" and "conciliation". In the last weeks of the greatest war in history, King wrote:

> There would have been no war had the principle of investigation before resort to Force been the guiding principle in the affairs of nations. What a momentous thought; what a responsibility upon those who in industrial or international relations may remain indifferent to this principle! Can we fight for one principle abroad, and act upon an opposite principle at home?[7]

It all seemed agreeably simple.

Mackenzie King, now leader of the opposition, re-entered the House of Commons in the autumn of 1919. Less than a year later, Sir Robert Borden, whose health had long been bad, was obliged to retire from public life (July 1920) after serving as Prime Minister for nearly nine years.[8] Borden was not a man of penetrating intellect or an original political thinker; but in his dour Nova Scotian fashion he had had a firm grasp of first principles. He was prepared to see Canada make great sacrifices for imperial causes in which the majority of the Canadian people believed; but he was determined that these sacrifices should purchase a share in imperial decision-making. This position was well defined before the war and was, as we have seen, in marked contrast to Laurier's. Increasingly, through the war and the making of peace, Borden maintained a steady pressure on the British government, with varying degrees of support from the other Dominion Prime Ministers. Unlike Hughes, he was almost always polite; but the pressure did not relax. The result was the position of effective influence which the Dominions had achieved in British councils by the armistice, and in the following year their appearance as national entities in the League of Nations. He had turned great world events to his country's national purposes, and had consolidated at the council table the victories won by Canadian soldiers in France and Flanders. The fighting men and the statesmen of 1914–19 were a new generation of Canadian founding fathers. If Borden's name is to be blazoned on the roll of Canada's great prime ministers, it is because of what he did to achieve a new position for her in the Empire and the world.

For half a year before his final retirement, Borden's health kept him away from public business. His successor as Prime Minister and leader of the Unionist party was not chosen, like King, by a convention. That method was novel in Canada and would have been difficult to compass in the light of the nature of the coalition. It was agreed that Borden should choose the new leader after consultation with members of the Unionist caucus and people outside Parliament. He soon found that the ministers' favourite was Sir Thomas White, though the backbenchers liked Arthur Meighen. White declined the Governor-General's offer of the premiership. The succession went to Meighen.[9]

Meighen was a man of distinguished abilities, but many people had doubts about him as a leader. He had been prominently associated with the government's emergency war legislation, including the Military Service Act, which he had drafted. In Quebec his name was synonymous with the policy of conscription. This he would never live down. He was a formidable debater. He detested Mackenzie King, who returned the feeling with interest. His attitudes on external policies remained to be developed. He had sat in the Imperial War Cabinet for a short time in 1918 (above, page 219), but had attended only three meetings and had never had the occasion or the need to speak. He represented Canada in the more mundane proceedings of the concurrent Imperial War Conference. He had not been a member of the Canadian team at the Paris Conference.[10] He thus had only a limited personal commitment to the new system of external relations with which Borden's name was associated.

CLIMATE OF OPINION

To assess accurately what "the people" of any community think about a given issue at a given time is as difficult as it is to decide why "the people" voted as they did in a particular election. One looks at the circumstances, one examines what public expressions of opinion are available, and one speculates. In recent times there are opinion polls to help, for whatever they may be worth. The fact remains that the thing the historian finds hardest to do is the thing that it is perhaps most important that he should be able to do: to look into the minds of men, as individuals or as groups.

It is desirable to form some notion of the state of Canadian opinion on the country's international position and policies at the end of the First World War, when the world crisis had forced Canada into playing a more active international role than she had ever essayed before. Perhaps the best starting point is the debate in the House of Commons in September 1919 on the Treaty of Versailles. The debate has been called brief and inadequate, but in fact a large number of members spoke, a wide variety of views were expressed, and the occasion gives us at least some idea of the channels in which opinion was presumably running.[11]

Sir Robert Borden opened the debate on September 2, moving a resolution approving the treaty. He summarized the treaty and outlined the Canadian part in the conference. He did not boast, though he had more reason for boasting than any other Canadian prime minister returning from a great international negotiation has ever had. He defined the position which he and his colleagues had taken in dignified and impressive words:

> On behalf of my country I stood firmly upon this solid ground; that in this, the greatest of all wars, in which the world's liberty, the world's justice, in short the world's future destiny were at stake, Canada had led the democracies of both the American continents. Her resolve had given inspiration, her sacrifices had been conspicuous, her effort was unabated to the end. The same indomitable spirit which made her capable of that effort and sacrifice made her equally incapable of accepting at the Peace Conference, in the League of Nations, or elsewhere, a status inferior to that accorded to nations less advanced in their development, less amply endowed in wealth, resources and population, no more complete in their sovereignty and far less conspicuous in their sacrifice.

Borden was supported by the other ministers who had played parts at Paris; also, most notably, by N. W. Rowell.[12] The President of the Council emphasized the achievement of new status, but was careful in allotting credit for it: "I do not claim that the Government of Canada has improved the status of the Dominion during this war, but what I say is that the troops of Canada at Ypres, Courcelette, Vimy Ridge, Passchendaele, Arras, Amiens, and Cambrai made such a place for Canada in the Empire and in Europe that any government here would have been false to its duty if it did not seek to maintain that place at the Peace Conference." He quoted Resolution IX of the Imperial War Conference (above, page 213), and declared, "We are recognized now as a nation of equal status with the Mother Country and other Dominions. The Constitutional Conference must work out the details."

The Liberals would have been better off in this debate if their new leader, Mackenzie King, had been in the House; but he had not yet found a seat. As it was, they spoke with a confused voice. Their convention in August had given them a platform as well as a leader; but its only reference to external affairs was a resolution on Canadian autonomy which did not help them much now:

> Resolved that we are strongly opposed to centralized Imperial control and that no organic change in the Canadian Constitution in regard to the relation of Canada to the Empire ought to come into effect until, after being passed by Parliament, it has been ratified by vote of the Canadian people on a Referendum.[13]

No mention was made of the League of Nations or any other concrete issue. And if any attempt was made to ensure that the party spoke with a united voice in the September debate it did not succeed.

D. D. McKenzie, the temporary leader, who had been defeated in the convention, made a curious speech[14] in which he said that the treaty should not be a party issue and went on to express serious doubts about the League of Nations, which he thought would bind Canada to actions not taken as a result of "the free will of the Canadian people"; he also said, "despite whatever we may say, or whatever ambitions we may attempt to put forward in the line of being a nation we are not a nation in the true sense of the term. We are part of a great Empire of which we are proud, and we are nothing else." At the end of the debate[15] W. S. Fielding, a Liberal elder statesman and, as we have noted, another defeated candidate for the leadership, took a rather similar line. His word for the proceedings of the Canadian government concerning the Peace Conference was "humbug", and he used it several times. "By their demand for separate recognition apart from the British Empire they are beginning—they may not have meant it so—to break up the British Empire." Canada was "a dependency of the British Crown". "Canada is not a nation, Canada cannot be a nation. When the hon. gentleman speaks of Canada standing on a position of equality with the Mother Country, it is apparent that the argument cannot be sustained for a single moment. There cannot be two parliamentary governments of equal authority in the Empire." To the argument that Sir Wilfrid Laurier had boasted that Canada was a nation, Fielding replied that Laurier had used the word in a different "sense". Fielding also took exception to Articles 10 and 16 of the League Covenant, which he said bound Canada to military action irrespective of her own wishes; and he moved an amendment to the resolution approving the treaty:

> That in giving such approval this House in no way assents to any impairment of the existing autonomous authority of the Dominion, but declares that the question of what part, if any, the forces of Canada shall take in any war, actual or threatened, is one to be determined at all times as occasion may require by the people of Canada through their representatives in Parliament.

Such a reservation had been suggested earlier in the debate[16] by another Liberal whose general approach to the treaty, nevertheless, was quite different from Fielding's. This was Ernest Lapointe, first elected to Parliament in 1904, who would be a member of every ministry headed by Mackenzie King and his trusted lieutenant in Quebec. "I am glad, indeed," said Lapointe, "that we had representatives at the Peace Conference. I do not share the opinion of those who claim that we had no business to be there. My criticism is rather in the opposite direction; my complaint is that our representatives were not there on a basis of perfect equality with those of the Mother Country." He went on to scoff at the Imperial War Cabinet; the people of Canada were, he said, "opposed to all schemes of centralization by which Canadian policies would be framed and decided upon outside Canada by any body of men in which Canada would have only one representative out of twelve":

> The right hon. the Prime Minister spoke in laudatory terms of the Imperial War Cabinet. He may be assured that any such representation or voice as Canada had in that body will not satisfy the Canadian people. His words of last year that the Imperial War Cabinet was a cabinet of governments* were grandiloquent words, and nothing else. There is no such thing as a cabinet of governments. There cannot be a cabinet unless there is also a parliament to which such cabinet is directly responsible.

Lapointe, not McKenzie or Fielding, was the spokesman of the Liberal future; indeed, as we shall see, of the Canadian future. But he also spoke for the Liberal past. In his refusal to see any possible advantage for Canada in the Imperial War Cabinet he echoed the views of the dead leader Laurier, who had written in one of his last letters to his friend and sup-

* Above, page 209.

porter Professor O. D. Skelton that economic discussions in which the Unionist ministers were rumoured to be involved in England would come to "nothing more real than their so called Imperial Cabinet".[17]

The violent controversy raging in the United States, and particularly in the Senate, over the question of American membership in the League of Nations, was enough to ensure that the League would be prominent in the Canadian debate, and that Article 10 would receive considerable attention. Borden admitted that the Canadian representatives in Paris did not think the treaty beyond criticism or the League Covenant "a perfect instrument"; but he and his colleagues breathed no word of the battle they had fought against Article 10. Had the facts been known they would certainly have had incalculable influence on the course of the debate.* As it was, the supposed menace which the League represented to Canadian autonomy turned up in a good many speeches, notably those of French-Canadian members. Rodolphe Lemieux, a former Liberal minister, argued that Canada should not substitute government from Geneva for the former government from London which had been outgrown; L.-T. Pacaud claimed that Article 10 placed the Canadian people "at the beck and call of a Council not responsible to the nation for its actions".[19] The fiercest attack on the League, however, came from an English-speaking MP from Quebec.[20] C. G. Power, later to be famous under the nickname "Chubby", was a Roman Catholic of Irish background who had been wounded overseas while serving as an infantry officer and had won the Military Cross. He would be a member of Mackenzie King's cabinet of 1935, and one of the most popular individuals who ever sat in the Canadian Parliament. Long afterwards he said in his autobiography that it was not sense of duty that took him into the army; he went because of "a desire for excitement and adventure".[21] Now he spoke as a Canadian nationalist and also an opponent of the League. "I have," he said, "neither the constitutional knowledge, the time nor the ability to discuss this matter at great length, but it strikes me that either we are a dependent nation, even though self-governing,—and in that case we have no business to sign the Treaty—or we are an independent, bound to the Mother Country only by ties of common interest, of blood and sentiment, and by a common

* Mr. Donald M. Page has pointed out that the opposition could have discovered the truth by reading an article by J. W. Dafoe published in the *Manitoba Free Press* earlier in the year.[18] Dafoe had represented the Canadian Department of Public Information at the Peace Conference.

King. For myself, I have no hesitation in proclaiming and approving of the latter proposition, and I think that this is the saner and truer conception of our status." Like Pacaud and others, he regarded the League as a menace to Canadian independence; he objected to the fact that the Canadian Parliament was being told that it could not amend the covenant, but must accept or reject it; and he hoped that Canada's next government would see to it that the country withdrew from the League. And he ended with a resounding declaration of isolationism:

> We as Canadians have our destiny before us not in continental Europe but here on the free soil of America. Our policy for the next hundred years should be that laid down by George Washington in the United States for the guidance of his countrymen—absolute renunciation of interference in European affairs—and that laid down by the other great father of his country in Canada, Sir Wilfrid Laurier—"freedom from the vortex of European militarism." I believe this policy to be the true expression of a Greater Canadianism. I believe the people of Canada will approve of this policy, namely, to let Europe be the arbiter of its own destiny while we in Canada, turning our energies to our own affairs, undertake our own peaceful development strong in the faith that we have within our national boundaries and within ourselves the material to become a great and powerful nation.
>
> I am convinced that our soldiers have returned from overseas more proud than ever before of that "Canada" badge which they bore so proudly on their shoulders; convinced, too, that they are as good men in peace and war as the poilu and Tommy Atkins, their Allies in many a desperate conflict, their comrades on many a blood-sodden field. They have learned nothing from European culture or continental civilization. The eagerness with which they demanded demobilization, their happy faces when they reached their native shores, were proof positive that above all they longed for their loved Canada, their home.

No doubt it would be a mistake to regard Power's attitude as representative of the country at large. Other ex-officers who spoke in the debate took different lines, seeing the League, as the government did, not as a menace to Canada but as the hope of mankind.[22] Power's Irish heredity doubtless coloured his views (he was the only member who brought the Treaty of Limerick into the discussion of the Treaty of Versailles) and doubtless also he was not unaware that these views were agreeable to a considerable proportion of the voters in his constituency of Quebec South. His opinions were narrow and might even be called ignorant—though

"European culture" and "continental civilization" were presented in very unfortunate guises to young Canadians of his generation. But if his reflections concerning the comparison between Canadians and their allies tend to the complacent, it is worth remembering that Sir Arthur Currie said much the same thing to Mackenzie King (above, page 238); if he was disposed to George Washington's view of entangling alliances, we may recall that Sir Robert Borden spoke in rather similar terms to the Imperial War Cabinet (above, page 272). Although young Major Power's views do not seem to have been widely noticed at the time—the *Canadian Annual Review* lists him merely as one who also spoke—isolationist prejudices like his were found in the minds of many Canadians in 1919, and by no means all of them lived in Quebec.

At the end of the Commons debate the Fielding motion calling for a reservation was rejected by a party vote, 102 to 70, and Borden's resolution was passed.[23]

Surveying the debate, one is impressed by the extraordinary variety of opinions. There was no sign of a national consensus and certainly none of a non-partisan or bi-partisan approach to external problems. It was a moment of great party bitterness, and the Liberal opposition, fresh from the heady experience of a national convention, had no intention of allowing the government any slightest meed of praise for what had been done in Paris. We have noticed the disunion among the Liberals—which their opponents did not fail to remark upon;[24] and there was every kind of permutation. Thus Power hated the League and almost every other connection that stood in the way of Canadian independence and isolation. French-Canadian backbenchers tended to agree with him. McKenzie and Fielding mistrusted the League but fully accepted the traditional colonial relationship to Britain. Lapointe had some reservations about the League but applauded the separate national status Canada seemed to have achieved and merely regretted that it had not been less equivocal. The government's supporters, generally speaking, saw (or said they saw) the League as a probable blessing and were pleased with the idea of an increasing Canadian share in the councils of a beneficent Commonwealth. The House of Commons spoke with a confusion of tongues, not surprising in a young country making its doubtful debut as a nation—apparently —among nations.

The new Liberal leader was acutely aware of the differences of opinion within his party that the debate had advertised; and after obtaining a seat in the Commons he took the first suitable opportunity to define the Liberal position in terms that in effect firmly repudiated the colonial position of McKenzie and Fielding. The chance came in March 1920, when N. W. Rowell, then Acting Secretary of State for External Affairs, laid before Parliament for approval before ratification the Treaty of Neuilly with Bulgaria (above, page 257). Offhand, as King remarked, it was a little difficult to see why this was done; for other subsidiary treaties had been approved by order-in-council. Rowell said that it was, in part, to enable Parliament to "reaffirm" its approval of the League of Nations, of the labour clauses of the treaties and the International Labour Organization, and of "the position and status accorded to Canada in the League of Nations and in the International Labour Organization and of its determination to maintain that status".[25] Presumably recent attacks on "that status" made in the United States (below, pages 306–07) were in Rowell's mind.

King's speech on March 16 was carefully prepared[26] and effective. The leader tactfully refrained from mentioning the views any individual Liberal had expressed in the earlier debate, but the stand he took was close to Lapointe's. He was prepared, he said, to give credit to Sir Robert Borden and his colleagues at Paris for doing their duty by standing firm for "the maintenance of Canada's status". But, he argued, "What we say is that Canada's status as a nation from the constitutional point of view was established long before the present Administration was formed and in spite of the opposition of some of its own members and their associates in the past." This status was, in fact, the work of Laurier.

> What, then, is the difference which exists between us and my hon. friend [Rowell], or any of those associated with him, in regard to this question of the status of Canada? So far as I can see, we have no difference on what is fundamental as respects our status. Our difference is that hon. gentlemen opposite, and in particularly my hon. friend, would have it appear, as I have already said, that our status is something newly acquired; that in some way or other which is inexplicable to us there has been a change within the last few years, and that we stand in a position now, from the legal and constitutional viewpoint, which we did not have before. We on this side of the House maintain that while there has been a clearer defining of the status of Canada, and while there has been unquestionably, and above all else, in the eyes of the world and from the international point of view, a recognition of the status of Canada through the splendid services of her armies overseas, and by

reason of the valiant part they played in the great war, all these circumstances have served to emphasize and strengthen and make permanent a status which we already had and which we intend to maintain.

King proceeded, at perhaps undue length, to quote from a speech made by Rowell in Montreal in 1912, when he was Liberal leader in Ontario. Rodolphe Lemieux had already quoted this speech during the September debate,[27] and King had evidently seen in it the means of making a debating point and embarrassing Rowell, the ex-Liberal. In 1912 Rowell had lauded the resolution of the Colonial Conference of 1907 changing the name of the conference to Imperial Conference as having "established the status of the Dominions as national entities". Rowell had said further,

I venture to suggest that when the history of our constitutional development is written among the great things that Sir Wilfrid Laurier has done none will appear greater than his perception of the fact that the status of Canada must be changed and that this change must be brought about, not by legislative enactment, but by the demand on our part for a new status, persisted in until the people of Canada were convinced of its necessity; persisted in until the statesmen of Great Britain were convinced that it was right. By this great achievement Sir Wilfrid has enlarged the liberties and improved the status of every Canadian citizen, and what he has done for Canada he has done for all the self-governing Dominions.

Rowell sturdily refused to take back anything he had said in 1912, or to admit that it was inconsistent with what he had said about what had been done in 1919. But King had established as the Liberal canon (and quite probably convinced himself) that Laurier, whom we have seen at every imperial gathering from 1897 onward insisting that Canada had nothing to ask and no improvements to suggest in the imperial structure (above, pages 56, 78, and 156), was the architect of the modern status of the Dominion.

Two other aspects of King's statement should be noted. First, he called up the bogey of centralization. Rowell, at the end of his speech, had said, "If we do not proceed along the line of equality of status and co-operation under a common sovereign, I submit that there are just two alternatives: Either dependency, with Great Britain controlling our foreign policy and the issues of peace and war, or independence, and we will not accept either alternative." King now said,

The thing about which we on this side of the House are alarmed is not independence or the maintenance of the status which we have as one of the nations comprising the British Empire. The thing we are concerned about and what we fear is the danger of swinging to the other extreme and developing a form of centralised Imperialism which we think would be thoroughly objectionable so far as the interests of this country are concerned. It is not to any status of Canada as one of the nations within the British Empire that we take exception. We wish to see that position maintained and strengthened; but we do not wish to see, through any insidious or other method, a condition of affairs brought about whereby the full autonomy of this country and of this Parliament will in any way be lessened or impaired by any scheme of Imperialism which will lead to a centralisation of the control of the British Empire, instead of the maintenance of the free self-governing position which we are privileged to enjoy at the present time.

We believe that position can be maintained by holding to the attitude of conference and consultation which was developed under the old Liberal administration; that it is possible for the British Empire to become, as regards the League of Nations, a league within a league, if you like, for the preservation of freedom amongst the different nations of the world.

The potential threat to Canada's autonomy, as King saw it, came from London; he did not choose to take note of the almost unanimous apprehension of the League of Nations expressed by his Quebec followers who had spoken in the debate the previous year. There had been "no difference of view", as he saw it, on the League of Nations and the labour clauses of the German treaty. "I am not aware, when they were being debated..., that a single exception was taken by any member of the House to the clauses relating to the League of Nations, and, in particular, to the labour clauses. . . . I believe there is only one opinion in this House and in this country. We all recognize that the League of Nations is in a formative stage, that its constitution is more or less nebulous at the present time, but that it has in it promise of great good for humanity and for mankind. We all desire to see the League of Nations made a success. . . ." It was tepid approval, but it was different from the hostility of Lemieux, Pacaud, and Power. A government headed by King was unlikely to take Canada out of the League as Power had hoped would happen.

Not uncharacteristically, but not without reason, King was pleased with his own performance. He recorded that both Fielding and McKenzie congratulated him. He wrote in his diary,[28] "I think I got our party out of the wrong lines of last session on this all important matter. . . . Rowell was effectively silenced as regards any *new* status Canada has acquired it gave me a great happiness to be able to refer to Grandfather's part in Canada's history, along with Sir Wilfrid's in the same speech. . . ." The mention of William Lyon Mackenzie had been in one of the quotations from Rowell's address of 1912. It was a very slight reference, but to be able to put it into the mouth of an opponent undoubtedly pleased King. His grandfather and Sir Wilfrid would continue to be, in his mind, his inspirers and patrons.

Generally speaking, the Canadian press, in its editorial comments on the problems of external policy, divided much as the House of Commons had.[29] The Commons debate in September 1919 aroused some additional interest in the subject, which had been fairly languidly regarded. Papers normally supporting the government as a general rule stood by it on these issues, accepting and applauding the ideas of a voice in the affairs of a reorganized Empire and of membership in the League. Some which had been doubtful about the League rallied to its cause as the debate proceeded. The Liberal press was divided, particularly on the question of the League. In the first instance the French-language Liberal journals—virtually all the French papers in Quebec—did not show great hostility to the League, but their comments during the parliamentary discussion were much more adverse to it. In the English-language Liberal press the League had strong friends, notably the still-influential Toronto *Globe*. And the *Manitoba Free Press** was beginning its long career as the foremost Canadian journalistic supporter of the League.

John W. Dafoe, editor of the *Free Press*, had returned from Paris (above, page 292) a friend of Sir Robert Borden and a believer in the League of Nations. He accepted Borden's claims concerning a new national status as well-founded; and while he had little use for the Treaty of Versailles as such, he saw the League as "the charter of the Future, the one star of hope shining in the overcast sky". He was not one of those who objected to Article 10; he saw its obligations as the price that had to be paid for peace. He took it on himself, in the columns of his paper and on the public platform, to fight for acceptance of the League idea. Using terms that would become fashionable only after another world war had opened many eyes, he told the Winnipeg Canadian Club in 1919, "There are 60,000 graves in France and Flanders, every one of which tells us that,

* The name was changed to *Winnipeg Free Press* in 1931.

for good or ill, we are in the world and must bear our part in the solution of its troubles."[30]

Dafoe, however, did not have an entirely free hand at the *Free Press*. The paper was still owned by our old acquaintance of Alaska days, Clifford Sifton, who had been knighted in 1915. Sifton was now a total nationalist and isolationist, who had markedly little enthusiasm for the League of Nations. He rode Dafoe on a loose rein, but he did take an interest in his newspaper's policies, and as long as he was there (he lived until 1929) Dafoe had to set bounds to his League enthusiasms.[31] Both men were strong nationalists—Dafoe increasingly so as time passed; but on the League they differed. Both were to play parts in shaping the policies of Mackenzie King's first administration.

Another nationalistic publicist who left a mark had his base in Ottawa. We have already made a passing reference to John S. Ewart (above, page 239). From 1904 onward he bombarded Canadians with arguments in favour of their country becoming, in some form, an independent nation. His style was too legalistic to command a large popular audience, but he never gave up. In the first instance he found his text in John A. Macdonald's desire to have the new political entity of 1867 labelled a kingdom, and the series of polemical papers in which he expounded the thesis that Canada would find her ultimate independent status in a personal union with the other Dominions and the United Kingdom under a common sovereign were published under the name *The Kingdom Papers*.[32] But the war changed all this. To Ewart the Imperial War Cabinet seemed an imperialistic sham, a revival of colonialism. It now seemed to him that genuine national freedom could be found only in proclaiming a Canadian republic; and *The Kingdom Papers* were succeeded in due time by *The Independence Papers*.[33] He convinced himself that the League of Nations, too, was part of an imperialist conspiracy, and Article 10 a device that would undermine Canadian autonomy. These views he developed in a series of articles in the Ottawa *Citizen* at the time when the Treaty of Versailles was before Parliament, and they were quoted at length by a French-Canadian Liberal, George Parent, during the debate in the Commons.[34]

Subsequently Ewart's opinions changed again. He found himself applauding the constitutional developments of the later twenties moving towards the Statute of Westminster. He reverted to the view that personal union was a respectable and satisfactory final goal, and by 1930 he was convinced that Sir Robert Borden "did more for the elevation of Canada's constitutional status than any other man".[35] Events had caught up with him, and the theories which quite lately had caused him to be described as a voice crying in the wilderness[36] became the current coin of the 1930s.

Dafoe and Sifton had much in common with Ewart, but they disliked his style and approach. Dafoe remarked, and Sifton agreed, that it was unfortunate that Ewart was not content to argue the nationalist case on the basis of abstract right. He ransacked history for illustrations of the danger of being associated as a subordinate with Great Britain in world affairs; he was particularly fond of representing British wars as unjust. "As a result he enrages those elements in our population which for sentimental or other reasons are pro-British; and he weakens his influence with a much larger number of Canadians who do not see why it is necessary to be so sharply critical of British policy and motives in setting forth the case for Canadian sovereignty."[37]

Mackenzie King had some contact with Ewart. His papers contain a series of questions prepared by Ewart, evidently with a view to being asked in the Commons debate of 1919. They include queries as to whether the Canadian representatives at Paris presented any representation against the imposition upon Canada of any specified obligation with reference to war, and whether the word "States" in the Covenant was changed to "Members of the League", and at whose instance.[38] These questions would have been very embarrassing to the government, but they were not asked. They may have represented unsolicited advice; but there is no accompanying correspondence. King, however, remained in touch with Ewart, and in 1922 we find the Prime Minister, as he had now become, consulting him as to the terms of a communication to Borden, who was representing Canada at the Washington Conference.[39] It may be that in 1919 King was a trifle chary of becoming associated with an avowed republican. Early in 1920 he recorded a conversation with A. R. McMaster, MP, who was "for a Canadian 'Republic' ". Possibly McMaster had been influenced by Ewart. Far back in 1837 King's revered grandfather had proclaimed what amounted to a Canadian republic on an island in the Niagara River. Now, however, the grandson's private comment on McMaster's remarks was, "I do not favor extreme views."[40] This approach to the issues of the day was to help ensure for William Lyon Mackenzie King a far more successful political career than had been achieved by William Lyon Mackenzie.

We should take some notice here of the appearance in Canada of organized bodies—pressure-groups, if you like—designed to influence public thinking on matters of external policy.

In Canadian society there was what may be called built-in support for certain attitudes in such matters. "Imperialist" views, in the sense at least of opinions favourable to the British connection and its maintenance and development, could always expect a friendly hearing in Ontario and, to a lesser but still important extent, in most other provinces of the Dominion. Isolationist attitudes were particularly well-established in French Canada, though French Canadians were far from having a monopoly of them. But what came to be called "collective security"—an international security system based on the League of Nations—had no natural, established body of support; and many people—academic people in particular—were painfully aware of the fact that in Canada there was comparatively little knowledge or informed discussion of international affairs. It was not surprising that concerned citizens came together to form societies devoted to these causes.

The League of Nations Society came into existence in Canada in 1921. It had its origin partly at least in urgings from the League of Nations Union in Britain, and specifically from Lord Robert Cecil. The idea was taken up with considerable enthusiasm by Canadian statesmen who had played leading parts in the events of 1919, notably N. W. Rowell. Sir Robert Borden became the society's first president. From this time onward the society made its voice heard in support of the League particularly and the ideals of peace and conciliation generally. It had some fierce critics. Borden's impeccable credentials as a Commonwealth statesman did not save it from violent attacks by the Toronto *Evening Telegram*, a crudely imperialist sheet. Yet one senior Conservative politician who certainly deserved the name of imperialist, Sir George Foster, was an extremely active member and supporter of the society.[41] The fact that some people of strong imperial sympathies were good friends of the League of Nations, while others were its sworn enemies, reminds us once more of the extraordinary variety of opinions on external matters in Canada after the First World War.

The League of Nations Society never acquired much strength in the province of Quebec. It had from the beginning a branch in Montreal, which passed through a good many vicissitudes; but that branch represented mainly the English-speaking minority. Two eminent French-Canadian public men, Raoul Dandurand and Ernest Lapointe, were active in the society, and Lapointe was its president for a time in the thirties while his party was in opposition; but in this respect they were not representative. The League of Nations continued to be viewed with suspicion in Quebec.[42]

The Canadian Institute of International Affairs was founded in 1928, growing out of involvement by interested Canadians in the activity of the British (later Royal) Institute of International Affairs and the Institute of Pacific Relations. Many of the people who were important in the League of Nations Society were also to be found working in the Institute, Borden and Rowell among them. The Institute's approach to its task, the cultivation of an informed knowledge of foreign affairs in Canada, was rather different from the society's. The latter sought, not very successfully, to build up a large membership among the public and exercise a direct influence on public opinion; the Institute, a more elitist body with a good deal of financial support from the business community, aimed to spread understanding of international problems among a limited influential group which might leaven the lump of the population at large. As time passed it published an increasing number of scholarly studies of international problems affecting Canada.[43]

This brief and disjointed survey of opinion may conclude with a notice of a pioneer book on Canadian external relations published in the year in which the CIIA was founded. Its authors were two McGill University professors, P. E. Corbett and H. A. Smith. Both had strong English connections, and Smith, a native Englishman, had returned home to take a chair at the University of London before the book was published. The volume's full title throws light on its content and approach: *Canada and World Politics: A Study of the Constitutional and International Relations of the British Empire*. It was Commonwealth-centred; this was both natural and (in English-speaking Canada) representative, in those days when the implications of the First World War were still being worked out in institutional terms. In some respects it tended, however, to look backward rather than forward; Smith contributed to it an appendix entitled "The Strategic Position of Canada", which noted the strategic weakness of the Canadian frontier with the United States, and observed that the possibility of a rupture with that country could not be entirely "dismissed from consideration". "If Canada were detached from the British Empire," wrote Smith, "there would be no great power whose vital interests would demand the protection of her independence, and the military control of the United States could not be effectively disputed." This sort of thinking, we shall see, was just on the point of becoming extinct at that moment.

The most remarkable, if not perhaps the most surprising aspect of the book, however, is what it omits. Its two authors, English-speaking Montrealers, say virtually nothing about the special views held in French Canada concerning the country's relationship to world politics, or the influence which those views had exerted in the past, and which they were certain to exert in the future.

Late in 1921 Newton W. Rowell, who had left the government when Meighen became Prime Minister in July 1920, delivered at the University of Toronto a series of lectures (Loring Christie had vetted them for him) which were later published under the title *The British Empire and World Peace*.* At the end of his discussion of "Canada and World Peace" he presented to the students in his audience, many of whom must have served in the war, what he called "a simple non-partisan political creed" of five points, which he evidently felt would ensure sound policies in internal and external affairs alike: the "establishment and maintenance of the spirit of Canadian national unity as opposed to sectionalism, whether racial, religious, geographical, or occupational"; co-operation between capital and labour "on a just and equitable basis", without class domination or class conflict; maintenance "of the full equality of status of the members of the Britannic Commonwealth, and the preservation of the unity essential to the strength and security of the whole"; maintenance also "of the most cordial relations between the Britannic Commonwealth and the United States of America and the recognition of Canada's position as an interpreter and reconciler between the two"; and finally, maintenance of "wholehearted co-operation with the League of Nations", the most "hopeful and practical experiment" yet devised as a substitute for war.[44]

This program, no less civilized and high-minded for being a bit obvious, combined in external matters Canadian traditional conceptions with the progress made as a result of the war and the labours of the Borden administration. It would have commended itself to much informed and

* The published version is in four parts: 1: "International Co-operation and World Peace"; 2: "The British Empire and World Peace"; 3: "Canada and World Peace"; and 4: "The Church and World Peace". It was natural enough at that day to give to the whole volume the title of Part 2.

"enlightened" opinion in English-speaking Canada (always that qualification!). Mackenzie King could have approved of it, though he would certainly have insisted on entering a caveat with respect to the unity of the Commonwealth, and one can imagine him making a strictly mental reservation about the word "wholehearted" in connection with the League. We can only speculate what the students who heard Rowell thought about it all. Doubtless a proportion of them, including some who had fought in France, were moved by his idealism and may have been ready to dedicate themselves, at least in moderation, to the good causes whose standard he raised. Doubtless also there were others who would have agreed with Chubby Power: to the devil with the Old World and its bloody battlefields, let us withdraw behind our own Great Wall.

THE NEIGHBOURS AND THE LEAGUE

Watching the neighbours is a great Canadian pastime; and the American political scene has seldom presented to observers north of the border a more absorbing (or, it may be added, a more depressing) spectacle than it did in 1919 and 1920. Then and in the years that followed, the American attitude towards the League of Nations affected Canada's view of the United States generally, and on the other hand that attitude certainly affected the Canadian public's own view of the League.

Under the United States constitution, the Treaty of Versailles, which as we know included the Covenant of the League of Nations, required to be approved by a two-thirds vote of the Senate. The President of the United States was regarded more than any other man as the father of the League; and it was generally considered at the time when the Treaty went to the Senate that it would be approved, though there might perhaps be reservations. Instead the Senate rejected the Treaty and the United States never joined the League of Nations, which in consequence was hamstrung from the beginning. Historians have not found it altogether easy to explain this "Great Betrayal".[45] We cannot discuss the question in detail here, but we must note what seem to be the chief factors in the unforeseen result.

It is generally agreed that Woodrow Wilson himself must bear a good part of the blame. He had made many political and personal enemies, and conciliation was an art he did not choose to practise, at least in this connection. He did not oppose all reservations, but he was utterly hostile to several which even some senators not unfriendly to the League idea considered vital. In the end, the Treaty and the League were defeated by the combined votes of those who hated the League and of friends of the League whom Wilson had asked not to vote for approval with reservations.

One of the evil geniuses of the moment was Senator Henry Cabot Lodge, Republican from Massachusetts, whom we saw as a member of the Alaska tribunal in 1903. We have also seen him supporting the League to Enforce Peace, which did much to popularize the idea of a League of Nations in the United States. But he was a Wilson-hater and a bitter partisan; and as chairman of the Foreign Relations Committee of the Senate he was powerful. While apparently not wishing to be known as a total foe of the League, he was one of the chief architects of its defeat. Some senators made no secret of the fact that they were determined to smash the League at all costs. These "irreconcilables" have been reckoned as sixteen in number: fourteen Republicans and two Democrats. Thanks largely to Lodge's management, they were strong in the Foreign Relations Committee.[46]

On September 10, 1919 the committee made a very hostile majority report to the Senate, recommending no less than forty-five textual amendments to the Covenant and four reservations. The Democratic minority recommended ratification without amendment or reservation. Debate in the Senate itself produced a result rather more moderate than the majority report: no amendments, but fourteen reservations, originally drafted in the Committee on Foreign Relations, which came to be known as the "Lodge reservations". On November 19 the Senate voted, Wilson having asked his supporters to vote against ratification with reservations. In two votes on the Treaty with the Lodge reservations it was defeated, 39–55 and 41–51. A motion to approve the Treaty without reservations was lost, 38–53. The question was revived in 1920, and in a vote on March 19 on ratification on the basis of a somewhat altered version of the Lodge reservations the Treaty won a simple majority, 49 to 35. It failed of the required two-thirds majority by seven votes. This was the end.

The nature of the proposed amendments and reservations is significant to our subject.[47] It may be said that the most important points to which these were directed were the following: the protection of unfettered American liberty of action under the Monroe Doctrine; the assurance of the free right of withdrawal from the League; protection against undue responsibility for other countries' territorial integrity or political independence under Article 10 or other articles; and, finally, unwillingness to accept the independent position of the British Dominions and India, which, it was contended, would give Britain six votes in the League Assembly while the United States had but one. This last point we must explore.

The majority report of the Senate Foreign Relations Committee made the matter the subject of its first amendment, saying,

> It is proposed so to amend the text as to secure for the United States a vote in the Assembly of the League equal to that of any other Power. Great Britain now has, under the name of the British Empire, one vote in the Council of the League. She has four additional votes in the Assembly of the League for her self-governing Dominions and Colonies which are, most properly, members of the League and signatories to the Treaty. She also has the vote of India, which is neither a self-governing Dominion nor a Colony, but merely a part of the Empire and which, apparently, was simply put in as a signatory and member of the League by the Peace Conference because Great Britain desired it . . . if Great Britain has six votes in the League Assembly, no reason has occurred to the Committee and no argument has been made to show why the United States should not have an equal number.[48]

Wilson quickly rejoined that the Dominions were autonomous states in all but foreign policy, and that, moreover, there was no danger of the United States being outvoted to its disadvantage in the Assembly, since except in the matter of the admission of new members to the League decisions of the Assembly or Council required unanimity.[49] But the issue would not go away; and as we have seen, there was only too much force in the criticism concerning India. In the debate in the Senate one of the irreconcilables, James A. Reed of Missouri, made great play with the assurance Sir Robert Borden had obtained from Wilson, Lloyd George, and Clemenceau (above, page 266), that the Dominions were eligible for election to the Council.[50] Thus a document which in Canada was almost a charter of liberties was represented in Washington as a reproach to the League and a menace to the United States. The "six British votes" continued to be a major complaint against the Covenant, and in the final form of the "Lodge reservations" No. 14 declared that until the Covenant was so amended as to give the United States a number of votes equal to the total that any member of the League with its dominions, colonies, etc., might be entitled to cast, the United States would not consider itself bound by any League decision in which any member "and its self-governing dominions, colonies or parts of empire" had cast more than one vote; while the United States assumed no obligation to be bound by any League decision arising out of any dispute between itself and any member of the League if such member, or any dominion, colony, etc., united with it politically had voted.[51]

This agitation had interesting echoes on the British side of the fence. W. H. Taft, Republican, ex-President and essentially friendly to the League, represented to Sir Robert Borden in July 1919 that concessions on the "six votes" were vital if the Treaty was to be ratified, and specifically suggested that Canada should abandon the right of being elected to the Council. Borden's reaction was adverse.[52] In September 1919 Viscount Grey of Fallodon (the Sir Edward Grey of prewar days) was sent to Washington as special ambassador to watch and perhaps influence the situation. President Wilson, who had suffered a stroke after collapsing during a speaking tour in which he appealed from the Senate to the American people, could not or would not see Grey. The ambassador was pretty clearly disposed on behalf of the British government to counsel the acceptance of some reservations in the interest of getting the United States into the League. On November 8 the Colonial Secretary in London cabled the Dominion governments that Grey was strongly urging the British cabinet to assist the supporters of the League in the Senate by making a public declaration of its belief that in the case of a "dispute likely to lead to a rupture" between a foreign power and a country of the British Empire which was a member of the League, "the representatives of all parts of the Empire would be debarred from voting". The cabinet had refused to take this action without the assent of the Dominions, and their views were asked accordingly. Lord Milner added that in spite of the contention in the United States that the Empire should at no time have more than one member on the League Council, the government had "definitely refused" to abandon the principle stated in the assurance given to Borden by Lloyd George, Wilson, and Clemenceau.[53]

On this question the Canadian cabinet divided. Borden, whose health was failing, as we have seen, was absent from Ottawa, as were several other ministers. Those in the capital told the Colonial Office that they were strongly opposed to Grey's suggestion, though they were unable to give a definite reply in the absence of the Prime Minister.[54] Borden thought differently, and in a meeting at New York a group of other ministers, including Rowell and Meighen, agreed with him.* Borden went on to Washington to confer with Grey. From their conference emerged a cable from Grey to the Foreign Office stating that Borden agreed that a question should be asked in the House of Commons concerning voting rights under Article 15, and that Borden and Grey thought that this reply should be made:

Members of League under Article 15 of Covenant do not vote upon a "dispute likely to lead to rupture" to which any of them are parties. All parts of British Empire will be parties to any such dispute in which any one of them is involved.

While, therefore, in common with His Majesty's Governments of other portions of the Empire, His Majesty's Government of United Kingdom firmly maintains rights of United Kingdom, of self-governing Dominions and of India as members of League, it is not understood or contended that in case of a dispute between any portion of the Empire and a foreign power likely to lead to a rupture, either United Kingdom or any of the self-governing Dominions or India would be entitled to vote thereon in Assembly.[55]

Grey remarked, "I entirely agree with Sir R. Borden, who feels that complete failure of Treaty in Senate, followed by a separate peace between United States and Germany, would be a calamity, and that nothing should be omitted which might help to avert it, however slight the chance."

In fact, no declaration was ever made; for both Australia and South Africa, replying to Lord Milner's dispatch of November 8, opposed such action.[56] The nearest thing to it was when Grey, after his return home, wrote a letter to *The Times* expressing what he called "only my personal opinion and nothing more". He wrote,

. . . If any part of the British Empire is involved in a dispute with the United States, the United States will be unable to vote, and all the parts of the British Empire, precisely because they are partners, will be parties to that dispute and equally unable to vote. But as regards their right to vote where they are not parties to a dispute, there can be no qualification, and there is very general admission that the votes of the self-governing Dominions would

* This is an interesting example of the working of the cabinet system. In this case the cabinet's decision was pretty clearly actually the Prime Minister's. If the ministers in Ottawa had taken strong issue with it, their only recourse would have been resignation.

in most cases be found on the same side as the United States. . . . Our object is to maintain the status of the self-governing Dominions, not to secure a greater British than American vote; and we have no objection in principle to an increase of the American vote.[57]

It all came to nothing.

The episode is interesting because of the light it throws on conceptions of the British Empire as it existed in 1919, and particularly on the views of Sir Robert Borden. His ideas were expressed in a memorandum for C. J. Doherty (Acting Prime Minister, and one of the ministers who had opposed Grey's suggestion), explaining his action. It seemed, he said, difficult, if not impossible, to justify other portions of the Empire voting in case of dispute between one portion and a foreign power:

Moreover, the case suggested arises in respect of a "dispute likely to lead to a "rupture". "Rupture" means war. So long as the United Kingdom, the Dominions and India are under one sovereignty all parts of the Empire are for that reason, technically and actually at war when once declared. This is perfectly consistent with the view that each Dominion shall take only such part in any war as its parliament may determine. The other party to the dispute cannot vote. The whole Empire will be involved in the war arising out of the rupture. It seems the logical conclusion that no part of the Empire should vote upon questions arising out of such dispute.[58]

Canada, in other words, while enjoying separate status as a nation in her own right in the League, remained a member of the British union, and that was a unit in matters of foreign policy—at least in such matters as might lead to war. N. W. Rowell thought that the League's admission of self-governing portions of an empire as members represented an important new departure in political science: "the other nations have recognized the unique character of the Britannic Commonwealth and have admitted the Dominions to the family of nations without involving separation or even the idea of separation from the parent state."[59] Neither Borden nor Rowell was disposed to question the Laurier maxim, "If England is at war we are at war and liable to attack". Yet Doherty had remarked at Paris that some Canadians looked askance at that doctrine even before 1914 (above, page 266). Given the new status the Dominion had now achieved, it was certain to be challenged before long, and not only by supposedly wrong-headed constitutionalists like John S. Ewart.

Canadians who were hostile to the League of Nations were undoubtedly pleased and encouraged by the United States Senate's rejection of it. But many other Canadians were profoundly shocked, and among them were those who had represented Canada at Paris. After the defeat of the Treaty on November 19, 1919, Borden wrote in his diary, "In foreign affairs the politicians of the U.S. act like children and do not recognize their responsibilities to their country and to the world." The Toronto *Globe* remarked that their countrymen would see through the senators who, claiming to be patriots, not partisans, had "placed the United States before all the world as the greatest of repudiating nations".[60] That the defeat was due in part to what Canadians saw as American unwillingness to recognize Canada's new world position as reflected in the League Covenant added a note of particular bitterness. Rowell remarked that the only important countries that had not accepted the Dominion's new position were the United States and Russia (which was also outside the League): "We in Canada thought the United States would be the first to recognize and approve and the last to object to this new principle."[61] The Senate's attitude seemed to be a blow, not only to internationalism as represented by the League, but to the sanguine hopes, entertained by so many Canadians, of the continuation of the wartime Anglo-Saxon alliance, an even greater guarantee, as they saw it, for world peace. Borden had expressed this characteristic Canadian idea in a message to the New York *Sun* in June 1919:

> not only is a League of Nations established, but there has been formed a virtual alliance between the two great English-speaking nations, the United States of America and the British Empire, in their determination to keep the peace of the world. That, I believe, is a great step; for I do believe, and I think you will believe, that these two nations have it within their power, if they are connected in purpose and in effort, to keep the peace of the world at all times in the future. They could have done that thing in the last weeks of July, 1914, and spared the world all the sacrifice and sorrow that it has since endured. Here are two nations, or rather two Commonwealths, committed to the same ideals of democracy, connected by like traditions, speaking the same language, having the same literature, the same customs and habits of life; and if these two Commonwealths cannot stand together to maintain the Peace of the world, then I do not think there is much hope for humanity in the years to come.[62]

This optimistic view of the British-American relationship, never well founded, could scarcely be persisted in after the events in the Senate that autumn. British and Canadian sentimentalists had not understood the United States nearly as well as they thought they had.

We have seen the Canadian delegation at Paris fighting against Article 10 and showing in a less extreme form much the same fear of responsibilities and entanglements that was later expressed by the American senators. But it did not occur to Borden and his colleagues to oppose the League of Nations generally or to suggest that Canada should not join it. For this there were good and obvious reasons. First, and doubtless most powerful, there was the League's enormous significance for Canadian national status. It was the means of establishing Canada's international personality, and those who understood and valued this development valued the League also. Secondly, Canada's painful losses in the war—far greater in proportion than those of the United States—had left their mark. On some people the effect was to drive them into embittered isolationism, but in general this was not true of men in the inner circle of politics, and particularly of those in Borden's government. They, and a good many of their fellow citizens, were inclined to give a fair try to an international experiment that might, with luck, be the means of preventing another holocaust such as that in which sixty thousand Canadians had just perished. Yet the difference between them and their southern neighbours was mainly simply one of degree. They had looked into Laurier's "vortex of European militarism", and they did not want to look again. The Canadian performance in the early sessions of the League Assembly (below, pages 326–29) would indicate that they had their own "reservations" about the League.

While the United States Senate was grappling with the question of the League the Canadian government was once more examining the problem of representation in Washington.

The institution early in 1918 of the Canadian War Mission had met the immediate need; but as soon as the war was over the question arose again. In December 1918 Rowell in Ottawa cabled Borden in London that it was expected the mission's business could be wound up by about January 1. "Council considers very essential that Canadian representation at Washington already secured through our War Mission should be continued and that arrangements should now be made for permanent Canadian Representative at Washington. What do you suggest?" Borden asked the advice of Loring Christie and O. M. Biggar, who jointly felt that it was both inadvisable and unnecessary to attempt any radical change at that moment, and that the mission could be retained for the time being. Borden accordingly replied to Rowell, "Suggest that present Mission be continued until Peace Treaty signed. At present there is absolutely no opportunity of discussing such a matter with Prime Minister or Foreign Secretary. Upon my return present Mission can be developed into permanent Mission."[63] In April 1919 the government asked funds from Parliament for the continuation of the mission on an interim basis.[64]

In the meantime the dovecotes had been fluttered by reports that Borden had been offered the British Embassy in Washington. Just what happened is far from clear. On February 14 Borden cabled in reply to an inquiry, "There was a confidential conversation on the subject but no announcement should be made at present. I merely said I could not consider it until after my return to Canada and necessary conference with our colleagues." Borden evidently found the idea not unattractive. In March the "Montreal financial district" was said to be anxious over a renewed rumour that Borden was considering the post. Sir Thomas White cabled, "These reports are harmful to you and embarrassing to us and should be contradicted. . . . The Union party cannot go on except under your continued leadership." This ended the affair. Borden telegraphed back, "You are authorized to state publicly that I am not considering the post of British Ambassador at Washington and that it is my intention to return to Canada and resume my duties as Prime Minister as soon as the work of the Peace Conference will permit."[65]

The person responsible for initiating the next stage of action seems to have been Sir Charles Gordon, chairman of the Canadian Trade Commission in Washington and acting chairman of the Canadian War Mission.[66] In September 1919 he discussed representation in Washington with Rowell, and subsequently sent him a strong letter on the subject.[67] "I wish to say," he wrote, ". . . that my experience in Washington has led me to believe that it is impossible for the British Embassy, with their limited knowledge of Canadian affairs and the fact that they are busy with so many other matters, to properly represent Canada in Washington." Gordon suggested the appointment of a High Commissioner, who would report to the British Ambassador and keep him informed, but who would himself conduct negotiations in Canadian matters with the United States authorities.

Almost inevitably, the task of producing a practicable scheme seems to have been confided to Christie, who took the view that since Canada had been accepted as a member of the League, her "right of legation" could hardly be contested. He plumped for a regular diplomatic title, Envoy Extraordinary and Minister Plenipotentiary.[68] His plan was "approved warmly" by the cabinet (except Sir George Foster, who may perhaps be described as the Conservative equivalent of W. S. Fielding).[69] Early in October it went to London through the Governor General.[70] It was prefaced by a brief argument: "a strong feeling has arisen in this country that effective steps should be taken to safeguard more thoroughly Canadian interests at Washington. The two countries adjoin each other upon a boundary line of nearly four thousand miles and the social and commercial intercourse is constantly increasing." The enormous increase in trade figures since 1900 was recalled. "Having regard to these facts my advisers have no doubt as to the necessity of distinctive representation. They are desirous of accomplishing it upon lines which will maintain and even emphasize the solidarity of the Empire but which will give to this country the distinctive representation which constitutional development in recent years both sanctions and demands."

The details of the scheme were put forward in the form of heads of an order-in-council:

> I. The Dominion of Canada shall be represented in the United States by a diplomatic agent duly accredited to the President of the United States to reside at Washington in the character of His Majesty's Envoy Extraordinary and Minister Plenipotentiary for Canada.
> II. The Canadian Minister shall be appointed by and be directly responsible to the Government of Canada. He shall receive his instructions from and shall report to the Secretary of State for External Affairs.
> III. The Canadian Diplomatic establishment at Washington under the direction of a Canadian Minister shall, subject to an agreement to be made with the Government of the United Kingdom, constitute a part of the establishment of His Majesty's Embassy.
> IV. The Canadian Minister shall conduct the negotiations and be the channel of communication at Washington in matters between the United States and His Majesty in respect of the Dominion of Canada.
> V. The Canadian Minister shall hereafter be the channel of communication in all matters between His Majesty's Embassy and the Dominion of Canada.

The remaining heads dealt with arrangements for "continuous consultation in all important matters of common concern" and "such necessary concerted action, founded on consultation" as the Minister and Ambassador may decide upon (note that these phrases are direct quotations from

Resolution IX of the Imperial War Conference, page 213 above); the importance of avoiding "confusion or embarrassment on the part of the Government of the United States in respect of channels of communication"; and the fact that the further negotiation of matters "now pending" between the United States and Canada would be handled "by and through the Canadian Minister".

The arrival of these proposals cannot have occasioned much surprise in London, but they met some resistance. The Colonial Office on the whole was sympathetic; Lord Milner sent to the Foreign Office a comment (it does not appear whether it represented his own conception or those of his officials) which suggested that in future the Embassy should be divided into two parts, one Canadian and one British, headed by co-equal officers. The Ambassador should in future be selected by the British and Canadian governments in consultation, Canada being "regarded as a field of selection for this post at least equal to the United Kingdom". Predictably, this "imaginative" suggestion did not commend itself highly to the Foreign Office. One official there thought it went "a long way towards establishing the virtual independence of Canada and as establishing a precedent which will not be overlooked by the other Dominions". Lord Curzon thought Milner's plan went "rather unnecessarily far".[71]

The British government's formal reply to the Governor General accordingly suggested amending the Canadian proposal in the direction of a more decided maintenance of imperial diplomatic unity. It accepted the desirability of "distinctive representation of Canada" and applauded the idea that it should take a form that would maintain and emphasize the solidarity of the Empire; with this in view, "the closest connection" between the Canadian representative and the Ambassador was desirable:

> The most convenient and suitable method of carrying out this object, in our opinion, would be for the Government of Canada to recommend and for the King to appoint a Minister plenipotentiary who would be next in rank in the Embassy to the Ambassador, and would have charge of Canadian affairs and conduct them with the United States Government, acting upon instructions from and reporting direct to the Canadian Government. He should take his place as Minister at the Embassy in charge of Canadian affairs, and the Government of the United States should be formally apprized by an official letter from the Secretary of State [for Foreign Affairs] of his appointment, accrediting the Canadian Minister, and empowering him to conduct Canadian affairs direct with the United States Government. The Canadian Minister would take charge of the Embassy in the absence of the Ambassador.

> In order to carry out this policy it would be essential that the Minister should reside and have his office within the precincts of the Embassy and that his Canadian Staff appointed like himself on the recommendation of the Canadian Government should have diplomatic status and be regarded as part of the diplomatic staff of His Majesty's Embassy with rank equivalent to that of their British colleagues of corresponding grades. In this way the solidarity of the Empire would be maintained and emphasized which could hardly be the case if a diplomatic agent for the Dominion of Canada were accredited independent[ly] to the President of the United States.[72]

The new arrangement would involve problems of accommodation; nevertheless, it was indicated that the Canadian branch of the Embassy could be established at once. If experience indicated a need for modifications, the whole matter could be discussed at the conference on the constitution of the Empire (suggested in Resolution IX) which it was expected would be held in 1920.

The similarities between the Canadian proposal and the British counter-proposal were perhaps more important than the differences. Both saw the Canadian establishment in Washington as part of the British Embassy, both expressed a desire to maintain the solidarity of the Empire. Under both, a Canadian minister supported by a Canadian staff would do Canada's business in Washington. But the British plan did have rather definite implications of subordination; the Canadian minister was not only to be part of the Embassy establishment, he was to be second-in-command. Christie did not make an issue of this. He observed that, practically, the British plan amounted to the same thing as the Canadian suggestion. The difference was in form: "that the first proposal treats Canada rather definitely as a separate State for diplomatic purposes; while the second, recognizing that there should be distinctive Canadian representation, at the same time treats the Empire as a unity for diplomatic purposes and weaves the new Canadian diplomatic service, so to speak, into the fabric of the present diplomatic service of the Empire." The Foreign Office regarded the matter of avoiding separate accreditation as important; the Canadians did not choose to consider the question very vital. The government accepted the British proposal, with the proviso that they considered it important that the Canadian representative should have the same precedence in the Washington diplomatic corps as the ministers of other countries resident there.[73]

The way was now open for discussion with the United States, and the British Embassy took the matter up. The State Department was friendly, though apparently there was some apprehension that advertising separate status for Canada might give Irish Americans an excuse to foment trouble between Britain and the United States. And "great difficulty" was seen in according a Canadian Minister the precedence which Ottawa thought so important. The Americans' advice was not to seek a firm decision on this point but to let the matter work itself out with the passage of time. The Canadian government accepted this polite refusal, for that was what it was. The same dispatch that informed the Colonial Office of this acceptance mentioned reports from England that suggested that people were thinking that the Canadian Minister would be a subordinate of the Ambassador. The Canadian comment was, "since he will be responsible to and take his instructions from the Canadian Government it is obvious that he cannot be a subordinate taking instructions from the Ambassador".[74] On this firm note the correspondence ended.

All parties being agreed, the Acting Prime Minister, Sir George Foster, announced the arrangement in the Canadian House of Commons on May 10, 1920. The Liberal opposition duly opposed, in a debate on May 17. Fielding made it clear that he disliked the whole idea of distinctive Canadian representation, but made it clear also that this was a personal opinion. The party leader, Mackenzie King, in a speech which may be called a landmark of party policy, took particular exception to the Canadian Minister taking charge of the British Embassy in the Ambassador's absence. There were, he said, dangers in this. The desire for Canadian representation had arisen from Canadian complaints of what British diplomatists had done for Canada. "Is our representative likely to be so perfect that he will always satisfy British opinion? Why not let British diplomatists manage British affairs and let us manage our own affairs?":

> There are two extreme views that may be taken in in regard to a matter of this kind. One is that the affairs of Canada should be managed exclusively by the British Embassy; the other that the Canadian representative should manage the British Embassy, for part of the time as is here proposed. What seems to be the more rational course is the middle one, that in matters between Canada and other countries Canada should manage her own affairs, and that in matters between Great Britain and other countries, Great Britain should manage her own affairs, always when necessary with co-operation and conference between the two.

On June 30 King moved to reduce the appropriation for representation at Washington from $80,000 to $50,000, the amount provided in the previous year. This, he said, was "as a protest primarily against having the Canadian Minister Plenipotentiary act at any time as British Ambassador in the absence of the British Ambassador." Fielding again expressed "grave doubts" about the wisdom of the whole proposition. King's amendment was lost 57 to 32. He refrained from attacking the proposition of making the Canadian establishment part of the British Embassy; overtly, at least, he objected only to the Minister acting on British business in the Ambassador's absence. His diary does nothing to explain his position further.

The Canadian government and the British government were agreed, the United States had accepted the idea, the Canadian parliament had approved; but no appointment was made, no Canadian Minister appeared in Washington until 1927. The reason for the Unionist government taking no action while it remained in office remains obscure. Borden's resignation was imminent when the House of Commons voted, but nothing was done during Meighen's year and a half in power. His papers are thin compared with Borden's or King's. He may have failed to find a suitable and willing appointee; he may not have been sufficiently interested, in the press of domestic business, to turn his attention to the matter.*

CULTIVATING THE GARDEN

In the summer of 1919 Canada welcomed the young Prince of Wales, who made an extensive tour of the country (August–November) and briefly visited the United States. The present writer, then thirteen, remembers this as a genuinely exciting moment for Canadians (and not only for thirteen-year-olds). Royal visits had been rare. Another Prince of Wales had visited Canada in 1860, and that, too, was a great affair; King George V and Queen Mary (as Duke and Duchess of Cornwall and York) had come in 1901; but this visit was something particularly special. The "Smiling Prince", winsome and charming, was very different from the haggard man who would abdicate the throne in 1936. He was welcomed for himself, and his inevitably modest war record was exaggerated and applauded; but he served also as a symbol of the ancient monarchy

* Sir Robert Borden's recorded remark, "You know, my successor was very lukewarm on the proposition",[75] might refer to Meighen in the cabinet, but the context suggests that the reference was rather to Mackenzie King's statements in the House of Commons.

to which Canadians owed allegiance, and the famous and formidable state that had once defended them, and beside whose forces so many of them had lately fought. The war had made the people of Canada nationally minded, but it had not made them anti-British; if anything, it had produced increased admiration and sentimental regard for the "Old Country". This contributed to make the Prince's long journey, as the *Manitoba Free Press* put it, "one continuous round of affectionate acclaim".[76] In a sense this emotional outburst was a final postscript to Canada's involvement in the Great War.

Whatever it signified, it did not mean a continuing and active interest in Canada's overseas connections and commitments. On the contrary, Canada was turning inwards upon herself, as the great effort of the war became a memory. The year 1919 was one of preoccupation with external problems. The return of the troops from abroad, the peace settlement and the League of Nations, the new status of Canada, the attitude of the United States to the League—these things had dominated the news. The year 1920 was different. It is almost comic to compare the *Canadian Annual Review of Public Affairs* for the former year with that for the latter. The 1919 volume abounds in headings relating to foreign and imperial affairs. In the 1920 volume there is not a single such title. It is as though the country had suddenly turned its back on the world outside. Home affairs—politics and the prospects of parties, railway nationalization, the state of business, economic problems of every sort—are what the book concerns itself with. It would be foolish to make too much of this, but foolish also to suggest that it did not reflect a trend of the times. Arthur Meighen assumed the direction of Canadian affairs at a moment when his countrymen, sated with sacrifice and doubtful of the fruits of idealism pursued across the seas, were turning to cultivate their own garden.

CHAPTER ELEVEN

MEIGHEN, CHRISTIE, AND TWO CONFERENCES, 1920-1921

THE NEW ADMINISTRATION AND ITS PROBLEMS

When Arthur Meighen took office as Prime Minister and Secretary of State for External Affairs on July 10, 1920, two relatively untried and mistrusted party leaders confronted each other in the political arena. Neither Meighen nor Mackenzie King possessed the sure allegiance of his own party. It seemed possible that neither would have a long political career. In fact, neither was ever to command the warm regard that had come to Macdonald or Laurier, or even, in lesser degree, to Borden. Neither the austere Meighen nor the awkward King had the personality to compel men's hearts. But King was to enjoy unparalleled political success, while Meighen was to be remembered as a perennial political failure. He was now beginning his one relatively secure period of power; and it was to last less than a year and a half.

He had many domestic problems: the shaky state of his Unionist party (now officially designated the "National Liberal and Conservative Party"); the growing revolt of the agricultural West against the government's tariff policies; the continuing alienation of French Canada; the railway question (for Meighen's ministry had to complete the implementation of the policy of nationalization applied to a great part of the country's rail mileage under Borden); and the endless general complexities of reconversion from a war to a peace economy. It was not surprising, in these circumstances, and in the absence of any serious international crisis, that external problems were pushed into the background.

They were still there, however, and sooner or later they would have to be dealt with. For the moment there were few urgent difficulties with the

United States. The trouble over the Dominions' status in the League of Nations had ended with the American rejection of the League; but the Republican landslide in the congressional and presidential elections of November 1920 which made Warren G. Harding President with a friendly Congress behind him presaged new increases in the U.S. tariff. The arrangement concerning Canadian representation in Washington remained to be implemented. And Prohibition, a war measure now in effect in the United States and in every Canadian province but Quebec,[1] was going to lead to infinite border difficulty.

And what was to come to the new Commonwealth? Its shape was to be determined, so said Resolution IX, by "a special Imperial Conference to be summoned as soon as possible after the cessation of hostilities" (above, page 213). It had not been summoned when Meighen took office. What was to be the relationship of Canada to imperial foreign policy? One question to which little attention was being given in Canada in 1920 was that of the Anglo-Japanese Alliance, extended for ten years after consultation with the Dominions during the Conference of 1911. Was it now to be further extended or was it to be abrogated? This matter would have to be dealt with shortly.

Closely allied with the question of Commonwealth organization was that of the defences of Canada. In the great conflict just concluded the Dominion's military effort had been closely integrated with the mother country's. Was this to continue in peacetime? Was Canada to maintain larger forces than before 1914? And what patterns were they to follow?

Finally, Canada's relationship to the League of Nations required some attention, if only to the extent of appointing delegates to the First Assembly, to be held in the autumn of 1920, and deciding what policies they were to pursue.

The cabinet that had to make these decisions was nearly the same as the one that had worked with Borden. An important exception was N. W. Rowell, who as we have already seen had left with Borden. Had he remained, his special interest and knowledge in the field of external affairs would probably have ensured a more active policy than Meighen actually followed. Three members of Borden's Paris team were still in the government—old Sir George Foster, C. J. Doherty, and Arthur Sifton; but Sifton died in office in January 1921, and Foster and Doherty retired when the ministry was reconstructed in the following September.[2] More important than most ministers was one civil servant, Loring Christie, who continued to serve as Legal Adviser in the Department of External Affairs.

In practice he was Meighen's general external adviser even more than he had been Borden's; Meighen's preoccupation with the domestic scene, and his relative lack of interest in affairs abroad, left the latter more than ever to Christie. Such "foreign" policy as Canada had under Meighen was largely of Christie's making.[3]

NOT MUCH DEFENCE

Theoretically, at least, a country's defence policies should be closely related to its external situation and policies. In Canada after the First World War uncertainty as to precisely what the Dominion's external situation was, and a general lack of interest in the question, militated against the formulation of a coherent military policy and resulted in practice in a return to colonial impotence.

At the outset of this study the point was made that the Canadians were an unmilitary people and that their Dominion of 1867 was almost entirely without a nation's normal equipment of self-defence. In 1914 the situation had not greatly changed. The great naval project of 1909 had misfired. The militia, while materially reformed so far as organization went, was still a body of amateurs with very little training; the regular component was only some three thousand strong.[4] On this slight foundation was erected the great military machine of 1914–18. Canada then became, for a brief moment, a military nation. It is interesting that this tremendous experience, which had such vast effects on so many departments of Canadian life, had so little influence on Canadian defence policy.

Some reasons for this seem fairly obvious. Canadians, like other people, hoped that the "war to end war" had really done just that; some of them, no doubt, thought that the League of Nations would ensure peace. Those who reflected that there had always been wars, and that they would probably continue, were not necessarily convinced that this implied preparedness. After all, unprepared Canada had played a great part in the war. As in 1812, her men had shown that civilians could fight with the best of them, or so it was believed. Had not General Currie, an undeniably competent Corps Commander, been a real estate agent in 1914? There were few to point to the evidence on the other side: the facts that the first Canadian Division did not enter the line until seven months after the war began, that the Canadian Corps did not attain its full strength of four divisions until 1916, that no qualified Canadian officer was available to take command of the 1st Division in 1914, that the Corps was not commanded by a Canadian until 1917, that the security of British Columbia in the first perilous weeks of war depended upon Japanese, Australian, and British ships (above, page 160), and that Canada never made much material contribution to the naval superiority that made victory possible.

Of course, there was something else. The cost of the war had not all been paid in blood. It had imposed on Canadians a financial burden unimagined in 1914. The net national debt just before war broke out was about $336 million, calculated as $42.64 for each resident of the country. By the spring of 1920 it had risen to about $2,249 million—or $262.84 per capita. Taxation had soared. In prewar Canada the expense of government had largely been met from customs and excise duties. Now direct taxation fell heavily upon the community. The income tax appeared in 1917, the sales tax in 1920; in 1921, for the first time, revenue from direct taxes exceeded that from the customs.[5] No government could disregard the cry that went up for economy; and in the aftermath of the elimination of the German menace, an obvious candidate for the axe was the defence forces.

The chief question-mark hung above the navy. It had no Canadian tradition behind it except a dubious political one; the good work done during the war by the east coast patrols (a force largely composed of trawlers and drifters) had made little impact on the public consciousness.[6] And attempts by the British Admiralty to influence Canadian naval policy probably did the Royal Canadian Navy more harm than good.

The Admiralty took the question up while the war was still in progress, laying before the Imperial War Conference a memorandum recommending a single imperial navy, under the control of one central authority, in peace or war. Strategically, it had never been hard to make a case for this; politically, in 1918, it had no hope whatever of acceptance by the Dominions; the world had moved on too far. Sir Robert Borden consulted his Canadian colleagues in London and subsequently the other Dominion Prime Ministers, and obtained—except from Lloyd of Newfoundland, who preferred to do his own negotiating—the premiers' assent to a joint memorandum which Borden sent to the First Lord of the Admiralty on August 15, 1918.[7] It briefly described the Admiralty plan as "not considered practicable". The Australian experience in the war had shown that a Dominion navy could operate in time of war "as part of a united navy under one direction and command established after the outbreak of war". (Thus Borden finally gave full support to the Laurier naval policy of 1910.) It was fully agreed that construction, armament, equipment, training, administration, and organization should "proceed upon the same lines in all the navies of the Empire". The memorandum also remarked that "hereafter" it might be necessary "to consider the establishment for war purposes of some supreme naval authority upon which each of the Dominions would be adequately represented". The Admiralty, after hearing from Borden that Canada was not prepared to accept its organization plan, had suggested that Viscount Jellicoe, the late First Sea Lord and commander of the Grand Fleet, should visit Canada and the other Dominions to advise on their naval policies. The Dominions collectively now said they would welcome visits by "a highly qualified representative of the Admiralty".

Lord Jellicoe's visit to Canada (November–December 1919) resulted in a report[8] which put forward four possible schemes for national naval development, ranging from one including two battle cruisers and costing $25 million annually, down to one designed merely to provide security for Canadian ports and composed mainly of torpedo craft, to cost only $5 million a year. The Canadian naval staff had itself made a study before Jellicoe's visit which arrived at a scheme for two successive seven-year programs of development which would leave the country with a force of seven cruisers and numerous smaller vessels; the cost was estimated at over $60 million for construction and nearly $16 million annually for upkeep.[9] It was soon to appear that every one of these plans, even Jellicoe's most modest one, was far beyond the compass of Canadian political reality.

Early in 1919 the Canadian government had accepted from Britain a gift of two submarines, part of the class built (or rather assembled) in Canada during the war.[10] With this act positive naval policy ended for the moment. It is clear that many of Borden's colleagues were afraid of the question. After the Jellicoe report, the cabinet, fortified by an offer of ships from the Admiralty, put before the Unionist parliamentary caucus a tentative program based upon Jellicoe's fourth and smallest plan. It is evident that the ministers were disunited and disinclined to give the sort of firm leadership that would have carried the caucus. In these circumstances the backbenchers, undoubtedly thinking as they usually are of the next election, gave a striking demonstration (March 20, 1920) of the traditional Canadian dislike of preparation for war in time of peace. Sir George Foster described it to Borden, who was absent:

Ballantyne [Minister of the Naval Service] went in with his modified $5m. per year programme sure of success, and gave a good explanation & sat down beaming for results. Well, the Caucus knocked it sky-high—only two or three favourable & those moderately so. The agreement was that he should present it, argue for it, & Ministers should say nothing—let the Caucus have its head. So the Caucus had its head & made a thorough job. But two or three of our Ministers broke faith, and told members he [sic] did not want it & Sir Henry [Drayton, Minister of Finance] even clapped applause when some Member hit it hard. . . .[11]

Ballantyne, thoroughly disgusted, began to take measures looking to a complete disbandment of the naval service; but after discussion with his colleagues he accepted a less drastic measure. Foster continues:

Well, we had a talk over it, and ended with a compromise. (a) To give the Minister a free hand to reorganise by notice of discontinuance of present staff. (b) Accept two destroyers and one cruiser from G.B. to replace the *Rainbow* & *Niobe** for training and protection purposes. (c) Keep up the [Royal Canadian Naval] College. (d) Defer Permanent Navy policy for the present. This I took to Caucus. . . and in less than half an hour got their unanimous consent. . . .[12]

Thanks to the avoidance of capital expenditure—the ships being a gift from Britain—this program was cheap. The actual cost of the naval service for each of the next two years was almost exactly $2 million.[13]

In spite of the casual manner in which they were arrived at, and in spite of the smallness of the establishment they authorized, in retrospect the decisions of March 1920 appear historic. For all the declaration that no decision on permanent policy was being made—a phrase that recalls the great prewar debate—the fact is that the policy laid down at this time proved permanent. There was to be a navy, however small, and it was to be a national Canadian navy, of the sort envisaged in Laurier's Naval Service Act of 1910 and in Borden's London memorandum of 1918. The Royal Canadian Navy between the two world wars was always tiny, and there were moments when its very existence was threatened; but it did continue to exist, and in 1939 it provided the essential nucleus for a great wartime development.

The militia was a different matter. It had a long tradition behind it; its units were part of the history of their towns and counties; it had always possessed a certain significance for the party political machines;[14] and it was the natural inheritor of the great military legacy of the Canadian

* These were the old cruisers purchased in 1910 (above, page 160).

Corps, which few Canadians were unaware of in the years after 1918. The citizen force—the Non-Permanent Active Militia—was maintained, and efforts were made to preserve within it the traditions of the fighting regiments of the Corps. In 1919 the statutory limit on the strength of the Permanent Force (the regular army) was raised to ten thousand, but the actual strength remained less than four thousand.[15]

There had been no air service before the war, but now even the most rudimentary defence clearly required one. A statute of 1919 set up an Air Board, to supervise "all matters connected with aeronautics", including, by implication rather than definition, military air activity. The policy which the board developed provided, almost inevitably in the light of the British government's decision of 1917 to set up the Royal Air Force, for an air arm independent of the militia and the navy.[16] The force in the beginning was to consist primarily of citizen volunteers undergoing annual training; the permanent element was very small. The total expenditure on the Air Board in the fiscal year 1920–21 was approximately $2 million, less than half of it devoted to the Canadian Air Force. Defence expenditure as a whole that year amounted to just under $31 million, of which nearly $27 million went to the militia service.[17]

One thing seems clear: the Canadians of that era were not aware of any likelihood of war. They had helped to scotch the threat from Germany; there seemed to be no other serious European danger at the moment. And they certainly were not disposed to take seriously any idea of menace from the United States. Even in the days when war with that country was a definite possibility, Canadians refused to believe in the necessity of large defensive preparations. Yet it is hard to believe that if they had considered an American war even remotely possible in 1919–21 they would not have favoured a much larger establishment than their representatives in Parliament showed themselves willing to accept. It is true that a military committee appointed to make recommendations concerning the postwar militia laid down a theoretical basis for it—an inflated establishment of eleven divisions and four cavalry divisions—which could only have applied to a war fought on the soil of Canada; but this remained purely theoretical and fewer than half of the units that would have been required to fill it were ever authorized.[18] It is true also that in 1920–21 work began secretly on "Defence Scheme No. 1", a plan for action in case of war with the United States (based on nineteenth-century British schemes) which has received of recent years more attention than it deserves.[19] It was a draft plan that was never reduced to final form and on which no work was done after 1926.[20] It seems to have been mainly the brain-child of one officer,[21] and while the attitude of mind which it reflected was still extant among civilians as well as soldiers (above, page 302) it was becoming exceptional. Certainly ordinary Canadians gave no thought whatever to the possibility of conflict with their friendly neighbours and late allies.

BEGINNINGS AT GENEVA

The first Assembly of the League of Nations was called to meet at Geneva in November 1920. In August Loring Christie sent the new Prime Minister a memorandum on the question of Canadian representation, arguing that there was a special case for sending a strong delegation.[22] Of the three delegates permitted, it was desirable that one should be a member of Parliament and a Minister or an ex-Minister. It would "seem well also" that one should be a French Canadian, and it was for consideration whether the opposition should be asked to nominate one—who might be the French Canadian.

Neither a French-Canadian nor an opposition representative was appointed. Members of Borden's former inner circle were anxious to go. Meighen consulted Borden and asked whether he himself would care to attend; Borden preferred not to. They agreed that Rowell, who had evidently indicated his willingness, was suitable. Foster and Doherty "urged their claims very strongly" and were appointed. No chairman was specifically indicated apart from the fact that Foster's name stood first in the appointing order-in-council, but as the senior privy councillor in the delegation he was the inevitable leader.[23] That did not keep Borden from warning Rowell against him. Foster, he said, "while at Paris did not seem to have an adequate conception of Canada's status and nationhood": "I say this in the strictest confidence and for the purpose of emphasizing my hope that the steps in advance which have already been taken and to which you have contributed so much will not be lost."[24]

The simple-minded might assume that the cabinet considered the policy to be followed at the Geneva meeting and instructed the delegation accordingly. In fact no such thing seems to have taken place. Borden understood that Foster and Doherty were to confer with him before leaving for Geneva; but, he wrote to Rowell, who was already overseas, "they did not do me the honour of inviting a conference".[25] To make matters worse, it is evident that the three distinguished delegates disliked one another fairly cordially. (The opposition subsequently derived some amusement from the fact that Rowell and Foster both made lengthy separate reports on the proceedings at Geneva to the House of Commons during the debate on the Address in February 1921.) Apart from this, the nearest thing to comedy generated by the Canadians at Geneva was their abstention from the tribute paid by the Assembly to one of the city's most famous citizens, Jean-Jacques Rousseau. Doherty's Catholic prejudices were probably the moving factor here.[26]

Loring Christie, who was present as an expert with the Canadian delegation, remarked that the First Assembly's most important achievement was the adoption of a scheme for a Permanent Court of International Justice. The original draft of this seemed to discriminate against the British Dominions (it was based on procedures connected with the Permanent Court of Arbitration set up by the Hague Conferences of 1899 and 1907, and made no provision for states not represented in it); but it was amended to ensure that their position concerning the nomination and election of judges and "all other rights and privileges" should be the same as that of all other members of the League.[27] The plan was approved by the Canadian Parliament in 1921, and the King ratified the Protocol of Signature concerning the Court, on behalf of the United Kingdom, Newfoundland and the Colonies, Canada, Australia, New Zealand, South Africa, and India, on July 16.[28]

What Canadian historians have chiefly remembered about the First Assembly is the fact that during it the Canadian attack on Article 10 of the League Covenant, launched at Paris in 1919, was renewed. On December 4 C. J. Doherty proposed a motion on behalf of Canada: "That Article x of the Covenant of the League of Nations be and is hereby struck out."[29] No final action was taken on it. The Assembly invited the League Council to appoint a committee to study the various proposed amendments and provide a report to be placed before the next Assembly. Sir Robert Borden was named as a member of this committee but regretted that he found it impracticable to act.[30]

This amendment seems in fact to have been entirely Doherty's own idea; it was his, not Canada's. The evidence comes mainly from Sir Robert Borden and is therefore secondhand, but there is nothing to contradict it in the terse and uninformative Canadian official records. In a letter to Rowell written from Ottawa on November 30 Borden speculated on the possibility of "modifications in the Covenant". "You know my objections to Article x," he wrote. "If that Article had been stricken out, as we proposed at the time, it is quite possible that the Treaty would have been ratified by the Senate of the United States, with some unobjectionable modifications."[31] But when the news of Doherty's motion arrived Borden was disturbed. It will be remembered that his government had said nothing to Parliament of its opposition to Article 10, and Borden evidently felt that it had committed itself, and Canada, to the whole Covenant. He now wrote to Rowell,

> With respect to Article X I may say to you in strict *confidence* that the position is not quite free from embarrassment. You remember the position which my Colleagues and I took at the Paris Conference. I am stronger than ever in the view which I then expressed. Yet we submitted the Treaty to Parliament, obtained its approval and many supporters of the Government strongly and earnestly defended the Article in question. So far as I can learn, the Government as a whole have not in any way determined upon the course which Mr. Doherty has followed. There might be a serious question as to whether the Government would have authorized such a course without a further reference to Parliament....
>
> However, the press seems to support not only your attitude* but that of Mr. Doherty....[32]

It seems pretty evident that Doherty acted without cabinet authority. It is hardly possible that he did not take his colleagues at Geneva into his confidence; but the very slight reference to Article 10 in the report made by Rowell to the House of Commons, and the fact that Foster made no such reference, suggest that they did not wish to be closely associated with his action. It is also significant that the initiative was not taken where it would have been natural, in the First Committee, charged with constitutional questions, where Rowell was the Canadian representative; the matter was raised by Doherty in plenary session.

It may be well to outline here the further history of Doherty's proposal. For the 1921 Assembly, evidently for reasons of economy, only two Canadian representatives were designated, Doherty and the High Commissioner in London, Sir George Perley.[34] Doherty's presence was a guarantee that the attack on Article X would be persisted in. The committee ap-

* Rowell's favourable publicity resulted from his opposing proposals that the League should concern itself with world distribution of raw materials, and that new international agencies on Finance, Transit, and Health should be set up at once. The Canadians saw these as involving probable interference in the internal affairs of member states.[33]

pointed by the Council recommended against Doherty's amendment; but in the First Committee of the Assembly (that concerned with constitutional matters) Doherty argued strongly in favour of it, and the upshot was that decision was again postponed. The matter, it was decided, would be dealt with by the next Assembly, with precedence over any other amendment.[35] Before that happened there had been a change of government in Canada, and the delegates to the 1922 Assembly were appointed by Mackenzie King's ministry.

One other matter about the machinery of the League caused questioning in Ottawa and London as it began to function: just how far was the British Empire or Commonwealth to be considered a unit vis-à-vis the League? A specific point was, who was to appoint the representative to which the "British Empire" was entitled on the Council of the League? The British government seem to have had no doubt, for when the Council met Lord Curzon was in attendance as the British representative. The Canadian government proceeded to point out, through the medium of an order-in-council forwarded to the Colonial Secretary, that they had nothing against Lord Curzon, but that they had been "in no way consulted" as to his selection. "The British Empire being a member of the Council of the League of Nations," they proceeded, "it appears to Your Excellency's Ministers but proper that the designation of its representative should be determined upon only after consultation with the Governments of the different nations composing the Empire." They also complained that the document convoking the meeting (issued by President Wilson in accordance with the Covenant) invited "Great Britain alone and not the British Empire".[36] It appears that London made no reply. By this time some people in Whitehall were doubtless beginning to wish that more attention had been paid to the Canadian suggestion that the United Kingdom as such should be specifically mentioned in the Covenant instead of merely the British Empire (above, page 269).

Before the First Assembly Rowell had some conversation on the matter with the Colonial Secretary, Lord Milner. After the Assembly he wrote Milner a personal letter (sending a copy to Meighen) suggesting that an early settlement of the question was desirable. A. J. Balfour, as "British Empire" representative on the Council, had taken positions relating to League mandates different on some points from those taken by the representatives of Canada and South Africa in the Assembly. Rowell remarked that had Balfour been representing the United Kingdom no exception could be taken to this; as it was, it could be argued that he was binding some Dominions "to a course of action of which they had expressly disapproved". Rowell wrote, "I have come to the conclusion myself that the only possible solution is that the representative on the Council should be the representative of Great Britain and not of the British Empire, and that until amendments are being made to the Covenant the position should be regularized by a statement in some form which would indicate that the representative of the British Empire on the Council did not represent those nations of the Empire which are members of the League, and that when the Covenant is being revised Great Britain should be substituted for the British Empire as the State to be represented on the Council."[37] In retrospect, the affair seems to reflect a fundamental difficulty: how could half a dozen supposedly co-equal communities around the world ever achieve unanimity on the day-to-day details of policy? Rowell's representation had no result; nearly five years later, O. D. Skelton, the new Under-Secretary of State for External Affairs, was complaining that lately at Geneva "a persistent attempt has been made to have Great Britain recognized as speaking or signing for the whole British Empire".[38]

There was some co-ordination and consultation at Geneva in 1920, but of a sort that Skelton would not have approved. The question of a preliminary meeting of the "British Empire Delegation" appears to have been first raised by Rowell, and was taken up by the Colonial Office, with the result that what was called the "38th Conference" of the Delegation (it was obviously regarded as a continuation of the meetings held at Paris the year before, and of meetings held in London in the early summer of 1920 preparatory to the Spa conference with Germany)* took place in London on November 5 with the British Prime Minister, Lloyd George, in the chair. Other meetings were held in London before the move to Geneva, and there were several at Geneva during the Assembly.[40] The "39th" meeting in London discussed procedure, and one of Rowell's recorded contributions may be quoted:

> It was important that the representatives of the Nations of the British Empire should not take any action or reach any conclusion which might [give]

* The Spa conference discussed matters arising out of the Versailles Treaty, particularly reparations. The British government suggested that each Dominion should "accredit a plenipotentiary in London who can represent their views and watch over their interests during discussions." The Canadian government designated Sir George Perley, the High Commissioner. There had been thirty-five meetings of the British Empire Delegation in Paris. The Spa meetings in London were called the 36th and 37th.[39]

support to the contention of the opponents of the League [in the United States] that the Covenant in effect gave six votes to Great Britain as against one to the United States. At the same time it was necessary, on the other hand, that there should be the closest possible consultation between the Dominions and the Mother Country on matters coming before the League, and he hoped that in all important matters the Dominions and the Home Government should reach a point where all would see eye to eye.[41]

This surely came close to prescribing two objects that were mutually exclusive.

When Lord Milner urged the desirability of the Empire Delegation holding meetings at Geneva, Lord Robert Cecil (who was representing South Africa) betrayed some doubts: "The only justification for having six votes was that the various Dominions would not necessarily always cast their votes in the same way." Milner rejoined that "They would merely meet for discussion, and not necessarily act *en bloc*."[42] This is what actually happened. As we have already seen, the various Empire delegations certainly did not "act *en bloc*" at Geneva.* Lord Curzon suggested the desirability of finding some better term to replace "British Empire Delegation" at the Assembly; and the papers circulated there by the British Secretariat were headed "British Delegations".[44]

A curious evidence of the unformed state of both Commonwealth and League relations in 1920 was the discussion of how communications between the League and the Dominions were to be handled. Sir James Allen of New Zealand took the view that "communication direct by the Dominion Governments with the League would be bound, sooner or later, to cause trouble". Rowell, a little further in advance, "did not think the Canadian Government had communicated with the League in respect of any important matter without informing the Secretary of State for the Colonies".[45] The idea, favoured by Allen, that there should be a clearing house in London for distributing League papers, was not carried out, but for a time all papers for Canada were sent through the High Commissioner in London. In 1921 the Secretary General of the League suggested that papers not necessarily calling for reply or any action by the Canadian government should thereafter be sent direct to Ottawa, while those

* The question of mandates was only one example. And even the Indian delegation showed independence. On the division in the First Committee as to whether non-permanent members of the Council should serve for four or for two years, Australia, Canada and India voted for two years, the "British Empire" for four. The two-year school of thought won, by a vote of 14 to 13.[43]

involving questions of policy should continue to be sent through the High Commissioner. Mr. Meighen approved this arrangement, specifying that both classes of documents should be addressed to the Secretary of State for External Affairs.[46]

PREPARING FOR AN IMPERIAL MEETING

As early as 1919 people were thinking about the next Imperial Conference. After all, the Imperial War Cabinet had agreed in 1917 that it was desirable that an imperial cabinet should meet annually, and the decision was clearly not meant to apply merely during the continuance of the war. Some Canadians conceived the idea that the next meeting might suitably take place in Ottawa. Perley seems to have originated the plan, and Rowell as Acting Secretary of State for External Affairs encouraged it. Leo Amery, acting as Colonial Secretary, sounded Lloyd George in January 1920. The British Prime Minister was doubtful whether the constitutional conference proposed in 1917 could be held before 1921, but remarked that there were a number of matters of imperial concern, including "the renewal in 1921 of the Anglo-Japanese treaty", which made it desirable that the Empire's prime ministers should meet during 1920. He was willing to go to Ottawa, but could not commit himself at present. When Rowell sent a formal invitation, the other Dominions were notably unenthusiastic both about a meeting in 1920 and a meeting in Ottawa. Smuts (who was now Prime Minister of South Africa, Botha having died in 1919) was willing to think of Ottawa as a site for the constitutional conference, but pointed out that the Dominions, having much business to transact with departments in London, normally found that a more suitable place for a conference. By November 1920 it had been agreed that a meeting would be held in London in mid-June of the following year.[47]

Nobody seemed quite sure, however, just what the body was that was going to meet. Lloyd George in his formal telegram spoke of "a meeting of the Imperial Cabinet . . . on the lines of the Imperial War Cabinet meetings in 1917–18". Meighen agreed that it would be desirable to hold "a meeting of what has been called the Imperial War Cabinet".[48] Writing to Leo Amery, he took the opportunity to nail the Union Jack to the mast:

> The term "Imperial Cabinet" is really open to no objections. None but a crank or a demagogue with an anti-British slant could take exception to it.

As for myself I have never catered to the vote that is afraid to raise the British flag or to name the British name and that course of all courses I never shall pursue....[49]

But the matter was really not so simple. Was the body that was going to meet an Imperial Cabinet, an Imperial War Cabinet, or (as some said) an Imperial Peace Cabinet? Or was it really one more in the long series of Imperial Conferences? In the end the officials keeping the records of the meeting that assembled in London on June 20, 1921 were extremely cautious. The confidential minutes called it simply "a Meeting of Representatives of the United Kingdom, the Dominions and India".[50] No one could take much exception to that. The published proceedings as laid before the British Parliament used the phrase "Conference of Prime Ministers and Representatives of the United Kingdom, the Dominions, and India".[51] Lloyd George nevertheless, in a statement to Parliament which had been approved by the members of the meeting, called it several times "the Imperial Cabinet".[52]

Meighen, for all his declared willingness to use the word "cabinet", almost entirely refrained from doing so in the discussion of the forthcoming meeting in the Canadian House of Commons in the spring of 1921. Presumably following a memorandum by Christie,[53] which pointed out that recent official correspondence from England referred to the gathering merely as a meeting of prime ministers, he took the line that it was a "special meeting of prime ministers", "not a meeting of the Imperial Conference".[54] He did once say that "any conference of prime ministers is in all its essentials a continuation of the idea of an Imperial cabinet".[55] These were doubtful distinctions. History has usually been content to call the affair the Imperial Conference of 1921.

In spite of his British gestures, Meighen clearly did not regard the meeting, under whatever name, as anything resembling a session of a central imperial executive whose decisions would be binding upon the member nations of the Empire. In his first parliamentary reference to it he said, "Necessarily any proposals resulting from the conference and affecting Canada must be subject to the approval of the Canadian Parliament."[56] Later he referred with apparent approval to Laurier's comments on the nature of the Imperial War Cabinet (above, page 217), saying,

... this is a conference—this is not an executive. Even the War Cabinet was not an executive; it was a consultative body and nothing more.... It was

> a consultative body, this is a consultative body. . . . That will be the nature of this conference, and in that respect it is on a parity with conferences held before, whether Imperial conferences or war cabinets. I can give the assurance, with all the emphasis that I can command, that no step whatever will be taken binding this country—indeed, no step can be taken, whatever might be the will of the representative of Canada, which would have force or effect before ratification by the Parliament of this Dominion.[57]

After this, there was little significance to the rejection by a party vote of a motion by Mackenzie King demanding that no steps should be taken at the meeting involving any change in Canada's relations to the Empire, or implying any obligation to undertake new naval or military expenditures.[58] The government argued that such a resolution was unprecedented and would tie the hands of the Canadian representative.

The agenda for the conference was discussed in the Canadian House of Commons,[59] and in the course of the discussion the government managed to make it clear that it shared the view expressed by Sir Robert Borden, now a private member, that "the occasion is altogether inopportune for considering the problems of Imperial defence".[60] The British government had suggested in January 1921 that there were four subjects "of first importance": the Anglo-Japanese Alliance ("As existing agreement expires July 13th 1921, this question is most urgent"); naval policy, including Lord Jellicoe's reports; "Common Imperial policy in Foreign Affairs"; and agenda and meeting place for the constitutional conference.[61] Meighen, disingenuously it must be said, concealed this from the House. (The blame, however, rests with Christie, who had supplied him with the summary of the correspondence from which he was clearly working.) He gave instead his own version of the four most important topics, substituting for naval policy "a general review of the main features of foreign relations, particularly as they affect the Dominions".[62] Basing his statement upon the earlier correspondence in the autumn of 1920, in which defence had not been mentioned, he was able to give the impression that the British authorities had referred to it merely as a matter of secondary importance. In view of the attitude with which the Canadian government was approaching the conference, it is not surprising that no important initiative in the field of defence resulted from it.

It was amply clear, on the other hand, that the question of the Anglo-Japanese Alliance was going to be important, and to it much Canadian attention was devoted, mainly by Christie, in the months before the conference. A policy began to take shape in Christie's mind during his trip to Europe for the meeting of the League Assembly in the autumn of 1920. In London on his way home he appears to have contrived a meeting with Lloyd George and put before him, without convincing him, the argument that the abandonment of the alliance was vital to the maintenance of sound Anglo-American and Canadian-American relations.[63] Sailing back to America in the *Aquitania*, he roughed out on paper the policy that Meighen pursued during the next six months.[64]

As Christie saw it, the decision on the renewal or termination of the alliance was enormously vital, "for on the one hand it has a direct bearing on the possibility of an English speaking concord and on the other it may have incalculable effects on the bonds of sympathy and understanding within the Empire itself". And he felt that "certain steps should be taken at once" in advance of the conference. Here is the plan as he sketched it:

> ... 11. Recognize that you cannot simply cancel Alliance & leave situation up in air. What alternative?
>
> B.E., U.S. Jap & China i.e. Pacific Powers—to pool interests in Far East. Initiative & dominant voice in this so far BE concerned to come from Pacific Dominions....
>
> How? Informal conversations in Wash. as soon as new Pres.* and his S[ecretary] of S[tate] installed. Place whole position before them with complete frankness. Discover wh[ether] poss[ible] to have conf[eren]ce of Pac. Powers to arrive at common policy in Far East....
>
> 12. How to be done? By a Canadian. Greater chances of success in dealing with Americans Sound them. Say this is what we believe. We want to know what you think before we go to London....

In Ottawa Christie developed these notes into one of his eloquent memoranda, which went to the Prime Minister on February 1, 1921.[65] After consideration by the cabinet, and discussion with Sir Robert Borden, a formal Prime-Minister-to-Prime-Minister message based upon it was sent to Lloyd George through the Governor General on February 15.[66]

"We feel," wrote Meighen, "that every possible effort should be made to find some alternative policy to that of renewal":

> Admitting that the Alliance has been useful in the past, it nevertheless seems true that the conditions have been so altered that the old motives no longer hold, while the objections have greatly increased. It is unnecessary to elaborate

* President Warren G. Harding, whose Secretary of State was Charles Evans Hughes.

those points at the moment, but I would emphasize the need of promoting good relations with the United States. In view of her tendency towards abandonment of attitude of isolation generally, her traditional special interest in China which is as great as ours, and of the increasing prominence of the Pacific as a scene of action, there is danger that a special confidential relationship concerning that region between ourselves and Japan to which she was not a party would come to be regarded as an unfriendly exclusion and as a barrier to an English speaking concord.

We should try, Meighen proceeded, "to attain our objects in the Far East in another way. Specifically we think we should terminate the Alliance and endeavour at once to bring about a Conference of Pacific Powers—that is Japan, China, the United States, and the British Empire represented by Great Britain, Canada, Australia and New Zealand—for the purpose of adjusting Pacific and Far Eastern questions. Such a straightforward course would enable us to end the Alliance with good grace and would reconcile our position in respect of China and the United States." In any case it seemed important to know before the coming conference what was possible in this direction:

Accordingly we suggest that a representative of the Canadian Government should get in touch with the new President and his Secretary of State as soon as possible after their inauguration and discover through informal confidential conversations whether any such policy is feasible. For this purpose I would nominate Sir Robert Borden who is willing to act.*

Meighen concluded by saying that this method of approach seemed appropriate because the Pacific Dominions were really more vitally concerned than the other parts of the Empire, and "because the proposal seems best calculated to succeed in Washington if put forward by Canada".

In London there had already been considerable heart-searching about the alliance, and some people in official circles there had ideas about it not very different from Christie's and Meighen's. Lord Curzon, the Foreign Secretary, had set up a committee of civil servants in his department, headed by Sir William Tyrrell, to report on the question. On January 21,

* It has been suggested[67] that Christie proposed the Borden trip as a "secret and independent Canadian move". But I see no evidence that he suggested acting behind the British government's back.

1921 the committee unanimously recommended that the alliance "should be dropped, and that in its stead should, if possible, be substituted a Tripartite *Entente* between the United States, Japan and Great Britain, consisting in a declaration of general principles which can be subscribed to by all parties without the risk of embarrassing commitments".[68] The committee added, "For the effective support and the ultimate success of those principles we must rely on the closest co-operation with the United States rather than with Japan." It explained that it had approached the matter not merely as a Far Eastern question, "but from the broader standpoint of world politics, which are dominated by our relations with the United States as constituting the prime factor in the maintenance of order and peace throughout the world."

Curzon, who undoubtedly considered himself in every sense the final authority on British foreign policy, was not convinced by his committee's arguments; and the Foreign Office was certain to oppose the dangerous innovation of allowing a ticklish negotiation to fall into Dominion hands. This was the line Curzon took when on February 18 the British cabinet discussed Meighen's cable. The Foreign Office and the Committee of Imperial Defence were studying the question, he said; there were strong arguments for renewing the alliance and Sir Auckland Geddes, the Ambassador in Washington, had, after initial doubts, recommended renewal. Winston Churchill, who had just become Colonial Secretary, favoured a more conciliatory tone towards the Canadian suggestion; Borden, he thought, might be invited to London.[69] Lloyd George incorporated this idea in his reply to Meighen,[70] which nevertheless rejected the latter's proposal pretty firmly. The British Prime Minister argued that presenting the plan for a Pacific conference to the United States government, however informally, would tie the hands of the coming meeting in London; and in any case the other Dominions would have to be consulted before such an initiative was taken.

The British attitude disgusted Christie, who proceeded to inquire "whether it should not be recognized that in matters of high policy respecting North America the voice of Canada should be predominant as far as the British Empire is concerned" (an exaggerated idea that was to turn up in Meighen's mouth at the conference) and to recommend that Canada should disregard Lloyd George and send Borden to Washington anyway.[71] Meighen was not prepared to go so far; but a stiff cable went off to London emphasizing "the very special Canadian position in this matter" and concluding, "We therefore are still strongly of the opinion that steps should be taken as soon as possible along the lines of our proposal." The answer indicated that the British had seen the danger of independent action by Canada; it urged that nothing of the sort be done "at this stage". The British reply was based to a considerable extent on a memorandum by M. W. Lampson of the Foreign Office, who also argued that the Canadian attitude was very close to that of the Foreign Office committee, and that "the policy of Anglo-American cooperation in the Pacific advocated by Canada is the right one". Lampson urged that the committee report should now be communicated to the Dominions. This was not done. On May 30, belatedly, the British cabinet made decisions about the alliance. At the coming conference it would "support the proposal that the President of the United States of America should be asked to summon a Conference of the Pacific Powers, but only after it had been made quite clear to Japan and to other Powers concerned that we had no intention of dropping the Alliance"; further, the period of renewal should be shorter than the ten years of the previous agreement and "its terms should be so drawn as not to be inconsistent with the Covenant of the League of Nations or liable to offend American susceptibilities".[72]

CONFRONTATIONS IN LONDON, 1921

Needless to say, Christie accompanied Meighen to London. The Minister of the Naval Service, C. C. Ballantyne, was present for the later sessions of the conference.

The less important aspects of the conference's work may be looked at first.[73] One was the question of the constitutional conference recommended in Resolution IX of 1917 (above, page 213). General Smuts argued strongly for holding such a conference, "to remove the obscurities which still cling to the situation". In South Africa he was faced with a separatist movement and felt that it could only be effectively dealt with by making it fully clear that the Empire was "a system of equal states working together on principles of equality and freedom". But Hughes of Australia and Massey of New Zealand were not friendly to the idea, and Meighen was not greatly interested; and the conference formally resolved that, "Having regard to the constitutional developments since 1917, no advantage is to be gained by holding a constitutional Conference."[74]

On defence, as already noted, there was no disposition to make commitments; the conference's decision was that the "method and expense" of naval cooperation were "matters for the final determination of the several

Parliaments concerned" and that recommendations should await the result of the disarmament conference which was shortly to take place.[75]

There was considerable discussion on the fundamental question of the coordination of foreign policy. No one at the conference really questioned the desirability of a unified policy for the Empire; but nothing was accomplished in the direction of creating consultative machinery to formulate it. Meighen suggested the appointment of a committee of the conference to consider the subject.[76] Lloyd George chose to disregard the suggestion. Meighen also put forward, at the outset of the discussion on foreign policy, three propositions on the matter. First, there should be "regular, and so far as possible, continuous" conferences between Britain, the Dominions, and India on questions of foreign relations; second, "the Ministry advising the King" (that is, the British ministry) should, in conducting foreign policy, have regard to the views of the Dominion and Indian governments; and third, "in spheres in which any Dominion is particularly concerned the view of that Dominion must be given a weight commensurate with the importance of the decision to that Dominion". Meighen added, "Speaking for Canada, I make this observation with particular reference to our relations with the United States."[77] We have seen that this idea originated with Loring Christie. It is hardly necessary to add that the apparent implication that Canada should be permitted to dictate the policies of the Empire on matters affecting relations with the United States was promptly challenged, particularly by W. M. Hughes.[78]

The conference's final statement on foreign policy is the closest an imperial gathering ever came to a formal endorsement of the principle of a unified imperial policy in foreign affairs:

> The discussions, which covered the whole area of foreign policy . . . proved most fruitful. . . . They revealed a unanimous opinion as to the main lines to be followed by British policy, and a deep conviction that the whole weight of the Empire should be concentrated behind a united understanding and common action in foreign affairs. In this context, very careful consideration was given to the means of circulating information to the Dominion Governments and keeping them in continuous touch with the conduct of foreign relations by the British Government. . . .[79]

This exaggerated both the unanimity of the conference and the attention paid to the process of consultation. Otherwise, it was not misleading; and the Canadian Prime Minister, like the other members of the conference, was evidently quite prepared to accept the concept of a common imperial foreign policy, formed as the result of consultation between the governments of the Empire,* but conducted by the British Foreign Office. Just how this last aspect of the matter would be affected by Canada's already declared intention of sending a representative to Washington remained to be seen.

In fact, the extraordinary difficulty likely to attend the formation of common policy had been strikingly demonstrated during the conference. The question of the Anglo-Japanese Alliance produced the most violent difference of opinion that had ever occurred in such a gathering.

That there were going to be differences had been clear for months, and not only to those who had seen the secret cables that had passed between London and Ottawa. Meighen did not commit himself in the House of Commons as to the attitude he would take; but he told the House that the importance of the alliance for Canada arose "in a very great degree, out of the very great interest of the United States in the renewal or the non-renewal thereof"; and he admitted under questioning the possibility that if the treaty were renewed it might, like the Anglo-French treaty of guarantee of 1919 (above, page 257), contain a provision that the treaty would not be binding upon Canada without the approval of the Canadian Parliament.[80] But N. W. Rowell in the same debate suggested in a carefully moderate speech that in view of the feeling existing in the United States it might be desirable "that this treaty should not be renewed, at least in its present form".[81] There was Canadian press comment to the same effect.[82] But indications of a different attitude came from Australasia. In a well-publicized utterance in the House of Representatives in Melbourne, Hughes, the Australian Prime Minister, proclaimed, "Our ideal at the Conference, as I see it, is a renewal of the Anglo-Japanese Treaty in such form, modified if that should be deemed proper, as will be acceptable to Britain, to America, to Japan, and to ourselves."[83] In the view of the makers of Canadian policy this ideal was unattainable.

At the very outset of the conference in London, Hughes hoisted the standard of renewal, still adding that everything possible should be done to avoid arousing apprehension in the United States.[84] On June 28 Lord Curzon surveyed the question, making it clear that he himself did not feel

* Meighen in this conference used the phrase "Commonwealth of Nations" more than once, but in general he and the other prime ministers, and the official documents of the conference, were content to use the old term "Empire".

prepared to abandon the alliance altogether. He gave the impression that his committee's suggestion, of replacing it with a tripartite agreement, had originated with the British Ambassador in Washington; he thought it was unlikely to be acceptable to the United States Senate or to American public opinion. He spoke politely of the Canadian suggestion of a conference, saying that such a meeting "might perfectly well be consistent with a renewal of the agreement in some form should it be considered desirable". Asked by Hughes what the British government's view was, the Foreign Secretary replied that the cabinet had been "inclined" to favour "renewal in a different form for a term of years, let us say four, capable of being either extended or dissolved at the end of that time". At this point Churchill interjected that this had been before receipt of the last telegrams from the Ambassador in Washington; Geddes now reported that the Secretary of State had told him "that he viewed the renewal of the Anglo-Japanese Alliance in any form with disquietude, because of the effect such renewal would inevitably have upon American opinion". Curzon noted that the Admiralty favoured renewal, "in a manner that will safeguard the suspicions of America"; and Balfour (Lord President of the Council) reported on behalf of the Standing Committee of the Committee of Imperial Defence, which had studied the problem, "We were clear that, from a strategic point of view, there could be no doubt whatever that it is to the advantage of this country to renew the Alliance." This would continue to be the case until Singapore was strengthened.

This galaxy of talent did not discourage Arthur Meighen. On the following day, June 29, he made a frontal attack on the alliance. He began by saying, "I feel compelled to oppose the renewal of the Alliance. I would regret to see the Treaty continued in any form at all." Canada, he said, felt that in the light of the treaty's effect upon British-American relations she had "a special right to be heard". In the awful event of war between the Empire and the United States, "Canada will be the Belgium". This was perhaps unnecessarily dramatic. But what followed was grim common sense:

> But we view this question not from the standpoint of the United States, we view it from this standpoint, that if, as I believe, the Foreign Secretary is sincere when he says that British-American friendship is the pivot of our world policy, it follows that in determining the wisdom from our own point of view of any engagement a major consideration must be its probable effect on that friendship.

From the beginning of the discussion I know that the Foreign Secretary has stated that any renewal should be in a form satisfactory to the United States, and that we must carry that country with us in any course that we take. Well, I am going to say this. I do not believe that it is possible to have an agreement in any form at all, however negative, that will be really satisfactory to the United States. . . .

Meighen went on to say forcibly that if renewal was intended "to create a combination against an American menace", there could be "no hope of ever carrying Canada into the plan". "We ourselves have got along with the United States for 100 years, and have overcome many difficulties, and we meet there a spirit which convinces us that we can still get along." He recalled his cable of February to Lloyd George suggesting a conference of Japan, the United States, the British Empire, and China. Asked by Balfour whether he had any ground for thinking that the United States would like to be "a third party to an agreement", he said that he had hoped to have it, but that Lloyd George's attitude had prevented the investigation which he had proposed. He thought nevertheless that the prospect was hopeful for a "broad, inclusive arrangement".

Billy Hughes was notoriously difficult and unpleasant. On this occasion, finding himself so firmly opposed, he burst into an excited emotional tirade. He questioned Meighen's interpretation of American opinion. He objected to the Empire's policy being "dictated by some other Power". He referred in hostile terms to the great American naval program.

. . . What does he offer us? Something we can grasp? What is the substantial alternative to the renewal of the Treaty? The answer is, that there is none. If Australia was asked whether she would prefer America or Japan as an ally, her choice would be America. But that choice is not offered her. As against the substance she is offered the shadow. She calls to America saying "Here are we with a coastline of 13,000 miles, with a great continent to defend, within three weeks of a thousand millions of Asiatics; will you come to us if we call?" But to the call of our young democracy in its remote isolation, there is no answer. Now let me speak plainly to Mr. Meighen on behalf of Australia. I, for one, will vote against any renewal of the Anglo-Japanese Alliance upon one condition and one only, and that is that America gives us that assurance of safety which our circumstances absolutely demand. . . . Mr. Meighen has not touched upon two facts which stand out; one, that America's real objection to this Treaty in any form is the fear of Japan; and the other, the hatred of Britain by certain sections in America. . . .

> ... If he [Meighen] will look at his own [defence] budget and ours he will see what it means to have a great nation like America as his neighbour, under whose wing the Dominion of Canada can nestle in safety....
>
> I do not wish to prolong the debate. I must regard Mr. Meighen's presentation of the case as not the case for the Empire, but as the case for the United States of America.... I am for the renewal of this Treaty, and I am against delay....

Subsequently General Smuts talked around the question without taking sides, and Massey on behalf of New Zealand aligned himself fully with Hughes, saying, "My country will not look to any other country than Britain for protection so long as the British Empire exists." For India the Maharao of Cutch, while recognizing that a tripartite understanding including the United States would be "the best thing" if it were practicable, strongly supported renewal. Meighen appeared to be in a minority of one.[85]

The sessions of June 29 clearly left Lloyd George, as chairman of the conference, in a position of extreme difficulty. The conference was threatened with breakdown as a result of the violent clash that had developed between the two senior Dominions. If their positions could not in some way be reconciled, the possibility had to be faced that Canada would simply be overborne by the majority, in which case Meighen (assuming that he did not leave the conference) would presumably insist that any treaty renewing the alliance should contain the provision already mentioned,* specifying that it should not apply to any Dominion whose Parliament had not approved it. Such an advertisement of disunity would be acutely embarrassing to the British government.

Lloyd George, a rather notable political conjurer, did in fact on June 30 pull out of his hat one of the most remarkable rabbits of his career. But before he did it he made a rather silly speech supporting Hughes:

> We must not insult Japan.... If we were beginning from the start, I do not know what we should do, but two years after the war, when this gallant little people in the East backed us through thick and thin, now to drop them—we cannot do it. I think the British Empire must behave like a gentleman. This is one plea I put in for the renewal of the Treaty with Japan....[86]

He then proceeded to his conjuring trick. The extreme urgency of the alliance question had been due to the fact that the British government's

* Both in Meighen's cable of April 1 to Lloyd George, and in the House of Commons on April 27.

legal advisers had taken the view that when Britain and Japan jointly informed the League of Nations in 1920 that they recognized the fact that the alliance, if continued after July 1921, must be in a form not inconsistent with the League Covenant, they in fact gave each other notice that the agreement would terminate at that time if not previously renewed.[87] The Imperial Conference was working against a deadline only a fortnight away.* Various people, including Meighen,[88] had thought the lawyers' opinion peculiar. A reversal of it would go a long way to resolve the impasse. On the morning of June 30 the British cabinet in an emergency meeting accepted Lloyd George's suggestion that the Lord Chancellor, Lord Birkenhead, the highest legal authority in the kingdom, should be asked to rule on the question. If he should decide that notice of denunciation had not been given, the Prime Minister said, "Mr. Meighen, instead of pleading for the non-renewal of the Alliance, would have to plead for the issue of a notice denouncing it."[89] Birkenhead did not take long to form his opinion. At the meeting of the conference at 4:30 that afternoon Lloyd George introduced him and invited him to give his ruling. It was definite:

> Prime Minister, I make no observations on the policy in the matter, but upon the technical matter on which you have asked my opinion for the purpose of this Conference I have no hesitation whatever in saying that we should adhere to the view that no denunciation has taken place.

The deadline had vanished. The alliance would continue to exist, in accordance with its terms, until one year after one side or the other formally denounced it. The fire had been largely taken out of the issue before the conference; it was no longer whether to renew or drop the alliance at once, but whether to allow it to remain in existence for the present. Lloyd George was "very pleased with himself".[90]

The cabinet meeting on June 30, faced with Curzon's report that Meighen had given the impression that Canada "would have to dissociate herself" from a decision to enter into any exclusive agreement with Japan, had taken another decision contributing to solution of the difficulty. It was agreed that the British representatives at the Imperial Conference should be authorized

* The British government proposed to Japan a three-month extension (from July 13) to give the conference time for discussion, but the crisis arose in the conference before the Japanese consent was received.

to propose or assent to the initiation of full and frank conversations with the Governments of both the United States of America and Japan with a view to some arrangement satisfactory to all parties.

Thus the renewal of the alliance lost the priority it had been given in the decision of May 30.[91] Meighen the day before had already urged "conversations with the United States at once and with any other nation which the Foreign Secretary thinks should come in".[92]

With the way thus prepared, the imperial meeting, in spite of continuing asperities between Meighen and Hughes, reached a compromise on July 1. It was decided that the Foreign Secretary should notify Japan of the new situation concerning the treaty: that Britain now held that no notice to denounce had been given and that it remained in effect. The League of Nations was to be informed that "we are dealing with the whole Eastern and Pacific question in a larger spirit"; any new arrangement would be in harmony with the Covenant, and in the meantime wherever the Covenant was in conflict with the treaty, the Covenant would prevail. The conference's agreement proceeded:

3. The Secretary of State for Foreign Affairs will approach the representatives in London of the United States of America, China and Japan in order to find out whether, the Anglo-Japanese Alliance, as modified ... [by the reference to the Covenant] being still in existence, they will enter into a Conference on the matter.
4. The Secretary of State for Foreign Affairs will report to the present meeting later on.
5. The British Government will not notify its intention to denounce until a settlement has been arrived at by the new Conference or a new Treaty has been drawn up by common agreement to replace the present one.[93]

Meighen had not abandoned his opposition to the treaty. Having perhaps been given a hint of the British cabinet's decision, he proposed the approach to the United States, Japan and China with a view to arranging a Pacific conference; but he was anxious that the life of the treaty should specifically be limited to one year. This would have involved denouncing it immediately. Lloyd George took the view that this "would be very undesirable before we enter into a Conference", and was clearly supported by the majority.[94] The conference in London ended with the Anglo-

Japanese Alliance still subsisting. Its early demise was probable but by no means certain.

The Japanese and Chinese when sounded by Curzon were not hostile to the idea of a Pacific conference. The Americans were determined not to let the diplomatic initiative pass to the British, and on July 11 President Harding announced publicly that he had invited Britain, Japan, France, and Italy to attend a conference on disarmament in Washington. This was a popular act with the American Congress and public, who were more than doubtful about the cost of the enormous program of naval construction which their country was pursuing. Harding at the same time proposed a separate meeting on Pacific and Far Eastern questions, which would be in effect the Pacific conference approved by the imperial gathering in London. The British government immediately put forward the idea that the Pacific meeting should be in London, perhaps even before the assembled Dominion statesmen went home; but the Americans would not agree.[95] Subsequently the British suggested a preliminary meeting in Washington, to discuss the agenda for the conference there. What happened then may perhaps be summarized in the rather bitter words of the published summary of the Imperial Conference:

> . . . The British Prime Minister and Foreign Secretary, together with the Dominion Prime Ministers, were prepared to attend such a meeting, if invited to do so by the American Government.
>
> The Japanese Government signified their willingness, if invited, to take part in the suggested conversations.
>
> The American Government, however, did not favour the idea, which was accordingly dropped.
>
> This conclusion was viewed with the utmost regret by the members of the Imperial Conference. . . .[96]

The final chapter in the history of the Anglo-Japanese alliance was written during the Washington Conference six months later, where it was replaced by the Four-Power Treaty.

It remains to say a word of retrospective comment about the treatment of the alliance by the Imperial Conference of 1921, and about the Canadian part in the affair.

The historical interpretation of this has gone from one extreme to the other. In 1935 J. B. Brebner, having no access to confidential records but making good use of newspaper reports, including the largely accurate account of events at the conference table which (to Lloyd George's great chagrin)[97] somebody leaked to the London *Times*, concluded that Meighen's assault on the alliance led the conference to decide to "shelve" it and that this was "the first notable occasion of a Dominion formulating the policy of the British Empire".[98] That this was exaggerated and inaccurate we have seen. It is nevertheless rather extraordinary that Brebner managed to reconstruct the conference with so high a degree of accuracy from the sources he had. On the other hand, more recent scholars, with all the documents available to them, seem to have over-reacted against Brebner. Meighen's influence on events has been minimized and it has even been argued that the exchange between Hughes and Meighen was a "temperate debate":[99] an interpretation calculated to surprise those who read the minutes and compare them with the tone of those of other imperial meetings.

It is quite clear that nobody at the conference insisted on continuing the alliance in its existing form, though Hughes' remarks suggest that he would have been glad to see this done had it been practicable. It is equally clear that men in the British Foreign Office shared the Canadian position in its essentials, taking the view that the alliance was a menace to good relations with the United States and that it should be replaced by a broader arrangement in which the United States should be included. They were, however, overruled by their political chief. There was considerable difference of opinion in British governmental circles. Nevertheless, it is hard to read the presentations made to the conference without concluding that but for Meighen's resolute and resounding attack, the meeting, instead of adopting an approach likely to lead to the supersession of the alliance, would almost certainly have decided to renegotiate it in the hope of making it less objectionable to the United States. The effect of Meighen's onslaught is, indeed, reflected in the record of the British cabinet meetings of May 30 and June 30 (above, pages 338, 344–45). The Canadians believed that any attempt to make the alliance acceptable to the United States was moonshine; and later events suggest that they assessed American opinion and policy more accurately than anybody else at the conference. Their opinion, however, was reinforced by Geddes' belated recognition of the true facts, mentioned by Churchill on June 28. Geddes' message of June 24 was referred to by Curzon in the cabinet meeting on the 30th and doubtless contributed materially to the result.

In terms of the great Commonwealth experiment that had been in progress since 1916, the Imperial Conference of 1921 was not an entirely encouraging portent. It is true that breakdown had been avoided and compromise achieved; yet the margin had been narrow. Without the happy expedient of the Lord Chancellor's new interpretation of the status of the Anglo-Japanese treaty, it might not have been possible to bridge the gulf between Canada and Australia. On another occasion, such a device might not lie to hand. Nor had the British government's attitude before the conference boded particularly well for the future. The frosty reception of the Canadian Prime Minister's initiative had made a bad impression in Ottawa; and had the Canadians known about the suppressed report of the Foreign Office committee, the impression would have been still worse. Consultation had been very imperfect, and the conference had produced no arrangements to improve it. The long-term prospect for an effective unified imperial foreign policy based on consultation might have seemed doubtful. Nevertheless, an encouraging episode lay just ahead.

THE WASHINGTON CONFERENCE

On August 11, 1921 invitations went out from Washington for "a conference on the subject of limitation of armaments, in connection with which Pacific and Far Eastern questions will also be discussed".[100] None was addressed to Canada or to any other Dominion; that to London ran, "the President invites the Government of Great Britain . . .". This was resented in some quarters, notably by General Smuts, who felt that the opportunity should be used to impress upon the Americans the reality of the Dominions' new status.[101] In view of the public emphasis placed on the diplomatic unity of the Empire by the recent London conference, however, Washington was perhaps hardly to be blamed. The Canadian government was very anxious to be represented, but it was quite satisfied with the policy adopted by Britain from the beginning, that the Dominions should nominate members of a British Empire Delegation which would function in the same manner as at Paris in 1919.[102] Meighen nominated Sir Robert Borden, the distinguished former Prime Minister, as the Canadian plenipotentiary. He was accompanied by Loring Christie as a member of the Delegation secretariat. When Maurice Hankey, the head of the secretariat, was recalled to England just before the end of the conference, Christie suceeded him as Secretary to the Delegation.[103] And when the time came to sign treaties, the Paris formula was followed (above, page 255). Again the phrase "United Kingdom" was not used. The names of the British government's delegates appeared after the King's titles; then

Borden's name followed, "for the Dominion of Canada", and the others in order.[104]

The leader of the British representatives was the urbane and accomplished Balfour, like Borden an ex-Prime Minister. The two old men found themselves agreeable colleagues, and within the British Empire Delegation at Washington there were none of the acerbities that had marred the conference in London. Meighen and Hughes were not present (Meighen was fighting an election). Australia was represented by Senator (later Sir) G. F. Pearce, a less abrasive character than Hughes. The delegation met almost daily (there were twenty-six meetings in all); matters of policy before the conference were discussed; and while there were differences of opinion on various points, substantial agreement on essentials was always reached.[105] Borden wrote afterwards, "a cordial and unvarying spirit of co-operation marked the action of the British Empire Delegation";[106] and this does not seem to have been mere window-dressing.

There is no need in this book to describe the work of the Washington Conference in great detail. Some attention must be given, however, to the final fate of the Anglo-Japanese Alliance.

Balfour came to Washington without any definite instructions on this matter from the British cabinet. He was, of course, familiar with the decisions of the Imperial Conference; and he knew that Lloyd George had made a statement in the House of Commons on August 18, somewhat in the spirit of his "gallant little people in the East" performance in the conference, indicating that Britain hoped to retain the alliance or replace it with something better. This was in part at least intended to reassure Japan as to Britain's continued friendship.[107] Beyond this, Balfour had an essentially free hand.

One thing the British government had made quite clear. Various minor powers were invited to the meeting in Washington.* These could have nothing to do with the discussion of the Anglo-Japanese Alliance or matters of policy "affecting the safety [of] Pacific Dominions and India". Such discussion, the Americans were bluntly told, could in Britain's view be "conducted with profit only between the three great Naval Powers".[108] On this basis Balfour went to work. His opening gambit was a draft tri-

* The participants were the five most important naval powers (the British Empire, the United States, Japan, France, and Italy) plus four other countries with interests in the Pacific: China, the Netherlands, Portugal, and Belgium, which had a concession at Tientsin and interests in Chinese railways.

partite "arrangement" by which Britain, the United States, and Japan agreed to respect one another's rights, and to consult with one another if imperilled by another power; while if their territorial rights were threatened any two of the three should be free to enter into a defensive military alliance. That is to say, the revival of the Anglo-Japanese Alliance would be a definite possibility.[109] This draft was doubtless what Hankey later called it, "a diplomatic opening".[110] Balfour showed it and others to the British Empire Delegation at a dinner meeting on November 10. By this time the British visitors had been told by Americans, including Root and Lodge, that continuance of the alliance would have a most unfortunate effect upon United States public opinion. Borden says that "various suggestions and criticisms" were made of the drafts Balfour exhibited, but it appears that the Empire representatives in general accepted his proposal.[111] He then showed it to the Americans (who were critical) and only somewhat later to the Japanese. The latter actually felt that there was too much of the old military alliance about it to be acceptable to the United States, and made suggestions accordingly. In the end what emerged was a treaty by which the parties agreed (a) to respect one another's rights concerning their "insular possessions and insular dominions" in the Pacific region, and in the event of controversy between them to resort to a conference of all of them; and (b) in the event of their rights being threatened by aggression by another power, to consult together on measures to be taken. The treaty was to remain in force for ten years, and thereafter to be subject to the right of any of the parties to terminate it on a year's notice. It was specifically provided that when the treaty was ratified, "the agreement between Great Britain and Japan, which was concluded at London on July 13, 1911, shall terminate".[112]

In marked contrast with the situation in London six months before, in Washington there was no serious difference of opinion within the British Empire Delegation about these arrangements, and Senator Pearce appears to have had no difficulty in obtaining his government's authority to sign the new treaty. It was discussed at length in the delegation only once, on December 7, when it was virtually complete. Some verbal improvements were suggested, and were incorporated in the final treaty.[113]

This turned out to be, not a tripartite but a four-power treaty. France was brought in on the insistence of the United States, whose negotiators seem to have felt that the arrangement would be more acceptable politically if the possibility were removed of two of the signatories, the old allies Britain and Japan, joining together against the third party. At any rate, the Anglo-Japanese Alliance was relegated to limbo, a result thoroughly agreeable to the government of Canada. Borden, formally requesting Meighen's authority to sign the four-power treaty on behalf of the Dominion, telegraphed the Prime Minister, "It is entirely in line with the proposal and purposes advocated by you at last summer's Conference."[114] It was Meighen's last taste of triumph. Though for the moment he still held the seals of office, he had already suffered a crushing defeat at the polls.

In accordance with Britain's insistence, the four-power treaty was negotiated outside the Washington Conference proper. But the Anglo-Japanese treaty had contained affirmations of the two countries' intention to maintain the independence and integrity of China and the "open door" policy there; and Balfour had taken the line that this matter should be dealt with separately by the conference as a whole, with China taking part. The result was a nine-power treaty, committing the signatories to the same general principles with respect to China as the preamble of the Anglo-Japanese treaty; indeed, there were two nine-power treaties, the second one dealing with the Chinese customs tariff.[115]

The most prominent question at Washington was, however, naval disarmament. At the very beginning Charles Evans Hughes, the American Secretary of State, made dramatic proposals for scrapping large numbers of battleships, built or building (leaving Britain, the United States, and Japan in a ratio of battleship strength of 5–5–3), and for a ten-year "naval holiday" in battleship construction. British sailors were appalled, and even Balfour was shaken. Canada had no battleships, and made no contribution to speak of to the Empire's naval strength; but Borden spoke up in the British Empire Delegation, and produced a strong memorandum, in favour of accepting the American scheme. The Canadian cabinet was momentarily alarmed by the thought of their country interfering in a matter so important to British security; but when it became apparent that in practice it was the naval officers Borden was opposing, and that the British political authorities at home were taking much the same line as he was, the objections were withdrawn.[116]

At a comparatively late date, on December 9, there was a sharp difference of opinion in the British Empire Delegation on the "naval holiday", the naval men still hoping to see it abandoned or much watered down, and getting considerable sympathy, it appeared, from everyone but Borden. The Canadian argued that the delegation could not now go back upon Balfour's acceptance of Hughes' plan "in spirit and in principle" on

November 15—a phrase which Borden said he put in Balfour's mouth.* Although Pearce had supported Borden's earlier action, now he and the New Zealand representative, Sir John Salmond, sided with the sailors. Borden wrote in his diary,

> ... Admiral [Sir Ernle] Chatfield, whom personally I like, indulged in some loose and foolish talk as to his willingness to fight [the] United States with an inferior fleet. He does not seem to realize that war between the two countries would mean the destruction of a civilisation already rocking under the impact of the late war.

To Borden, the man who had seen a British-American alliance as the key to world peace, this must have been a particularly bitter pill.

Sir Robert might be in a minority of one in Washington, but in London Lloyd George and Curzon still took the same attitude as he did. In the end a naval disarmament treaty incorporating the essence of Secretary Hughes' program was signed by the United States, the British Empire, Japan, France, and Italy. With some qualifications† the ten-year holiday in battleship construction was accepted.[117] An agreement to maintain the status quo with respect to fortifications and naval bases in certain Pacific areas prevented the United States from strengthening the Philippines, and Britain from strengthening Hong Kong. The general result was material temporary relaxation of international tensions, and very important economies.

The whole episode, of course, reflects Britain's declining world position. Early in the century she had recognized that she could not maintain

* In his "Notes" for November 15 Borden wrote, "... before he spoke I had the opportunity of urging upon him the importance of making no reservation, and, just as the Chairman's gavel called the meeting to order, I said to him 'declare that you accept the American proposal in spirit and in principle'. It was with a great deal of satisfaction that I heard him use that exact expression ..." Newspaper accounts of Balfour's speech do not include these words, but they were probably based on a previously prepared text.

† The Japanese were allowed to keep the *Mutsu*, a new battleship scheduled by Hughes for scrapping, the United States completed the *Colorado* and *Washington*, which had also been on the scrapping list, and the British were permitted to proceed with the construction of two replacement battleships, which became H.M. ships *Nelson* and *Rodney*, though on a smaller scale than had been planned. *Nelson* and *Rodney* became known as the Cherry-Tree Class, having been cut down by Washington.

naval supremacy throughout the world (above, page 125). Now she abandoned the policy of maintaining an unequalled fleet. Lloyd George and Curzon realized that she had not the resources to engage in naval competition with the United States. Henceforth she would face the problem of attempting to defend world-wide interests with limited and inadequate means.

There is a rather striking parallel between Meighen's action in London on the Anglo-Japanese alliance and Borden's in Washington on the naval holiday. In both cases the Canadian functioned within the Commonwealth circle as the interpreter and defender of United States policy, and the spokesman of the conception of friendship and co-operation with the United States as the real, and not merely theoretical, foundation of Commonwealth foreign policy. It is not clear that Borden's interventions had any decisive effect. After all, the British statesmen who had to make the decisions on naval policy were doubtless as capable as he was of seeing the chief points he made in his memorandum and elsewhere—that the American initiative on naval disarmament was courageous as well as dramatic and had caught the imagination of ordinary people in many countries, and that it was very undesirable for the Empire to give less than whole-hearted acceptance to it; and that it had to be remembered that the United States possessed the economic resources to outbuild the Empire in any competition in naval construction. But in the record of Canadian policy these positions are significant, and give some substance to the widespread idealistic notion that Canada had a special part to play as an "interpreter and reconciler" between Commonwealth and Republic.

Borden had gone to Washington as the representative of Arthur Meighen's government, but before the Washington Conference was over that government was no more. On December 29, 1921 Mackenzie King's first ministry took office. Borden had already written the Prime Minister-elect offering to relinquish his appointment in favour of "some one more thoroughly in your confidence than I can claim to be". King replied, not too graciously, telling Borden to "consider it the wish" of the new government that he should continue to serve "as a Member of the British Empire Delegation". He added, "If at all in doubt as to the policy or course which you think the Government might wish to have pursued, kindly defer action until opportunity has been had for communication with Ottawa."[118]

An exchange a few weeks later reflects the suspicious attitude of mind with which King was to approach the problems of Commonwealth relations. He thought he discovered in "the secret correspondence" that

Meighen had agreed to or indeed had made proposals "which may commit Canada along lines of Naval defence in a manner never intended and not likely to be countenanced by Parliament".[119] He had apparently been looking at letters concerning the four-power treaty, and was apprehensive lest Meighen might have made commitments during the conference in London (which it is quite clear he had not). To King, naval policy immediately recalled the bitter controversies of 1909–13. He consulted John S. Ewart (above, page 299) and wrote what seems a rather excited letter to Borden, asking for full details of any "understandings or agreements" on naval policy between members of the British Empire Delegation before the naval treaty was signed. In particular, the treaty was not to be signed on behalf of Canada if "by implication or otherwise, it contravenes, restricts or abridges in any way" any of the provisions of Laurier's Naval Service Act of 1910. What he was worried about, evidently, was the power of the Canadian government in an emergency to decide whether to withhold its ships or to place them at the disposal of the Admiralty.[120] One cannot help feeling, however, that he was glorying in the opportunity to use his newly acquired power to humiliate one of the fallen Tories.

Borden replied stiffly, on the basis of a memorandum by Christie. On decisions in London, he referred King to the official proceedings of the Imperial Conference (above, pages 338–39). As for agreements and understandings concerning imperial co-operation in naval defence, this question had never been discussed in the British Empire Delegation. "It was quite unnecessary to discuss it and so far as I am aware no member of the British Empire Delegation was authorised to discuss any such question." Borden added, "The Naval Treaty as I understand it imposes no obligation upon Canada except to restrict the naval armament which otherwise she would be at liberty to undertake." This reply King found "reassuring".[121] However, he went on to ask questions about the ratification of the treaties. Borden had said that all the treaties would be "subject to ratification [*sic*] by the Canadian Government". Was this a matter of form or an act of significance? Borden replied that the treaty provided that it should be ratified in accordance with the constitutional methods of the contracting parties. It was for Canada to decide the method, and to require that the treaties should provide for approval by Parliament (as King had suggested) was impracticable.[122] In the end the same procedure was followed as with the treaties of 1919: approval by resolution of the Canadian Senate and House of Commons, followed by an order-in-council humbly moving the King to ratify in respect of the Dominion of Canada.[123] (Neither King nor Borden in their correspondence had noted that ratification was a prerogative of the Crown.)

In due course Sir Robert Borden submitted a detailed report on the Washington Conference, which was placed before Parliament.[124] It was presumably mainly in the words of Loring Christie. It expressed almost complete satisfaction with the British Empire Delegation as a means of reconciling the individual interests of the various nations of the Empire with the imperial diplomatic unity which Borden accepted as vital:

> Doubtless the scheme will be susceptible of improvement as time goes on, but speaking broadly I believe the experience of this Conference has again justified it as a means whereby under our present constitutional system the Empire can effectively act at international gatherings. The formal aspects of the Treaties and of our appearance at the Conference recognize both the principle of unity and that of co-ordinate autonomy; but neither could be real without effective means whereby in advance of action the views of all would be fully and frankly exchanged and considered in common. The organization of the British Empire Delegation provided that means.

Borden, in fact, took the view that the events at Washington had proved that a unified imperial foreign policy, based on consultation, was practicable as well as desirable, and he looked to a future in which the Commonwealth would continue to function effectively with the machinery that had worked so smoothly at the Peace Conference of Paris and the Disarmament Conference. But the meeting at Washington was the last occasion when a serious effort was made to use that machinery or apply those principles. New men with different ideas were already in power at Ottawa.

APPENDIX A

CANADIAN EXTERNAL TRADE–STATISTICS OF IMPORTS AND EXPORTS, 1868-1921

(SOURCE: Canada Year Book, 1922–23)

Exports to the United Kingdom, to the United States and to other Countries of Merchandise, the Produce of Canada, 1868–1921

Fiscal Year	Exports to United Kingdom	Per cent Can. Exports to U.K. to Total Can. Exports (mdse.)	Exports to United States	Per cent Can. Exports to U.S. to Total Can. Exports (mdse.)	Exports to Other Countries	Total Exports of Canadian Produce
1868	$17,905,808	36.9%	$25,349,568	52.3%	$5,249,523	$48,504,899
1869	20,486,389	39.1	26,717,656	51.0	5,196,727	52,400,772
1870	22,512,991	38.1	30,361,328	51.4	6,169,271	59,043,590
1871	21,733,556	37.7	29,164,358	50.6	6,732,110	57,630,024
1872	25,223,785	38.3	32,871,496	49.9	7,735,802	65,831,083
1873	31,402,234	41.0	36,714,144	48.0	8,421,647	76,538,025
1874	35,769,190	46.6	33,195,805	43.3	7,777,002	76,741,997
1875	34,199,134	49.1	27,902,748	40.0	7,607,941	69,709,823
1876	34,379,005	47.4	30,080,738	41.5	8,031,694	72,491,437
1877	35,491,671	52.2	24,326,332	35.8	8,212,543	68,030,546
1878	35,861,110	52.7	24,381,009	35.9	7,747,681	67,989,800
1879	29,393,424	47.1	25,491,356	40.8	7,546,245	62,431,025
1880	35,208,031	48.3	29,566,211	40.6	8,125,455	72,899,697
1881	42,637,219	50.8	34,038,431	40.5	7,269,051	83,944,701
1882	39,816,813	42.3	45,782,584	48.6	8,538,260	91,137,657
1883	39,538,067	45.1	39,513,225	45.1	8,651,139	87,702,431
1884	37,410,870	46.9	34,332,641	43.0	8,089,587	79,833,098
1885	36,479,051	46.1	35,566,810	44.9	7,085,874	79,131,735
1886	36,694,263	47.2	34,284,490	44.1	6,777,951	77,756,704
1887	38,714,331	47.8	35,269,922	43.6	6,976,656	80,960,909

Fiscal Year	Exports to United Kingdom	*Per cent Can. Exports to U.K. to Total Can. Exports (mdse.)*	Exports to United States	*Per cent Can. Exports to U.S. to Total Can. Exports (mdse.)*	Exports to Other Countries	Total Exports of Canadian Produce
1888	$33,648,284	41.3 %	$40,407,483	49.6 %	$ 7,326,305	$ 81,382,072
1889	33,504,281	41.7	39,519,940	49.2	7,248,235	80,272,456
1890	41,499,149	48.7	36,213,279	42.5	7,545,158	85,257,586
1891	43,243,784	48.8	37,743,430	42.6	7,684,524	88,671,738
1892	54,949,055	55.5	34,666,070	35.0	9,417,341	99,032,466
1893	58,409,606	55.4	37,296,110	35.4	9,783,082	105,488,798
1894	60,878,056	58.6	32,562,509	31.4	10,411,199	103,851,764
1895	57,903,564	56.3	35,603,863	34.6	9,321,014	102,828,441
1896	62,717,941	57.2	37,789,481	34.4	9,200,383	109,707,805
1897	69,533,852	56.2	43,664,187	35.3	10,434,501	123,632,540
1898	93,065,019	64.4	38,989,525	27.0	12,494,118	144,548,662
1899	85,113,681	62.0	39,326,485	29.0	12,920,626	137,360,792
1900	96,562,875	57.1	57,996,488	34.2	14,412,938	168,972,301
1901	92,857,525	52.3	67,983,673	38.3	16,590,188	177,431,386
1902	100,347,345	55.8	66,567,784	34.0	20,104,634	196,019,763
1903	125,199,980	58.4	67,766,367	31.6	21,435,327	214,401,674
1904	110,120,892	55.5	66,856,885	33.7	21,436,662	198,414,439
1905	97,114,867	50.9	70,426,765	36.9	23,313,314	190,854,946
1906	127,456,465	54.1	83,546,306	35.5	24,481,185	235,483,956
1907[1]	98,691,186	54.7	62,180,439	34.4	19,673,681	180,545,306
1908	126,194,124	51.1	90,814,871	36.8	29,951,973	246,960,968
1909	126,384,724	52.1	85,334,806	35.2	30,884,054	242,603,584
1910	139,482,945	50.0	104,199,675	37.3	35,564,931	279,247,551
1911	132,156,924	48.2	104,115,823	38.0	38,043,806	274,316,553
1912	147,240,413	50.7	102,041,222	35.2	40,942,222	290,223,857
1913	170,161,903	47.8	139,725,953	39.3	45,866,744	355,754,600
1914	215,253,969	49.9	163,372,825	37.9	52,961,645	431,588,439
1915	186,668,554	45.6	173,320,216	42.3	49,430,066	409,418,836
1916	451,852,399	60.9	201,106,488	27.1	88,651,751	741,610,638
1917	742,147,537	64.5	280,616,330	24.4	128,611,901	1,151,375,768
1918	845,480,069	54.9	417,233,287	27.0	277,314,432	1,540,027,788
1919	540,750,977	44.5	454,873,170	37.4	220,819,659	1,216,443,806
1920	489,152,637	39.5	464,028,183	37.4	286,311,278	1,239,492,098
1921	312,844,871	26.3	542,322,967	45.6	333,995,863	1,189,163,701

[1] Nine months.

Imports from the United Kingdom, from the United States and from other Countries of Merchandise entered for Home Consumption, 1868–1921

Fiscal Year	*Imports from United Kingdom*	*Per cent Imports from U.K. to Total Imports (mdse.)*	*Imports from United States*	*Per cent Imports from U.S. to Total Imports (mdse.)*	*Imports from Other Countries*	*Total Imports for Home Consumption*
1868	$37,617,325	56.1%	$22,660,132	33.8%	$6,812,702	$67,090,159
1869	35,496,764	56.2	21,497,380	34.0	6,160,797	63,154,941
1870	37,537,095	56.1	21,697,237	32.4	7,667,742	66,902,074
1871	48,498,202	57.6	27,185,586	32.3	8,530,600	84,214,388
1872	62,209,254	59.7	33,741,995	32.1	9,004,118	104,955,367
1873	67,996,945	54.6	45,189,110	36.3	11,323,074	124,509,129
1874	61,424,407	49.9	51,706,906	42.0	10,049,574	123,180,887
1875	60,009,084	51.1	48,930,358	41.7	8,469,126	117,408,568
1876	40,479,253	43.8	44,099,880	47.7	7,933,974	92,513,107
1877	39,331,621	41.8	49,376,008	52.5	5,418,765	94,126,394
1878	37,252,769	41.2	48,002,875	53.1	5,140,207	90,395,851
1879	30,967,778	39.3	42,170,306	53.6	5,564,435	78,702,519
1880	33,764,439	48.3	28,193,783	40.3	7,942,320	69,900,542
1881	42,885,142	47.4	36,338,701	40.6	11,264,486	90,488,329
1882	50,356,268	45.3	47,052,935	42.3	13,735,981	111,145,184
1883	51,679,762	42.4	55,147,243	45.3	15,034,491	121,861,496
1884	41,925,121	39.6	49,785,888	47.0	14,261,969	105,972,978
1885	40,031,448	40.1	45,576,510	45.7	14,147,817	99,755,775
1886	39,033,006	40.7	42,818,651	44.6	14,140,480	95,992,137
1887	44,741,350	42.6	44,795,908	42.6	15,569,952	105,107,210
1888	39,167,644	38.9	46,440,296	46.1	15,063,688	100,671,628
1889	42,251,189	38.7	50,029,419	45.9	16,817,588	109,098,196
1890	43,277,009	38.8	51,365,661	46.0	17,039,903	111,682,573
1891	42,018,943	37.7	52,033,477	46.7	17,481,534	111,533,954
1892	41,063,711	35.7	51,742,132	44.9	22,354,570	115,160,413
1893	42,529,340	36.9	52,339,796	45.4	20,301,694	115,170,830
1894	37,035,963	34.0	50,746,091	46.5	21,288,857	109,070,911
1895	31,059,332	30.9	50,179,004	49.8	19,437,555	100,675,891
1896	32,824,505	31.2	53,529,390	50.8	19,007,266	105,361,161
1897	29,401,188	27.6	57,023,342	53.5	20,193,297	106,617,827
1898	32,043,461	25.4	74,824,923	59.2	19,438,778	126,307,162
1899	36,966,552	24.7	88,506,881	59.2	23,948,983	149,422,416
1900	44,280,041	25.7	102,224,917	59.2	26,146,718	172,651,676
1901	42,820,334	24.1	107,377,906	60.3	27,732,679	177,930,919
1902	49,022,726	25.0	115,001,533	58.4	32,713,545	196,737,804
1903	58,793,038	26.2	129,071,197	57.3	37,230,574	225,094,809
1904	61,724,893	25.3	143,329,697	58.7	38,854,825	243,909,415
1905	60,342,704	24.0	152,778,576	60.6	38,842,934	251,964,214

Fiscal Year	*Imports from United Kingdom*	*Per cent Imports from U.K. to Total Imports (mdse.)*	*Imports from United States*	*Per cent Imports from U.S. to Total Imports (mdse.)*	*Imports from Other Countries*	*Total Imports for Home Consumption*
1906	$69,183,915	24.4%	$169,256,452	59.6%	$45,299,913	$283,740,280
1907[1]	64,415,756	25.8	149,085,577	59.5	36,724,502	250,225,835
1908	94,417,320	26.8	205,309,803	58.2	52,813,756	352,540,879
1909	70,682,600	24.5	170,432,360	59.0	47,479,236	288,594,196
1910	95,337,058	25.8	218,004,556	58.9	56,976,585	370,318,199
1911	109,934,753	24.3	275,824,265	60.8	66,965,585	452,724,603
1912	116,906,360	22.4	331,384,657	63.4	74,113,658	522,404,675
1913	138,742,464	20.7	436,887,315	65.0	95,577,275	671,207,234
1914	132,070,406	21.4	396,302,138	64.0	90,821,454	619,193,998
1915	90,157,204	19.8	297,142,059	65.2	68,656,645	455,955,908
1919	77,404,361	15.2	370,880,549	73.0	59,916,224	508,201,134
1917	107,096,735	12.7	665,312,759	78.6	74,041,384	846,450,878
1918	81,324,283	8.4	792,894,957	82.3	89,313,338	963,532,578
1919	73,035,118	8.0	750,203,024	81.6	96,473,563	919,711,705
1920	126,362,631	11.9	801,097,318	75.3	137,068,174	1,064,528,123
1921	213,973,562	17.3	856,176,820	69.0	170,008,500	1,240,158,882

[1] Nine months.

APPENDIX B

EXPORTS FROM CANADA TO THE UNITED KINGDOM AND THE UNITED STATES–SELECTED IMPORTANT COMMODITIES, 1887-1920

This table has been compiled for this book from the tables covering a few years each published annually, beginning in 1888, in the Canadian *Statistical Abstract and Record* and its successors the *Statistical Year-Book of Canada* and the Canada Year Book. The year 1887 is included as being the earliest for which figures are available; thereafter the arrangement is by decades. In general, only the largest items have been included. The original tables are not on strictly comparable bases throughout, and it has been necessary to take a few liberties to maintain uniformity and simplicity; but it is believed that these have not involved any serious misrepresentation.

These apparently dull statistics present in microcosm the changing pattern of Canada's external trade, which reflected the development of the national economy. Notable major changes are the enormous growth of the export trade in wheat and wheat flour, mainly to the United Kingdom, and the rise after 1890 of the great pulp and paper industry, finding its market primarily in the United States. One sees the influence of technology and the influence of politics. Britain was a free-trade country, but distance made it difficult to send perishable produce thither. But in the last decade of the nineteenth century the introduction of cold storage and refrigerated steamships produced a dramatic increase in sales of Canadian butter, eggs, and bacon to the United Kingdom at the moment when the Dingley Tariff of 1897 suddenly strangled egg exports to the United States. The manner in which the American tariff excluded much Canadian produce for a great part of the period is evident. On the other hand, the export figures for 1920 reflect the effect of the liberal Underwood

Tariff of 1913, at the moment when it was shortly to be superseded by much higher rates imposed by a Republican Congress. Canadian sales of horses to Britain, normally minimal, suddenly rise strikingly in 1900 as a result of the South African War. The decennial arrangement of the table prevents it from reflecting the great expansion of exports of manufactured goods (chiefly shells) to Britain during the First World War, 1914–18; see the total export figures in Appendix A.

One observes the fundamental fact that in 1920 Canada's external trade is still dominated by a few great staple articles, among which wheat and newsprint paper are prominent. Her exports are in the main natural products or manufactures directly based upon natural products. A parallel table of Canadian imports from Britain and the United States would show a heavy representation of manufactured goods, notably under the general headings "Iron and its Products" and "Fibres, Textiles and Textile Products".

(Table overleaf.)

Values in Canadian Dollars

	1887		1890		1900		1910		1920	
	U.K.	U.S.	U.K.	U.S.	U.K.	U.S.	U.K.	U.S.	U.K.	U.S.
Fish	685,986	2,026,913	2,096,314	2,052,565	3,530,495	3,641,373	5,136,215	4,627,051	9,815,979	17,180,250
Horses	38,230	2,214,338	17,925	1,887,895	517,641	222,626	66,815	453,185	36,045	493,638
Cattle	5,344,375	887,756	6,565,315	104,623	7,579,080	1,401,137	9,979,918	642,674	70,200	42,995,963
Furs, undressed	1,341,561	336,197	1,153,280	396,453	1,438,210	287,400	1,518,092	1,925,444	3,939,539	16,540,822
Cheese	7,065,983	30,667	9,349,731	6,425	19,812,670	4,836	21,481,566	23,995	25,720,370	1,575,264
Butter	757,261	17,207	184,105	5,059	4,947,000	5,044	587,493	199,854	2,323,479	5,712,727
Eggs		1,821,364	820	1,793,104	1,447,030	2,621	9.333	11,551	3,309,364	70,514
Bacon	870,430	17	606,251	81	12,469,209	1,235	6,422,747	7,338	69,293,178*	424,639
Lumber	7,101,121	7,373,103	9,693,830	7,840,971	12,822,910	9,165,131	10,024,960	23,927,619	27,300,284	44,922,022
Timber, square	2,157,988	10,677	4,274,500	4,491	1,969,968	36,412	907,759	21,103	1,472,174	103,795
Wood Pulp					562,178	1,193,753	931,150	4,012,838	5,014,400	31,316,753
Paper							912,474	1,291,880	4,813,577	50,367,339
Leather	388,678	28,636	644,501	8,653	1,406,029	19,636	1,161,999	60,577	9,233,152	4,858,724
Barley	5,827	5,245,968	12,017	4,582,562	810,917	77,754	744,470	66,608	18,138,354	1,153,933
Wheat	4,278,417	265,940	379,893	6,589	11,350,942	58,305	49,267,736	1,883,647	122,108,193	14,000,932
Wheat Flour	1,582,147	17,572	387,309	32,055	1,665,708	12,993	8,872,698	571,938	61,494,045	337,514
Coal	72,245	1,252,867	78,417	2,126,000	64,078	4,026,605	33,842	3,798,623	1,651,188	5,700,441
Silver	8,450	16,487	17,600	184,015	3,496	1,350,557	2,255,790	12,015,356	3,805,195	5,408,520

* Includes hams.

REFERENCES

CHAPTER 1: THE NEW "NATION", 1867

1. Speech of John A. Macdonald, February 6, 1865, *Parliamentary Debates on the Subject of the Confederation of the British North American Provinces* (Quebec, 1865), p. 27.
2. Ibid., p. 44.
3. Sir Robert Herbert, ed., *Speeches on Canadian Affairs by Henry Howard Molyneux, Fourth Earl of Carnarvon* (London, 1902), p. 128.
4. Monck to Carnarvon, September 7, 1866; published in C. P. Stacey, "Lord Monck and the Canadian Nation," *Dalhousie Review*, July 1934.
5. Stanley to Sir Frederick Bruce, March 23, 1867, Derby Papers, transcripts in Public Archives of Canada. See C. P. Stacey, "Britain's Withdrawal from North America, 1864–1871," *Canadian Historical Review*, September 1955.
6. Monck to Buckingham, August 1868, in Stacey, "Lord Monck and the Canadian Nation."
7. *Canada Year Book*, 1907, pp. 2-3, 8; ibid., 1938, p. 138.
8. CYB, 1907, p. 10.
9. Mason Wade, *The French Canadians, 1760–1967*, rev. ed., 2 vols. (Toronto, 1968), 1: 47.
10. Leopold Lamontagne, "Habits gris et chemise rouge," *Canadian Historical Association Report*, 1950.
11. J. B. Brebner, *North Atlantic Triangle: The Interplay of Canada, the United States and Great Britain* (New Haven, 1945).
12. U.S. Bureau of the Census, *Historical Statistics of the United States, Colonial Times to 1957* (Washington, 1960), pp. 7-8. B. R. Mitchell, with Phyllis Deane, *Abstract of British Historical Statistics* (Cambridge, 1962), pp. 6-7.
13. Robin W. Winks, *Canada and the United States: The Civil War Years* (Baltimore, 1960); William D'Arcy, *The Fenian Movement in the United States, 1858–1886* (Washington, 1947); Brian Jenkins, *Fenians and Anglo-American Relations during Reconstruction* (Ithaca, N.Y., 1959); and C. P. Stacey, *Can-*

ada and the British Army, 1846–1871: A Study in the Practice of Responsible Government, rev. ed. (Toronto, 1963).

14. C. P. Stacey, "Fenianism and the Rise of National Feeling in Canada at the time of Confederation," CHR, September 1931.
15. Stacey, *Canada and the British Army*, p. 193.
16. Ibid., chapters 9 and 10. Cf. Stacey, "Britain's Withdrawal from North America."
17. Stacey, *Canada and the British Army*, p. 227.
18. Sessional Papers, Canada, 1872, no. 26, pp. 3-4.
19. Ibid., pp. 94, 112. "Statement of Expenditure for the Militia and Defence of the Dominion of Canada . . . from 1867 to 1890, inclusive," Department of Militia and Defence, December 3, 1890.
20. Stacey, *Canada and the British Army*, p. 255; Sessional Papers, "Statement of Expenditure."
21. *Weekly Globe*, August 26, 1870.
22. C. P. Stacey, "The Myth of the Unguarded Frontier, 1815–1871," *American Historical Review*, October 1950.
23. CYB, 1907, pp. 178-85.
24. Ibid.
25. Ibid., p. 186.
26. *Historical Statistics of the United States*, pp. 550-51; *Statistical Abstract of the United States*, 1969, pp. 814-17.
27. Quoted in *Globe and Mail*, Toronto, September 25.
28. O. D. Skelton, *The Life and Times of Sir Alexander Tilloch Galt* (Toronto, 1920), p. 272.
29. CYB, 1907, pp. 124, 182.

CHAPTER 2: MACDONALD AND THE PURSUIT OF NATIONAL POLICIES, 1867–1896

1. Macdonald to Gen. Sir Hastings Doyle, June 16, 1869, PAC, Macdonald Papers, Private Letter Book No. 12, pp. 890-91.
2. C. P. Stacey, "The Military Aspect of Canada's Winning of the West, 1870–1885," CHR, March 1940; Stacey, *Canada and the British Army*, pp. 230-41. Alvin C. Gluek, Jr., *Minnesota and the Manifest Destiny of the Canadian Northwest: A Study in Canadian-American Relations* (Toronto, 1965).
3. Samuel Flagg Bemis, *A Diplomatic History of the United States*, 5th ed. (New York, 1965), pp. 397-99. See Victor J. Farrar, *The Annexation of Russian America to the United States*, new ed. (New York, 1966).
4. Thomas A. Bailey, "Why the United States Purchased Alaska," *Pacific Historical Review*, III (March 1934).
5. Monck to Macdonald, February 10, 1871, Macdonald Papers, PAC, Vol. 167.
6. Allan Nevins, *Hamilton Fish: The Inner History of the Grant Administration* (New York, 1936), pp. 425-26. This book provides perhaps the best general account of the negotiation.

7. Department of External Affairs, *Treaties and Agreements affecting Canada in Force between His Majesty and the United States of America, 1814–1925* (Ottawa, 1927), pp. 15-17.
8. *Papers relating to the Foreign Relations of the United States transmitted to Congress with the Annual Message of the President, December 5, 1870* (Washington, 1870), pp. 9-13.
9. Notably Goldwin Smith, *The Treaty of Washington* (Ithaca, 1941), and Donald Creighton, *John A. Macdonald, The Old Chieftain* (Toronto, 1955), chapter 3.
10. *Treaties and Agreements affecting Canada*, pp. 37-49.
11. Nevins, *Fish*, p. 477.
12. February 21, 1871; quoted in Smith, *Treaty of Washington*, p. 44.
13. Creighton, *The Old Chieftain*, pp. 84-85.
14. Ibid., p. 100.
15. Smith, *Treaty of Washington*, pp. 87-88.
16. Creighton, *The Old Chieftain*, p. 87.
17. Smith, *Treaty of Washington*, p. 79.
18. James O. McCabe, *The San Juan Water Boundary Question* (Toronto, 1964).
19. Sir Joseph Pope, *Memoirs of the Right Honourable Sir John Alexander Macdonald*, rev. ed. (Toronto, 1930), p. 469. Much of Macdonald's Washington correspondence is printed in this old biography.
20. Gladstone to Granville, October 14, 1870; quoted in Nevins, *Fish*, p. 432.
21. Creighton, *The Old Chieftain*, chapter 4.
22. Pope, *Memoirs*, p. 464.
23. Smith, *Treaty of Washington*, p. 88.
24. Pope, *Memoirs*, p. 465.
25. Ibid., p. 474.
26. Smith, *Treaty of Washington*, p. 121.
27. Clarendon to the Queen, May 1, 1869, G. E. Buckle, ed., *The Letters of Queen Victoria*, Second Series, 2 vols. (London, 1926), 1: 594-95.
28. *Daily Globe*, Toronto, May 4, 1872. At this time there was no official Canadian *Hansard*.
29. *Parliamentary Debates, Dominion of Canada . . . 1872* (Ottawa: Robertson, Roger and Co., (see note 28) 1872), pp. 647-48 (May 16).
30. Nevins, *Fish*, p. 448.
31. Ibid., p. 424.
32. Sumner's memorandum for Fish, January 17, 1871, ibid., pp. 440-41.
33. Ibid., p. 426.
34. G. P. de T. Glazebrook, *A History of Canadian External Relations*, rev. ed., 2 vols. (Toronto, 1966), 1: 120-23. Nevins, *Fish*, Appendix II; J. M. S. Careless, *Brown of the Globe* (Toronto, 1963), 2: 311-22. Various documents in C. W. de Kiewiet and F. H. Underhill, eds., *Dufferin-Carnarvon Correspondence, 1874–1878* (Toronto, 1955). Creighton, *The Old Chieftain*, pp. 184-85.
35. Fish to R. G. Watson, July 18, 1874, *Foreign Relations of the United States, 1874*, pp. 563-64.

36. Fish to Thornton, February 11, 1875, ibid., 1875, p. 653.
37. W. P. M. Kennedy, ed., *Documents of the Canadian Constitution, 1759–1915* (Toronto, 1918), documents CLXXXIII-IV; F. H. Underhill, "Edward Blake and Canadian Liberal Nationalism," in R. Flenley, ed., *Essays in Canadian History Presented to George MacKinnon Wrong* (Toronto, 1939), and "Edward Blake, the Supreme Court Act, and the Appeal to the Privy Council, 1875–6," CHR, September 1938.
38. 42 Vict., Chap. 15, May 15, 1879.
39. *Debates, House of Commons*, March 14, 1879.
40. Creighton, *The Old Chieftain*, pp. 257-58.
41. Ibid., p. 267. On the salt preference, see Orville John McDiarmid, *Commercial Policy in the Canadian Economy* (Cambridge, Mass., 1946), pp. 139, 163.
42. Section 6.
43. Section 12.
44. Glazebrook, *External Relations*, 1: 130-31; Creighton, *The Old Chieftain*, pp. 255-60. Tilley's budget speech, March 14, 1879.
45. Glazebrook, *External Relations* 1: 131-4; Creighton, *The Old Chieftain*, pp. 256, 269-80; Morden H. Long, "Sir John Rose and the Informal Beginnings of the Canadian High Commissionership," CHR, March 1931. There is a careful account of the whole affair in David M. L. Farr, *The Colonial Office and Canada, 1867–1887* (Toronto, 1955), chapter 8. H. Gordon Skilling, *Canadian Representation Abroad: From Agency to Embassy* (Toronto, 1945), chapter 3.
46. Document No. 12 in Department of External Affairs, *Documents on Canadian External Relations*, Vol. I, 1909–1918 (Ottawa, 1967).
47. Ibid.; Glazebrook, *External Relations* 1: 134-35. Creighton, *The Old Chieftain*, p. 291.
48. C. P. Stacey, "The Backbone of Canada," CHA *Report*, 1953.
49. CYB, 1907, p. 348.
50. Sir John Clapham, *An Economic History of Modern Britain: Machines and National Rivalries (1887–1914)* (Cambridge, 1951), p. 5.
51. Glazebrook, *External Relations*, 1: 141.
52. Creighton, *The Old Chieftain*, p. 477.
53. Brown, *Canada's National Policy*, p. 62.
54. Glazebrook, *External Relations* 1: 142.
55. Brown, *Canada's National Policy*, pp. 66-69.
56. Ibid., p. 92.
57. Ibid., pp. 77-81. The treaty is Schedule A to the Canadian assenting statute (51 Vict., Chap. 30, May 4, 1888); the *modus vivendi* is Schedule B.
58. Brown, *Canada's National Policy*, pp. 82-90.
59. *Annual Register*, 1888, pp. 407-08.
60. Brown, *Canada's National Policy*, pp. 46-47.
61. Ibid., pp. 105-14. Cf. Charles C. Tansill, *Canadian-American Relations, 1875–1911* (New Haven, 1943), chapter 11.
62. Tansill, *Canadian-American Relations*, pp. 321-29. Treaty, *Treaties and Agreements affecting Canada*, pp. 85-89.

63. Award, *Treaties and Agreements affecting Canada*, pp. 89-95; Tansill, *Canadian-American Relations*, map opposite page 267.
64. Convention and award, *Treaties and Agreements affecting Canada*, pp. 98-104. Tansill, *Canadian American Relations*, pp. 345-47.
65. Brown, *Canada's National Policy*, chapter 6. Creighton, *The Old Chieftain*, chapter 15. O. D. Skelton, *Life and Letters of Sir Wilfrid Laurier*, 2 vols. (Toronto, 1921), 1: chapter 8.
66. Brown, *Canada's National Policy*, chapter 8. Skelton, *Laurier*, 1: 418-22 and chapter 9.
67. W. F. Monypenny and G. E. Buckle, *The Life of Benjamin Disraeli*, 2 vols. (New York, 1929), 1: 1201 and 2: 210.
68. C. P. Stacey, *The Military Problems of Canada* (Toronto, 1940), pp. 65-66. Papers concerning the defensive measures of 1878, and memorandum by Lt.-Gen. Sir Patrick MacDougall, February 27, 1882, Macdonald Papers, PAC, vol. 100.
69. See Alice R. Stewart, "Sir John A. Macdonald and the Imperial Defence Commission of 1879," CHR, June 1954.
70. C. P. Stacey, "Canada and the Nile Expedition of 1884–85," CHR, December 1952. Stacey, ed., *Records of the Nile Voyageurs, 1884–1885* (Toronto, 1959).
71. Stacey, "Canada and the Nile Expedition."
72. Macdonald to Lord Melgund, February 10, 1885: see C. P. Stacey, "John A. Macdonald on Raising Troops for Imperial Service, 1885," CHR, March 1957.
73. March 12, 1885; see Stacey, "Canada and the Nile Expedition." Published in Sir Joseph Pope, ed., *Correspondence of Sir John Macdonald* (Toronto, n.d.), pp. 337-38.
74. February 20, 1885.
75. The proceedings of the Conference, including the preliminary correspondence, are in the British Parliamentary Papers, 1887, C. 5091. For extended extracts, see Maurice Ollivier, ed., *The Colonial and Imperial Conferences from 1887 to 1937*, 3 vols. (Ottawa, 1954), 1: 3-61. John Edward Kendle, *The Colonial and Imperial Conferences, 1887–1911* (London, 1967), pp. 7-13.
76. Creighton, *The Old Chieftain*, pp. 475-80.
77. For Campbell's statement, see Ollivier, *Conferences 1887–1937*, 1: 38-44. For Sir Henry Holland's circular dispatch on the results of the conference, July 23, 1887, see ibid., 8-13.
78. Ibid., 32-36.
79. The correspondence, and the order-in-council (PC 358, February 7, 1894), are in Governor-General's Numbered File No. 221, PAC, RG 7, G 21.
80. Ripon to Aberdeen, No. 147, June 6, 1944, ibid. Many of the documents relating to the conference are in Sessional Papers, Canada, 1894, No. 5B. Cf. British Parliamentary Papers, 1894, C. 7553, Ollivier, *Conferences, 1887–1937* 1: 65-124. Kendle, *Conferences 1887–1911*, pp. 17-18.
81. Ollivier, *Conferences 1887–1937*, 1: 74-75, 71.
82. Mackenzie Bowell's opening speech to the Conference, SP, 1894, No. 5B, pp. 21-27, misdates the address to the Crown as 1892. The Commons debate on it

was on September 30, 1891. For early correspondence on the treaties, and the British government's rejection of the address, see SP, 1892, Nos. 24 and 24a.

83. R. A. Shields, "Imperial Policy and the Ripon Circular of 1895," CHR, June 1966.
84. Dated June 28, 1895; printed in A. B. Keith, ed., *Selected Speeches and Documents on British Colonial Policy, 1763–1917*, 2 vols. (London, 1918), 2: 156-64. Both the "circular" and the dispatch of the same date concerning the resolutions of the conference are in Foreign Office confidential print No. 6650, Historical Division, Dept. of External Affairs (1–1894–1897/1). Cf. A. B. Keith, *Imperial Unity and the Dominions* (Oxford, 1916), pp. 264-66.
85. Farr, *The Colonial Office*, p. 236.
86. Ibid., p. 230.
87. For text of treaty, see Schedule A to the French Treaty Act, 1894 (57-58 Vict., Chap. 2, July 23, 1894).
88. 58-59 Vict., Chap. 3, July 23, 1895. See R. A. Shields, "Sir Charles Tupper and the Franco-Canadian Treaty of 1895: A Study of Imperial Relations," CHR March 1968. The correspondence with the Colonial Office is in Foreign Office confidential print No. 6650. See particularly Ripon to Aberdeen, June 1, 1895, p. 83.
89. *Papers relating to the Foreign Relations of the United States . . . transmitted to Congress December 2, 1895* (Washington, 1896), pp. 545-62. See also *The Times*, London, December 18, 1895.
90. James D. Richardson, A *Compilation of the Messages and Papers of the Presidents* (Washington, 1898), 9: 655-58. On the whole incident, see Thomas A. Bailey, A *Diplomatic History of the American People* (New York, 1940), Chapter 29.
91. *Times*, London, December 20, 1895.
92. Ibid., December 21 and 24, 1895. W. A. Swanberg, *Pulitzer* (New York, 1967), pp. 197-200.
93. *Globe*, Toronto, December 25, 1895.
94. Edward P. Crapol, *America for Americans: Economic Nationalism and Anglophobia in the Late Nineteenth Century* (Westport, Conn., 1973), p. 211. The source is a memorandum of a cabinet meeting of January 11, 1896.
95. A. R. Dickey, *Debates, House of Commons*, April 21, 1896.
96. Aberdeen to Chamberlain, January 3, 1896, PAC, G Series.
97. Statements of George E. Foster and A. R. Dickey, *Debates, House of Commons*, April 21, 1896.

CHAPTER 3: LAURIER, NATIONALISM, AND IMPERIALISM

1. Carl Berger, *The Sense of Power: Studies in the Ideas of Canadian Imperialism, 1867–1914* (Toronto, 1970), p. 259.
2. Ibid., p. 260.
3. Ibid., p. 5.
4. D. Owen Carrigan, comp., *Canadian Party Platforms, 1867–1968* (Toronto, 1968), pp. 34-36.

5. 60–61 Vict., Chap. 16, June 29, 1897.
6. Foreign Office confidential print No. 7020, May 1898, "Correspondence respecting the Canadian Preferential Tariff. 1897" (Historical Division, Department of External Affairs, 1—1894–1897/1). Confidential *Report* of the Colonial Conference of 1897, Colonial Office confidential print Miscellaneous No. 111, September 1897, RG 7, G 21, Vol. 80, PAC.
7. The published *Proceedings* of the Conference as presented to the British Parliament are C. 8596, 1897. For the complete record, see confidential print Miscellaneous No. 111, September 1897. On Chamberlain as Colonial Secretary, see J. L. Garvin, *The Life of Joseph Chamberlain*, 3 (London, 1934).
8. Lucien Pacaud, ed., *Sir Wilfrid Laurier: Lettres à mon père et à ma mère, 1867–1919* (Arthabaska, P.Q., 1935), pp. 272-74 (April 12, 1900).
9. Confidential print Miscellaneous No. 111, pp. 10 *ff*.
10. Ibid., p. 110.
11. Ibid., p. 107.
12. Ibid., pp. 61-62.
13. Norman Penlington, *Canada and Imperialism, 1896–1899* (Toronto, 1965), pp. 220-24.
14. Ibid., pp. 226-33. *Correspondence relating to the Despatch of Colonial Military Contingents to South Africa, printed by order of Parliament* (Ottawa, 1900), p. 1 *ff*.
15. Public Record Office, London, C.O. 42/869 (microfilm, PAC). Cf. Minto to Chamberlain, October 20, 1899, ibid.
16. Minto to Chamberlain, October 20, 1899.
17. *Correspondence relating to the Despatch of Colonial Military Contingents*, pp. 5-7. Curiously enough, I have failed to find this famous dispatch in the Colonial Office records. Version as received, RG 7, G 21, file 233 (3).
18. Penlington, *Canada and Imperialism*, p. 236.
19. Ibid., Appendix F and pp. 241-51.
20. Sir John Willison, *Reminiscences Political and Personal* (Toronto, 1919), pp. 304-05.
21. *Globe* (Toronto), October 12, 1899.
22. Laurier Papers, vol. 127.
23. Ibid.
24. *Globe*, October 13 and 14, 1899.
25. Penlington, *Canada and Imperialism*, p. 257.
26. Minto to Chamberlain, October 20, 1899.
27. Tarte to J. Castell Hopkins, November 1, 1899; *Globe*, November 8, 1899.
28. Memorandum by Minto, November 16, 1899, Minto Papers, vol. 1 PAC, MG, 27, II, B 1, vol. 1.
29. Penlington, *Canada and Imperialism*, p. 257.
30. Laurier to John Cameron, *London Advertiser*, October 14, 1899, Laurier Papers, vol. 127.
31. Penlington, *Canada and Imperialism*, p. 258.
32. CO 42/869.
33. Ibid.

34. Ibid.
35. Ibid.
36. Ibid. Quoted in *Correspondence relating to the Despatch of Colonial Military Contingents*, p. 29.
37. House of Commons, March 13, 1900, quoting a letter to Laurier.
38. CO 42/869.
39. Ibid.
40. L[ansdowne] to Chamberlain, October 15 [1899], ibid.
41. Knox (War Office) to Under Secretary of State, Colonial Office, October 17, 1899, CO 42/873.
42. Minto to Laurier, October 16, 1899, Laurier Papers, vol. 127.
43. Scott to Laurier, October 16, 1899, ibid.
44. October 16, 1899.
45. Laurier to Scott, October 15, 1899 (clearly an error for October 17), Laurier Papers, vol. 127.
46. Scott to Laurier, October 18, 1899, ibid.
47. Minto to Chamberlain, received October 18, 1899, CO 42/869.
48. Ibid.
49. Department of Militia and Defence, *Supplementary Report: Organization, Equipment, Despatch and Service of the Canadian Contingents during the War in South Africa* (Sessional Paper No. 35a, 1901), Report of the Major General, pp. 3-4.
50. "Canada's Aid to the Empire," pp. 94-95, Sessional Paper No. 35a, 1903.
51. Penlington, *Canada and Imperialism*, p. 230.
52. Sessional Paper No. 35a, 1901, p. 12.
53. *The Great Boer War* (ed. Toronto, 1901), p. 284. On the First Contingent generally, see Desmond Morton's excellent *The Canadian General: Sir William Otter* (Toronto, 1974), pp. 160-236.
54. Minto to Chamberlain, November 21, 1899, CO 42/869.
55. War Office to Colonial Office, December 23, 1899, CO 323/447.
56. Sessional Paper No. 35a, 1901.
57. Sessional Paper No. 35a, 1903, p. 10.
58. "Canada's Aid to the Empire."
59. John Buchan's not very satisfactory *Lord Minto, A Memoir* (London, 1924) gives Minto the credit for the Canadian contingents not being "split up among British regiments," and on this point it appears to be right.
60. Penlington, *Canada and Imperialism*, pp. 241, 257, 233.
61. Ibid., p.260.
62. Carman Miller, "English-Canadian Opposition to the South African War as seen through the Press," CHR, December 1974.
63. Debates, House of Commons, March 13, 1900, pp. 1794-1847. For Bourassa's letter to Laurier, October 29, 1899, see Robert Craig Brown and Ramsay Cook, *Canada 1896–1921; A Nation Transformed* (Toronto, 1974); O. D. Skelton, *Life and Letters of Sir Wilfrid Laurier*, 2 vols. (Toronto, 1921), 2: 97-109; Joseph Schull, *Laurier, The First Canadian* (Toronto, 1966), pp. 380-91. Robert

Rumilly, *Henri Bourassa: La vie publique d'un grand canadien* (Montreal, n.d.), chapter 5.

64. Minto to Chamberlain, April 14, 1900; Paul Stevens, "Wilfrid Laurier: Politician," M. Hamelin, ed., *The Political Ideas of the Prime Ministers of Canada* (Ottawa, 1969), p. 73.
65. Memorandum by Laurier for the Governor General, April 9, 1900, Minto Papers, Vol. 1.
66. O. D. Skelton, *The Day of Sir Wilfrid Laurier*, "Chronicles of Canada" (Toronto, 1916), pp. 187-88.
67. Minutes of Proceedings and Papers Laid Before the Conference, Colonial Office confidential print Miscellaneous No. 144, October 1902 (Historical Division, Department of External Affairs, 1–1902/1). Ollivier, *Colonial and Imperial Conferences*,, *1887–1937*, I, pp. 149-209, contains Chamberlain's opening address and most of the items of Canadian interest. Julian Amery, *The Life of Joseph Chamberlain*, 4 (London, 1951), chapters 93-94, deals with the conference, including Laurier's dealings with Chamberlain on imperial preference.
68. Amery, *Chamberlain*, 4: 416-17.
69. Ibid., pp. 523, 520-21.
70. Ibid., 5 (London, 1969), chapters 98-99.
71. Ibid., chapter 107.
72. R. C. K. Ensor, *England, 1870–1914* (Oxford, 1936), pp. 386-89.
73. 6-7 Edward VII, Chap. 11, April 12, 1907. See Orville John McDiarmid, *Commercial Policy in the Canadian Economy* (Cambridge, Mass., 1946), p. 221.
74. The Minutes of Proceedings of the 1907 Conference are in British Parliamentary Papers, Cd. 3523 (May 1907). A confidential version of the proceedings of the 13th, 14th, and 15th days, containing passages which the conference decided should not be published, was printed separately. For long extracts, see Maurice Ollivier, ed., *The Colonial and Imperial Conferences from 1887 to 1937*, 3 vols. (Ottawa, 1954), 1:213-324.
75. For a defence of Elgin and his partnership with Churchill, see Ronald Hyam, *Elgin and Churchill at the Colonial Office, 1905–1908* (London, 1968).
76. Reproduced in Skelton, *Laurier*, 2, opposite p. 64. Also in the present book.
77. Cd. 3523, p. 7.
78. See John Edward Kendle, *The Colonial and Imperial Conferences, 1887–1911* (London, 1967), chapter 5.
79. Richard A. Preston, *Canada and "Imperial Defense"* (Durham, N.C., 1967), pp. 317-20.
80. The Japanese Treaty Act, 1906, 6-7 Edward VII, Chap. 50, January 30, 1907. The convention of 1906 and the treaty and convention of 1894–95 form a schedule to the act.
81. July 4, 1907: see A. B. Keith, ed., *Selected Speeches and Documents on British Colonial Policy, 1763–1917*, 2 vols. (London, 1918), 2: 165-66.
82. The convention is a schedule to the French Convention Act, 1908, 7-8 Edward VII, Chap. 28, April 3, 1908.

CHAPTER 4: LAURIER AND THE AMERICANS, 1896–1909

1. F. W. Taussig, *The Tariff History of the United States*, 8th revised ed. (New York, 1964), p. 358.
2. See R. C. Brown, *Canada's National Policy*, chapter 9.
3. Ibid., chapter 10; C. S. Campbell, *Anglo-American Understanding, 1898–1903* (Baltimore, Md., 1957), chapter 3. This is an excellent book.
4. Brown, *Canada's National Policy*, p. 341. Villiers (FO) to Colonial Office, December 10, 1897, and Chamberlain to Gov. Gen., December 17, 1897, PRO, CO 42/854 (PAC, microfilm reel B-773).
5. See the summary in Fairbanks to Laurier, July 18, 1901, O. D. Skelton, *Life and Letters of Sir Wilfrid Laurier*, 2 vols. (Toronto, 1921), 2: 133-34.
6. Brown, *Canada's National Policy*, pp. 381-85; Campbell, *Anglo-American Understanding*, pp. 107-12.
7. Ibid., pp. 112-19; Brown, *Canada's National Policy*, pp. 385-91. Skelton, *Laurier*, 2: 130.
8. Brown, *Canada's National Policy*, 392-96. The *modus vivendi* is No. 19 in the British Treaty Series, 1899 (copies in RG 7, G 21, Vol. 84, No. 173, Vol. 6 (b), PAC). On the garrison at Pyramid Harbor, see Chamberlain to Minto, June 20, 1899, and enclosures, RG 7, G 21, Vol. 83, No. 173, vol. 5 (b), PAC.
9. Norman Penlington, *Canada and Imperialism, 1896–1899* (Toronto, 1965), p. 130.
10. Brown, *Canada's National Policy*, pp. 396-401.
11. See, e.g., the debate in the House of Commons on March 21, 1899.
12. Campbell, *Anglo-American Understanding*, pp. 120-33. On the Hay-Pauncefote treaties generally, see Thomas A. Bailey, A *Diplomatic History of the American People* (New York, 1940), pp. 533-35.
13. Campbell, *Anglo-American Understanding*, p. 190.
14. Chamberlain to Minto, January 30, 1900, ibid., pp. 191-92.
15. Ibid., chapter 11. These matters are briefly and rather unsatisfactorily treated in Skelton, *Laurier*, 2: 139-41. The two draft treaties are in RG 7, G 21, Vol. 84, No. 173, Vol. 6 (c).
16. Campbell, *Anglo-American Understanding*, p. 253.
17. Ibid., pp. 256-58. Allan Nevins, *Henry White: Thirty Years of American Diplomacy* (New York, 1930), pp. 192-93. Lansdowne to Raikes (British chargé d'affaires, Washington), July 16, 1902, is in John A. Munro, ed., *The Alaska Boundary Dispute* (Toronto, 1970), p. 38. This is a collection of documents covering the final stage of the question.
18. John W. Dafoe, *Clifford Sifton in Relation to His Times* (Toronto, 1931), p. 217.
19. Campbell, *Anglo-American Understanding*, pp. 259-68.
20. Skelton, *Laurier*, 2: 142.
21. Hay to White, September 20, 1903, Campbell, *Anglo-American Understanding*, p. 333. Also in A. E. Campbell, *Great Britain and the United States, 1895-1903* (London, 1960), p. 111.

22. Text of treaty, which was virtually unaltered from the draft, *Treaties and Agreements affecting Canada in Force between His Majesty and the United States of America*, pp. 149-52. For Roosevelt's remarks concerning the preamble, see Roosevelt to G. F. W. Holls, February 3, 1903, Elting E. Morison, ed., *The Letters of Theodore Roosevelt*, 3 vols. (Cambridge, Mass., 1951), 3: 418.
23. Campbell, *Anglo-American Understanding*, pp. 307-13. Minto's memorandum, January 19, 1903, of conversation with Laurier same date, Minto Papers, Vol. 2.
24. Laurier's letter to Herbert, February 20, 1903, is in Laurier Papers, PAC, 70454-5. His letter to Hay is quoted in Howard K. Beale, *Theodore Roosevelt and the Rise of America to World Power* (Baltimore, 1956), p. 119; the reply is in Laurier Papers, 71513-16.
25. Laurier Papers, 70446-53.
26. Campbell, *Anglo-American Understanding*, pp. 315-17. Balfour to the King, February 24, 1903, PRO, CAB 41, Vol. 28 (PAC, film B-3830).
27. Campbell, *Anglo-American Understanding*, p. 304. Balfour to the King, n.d. [March 1903] and March 10, 1903, CAB 41, Vol. 28.
28. Campbell, *Anglo-American Understanding*, pp. 326-29; Beale, *Roosevelt*, pp. 126-29. Roosevelt's letter of instruction, March 17, 1903, is in Morison, *Letters*, 3: 448-49.
29. White to Hay, October 20, 1903, Nevins, *Henry White*, pp. 200-201. On errors in this letter as published by Nevins, see Campbell, p. 335 *n*. For Roosevelt's own view of the reasons for the result, see his letter to his son Theodore, October 20, 1903, Morison, *Letters*, 3: 634-35.
30. On the episode at large, see Norman Penlington, *The Alaska Boundary Dispute: A Critical Reappraisal* (Toronto, 1972), and F. W. Gibson, "The Alaskan Boundary Dispute," CHA *Report*, 1945. The award (October 20, 1903) is printed in *Treaties and Agreements affecting Canada in Force between His Majesty and the United States of America*, pp. 153-54.
31. Minto to Lyttelton, November 19, 1903, Munro, *Alaska Boundary Dispute*, pp. 98-99.
32. Ibid., pp. 62-64.
33. October 21, 1903, ibid., p. 91. Other newspaper comments, ibid.
34. Minto to Lyttelton, October 25, 1903, ibid., pp. 190-01.
35. Kenneth Bourne, *Britain and the Balance of Power in North America, 1815-1908* (Berkeley and Los Angeles, 1967), p. 350.
36. George Monger, *The End of Isolation: British Foreign Policy, 1900-1907* (London, 1963), pp. 11, 72 *n*.
37. Bourne, *Britain and the Balance of Power*, p. 342.
38. Dafoe, *Sifton*, pp. 221-22.
39. Minto's record of conversation with Sifton, November 11, 1903; Minto to Lyttelton, November 19, 1903, Munro, pp. 79-83, 98-99.
40. Dafoe, *Sifton*, p. 212.
41. Statement in House of Commons, March 14, 1904. See Alvin C. Gluek, Jr.,

"Pilgrimages to Ottawa: Canadian-American Diplomacy, 1903–13," CHA *Historical Papers*, 1968.

42. Lord Grey to Sir Edward Grey, Vol. 7, December 7, 1906, Grey Papers, PAC (MG 27, II, B 2), folios 001856-80.
43. Paging as in the Governor General's copy, PAC, RG 7, G 21, Vol. 93, file 192A. Grey to Laurier, April 3 and 4, 1906, are in Grey Papers, Vol. 1, folios 000261-4.
44. Gluek, "Pilgrimages." See also Peter Neary, "Grey, Bryce, and the Settlement of Canadian-American Differences, 1905–1911," CHR, December 1968.
45. Gluek, "Pilgrimages." James Morton Callahan, *American Foreign Policy in Canadian Relations* (New York, 1937), chapter 20, cannot be said to be a very satisfactory account, but it contains a good deal of detail on various aspects. Skelton, *Laurier*, 2: 359-64, is very general. See also Jessup, *Root*, 2: chapter 30. On Laurier's views, R. MacG. Dawson, *William Lyon Mackenzie King*, I, *1874–1923* (Toronto, 1958), 154; and Grey to Bryce, December 26, 1907, Grey Papers, Vol. 8. Cf. King Diary, 1912, "Talk with Sir Wilfrid in car, Sept. 16th 12." Paper in response to Root's: covering letter, Laurier to Grey, September 29, 1906, Grey Papers, Vol 2; and text (September 25, 1906), Pope Papers, PAC (MG 30, E.1, Vol. 120, file 38, v. 4).
46. Document No. 575, *Documents on Canadian External Relations* (DCER), 1.
47. Ibid., Documents 569-75. Special Agreement and Award, *Treaties and Agreements*, pp. 319-48.
48. Skelton, 2: 363. Tansill, *Canadian-American Relations*, pp. 118-20.
49. Ibid., pp. 364-71. DCER, 1: Documents 631-65. Treaty, *Treaties and Agreements*, pp. 374-76.
50. Instructions, Laurier to Pope, May 8, 1911, DCER, 1: Document 671.
51. Ibid., Document 679 (May 25, 1911).
52. Treaty, *Treaties and Agreements*, pp. 391-96. Pope to Laurier, July 17, 1911, DCER, 1: Document 703.
53. *Treaties and Agreements*, pp. 299-310.
54. Ibid., pp. 352-54. Correspondence, DCER, 1: 385-418. Alvin C. Gluek, Jr., "The Passamaquoddy Bay Treaty, 1910: A Diplomatic Sideshow in Canadian-American Relations," CHR, March 1966. This article also discusses the Root-Bryce Canadian negotiations generally.
55. Documents on PAC, RG 15, H 1., Vol. 70, file 246 (Dept. of the Interior). Orders-in-Council of January 8, 1896 and October 27, 1902, both in ibid., Vol. 261, file 3970.
56. Orders-in-council and dispatches, PAC, RG 7, G 21, Vols. 143-44, files 268 (2) and (3). PC 2106, November 21, 1905.
57. Root to Durand, May 3, 1906, as per note 43 above.
58. Alan O. Gibbons, "Sir George Gibbons and the Boundary Waters Treaty of 1909," CHR, June 1953: Gibbons to George Clinton, April 6, 1906, and to Laurier, February 15, 1907.
59. Enclosure to Esmé Howard to Lord Grey, June 20, 1907, PAC, RG 7, G 21, Vol. 144, file 268 (3).
60. Bryce to Sir E. Grey, with enclosures, December 13, 1907, ibid.

61. Bryce to Sir E. Grey, January 4, 1908, ibid., file 268 (4).
62. Howard to Sir E. Grey, July 15, 1908, ibid.
63. Gibbons to Laurier, July 6, 1908, Gibbons, "Sir George Gibbons and the Boundary Waters Treaty of 1909."
64. Laurier to Gibbons, July 8, 1908, ibid.
65. *Report of the International Waterways Commission . . . Buffalo, N.Y., November 15, 1906*, PAC, RG 7, G 21, Vol. 144, file 268 (3).
66. Gibbons to Laurier, August 25, 1908, ibid., file 268(4).
67. *Treaties and Agreements*, pp. 312-19.
68. Laurier to Gibbons, April 20, 1909, Gibbons, "Sir George Gibbons and the Boundary Waters Treaty." Aylesworth memorandum, May 27, 1909, DCER, 1: 388-95.
69. DCER, 1: 414. On the episode generally, and Anderson's role particularly, see N. A. F. Dreisziger, "The International Joint Commission . . . 1895–1920" (Ph.D. thesis, University of Toronto, 1974).
70. G. V. LaForest, *Disallowance and Reservation of Provincial Legislation* [Ottawa], (1955), appendices.
71. Robert Craig Brown and Ramsay Cook, *Canada 1896–1921: A Nation Transformed* (Toronto, 1974), pp. 68-70. Dawson, 1: 146-47. DCER, 1: 593. Maurice Pope, ed., *Public Servant: The Memoirs of Sir Joseph Pope* (Toronto, 1960), pp. 191-203.
72. Laurier Papers, PAC, Vol. 755, folios 215975-82. Cf. Dawson, *King*, 1: 151-66, which quotes King's diary on the affair.
73. Dawson, *King*, 1: 155-66. G. M. Trevelyan, *Grey of Fallodon* (London, 1937), p. 230.
74. Laurier Papers, PAC, Vol. 755, folios 215975-82.
75. Grey to Laurier, February 5, 1908, Grey Papers, Vol. 3, folios 000703-4.
76. Dawson, *King*, 1: 192-97. DCER, 1: 591-607. Brown and Cook, *Canada 1896–1921*, p. 70.
77. Ibid., p. 68.
78. DCER, 1: Document 1. Also published in *External Affairs*, March 1966.
79. See F. A. Coghlan, "James Bryce and the Establishment of the Department of External Affairs," CHA *Historical Papers*, 1968.
80. Bryce to Grey, December 14, 1907 (copy), Grey Papers (PAC, MG 27, II, B 2, vol. 8).
81. Coghlan, "James Bryce," n. 126.
82. August 10, 1908, Grey Papers, vol. 8.
83. August 22, 1908, ibid.
84. Draft covered by Pope to "Hanby" (Hanbury-Williams?), February 6, 1909, file 1840-C.1, office of the Secretary to the Governor General. I am indebted to Mr. Esmond Butler, Secretary to His Excellency, for permission to see and use this file.
85. 8-9 Edward VII, Chap. 13, May 19, 1909 (it is Document 2 in DCER, 1).
86. The most important parliamentary discussion was in the Commons on March 4, 1909. Grey to Laurier, May 6, 1909 (copy), and Laurier to Grey, same date, both in Grey Papers, vol. 4.

87. Grey to Laurier, May 7, 1909, file 1840-C.1.
88. Crewe to Grey, Confidential, June 5, 1909, ibid.
89. Harcourt to Connaught, March 9, 1912; Borden to Connaught, March 14, 1912; Connaught to Harcourt, Secret, March [*sic*] 1912, all in ibid.
90. F. H. Soward, *The Department of External Affairs and Canadian Autonomy, 1899–1939* (Canadian Historical Association Booklets, No. 7, Ottawa, 1956). Various passages in James Eayrs, *The Art of the Possible: Government and Foreign Policy in Canada* (Toronto, 1961).

CHAPTER 5: EXTERNAL RELATIONS AND THE FALL OF LAURIER

1. *Canadian Annual Review*, 1907, p. 398.
2. *Canada Year Book*, 1925, pp. xxvi-vii, 314, 411. *Statistical Year Book of Canada*, 1904, 332, 337. CYB, 1906, 186, 197. W. T. Easterbrook and Hugh G. J. Aitken, *Canadian Economic History* (Toronto, 1958), pp. 482-86, 538-46. V. W. Bladen, *An Introduction to Political Economy*, revised ed. (Toronto, 1956), chapters 6-7. John A. Guthrie, *The Newsprint Paper Industry, An Economic Analysis* (Cambridge, Mass., 1941).
3. CYB, 1938, pp. xxxviii-ix.
4. Ian H. Nish, *The Anglo-Japanese Alliance: The Diplomacy of Two Island Empires, 1894–1907* (London, 1955), p. 353.
5. Annual Reports, Department of Militia and Defence, year ended June 30, 1893, p. 43, and year ended June 30, 1894, Financial Statement and p. iv.
6. Arthur J. Marder, *The Anatomy of British Sea Power: A History of British Naval Policy in the Pre-Dreadnought Era, 1880–1905* (New York, 1940), chapter 26. Summary of the new program, *Annual Register*, 1904, pp. 227-28. C. S. Mackinnon, "The Imperial Fortresses in Canada: Halifax and Esquimalt, 1871–1906" (Ph.D. thesis, University of Toronto, 1965), pp. 550-51.
7. Mackinnon, "Imperial Fortresses," chapter 8. Kenneth Bourne, *Britain and the Balance of Power in North America 1815–1908* (Berkeley and Los Angeles, 1967), chapter 10. Richard A. Preston, *Canada and "Imperial Defense"* (Durham, N.C., 1967), pp. 336-43. G. N. Tucker, *The Naval Service of Canada: Its Official History*, 2 vols. (Ottawa, 1952), 1: 104-05, 160-61. C. P. Stacey, *The Military Problems of Canada* (Toronto, 1940), pp. 69-70.
8. Arthur J. Marder, *From the Dreadnought to Scapa Flow: The Royal Navy in the Fisher Era, 1904–1919*, Vol. I, *The Road to War, 1904–1914* (London, 1961), chapter 7. Sir Charles Lucas, ed., *The Empire at War* (London, 1921), 1: 191-94. Donald C. Gordon, *The Dominion Partnership in Imperial Defense, 1870–1914* (Baltimore, 1965), chapters 9-10.
9. Borden to L. J. Maxse, editor of the *National Review*, May 10, 1909, Borden Papers, vol. 406. I owe this reference to Mr. G. N. Hillmer.
10. *House of Commons Debates*, March 29, 1909, col. 3511.
11. CAR, 1909, pp. 92-93, 102. Tucker, *Naval Service*, 1: 131.
12. *Imperial Conference. Conference with Representatives of the Self-Governing*

Dominions on the Naval and Military Defence of the Empire, 1909 (Canadian reprint, Sessional Paper No. 29a, 1910). See also the secret *Minutes of Proceedings* (Dominions No. 15, Imperial Conference Secretariat, October 1909).

13. See DCER, 1: 231.
14. Canada Sessional Paper 29a, 1910, p. 21.
15. Ibid., pp. 23-25.
16. DCER, 1: 243.
17. Ibid., 242-45. Cf. Sessional Paper No. 29a, 1910, pp. 26-28.
18. Tucker, *Naval Service*, 1: 131.
19. *Le Devoir*, January 17, 1910, quoted in Mason Wade, *The French Canadians, 1760–1967* (Toronto, 1968), 1: 568.
20. 9-10 Edward VII, Chap. 43, May 4, 1910.
21. O. D. Skelton, *The Life and Letters of Sir Wilfrid Laurier* (Toronto, 1921), 2: 337-40.
22. *Minutes of Proceedings of the Imperial Conference, 1911*, British Parliamentary Papers, Cd. 5745. A large part of the discussion of Ward's motion is reprinted in A. B. Keith, *Selected Speeches and Documents on British Colonial Policy, 1763–1917*, 2 vols. (London, 1918), 2: 247-303.
23. John Edward Kendle, *The Colonial and Imperial Conferences, 1887–1911* (London, 1967), chapter 10. Cf. Lord Hankey, *The Supreme Command, 1914–1918*, 2 vols. (London, 1961), 1: 125-32.
24. Public Record Office, London, CAB 2/2: Committee of Imperial Defence, minutes of 111th meeting, May 26, 1911, 112th meeting, May 29, 1911, and 113th meeting, May 30, 1911. Kendle, *Colonial and Imperial Conferences*, pp. 194-98. Roskill, *Hankey, Man of Secrets*, 1: 106-07.
25. *Report of a Committee of the Imperial Conference convened to discuss Defence (Military) at the War Office. June 14 and June 17, 1911.* Covered by Harcourt to Lord Grey, July 14, 1911, PAC, RG 7, G 21, file no. 311, vol. 3(a).
26. June 1911: Canada Sessional Paper No. 40d, 1912. In Keith, *Selected Speeches and Documents*, 2: 304-07.
27. C. P. Stacey, *Arms, Men and Governments: The War Policies of Canada, 1939–1945* (Ottawa, 1970), p. 309.
28. F. W. Taussig, *The Tariff History of the United States*, 8th ed. (New York, 1964), p. 407.
29. L. Ethan Ellis, *Reciprocity, 1911: A Study in Canadian-American Relations* (New Haven, 1939), chapter 3.
30. Ibid., pp. 20-27. Cf. John A. Dafoe, *Clifford Sifton in Relation to His Times* (Toronto, 1931), pp. 359-61. CAR, 1910, pp. 263-83.
31. Skelton, *Laurier*, 2: 364-66. Taussig, *Tariff History*, pp. 404-05. Ellis, *Reciprocity 1911*, pp. 35-43. The changes in the Canadian tariff were effected by 9-10 Edward VII, Chap. 16, May 4, 1910.
32. Background of the meeting, *Globe*, Toronto, March 19, 1910. Speeches of Grey and Taft, account of the conference, and Taft's message, ibid., March 21, 1910. For Macdonald's role, see statement of Fielding in House of Commons, April 6, 1910. Documents including exchange of telegrams between

Taft and Fielding, March 18, 1910, DCER, 1: 771-72. Henry F. Pringle, *The Life and Times of William Howard Taft*, 2 vols. (New York, 1939), 2: 586.

33. Ellis, *Reciprocity, 1911*, pp. 53-71. For details of the agreement, see the U.S. statute enacting it, Sixty-Second Congress, Sess. 1, Chap. 3, July 26, 1911. The Canadian tariff of 1907 is in 6-7 Edward VII, Chap. 11.
34. Ellis, *Reciprocity, 1911*, chapters 8-9. Pringle, *Taft*, 2: chapter 31.
35. Dafoe, *Sifton*, pp. 362-63. Skelton, *Laurier*, 2: 369-70.
36. The reciprocity battle is described in much detail in CAR, *1911*, pp. 1-270. See also Robert Craig Brown, *Robert Laird Borden, A Biography* (Toronto, 1975), chapter 9.
37. Ellis, *Reciprocity, 1911*, pp. 96, 114, chapters 10-11. Pringle, *Taft*, 2: 589-92. CAR, *1911*, pp. 62 ff. Dafoe, *Sifton*, chapter 13.
38. *Gazette* (Montreal), June 4, 1945. D. Owen Carrigan, comp., *Canadian Party Platforms, 1867–1968* (Toronto, 1968), pp. 63-67.
39. Cahan to Grattan O'Leary, November 25, 1930, Cahan Papers, vol. 1, PAC. I owe this reference to Mr. Hillmer.
40. J. Murray Beck, *Pendulum of Power: Canada's Federal Elections* (Scarborough, Ont., 1968), pp. 120-35.

CHAPTER 6: THE FIRST YEARS OF BORDEN, 1911–1914: A NEW DIRECTION

1. Sir John Willison, *Reminiscences Political and Personal* (Toronto, 1919), p. 307; cf. J. Murray Beck, *Pendulum of Power* (Scarborough, Ont., 1968), p. 94.
2. M. C. Urquhart and K. A. H. Buckley, *Historical Statistics of Canada* (Toronto, 1965), p. 27.
3. *Canadian Annual Review, 1911*, p. 295. I had the advantage of reading in advance of publication Professor Brown's chapter 10 of Robert Craig Brown and Ramsay Cook, *Canada 1896–1921: A Nation Transformed* (Toronto, 1974). On Borden, Robert Craig Brown, *Robert Laird Borden, A Biography*, 1 (Toronto, 1975).
4. *Annual Register, 1913*, p. 476.
5. Laurier to Gibbons, November 30, 1911, Sir G. C. Gibbons Correspondence, Vol. 3 (PAC, MG 30, B 3). Cf. C. J. Chacko, *The International Joint Commission between the United States of America and the Dominion of Canada* (New York, 1932), pp. 81-84.
6. Grey to Laurier, January 4, 1908 [1909], Laurier Papers, Vol. 734. DCER, I, Documents 516 and 556-59. List of "dockets" (topics referred to the commission), L. M. Bloomfield and Gerald F. Fitzgerald, *Boundary Waters Problems of Canada and the United States* (Toronto, 1958), pp. 65-205.
7. Charles A. Beard and Mary R. Beard, *The Rise of American Civilization* (New York, 1930), 2: 607. Cf. F. W. Taussig, *The Tariff History of the United States*, 8th revised ed. (New York, 1964), chapter 9. Orville John McDiarmid, *Commercial Policy in the Canadian Economy* (Cambridge, Mass., 1946), p. 237.

8. Sixty-Third Congress, Sess. I, Chap. 16, "An Act to reduce tariff duties and to provide revenue for the Government, and for other purposes," October 3, 1913; Free List. John A. Guthrie, *The Newsprint Paper Industry, An Economic Analysis* (Cambridge, Mass., 1941), pp. 46, 57, 222. H. V. Nelles, *The Politics of Development: Forests, Mines & Hydro-Electric Power in Ontario, 1849–1941* (Toronto, 1974), p. 346.
9. Donald M. Page, "Canadians and the League of Nations before the Manchurian Crisis" (Ph.D. thesis, University of Toronto, 1972), pp. 46-54. James A. Macdonald, *The North American Idea* (The Cole Lectures for 1917 delivered before Vanderbilt University, New York, 1917). King Diary, February 11, 1913. Personal recollection.
10. Gilbert Norman Tucker, *The Naval Service of Canada: Its Official History*, 2 vols. (Ottawa, 1952), 1: 170-78.
11. Minutes, 113th meeting CID, p. 20.
12. Minutes, 119th meeting CID, August 1, 1912; extract in DCER, 1: 267-70.
13. *Minutes of Proceedings*, p. 24 (May 23, 1911).
14. Harcourt to Sir H. Just, August 26, 1912, CO 537/576, microfilm in PAC.
15. Tucker, *Naval Service*, 1: 178-87. Borden Diary, July-August 1912. (I owe access to this diary to the kindness of Mr. Henry Borden and the good offices of Mr. Robert Craig Brown.) Arthur J. Marder, *From the Dreadnought to Scapa Flow* (London, 1961), 1: 295-98.
16. Tucker, *Naval Service*, 1: 181. On visit to CID, Borden to Seely, August 29, 1912, Borden Papers, folio 8072.
17. Text of bill, Tucker, *Naval Service* 1: Appendix IX. Ibid., pp. 186-88.
18. The secret memorandum is in ibid., Appendix VIII.
19. On Naval Service Act, *Debates*, House of Commons, March 4, 1912. For Borden's ideas on approach to permanent naval policy, his memorandum for the Governor General, March 24, 1913, DCER, 1: Document 404. On shipbuilding, Borden to Churchill, November 2, 1912, Borden Papers, folio 8100.
20. Tucker, *Naval Service*, 1: chapter 9. O. D. Skelton, *The Life and Letters of Sir Wilfrid Laurier*, 2 vols. (Toronto, 1921), 2: chapter 17. Donald C. Gordon, *The Dominion Partnership in Imperial Defense, 1870–1914* (Baltimore, 1965), pp. 263-67. Brown and Cook, *A Nation Transformed*, pp. 207-08. As one would expect, the whole affair is badly garbled in Randolph S. Churchill, *Winston S. Churchill*, 2 vols. (London, 1966-67), 2: 665.
21. C. P. Stacey, *The Military Problems of Canada* (Toronto, 1940), pp. 81-84. Tucker, *Naval Service*, 1: chapters 11-12.
22. Arthur W. Jose, *The Royal Australian Navy, 1914–1918*, "Official History of Australia in the War of 1914–1918," Vol. 9, 7th ed. (Sydney, 1939).
23. *Minutes of Proceedings of the Imperial Conference, 1911*, p. 71.
24. Harcourt to the Duke of Connaught, with enclosure, December 11, 1912, Borden Papers, folios 8113-16. Telegraphed text, December 10, 1912, DCER, 1: Document 401. On consideration by the cabinet, Harcourt to Just, August 26, 1912, CO 537/576, microfilm in PAC.
25. Lord Hankey, *The Supreme Command, 1914–1918*, 2 vols. (London, 1961).

Franklyn Arthur Johnson, *Defence by Committee* (London, 1960). *The Memoirs of General the Lord Ismay* (London, 1960). Samuel R. Williamson, Jr., *The Politics of Grand Strategy: Britain and France Prepare for War, 1904–1914* (Cambridge, Mass., 1969). Nicholas d'Ombrain, *War Machinery and High Policy: Defence Administration in Peacetime Britain, 1902–1914* (Oxford, 1973). This last book argues that the Committee of Imperial Defence was unimportant after 1906–09, but says little about the Dominions' relationship to it in 1911–14.

26. Fielding to Laurier, March 18 and 19, 1913, Laurier Papers. Borden to the Duke of Connaught, March 24, 1913, DCER, 1: Document 404. *Parliamentary Debates*, House of Commons, United Kingdom, March 26, 1913.
27. Documents in Borden Papers, folios 8141-3. Minutes, 124th meeting CID, August 5, 1913, CAB 2/3.
28. Johnson, *Defence by Committee*, p. 124; but see Richard A. Preston, *Canada and "Imperial Defense"* (Durham, N.C.), p. 460.
29. PC 1421, June 2, 1914, PAC.
30. Borden to Harcourt, June 6, 1914, Perley Papers, Vol. 1, PAC.
31. 2 George V, Chap. 22, April 1, 1912; printed in DCER, 1: document 15.
32. *Curriculum vitae* signed with Christie's initials, Borden Papers, vol. 264, folio 148417.
33. Innes to Borden, May 22, 1912, Borden Papers, OC 138, folios 8277-80. Robert Bothwell, "Loring Christie: The Failure of Bureaucratic Imperialism", Harvard University Ph.D. thesis, 1972.
34. Memo by Christie, December 10, 1914 [1913?], Borden Papers, OC vol. 659, folios 67875-80. I owe this reference to Mr. Robert Bothwell.
35. C. P. Stacey, "Nationality: the Experience of Canada," CHA *Historical Papers*, 1967, Carroll Quigley, "The Round Table Groups in Canada, 1908–38," CHR, September 1962.
36. Borden Diary, July 20, 1912. John Edward Kendle, *The Colonial and Imperial Conferences, 1887–1911*, pp. 200-01.
37. Stacey, *Military Problems of Canada*, pp. 75-76.
38. W. T. Easterbrook and Hugh G. J. Aitken, *Canadian Economic History* (Toronto, 1958), p. 486. Cf. CAR, *1913*, pp. 17-24. On unemployment in Toronto late in 1914, see the speech by Mayor H. C. Hocken in Paul Rutherford, ed., *Saving the Canadian City: The First Phase, 1880–1920* (Toronto, 1974), pp. 207-08.
39. Urquhart and Buckley, *Historical Statistics of Canada*, p. 199.
40. See Laurier to Philippe Roy, June 15, 1916, C. P. Stacey, ed., *The Arts of War and Peace, 1914–1945* ("Historical Documents of Canada", V, Toronto, 1972), Document 219.

CHAPTER 7: THE WORLD EXPLODES, 1914–1916

1. Winston S. Churchill, *The World Crisis*, one-vol. ed. (New York, 1931), p. 92.
2. DCER, 1: 643-55; Borden Diary, July 23, 1914.

3. Borden Diary, dates cited.
4. Stephen W. Roskill, *Hankey, Man of Secrets* (London, 1970), 1: 136; Samuel R. Williamson, Jr., *The Politics of Grand Strategy: Britain and France Prepare for War, 1904–1914* (Cambridge, Mass., 1969), p. 344. Minutes, 128th Meeting CID, July 14, 1914, PRO, CAB 2/3. Asquith to the King, July 25, 1914, PRO, CAB 41, vol. 35 (PAC, film B—3833).
5. Borden Diary, August 1, 1914; DCER, 1: 137. Asquith to the King, August 18, 1914, PRO, CAB 41, vol. 35.
6. The account of the development of events in G. P. Gooch, *History of Modern Europe, 1878–1919* (London, 1923), pp. 549-52, is still useful. The standard more recent versions are Sidney Bradshaw Fay, *The Origins of the World War*, 2-vol. ed. (New York, 1934), and Luigi Albertini, *The Origins of the War of 1914*, 3 vols. (London, 1952–57).
7. Borden Diary, August 4, 1914.
8. C. P. Stacey, ed., *Historical Documents of Canada*, vol. 5, *The Arts of War and Peace*, p. 549.
9. Ibid., pp. 549-50. DCER, 1: 38-43. Asquith to the King, August 16, 1914, CAB 41, vol. 35.
10. G. W. L. Nicholson, *Canadian Expeditionary Force, 1914–1919* (Ottawa, 1962), p. 18.
11. Stacey, *The Arts of War and Peace*, p. 68.
12. O. D. Skelton, *The Life and Letters of Sir Wilfrid Laurier* (Toronto, 1921), 2: 428. *Debates, House of Commons*, Special War Session, 1914, p. 10.
13. *Canadian Annual Review*, 1914, pp. 140-41.
14. Borden Diary.
15. Nicholson, *Canadian Expeditionary Force*, pp. 29-31.
16. DCER, 1: 52.
17. D. J. Goodspeed, ed., *The Armed Forces of Canada, 1867–1967* (Ottawa, 1967), pp. 76-90.
18. Governor General to Colonial Secretary, October 6, 1914, DCER, 1: 51.
19. Acting High Commissioner to Prime Minister, May 29, 1915, ibid., 73-74.
20. War Office to Colonial Office, June 24, 1915, ibid., 79-80.
21. Sir James E. Edmonds, *Military Operations, France and Belgium, 1918* ("History of the Great War based on Official Documents") (London, 1935), 1: 13 and 48.
22. Acting High Commissioner to Prime Minister, June 10, 1915, ibid., 74. Deputy Minister of Militia and Defence to Secretary, Governor General, July 19, 1915, ibid., 87. On Hughes' letter, Nicholson, *Canadian Expeditionary Force*, p. 114.
23. Ibid., 133.
24. The story is told in A. Fortescue Duguid, *Official History of the Canadian Forces in the Great War, 1914–1919, General Series* (Ottawa, 1938), 1: 126-27. For comment, see Nicholson, *Canadian Expeditionary Force*, p. 35.
25. Ibid., pp. 28-29. Cf. DCER, 1: 44-47. Stacey, *The Arts of War and Peace*, pp. 560-62.

26. Nicholson, *Canadian Expeditionary Force*, pp. 114-15, 147, 135. 188, 230-31.
27. DCER, 1: 51-52, 57, 60.
28. Ibid., 59.
29. Borden to Perley, November 25, 1914, ibid., 59.
30. This whole affair is described in Gaddis Smith, *Britain's Clandestine Submarines, 1914–1915* (New Haven, Conn., 1964).
31. Ibid., p. 93.
32. DCER, 1: 63-64.
33. Ibid., 64.
34. Borden to Perley, April 7, 1915 and April 10, 1915, ibid, 66-67.
35. Smith, *Britain's Clandestine Submarines*, p. 127.
36. DCER, 1: 65.
37. PC 3189, January 30, 1917, ibid., 158-59.
38. Colonial Secretary to Governor General, May 19, 1917, ibid., 163; cf. 167.
39. Perley to Borden, March 4, 1916, ibid., 116-18; Borden to Perley, October 28, 1916, ibid., 144-47.
40. *Mail and Empire*, Toronto, December 7, 1914.
41. Ibid., December 8, 1914.
42. *Star* (Montreal), December 8, 1914, quoted in Smith, *Britain's Clandestine Submarines*, pp. 92-93.
43. Tel. January 14, 1915, Borden Papers, vol. 33, folio 13592.
44. Copy, ibid., vol. 172, folios 93475-80.
45. Minutes, ibid., vol. 23, folio 7948 B.
46. Minutes, PRO, CAB 2/3.
47. Perley to Borden, January 27, 1915, Borden Papers, vol. 172, folio 93486.
48. Roskill, *Hankey*, 1: 156.
49. Perley to Hankey, January 18, 1915, Borden Papers, vol. 172, folios 93472-4.
50. Report of Sub-Committee on War Trade Department, meeting March 30, 1915, and Report of Sub-Committee on transfer of flags, August 31, 1915, Borden Papers, vol. 23, folios 7949 A and 7992.
51. Borden to C. H. Cahan, February 1, 1915, Borden Papers, vol. 23, folios 7944-5.
52. DCER, 1: 284-85.
53. See, e.g., letter to Cahan, February 1, 1915, Borden Papers.
54. Borden Papers, vol. 172, folio 93487.
55. Cahan to Borden, January 30, 1915, ibid., vol. 23, folios 7941-3. Perley to Borden, February 16, 1915, DCER, 1: 285.
56. [Borden] to Perley, October 19, 1914; Perley to Borden, October 23, 1914, Borden Papers, vol. 33.
57. Perley to Borden, November 9, 1914, ibid. DCER, 1: 61, 64.
58. Tel. Borden to Law, August 30, 1912, photocopies from Bonar Law Papers, PAC, MG 27, II, A1.
59. Ibid.
60. Law to Borden, Private, June 5, 1915, ibid.
61. DCER, 1: 288-90.
62. Borden Diary, July-August 1915.

63. Borden *Memoirs*, 2 vols. (Toronto, 1938), 1: 500.
64. Ibid., 507-08.
65. DCER, 1: 93-94.
66. Perley to Law, Law to Perley, November 3, 1915, ibid., 95-96.
67. Perley to Borden, November 5, 1915, ibid., 97.
68. PC 36, ibid., 107-08.
69. Nicholson, *Canadian Expeditionary Force*, Appendix C. Cf. C. P. Stacey, *The Military Problems of Canada* (Toronto, 1940), p. 77.
70. For some discussion of the significance of the adoption of the 500,000-man ceiling, see Stacey, *The Arts of War and Peace*, p. 566.
71. Borden *Memoirs*, 2: 622-23; also in DCER, 1: 104.
72. Borden Papers, vol. 172, folio 93512 (January 12, 1916). In DCER, 1: 104 *n*.
73. Borden Papers, vol. 23, folios 7968-75.
74. "Schedule of Enclosures," Bonar Law Papers, PAC.
75. Borden Papers, vol. 165, folio 89580.
76. See the excellent account in Nicholson, *Canadian Expeditionary Force*, pp. 379-82, including Currie to Lt.-Gen. Sir H. A. Lawrence, March 27, 1918 (from Kemp Papers, PAC). Derby to Haig, November 9, 1917, is in Robert Blake, ed., *The Private Papers of Douglas Haig, 1914–1919* (London, 1952), p. 266; for Haig's resentment see ibid., pp. 303-04, 319.
77. *Report of the Ministry, Overseas Military Forces of Canada, 1918* (London, n.d.). Quoted in Stacey, *The Arts of War and Peace*, pp. 554-55. I am grateful to Richard Gibson for the use of his graduate paper, "The Canadian Section, British General Headquarters: Its Origin and Development."
78. DCER, 1: 165-66.
79. Hugh M. Urquhart, *Arthur Currie, The Biography of a Great Canadian* (Toronto and Vancouver, 1950).
80. C. P. Stacey, "The Staff Officer: A Footnote to Canadian Military History," *Canadian Defence Quarterly*, Winter 1973/74.
81. PC 2651, October 28, 1916, DCER, 1: 147-49.
82. Nicholson, *Canadian Expeditionary Force*, pp. 209-12. For a summary of the subject generally, see A. F. Duguid, *Official History of the Canadian Forces in the Great War, 1914–1919, General Series* (Ottawa, 1938), 1: Appendix 8: "The Growth and Control of the Overseas Military Forces of Canada."
83. G. N. Tucker, *The Naval Service of Canada: Its Official History*, 2 vols. (Ottawa, 1952), 1: 254, and chapter 11 generally.
84. Sydney F. Wise, "The Borden Government and the Formation of a Canadian Flying Corps, 1911–1916," in Michael Cross and Robert Bothwell, eds., *Policy by Other Means* (Toronto, 1972), p. 144.
85. Ibid. Stacey, *Military Problems of Canada*, p. 81. Alan Sullivan, *Aviation in Canada, 1917–1918* (Toronto, 1919). Various documents in DCER, vol. 1.
86. Lash to Borden, September 16, 1915; Borden to Lash, January 21, 1916, Borden Papers, vol. 23, folios 7950, 7965.
87. Ibid., vol. 66, folios 33624-52.
88. Lash to Borden, April 28, 1916, ibid., folio 33657.

89. Lash to Borden, June 1, 1916, enclosing paper, ibid., folios 33662-728.
90. Angus Duncan Gilbert, "The Political Influence of Imperialist Thought in Canada, 1899–1923" (Ph.D. thesis, University of Toronto, 1974), chapter 10.
91. Lash to Borden, November 1, 1916; Borden to Lash, November 3, 1916, Borden Papers, vol. 66, folios 33729-31.

CHAPTER 8: COMMONWEALTH AND ANGLO-SAXON ALLIANCE, 1917–1918

1. A. J. P. Taylor, *English History, 1914–1945* (Oxford, 1965), p. 73.
2. DCER, 1: 153.
3. *War Memoirs of David Lloyd George*, 2-vol. ed. (London, 1938), 1: 1026.
4. DCER, 1: 302-03.
5. Ibid., 304.
6. Taylor, *English History*, p. 82.
7. Stephen W. Roskill, *Hankey, Man of Secrets* (London, 1970), 1: 148.
8. Borden to Lloyd George, from Paris, May 13, 1919, Borden Papers, OC 474, folio 49386. Robert Bothwell, "Loring Christie: The Failure of Bureaucratic Imperialism" (Ph.D. thesis, Harvard University, 1972), p. 211 (Christie to George M. Wrong, December 30, 1919).
9. Borden Diary, January 25, 1917.
10. Lloyd George *War Memoirs*, 1: 1034.
11. Borden Diary, February 28, and March 1, 1917. Minutes of first meeting of Imperial War Cabinet, March 20, 1917.
12. Borden Diary, March 6, 1917.
13. *The War Cabinet, Report for the Year 1917*, British Parliamentary Papers, Cd. 9005, 1918; extract in C. P. Stacey, *Historical Documents of Canada*, Vol. 5, *The Arts of War and Peace* (Toronto, 1972), pp. 363-69. Cf. Lloyd George *War Memoirs*, 1: 1044-45.
14. The published *Extracts* from the minutes of the Imperial War Conference are in British Parliamentary Papers, Cd. 8566, 1917. The portion of the proceedings which remained confidential was printed by the Imperial Conference Secretariat, June 1917. Both prints, bound together, are in Sir George Foster's papers, PAC, MG 27, II, D 7, vol. 45.
15. Nicholas Mansergh, *The Commonwealth Experience* (London, 1969), p. 173. L. S. Amery, *My Political Life* (London, 1953), 2: 91.
16. *Procès-verbal of the First Meeting of the Imperial War Cabinet*, March 20, 1917 (Historical Division, Dept. of External Affairs). Cf. Lloyd George *War Memoirs*, 1: Appendix A.
17. *The War Cabinet, Report for the Year 1918*, British Parliamentary Papers, Cmd. 325, 1918.
18. *The War Cabinet, Report for the Year 1917*.
19. Minutes of 14th meeting of Imperial War Cabinet, May 2, 1917.
20. *Procès-verbal*, note 16 above.

21. Minutes of 8th meeting of Imperial War Cabinet, April 5, 1917, and Appendix.
22. Minutes of 9th meeting of Imperial War Cabinet.
23. Cf. Minutes of 4th meeting of Imperial War Cabinet, March 27, 1917 (reference to War Cabinet minutes of January 31, 1917).
24. Minutes of 10th meeting of Imperial War Cabinet.
25. Ibid., 12th meeting, April 26, 1917.
26. Ibid., 13th meeting, May 1, 1917.
27. Cd. 8566 (note 14 above), pp. 40-61. See also Maurice Ollivier, *The Colonial and Imperial Conferences, from 1887 to 1937* (Ottawa, 1954), 2: 194-216.
28. Mansergh, *Commonwealth Experience*, p. 19. King Diary, PAC, September 12, 1923.
29. Sir Keith Hancock, *Smuts*, Vol. 1: *The Sanguine Years* (Cambridge, 1962), 429-30. Sir Keith Hancock, "Empire, Commonwealth, Cosmos and His Own Place: The Smutsian Philosophy," *Round Table*, no. 240, November 1970.
30. Borden *Memoirs*, 2 vols. (Toronto, 1938), 2: 668.
31. Cd. 8566 (note 14 above).
32. Department of External Affairs, Imperial War Conference, 1917, Conference Papers, Folder 15A. This file was presumably originally a unit of the Christie Papers.
33. This is done by R. Craig Brown and Robert Bothwell in "The 'Canadian Resolution'" in Michael Cross and Robert Bothwell, eds., *Policy by Other Means* (Toronto, 1972), pp. 163-78.
34. Borden Diary, March 19 and 21, 1917.
35. Ibid., March 22, 1917.
36. Brown and Bothwell, "The 'Canadian Resolution'".
37. Lloyd George Papers, quoted in ibid.
38. Brown and Bothwell, "The 'Canadian Resolution'", p. 172. Minutes of [British] War Cabinet, March 1917.
39. Ibid. Cd. 8566.
40. Borden Diary, May 17, 1917.
41. Borden *Memoirs*, 2: chapters 31-34. O. D. Skelton, *Life and Letters of Sir Wilfrid Laurier*, 2 vols. (Toronto, 1921), 2: chapter 19. *Guide to Canadian Ministries since Confederation, July 1, 1867–January 1, 1967* (Ottawa, 1967), pp. 35-39.
42. Perley to Borden, August 15, 1914, DCER, 1: 18-22. Borden *Memoirs*, 2: 681-82. *Guide to Canadian Ministries*, pp. 35-39.
43. L. S. Amery, "The Future of the Imperial Cabinet System" (June 29, 1918), DCER, 1: 333-44.
44. Documents in DCER, 1: 318-22.
45. Ibid., 321. Borden *Memoirs*, 2: 806. *Shorthand Notes of the Fifteenth Meeting of the Imperial War Cabinet . . . June 11, 1918* (Historical Division, Dept. of External Affairs).
46. *Shorthand Notes of the Fifteenth Meeting.*

47. *Shorthand Notes of the Sixteenth Meeting of the Imperial War Cabinet . . . June 13, 1918* (Historical Division, Dept. of External Affairs). Cf. Borden's memorandum on the episode, June 15, 1918, DCER, 1: 201-03; also in Borden *Memoirs*, 2: 808-12. For a longer extract from the minutes of Borden's statement, see Stacey, *The Arts of War and Peace*, pp. 556-60.
48. Lord Hankey, *The Supreme Command, 1914–1918*, 2 vols. (London, 1961), 2: 816.
49. Borden *Memoirs*, 2: 813.
50. Ibid., 813-14.
51. *Shorthand Notes*, 16th meeting of Imperial War Cabinet.
52. Hankey, *Supreme Command*, 2: 816.
53. Minutes, 17th, 18th, and 19th meetings of Imperial War Cabinet.
54. Hankey, *Supreme Command*, 2: 816-17.
55. Roskill, *Hankey*, 1: 566.
56. Ibid., 565.
57. Hankey, *Supreme Command*, 2: 832.
58. Borden Papers, vol. 122; Part II, which embodies the conclusions, is folios 66358-78. The date is August 14, 1918.
59. Hankey, *Supreme Command*, 2: 829.
60. Borden *Memoirs*, 2: 815-17.
61. Minutes, 3rd and 31st meetings of Imperial War Cabinet.
62. See the discussion in Robert Craig Brown, "Sir Robert Borden, the Great War and Anglo-Canadian Relations," in John S. Moir, ed., *Character and Circumstance: Essays in Honour of Donald Grant Creighton* (Toronto, 1970).
63. Minutes, 27th and 28th meetings of Imperial War Cabinet, July 25 and 30, 1918.
64. This was actually done with seven meetings, Nos. 30-36 of the Imperial War Cabinet, August 13–November 5, 1918, both inclusive. The last meeting Borden attended was No. 32, August 15.
65. Bothwell, "Loring Christie," pp. 83-98. Borden Diary, December 22-23, 1915, November 18, 1916.
66. Ernest R. May, *The World War and American Isolation, 1914–1917* (ed. Chicago, 1966).
67. Lansing to Spring-Rice, January 18, 1916, copy in Borden Papers, vol. 66, OC 306, folios 33511-14.
68. Spring-Rice to Borden, September 17, 1916, ibid., folios 33522-3.
69. Borden Diary, September 21, 1916.
70. Borden to Spring-Rice, September 22, 1916, Borden Papers, OC 306, folios 33524-5. Correspondence with Colonial Secretary, same file.
71. May, *World War and American Isolation*, pp. 365-70.
72. Bothwell, "Loring Christie," pp. 105-06.
73. Borden to High Commissioner in London, October 13, 1917, DCER, 1: 24. The whole subject is thoroughly covered in Robert Bothwell, "Canadian Representation at Washington: a Study in Colonial Responsibility," CHR, June 1972.
74. Bothwell, "Canadian Representation." Documents in DCER, 1: 24-27.

75. W. G. Ross to C. C. Ballantyne, January 14, 1918, Dept. of External Affairs file 996-1918, PAC, RG 25, D 1.
76. Harris to Borden, January 19, 1918, Borden Papers, vol. 95, OC 483, folios 50244-7.
77. PC 272, February 2, 1918, DCER, 1: 32-34.
78. Governor General to Colonial Secretary, February 6, 1918, ibid., 35.
79. Bothwell, "Canadian Representation."
80. Borden *Memoirs*, 2: 769-73. Borden to Governor General, March 6, 1918, Borden Papers, vol. 95, OC 484, folios 50535-9.
81. Harris to Borden, May 17, 1918, Borden Papers, vol. 164, RLB 17, folio 89479.
82. C. P. Stacey, *The Military Problems of Canada* (Toronto, 1940), 84. Sydney F. Wise, "The Borden Government and the Formation of a Canadian Flying Corps, 1911–1916," in Cross and Bothwell, eds., *Policy by Other Means.*
83. Elie Halévy, A *History of the English People,* Epilogue Vol. I, 1895–1905 (London, 1929), 52.
84. This feeling is forcefully described in H. L. Keenleyside, *Canada and the United States* (New York, 1929). The original edition of this book is in many ways better than the revised one of 1952.
85. *Fifth Census of Canada, 1911*, 2: Table 7.
86. Ibid.
87. *Canada Year Book*, 1938, p. 146.
88. CYB, 1934–35, pp. 219-20.
89. Stacey, *The Arts of War and Peace*, pp. 568-69 (*Debates*, House of Commons, April 25, 1918).
90. This is described by Miss Barbara Wilson in a volume on Ontario in the First War, prepared for the Champlain Society, which she has kindly allowed me to see in advance of publication.
91. House of Commons, March 13, 1900.
92. King Diary, May 30, 1919.
93. G. W. L. Nicholson, *The Gunners of Canada* (Toronto/Montreal, 1967), 1: 325. Information from the late Brigadier G. A. McCarter.
94. Sir Robert Borden, *Letters to Limbo*, ed. Henry Borden (Toronto, 1971), p. 6.

CHAPTER 9: THE PEACE AND THE LEAGUE

1. DCER, 1: 218.
2. Borden to Lloyd George, October 28 and 29, 1918, ibid., 218.
3. Lloyd George to Borden, November 3, 1918, ibid., 219. Other documents, ibid., 219-20. Borden *Memoirs*, 2 vols. (Toronto, 1938), 2: 860-65.
4. Churchill, *The World Crisis*, one-vol. ed. (New York, 1931), pp. 845-46. For the process of negotiating the armistice, Lloyd George *War Memoirs*, 2-vol. ed. (London, n.d.), 2: chapter 85. Terms of the armistice, *Papers Relating to the Foreign Relations of the United States: 1919: The Paris Peace Conference*, 11 vols. (Washington, 1942), 2: 1-11.
5. L. F. Fitzhardinge, "Hughes, Borden, and Dominion Representation at the

Paris Peace Conference," CHR, June 1968. Hughes to Borden, November 10, 1918, DCER, 1: 220.
6. Minutes of Imperial War Cabinet, meetings nos. 37, 40 and 43.
7. Ibid., no. 37.
8. Ibid., no. 38.
9. Acting Prime Minister to Borden, December 4, 1918, R. A. MacKay, ed., *Documents on Canadian External Relations*, Vol. 2, *The Paris Peace Conference of* 1919 (Ottawa, 1969) (hereafter DCER, 2), 7.
10. Fitzhardinge, "Hughes, Borden, and Dominion Representation." Borden *Memoirs*, 2: 871-72.
11. Quoted in Minutes of Imperial War Cabinet, meeting no. 48, December 31, 1918.
12. "Notes of an Allied Conversation," December 3, 1918.
13. Minutes of Imperial War Cabinet, meeting no. 48.
14. Fitzhardinge, "Hughes, Borden, and Dominion Representation."
15. Borden to Acting Prime Minister, January 2, 1919, Canada, Sessional Papers, no. 41j, Special Session 1919 (quoted in C. P. Stacey, *Historical Documents of Canada*, Vol. 5, *The Arts of War and Peace* (Toronto, 1972), p. 376). The date is probably that of receipt rather than of dispatch, as Borden speaks of a cabinet meeting "to-day" which is clearly that of December 31.
16. H. W. V. Temperley, ed., *History of the Peace Conference at Paris*, 6 vols. (London, 1920–24). A still valuable summary is G. P. Gooch, *History of Modern Europe, 1878–1919*, chapter 19. On Canadian aspects, G. P. deT. Glazebrook, *Canada at the Paris Peace Conference* (Toronto, 1942). Important documents in *Foreign Relations of the United States: The Paris Peace Conference*, 1919 (Washington, 1942).
17. Report by Lloyd George, minutes of meeting no. 1 of British Empire Delegation, January 13, 1919 (PAC, Foster Papers, MG 27, II, D 7, vol. 62); also in DCER, 2: 26-28. "General Memorandum" No. 2, January 15, 1919, forwarded by Borden for information of cabinet, DCER, 2: 188-91.
18. "General Memorandum" No. 2.
19. Minutes of meeting no. 1 of BED, January 13, 1919 (extract in DCER, 2: 26-28). Borden *Memoirs*, 2: 899. Cf. "General Memorandum" No. 2.
20. "Secretary's Notes of a Conversation held in M. Pichon's Room at the Quai d'Orsay on Monday, January 13, 1919, at 4 P.M." (IC 106) (Foster Papers, vol. 47).
21. Minutes of meeting no. 3 of BED, January 23, 1919.
22. "Secretary's Notes . . . January 13, 1919. . . ."
23. Prime Minister to Acting Prime Minister, January 20, 1919, and Memorandum by Prime Minister, same date, DCER, 2: 30-31.
24. "Preliminary Peace Conference . . . Protocol No. 1. Plenary Session of January 18, 1919," Annex II. (Foster Papers, vol. 47).
25. Minutes of meeting no. 3 of BED, and of minutes of plenary session of Preliminary Peace Conference, January 25, 1919; extracts, DCER, 2: 36-37 and 39-40.

26. "Secretary's Notes of a Conversation held in M. Pichon's Room at the Quai d'Orsay, Paris, on Tuesday, April 15, 1919, at 3 P.M." (IC 171) (Foster Papers, vol. 47); cf. Borden to Lloyd George, April 16, 1919, DCER, 2: 116-17.
27. Published in *External Affairs*, April 1964; extract in Stacey, *The Arts of War and Peace*, pp. 379-85.
28. List of bodies and representatives, DCER, 2: 71-72.
29. Borden *Memoirs*, 2: 910 *ff*. Robert Bothwell, "Loring Christie: The Failure of Bureaucratic Imperialism" (Ph.D. thesis, Harvard University, 1972), 267, citing minute by Crowe on FO 371/7909/12276, November 6, 1923.
30. Documents in DCER, 2: 38-40.
31. List, ibid., 71-72.
32. Minutes of Imperial War Cabinet, meeting no. 40, December 3, 1918 (extract in DCER, 2: 6-7).
33. Committee of Imperial War Cabinet on Indemnity, December 9, 1918, extract in ibid., 9-10. Cf. minutes of Imperial War Cabinet, meeting no. 46, December 24, 1918, extract in ibid., 15-16.
34. Borden to Acting Prime Minister, March 14, 1919, ibid., 88.
35. See Lloyd George's remarks at the Imperial Conference of 1921, July 12, 1921 (extract in Stacey, *The Arts of War and Peace*, pp. 407-09), and his book *The Truth about the Peace Treaties*, 2 vols. (London, 1939), 1: chapter 16.
36. Lloyd George, *The Truth About the Peace Treaties*, 1: 675-91.
37. Minutes of meetings nos. 33 and 34 of British Empire Delegation, June 1 and 2, 1919. Extracts in Lloyd George, *The Truth about the Peace Treaties*, 1: chapter 16, and (Canadian portions) DCER, 2: 158-59.
38. Memorandum by Borden (WCP 242), March 12, 1919, DCER, 2: 72-73: also quoted in Stacey, *The Arts of War and Peace*, pp. 377-78. Cf. "General Memorandum" No. 12, DCER, 2: 211.
39. Extract from preamble, DCER, 2: 161-62.
40. Prime Minister to Acting Prime Minister, April 9, 1919, and text of Borden's Full Power, ibid., 109-10.
41. Memorandum, May 12, 1919, ibid., 155-57.
42. W. Stewart Wallace, *The Memoirs of the Rt. Hon. Sir George Foster* (Toronto, 1933), pp. 201-02. *Canadian Annual Review*, 1919, p. 82, notes Sifton's return but says Foster and Doherty signed the treaty!
43. *The Treaty of Peace between the Allied and Associated Powers and Germany* . . . (HMSO, London, 1919) (copy in PAC, RG 25, G-1, vol. 1252, file 1920-5). Signatures reproduced in facsimile.
44. Minutes of meeting no. 30 of BED, May 5, 1919; extract in DCER, 2: 147-48. Borden to Acting Prime Minister, May 5, 1919, ibid, 148-49.
45. Lloyd George and Balfour to Clemenceau, May 5, 1919, enclosed in Lloyd George to Borden, May 10, 1919, ibid., 153-54.
46. Treaties printed in *Treaty of Peace between the Allied and Associated Powers and Germany*, pp. 442-51.
47. Thomas A. Bailey, A *Diplomatic History of the American People* (New York, 1940), p. 663.

48. Governor General to Governor General of South Africa, August 24 and 26, 1919, DCER, 2: 173. Borden *Memoirs*, 2: 996.
49. Canada, Sessional Papers, Special Session 1919, No. 41 1. Ibid., 1920, list of papers (treaties not printed). Report of Under Secretary of State for External Affairs for years ending March 31, 1920 and March 31, 1921, Sessional Paper No. 34, 1921 and 1922. Glazebrook, *Canada at the Paris Peace Conference*, p. 108. Documents in DCER, 3: 69-73.
50. F. P. Walters, A *History of the League of Nations*, 1-vol. ed. (London, 1967), p. 18. On the contribution of private researchers and propagandists and the societies in England, see Leonard Woolf, *Beginning Again, An Autobiography of the Years* 1911–1918 (London, 1964), pp. 183-92. Donald M. Page, "Canadians and the League of Nations before the Manchurian Crisis" (Ph.D. thesis, University of Toronto, 1972). G. M. Trevelyan, *Grey of Fallodon* (London, 1937), p. 395.
51. Walters, *League of Nations*, p. 20. Text of the Fourteen Points, Samuel Flagg Bemis, A *Diplomatic History of the United States* (ed. New York, 1936), pp. 619-20.
52. Minutes of Imperial War Cabinet, meeting no. 30, August 13, 1918.
53. David Hunter Miller, *The Drafting of the Covenant*, 2 vols. (New York, 1928), 1: 3, 8-17. The Phillimore report (March 20, 1918) is Document 1 in Vol. 2.
54. "A League of Nations," with covering memorandum dated Foreign Office, October 5, 1918 (Foster Papers, vol. 45).
55. "The League of Nations. A Programme for the Peace Conference" (British official print, December 16, 1918), ibid.
56. Walters, *League of Nations*, p. 26. Miller, *Drafting of the Covenant*, I, p. 35.
57. Minutes of meeting no. 3 of BED, January 23, 1919. Borden to Lloyd George, February 6, 1919; P. H. Kerr to Lloyd George, February 8, 1919; Doherty to Secretary, Committee on Position of Dominions and India in League of Nations, January 27, 1919. Documents in DCER, 2: 53-54, 42-43.
58. Ibid., 44-48.
59. Borden *Memoirs*, 2: 920. Bothwell, "Loring Christie," pp. 183 *ff*.
60. Miller, *Drafting of the Covenant*, 2: 327-35.
61. Ibid., 106-16.
62. Doherty to Cecil, January 30, 1919, ibid., 50.
63. Ibid., 58-63 [February 22, 1919].
64. Bothwell, "Loring Christie," pp. 184-95. Rowell to Borden, March 27, 1919, Borden Papers, RLB 26a.
65. DCER, 2: 73-87 (WCP 245, March 13, 1919).
66. Borden to Wilson, March 14, 1919, ibid., 88.
67. Ibid., 92-94.
68. Miller, *Drafting of the Covenant*, 1: 354 *ff*. Hughes' paper, March 21, 1919, ibid., 363-68.
69. Ibid., 2: 684.
70. Ibid., 2: 288; 1: 279-89.
71. Minutes of meeting no. 26 of BED, April 21, 1919.

72. DCER, 2: 150-51 and frontispiece (facsimile of document).
73. Article 7 of draft Labour Convention (which ultimately became Article 393 of Treaty of Versailles). Memorandum by Arthur Sifton, WCP 440 (covering note April 2, 1919), ibid., 101-04.
74. *Foreign Relations of the United States: The Paris Peace Conference, 1919* (Washington, 1943), 3: 240-60 (Minutes of Plenary Session No. 4, April 11, 1919).
75. Borden to Lloyd George, April 29, 1919, DCER, 2: 135-36.
76. Minutes of meeting no. 30 of BED, May 5, 1919; extract, DCER, 2: 147-48.
77. Borden to Lloyd George, May 6, 1919, ibid., 149-50.
78. Hankey to Secretary General of Peace Conference, May 6, 1919, ibid., 151.
79. Borden to Lloyd George, and enclosure, April 27, 1919, ibid., 130-31. Cf. Borden *Memoirs*, 2: 954-60.
80. Bothwell, "Loring Christie," quoting Christie, "Notes on the Right of Legation and International Personality in relation to Canada," March 16, 1918, Christie Papers, PAC, vol. 2.
81. *Foreign Relations . . . 1919*, 3: 484.
82. Minutes of Imperial War Cabinet, meeting no. 47, December 30, 1918.
83. *Foreign Relations . . . 1919*, 3: 503.
84. Borden to Lloyd George, May 2, 1919, DCER, 2: 142.
85. Borden to Acting Prime Minister, May 6, 1919, ibid., 152.
86. Walters, *League of Nations*, p. 117.
87. Borden to Sifton, July 9, 1919; other communications quoted in DCER, 2: 165-66.
88. Milner to Borden, July 23, 1919, ibid., 166-67.
89. Borden to Milner, July 29, 1919, ibid., 167.
90. *Parliamentary Debates*, House of Commons, Great Britain, July 21, 1919. Borden to Milner, August 4, 1919, DCER, 2: 168.
91. PC 1907, ibid., 175. Stacey, *The Arts of War and Peace*, p. 386.
92. Extracts, DCER, 2: 176-77.
93. Notes on the Conference (in *External Affairs*, April 1964, and Stacey, *The Arts of War and Peace*, pp. 379-85).
94. The best summary of the Canadian military relationship to the Russian intervention is in G. W. L. Nicholson, *Canadian Expeditionary Force, 1914–1919*, chapter 16. See also John Swettenham, *Allied Intervention in Russia, 1918–1919, and the Part Played by Canada* (Toronto, 1967). The most recent book, based on a wide range of sources, is Roy MacLaren, *Canadians in Russia, 1918–1919* (Toronto, 1976).
95. Capt. W. W. Murray, "Canadians in Dunsterforce," *Canadian Defence Quarterly*, January 1931–January 1932. On origins of Canadian participation, Kemp to Borden, February 24, 1918, Swettenham, *Allied Intervention*, pp. 43-44.
96. Minute by Lt.-Gen. Sir R. Turner, July 17, 1918, Borden Papers, file OC 518 (1); Borden's concurrence, same date, ibid. Nicholson, *Canadian Expeditionary Force*, pp. 510-12.

97. Ibid., pp. 512-13.
98. Richard H. Ullman, *Anglo-Soviet Relations, 1917–1921: Intervention and the War* (Princeton, 1961), chapter 7.
99. Memo by Maj.-Gen. P. de B. Radcliffe, Director of Military Operations, War Office, for Minister of Militia and Defence, July 12, 1918, Borden Papers, file OC 518 (1).
100. Borden to cabinet, July 25, 1918, ibid. PC 1983, August 12, 1918, DCER, 3: 207. Nicholson, *Canadian Expeditionary Force*, pp. 517-20.
101. Mewburn to Borden, July 12, 1918, Borden Papers, file OC 518 (1). Borden to Mewburn, August 13, 1918, ibid. PC 2595, October 21, 1918, DCER, 1: 211-13.
102. *Dana Wilgress Memoirs* (Toronto, 1967), pp. 13-16, 22-29, 49-56. Wallace, *Memoirs of Sir George Foster*, pp. 165-66. C. F. Just, "Economic Mission to Siberia," August 29, 1918, Foster Papers, file 73; see Gaddis Smith, "Canada and the Siberian Intervention, 1918–1919," AHR, July 1959, and Aloysius Balawyder, *Canadian-Soviet Relations between the World Wars* (Toronto, 1972).
103. "Memorandum respecting the Organization and Status of the Proposed Canadian Siberian Expeditionary Force," with covering letter Mewburn to Borden, September 12, 1918, Borden Papers, file OC 518 (1), folios 56190-95 A.
104. November 14, 1918, DCER, 3: 51.
105. Borden to White, November 24, 1918 and December 9, 1918, ibid., 52-53, 57-58, and communications from Ottawa, particularly White to Borden, November 29, 1918, ibid., 55.
106. Ibid., 58.
107. Nicholson, *Canadian Expeditionary Force*, pp. 520-22. For part of the correspondence, see James Eayrs, *In Defence of Canada*: Vol. 1, *From the Great War to the Great Depression* (Toronto, 1964), chapter 1.
108. Minutes of meeting no. 8 of BED, February 17, 1919.
109. Nicholson, *Canadian Expeditionary Force*, pp. 521-23.
110. DCER, 3: 66-67.
111. Sifton to Borden, May 5, 1919, Borden Papers, file OC 518 (2), folio 56432. Borden to Churchill, May 5, 1919, ibid., folio 56433.
112. DCER, 3: 67-68. Nicholson, *Canadian Expeditionary Force*, pp. 516, 523.
113. Churchill to Borden, July 21, 1919, and Foster (Acting Prime Minister) to Churchill, July 22, 1919, DCER, 3: 68. Nicholson, *Canadian Expeditionary Force*, p. 517. On the experience of the artillery, see Leonid I. Strakhovsky, "The Canadian Artillery Brigade in North Russia, 1918–1919," CHR, June 1958.
114. White to Borden, November 25, 1918, DCER, 3: 53.
115. Crerar to White, November 22, 1918, Borden Papers, file OC 518 (1), folios 56231-33.
116. White to Borden, November 25, 1918.
117. DCER, 3: 57.
118. Ibid., 56 (December 4, 1918).

CHAPTER 10: REACTION FROM THE HEROIC AGE, 1919–1920

1. King Diary, February 18-22, 1919.
2. R. MacGregor Dawson, *William Lyon Mackenzie King, A Political Biography, 1874–1923* (Toronto, 1958), p. 307.
3. On this period of King's life there are two books: H. S. Ferns and B. Ostry, *The Age of Mackenzie King: The Rise of the Leader* (London and Toronto, 1955), violently prejudiced against King; and F. A. McGregor, *The Fall & Rise of Mackenzie King: 1911–1919* (Toronto, 1962), by an old associate of King and much more sympathetic. See also C. P. Stacey, *A Very Double Life: The Private World of Mackenzie King* (Toronto, 1976). On the speech of 1920, see King Diary, April 20, 1920, and preceding days.
4. New edition, Toronto, 1973, ed. David Jay Bercuson.
5. King Diary, September 21, 1918.
6. 6-7 Edward VII, March 22, 1907.
7. *Industry and Humanity*, ed. 1973, p. 333.
8. Borden *Memoirs*, 2 vols. (Toronto, 1938), 2: 1031-40.
9. Ibid., 1031-40. Roger Graham, *Arthur Meighen*, Vol. 1: *The Door of Opportunity* (Toronto, 1960), chapter 11. Dawson, *King*, pp. 339-42. Robert Craig Brown, "The Political Ideas of Robert Borden," in Marcel Hamelin, ed., *The Political Ideas of the Prime Ministers of Canada* (Ottawa, 1969).
10. Graham, *Meighen*, 1: chapters 6, 8. Minutes of Imperial War Cabinet, meetings nos. 15 (June 11, 1918), 16 (June 13, 1918) and 17 (June 14, 1918).
11. *Debates*, House of Commons, second session, 1919, September 2, 8, 9, and 11. Extended summary of the debate, *Canadian Annual Review*, 1919, pp. 101-09.
12. September 9.
13. C. P. Stacey, ed. *Historical Documents of Canada*, Vol. 5. *The Arts of War and Peace* (Toronto, 1972), p. 42.
14. *Debates*, House of Commons, September 8.
15. Ibid., September 11.
16. Ibid., September 9.
17. Laurier to Skelton, November 25, 1918, Laurier Papers, vol. 727.
18. Donald M. Page, "Canadians and the League of Nations before the Manchurian Crisis" (Ph.D. thesis, University of Toronto, 1972), p. 134. *Manitoba Free Press*, May 3, 1919.
19. *Debates*, House of Commons, September 10 and 8.
20. Ibid., September 11.
21. *A Party Politician: The Memoirs of Chubby Power* (Toronto, 1966), p. 42.
22. Notably Lt.-Col. C. W. Peck, VC (September 11).
23. *Debates*, House of Commons, September 11, 1919.
24. Speech of Rowell, September 9.
25. *Debates*, House of Commons, March 11, 1920.
26. King Diary, March 13, 1920.
27. September 10, 1919.

28. March 16, 1920.
29. I rely here mainly on Mr. Page's thesis, "Canadians and the League," pp. 123-43.
30. Ramsay Cook, *The Politics of John W. Dafoe and the Free Press* (Toronto, 1963), pp. 88-92.
31. Ibid., p. 92.
32. Vol. 1, Ottawa, 1912. Vol. 2, Toronto, n.d. [1917?]. Ewart's publications are a bibliographer's nightmare. On Ewart generally, see Frank H. Underhill, "The Political Ideas of John S. Ewart," CHA *Report*, 1933; J. W. Dafoe, "The Views and Influence of John S. Ewart," CHR, June 1933; and Douglas L. Cole, "John S. Ewart and Canadian Nationalism," CHA *Historical Papers*, 1969.
33. *The Independence Papers*, Vol. 1, 1925–1930 [Ottawa, 1930?]. Vol. 2, 1927–1932 (n.p., n.d., typewritten title-page).
34. *Citizen* (Ottawa), August 26–September 1, 1919. Speech of George Parent, *Debates*, House of Commons, September 11, 1919.
35. *Independence Papers*, 2: no. 8, "Canada's Constitutional Status" (Rotary Club, Ottawa, July 7, 1930).
36. P. E. Corbett and H. A. Smith, *Canada in World Politics* (London, 1928), p. 166.
37. Dafoe to Sifton, February 12, 1923, quoted in Ramsay Cook, ed., *The Dafoe-Sifton Correspondence, 1919–1927* (Manitoba Record Society, 1966), pp. 150-53.
38. King Papers, PAC, MG 26, J 4, vol. 28, file 155.
39. King Diary, January 28, 1922.
40. Ibid., March 10, 1920.
41. Page, "Canadians and the League," chapter 4.
42. Ibid. I am grateful to Miss Mary McTavish for the use of an essay, "The League of Nations Society in Canada and the Development of Canadian Interest in International Affairs," which she wrote when taking my graduate course in 1972.
43. Carter Manny, "The Canadian Institute of International Affairs, 1928 to 1939: An Attempt to "Enlighten" Canada's Foreign Policy" (Harvard BA thesis, 1971). McTavish essay.
44. Newton W. Rowell, *The British Empire and World Peace, Being the Burwash Memorial Lectures . . . University of Toronto, November, 1921* (Toronto, 1922), p. 210. On the lectures as delivered, *The Varsity*, University of Toronto, November 23, 25 and 28, 1921. Margaret Prang, *N. W. Rowell, Ontario Nationalist* (Toronto, 1975), pp. 380-83.
45. Thomas A. Bailey, *Woodrow Wilson and the Great Betrayal* (New York. 1945); Ralph Stone, *The Irreconcilables: The Fight against the League of Nations* (New York, 1973); F. P. Walters, *A History of the League of Nations* (London, 1967), chapter 6; H. Barrett Learned, "The Attitude of the United States Senate towards the Versailles Treaty: 1918–20," in H. W. V. Temperley, ed., *History of the Peace Conference of Paris*, vol. 6 (London, 1924); Samuel Flagg Bemis, *A Diplomatic History of the United States* (New York, 1936), chapter 34.

46. Stone, *The Irreconcilables*, pp. 1, 97-99.
47. The different versions of the "Lodge reservations" are printed in Bailey, *Great Betrayal*, pp. 387-93.
48. CAR, 1919, p. 96.
49. Ibid. (statement at San Francisco, September 18, 1919).
50. Stone, *The Irreconcilables*, p. 134.
51. Bailey, *Great Betrayal*, p. 392.
52. Page, "Canadians and the League," pp. 144-45.
53. On the Grey mission, see Bailey, *Great Betrayal*, pp. 233-42. Milner to Devonshire, November 8, 1919, DCER, 3: 383-84.
54. Page, "Canadians and the League," p. 146. Doherty to Milner, November 10, 1919, Borden Papers, OC 667.
55. Grey to Foreign Secretary, November 14, 1919, DCER, 3: 384-85. Borden *Memoirs*, 2: 1009-12.
56. Colonial Secretary to Governor General, January 9, 1920, DCER, 3: 386.
57. *The Times* (London), January 31, 1920. See the discussion in Bailey, *Great Betrayal*, pp. 236-42.
58. Borden *Memoirs*, 2: 1012-13. In Borden Papers, OC 667 (Borden to Doherty, November 15, 1919).
59. Rowell, *The British Empire and World Peace*, p. 179.
60. November 21, 1919.
61. Rowell, *The British Empire and World Peace*, p. 179.
62. CAR, 1919, pp. 110-11.
63. Tel. P59, Rowell to Borden, December 10, 1918; Borden to [Acting] P.M., December 13, 1918 both in PAC, RG 25, D 1, Box 265119, file 603; [L. C. Christie], "Memorandum for Sir Robert Borden," December 12, 1918, ibid., Box 265106, file 996.
64. Robert Bothwell, "Canadian Representation at Washington: A Study in Colonial Responsibility," CHR, June 1972.
65. Borden to [Acting] P.M., February 14, 1919; Blount to Christie, March 14, 1919; White to Borden, March 24, 1919; Borden to [Acting] P.M., March 26, 1919 (all in Borden Papers, vol. 111, OC 353).
66. PC 55, January 11, 1919, appointing Gordon Acting Chairman of War Mission, and his report on the mission for year ending December 31, 1919, PAC, RG 25, G 1, vol. 1255, file 40-A.
67. Gordon to Rowell, September 17, 1919, DCER, 3: 4-6.
68. "Note on the Title and Status of the Proposed Canadian Agent at Washington," September 19, 1919, ibid., 6-7.
69. Bothwell, "Canadian Representation."
70. Devonshire to Colonial Secretary, October 3, 1919, Borden Papers, Memoir Notes, folios 3900-02, printed in Stacey, *The Arts of War and Peace*, pp. 468-70. Slightly different text, DCER, 3: 7-9.
71. Bothwell, "Canadian Representation."
72. Milner to Devonshire, October 28, 1919, Borden Papers, Memoir Notes, folios 3906-8, printed in Stacey, *The Arts of War and Peace*, pp. 470-71; DCER, 3: 9-10.

73. Bothwell, "Canadian Representation." Devonshire to Colonial Secretary, December 20, 1919, DCER, 3: 10-11.
74. Administrator to Colonial Secretary, May 6, 1920, ibid., 21. Correspondence on discussions with U.S. State Dept., ibid., 13-20.
75. Dafoe to Sifton, March 30, 1922, Cook, *Dafoe-Sifton Correspondence*, p. 114.
76. September 6, 1919 (quoted in CAR, *1919*, p. 291).

CHAPTER 11: MEIGHEN, CHRISTIE, AND TWO CONFERENCES, 1920–1921

1. C. P. Stacey, ed., *Historical Documents of Canada*, Vol. 5. *The Arts of War and Peace* (Toronto, 1972), pp. 179-89.
2. Public Archives of Canada, *Guide to Canadian Ministries since Confederation*, pp. 40-42. Roger Graham, *Arthur Meighen*, Vol. 2: *And Fortune Fled* (Toronto, 1963), pp. 114-15.
3. Robert Bothwell, "Loring Christie: The Failure of Bureaucratic Imperialism" (Ph.D. thesis, Harvard University, 1972), chapter 7. Cf. Graham, *Meighen*, 2: 215.
4. C. P. Stacey, *The Military Problems of Canada* (Toronto, 1940), pp. 66-70, 75-6.
5. *Canada Year Book, 1938*, pp. 835, 860-61; Stacey, *The Arts of War and Peace*, pp. 252-57.
6. G. N. Tucker, *The Naval Service of Canada, Its Official History*, 2 vols. (Ottawa, 1952), 2: chapter 11.
7. DCER, 1: 355-56. Cf. Borden *Memoirs* (Toronto, 1938), 2: 841-43, and Stacey, *Military Problems of Canada*, p. 89.
8. *Report of Admiral of the Fleet Viscount Jellicoe of Scapa . . . on Naval Mission to the Dominion of Canada* (Ottawa, 1920). Two additional volumes of the report, kept secret at the time, are in Department of National Defence file HQS 3220.
9. Tucker, *Naval Service*, 1: 306-09. James Eayrs, *In Defence of Canada*: Vol. 1, *From the Great War to the Great Depression* (Toronto, 1964), 151-54.
10. Tucker, *Naval Service*, 1: 316-17.
11. Foster to Borden, March 25, 1920, Eayrs, *In Defence of Canada*, 1: 163-64.
12. Ibid.
13. Stacey, *The Arts of War and Peace*, p. 523.
14. Desmond Morton, *Ministers and Generals: Politics and the Canadian Militia, 1868–1904* (Toronto, 1970).
15. Stacey, *Military Problems of Canada*, p. 88. Eayrs, *In Defence of Canada*, 1: 65-66.
16. The most complete account of the early years of the RCAF is Eayrs, *In Defence of Canada*, 1: chapter 5.
17. Stacey, *The Arts of War and Peace*, p. 523.
18. C. P. Stacey, *Six Years of War* (Official History of the Canadian Army in the Second World War), vol. 1 (Ottawa, 1955), pp. 4-5.

19. Eayrs, *In Defence of Canada*, 1: 70-78.
20. Stacey, *Six Years of War*, pp. 29-30.
21. Eayrs, *In Defence of Canada*, 1: 70-78.
22. "Canadian Representation at First Meeting of the Assembly of the League of Nations . . . ," August 17, 1920 (corrections in Christie's hand), Christie Papers, PAC, MG 30, E 15, vol. 6, folios 5049-50.
23. Borden to Rowell, October 2, 1920, Rowell Papers, PAC, MG 27, II, D 13, vol. 8, file 38. Appointing order-in-council, PC 2609, October 26, 1920, PAC, RG 2, series 1, vol. 1605.
24. Borden to Rowell, October 2, 1920, Rowell Papers, vol. 8, file 38.
25. Borden to Rowell, December 14, 1920, ibid.
26. *Debates*, House of Commons, February 16, 1921 (Foster) and February 18, 1921 (Rowell). *League of Nations: The Records of The First Assembly. Plenary Sessions* (Geneva, 1920).
27. L. C. Christie's "Notes on the First Assembly of the League of Nations, Held at Geneva, Switzerland, November 15th to December 18th, 1920," copies in Christie Papers, vol. 6, and in Dept. of External Affairs file 65-A-1921, vol. 3, PAC, RG 25, G 1, vol. 1286). (In vol. 4 of the same External file is Foster's "Report of the Delegates appointed to Represent Canada at the First Assembly of the League of Nations"; it is identical with the Christie "Notes.") *League of Nations: The Records of the First Assembly. Meetings of the Committees* (Geneva, 1920), pp. 331 *ff*., 432, 538.
28. DCER, 3: 476.
29. Printed document recording motion, External file 65-1921, vol. 1, sec 1.
30. Note by Secretary General of League, March 19, 1921, ibid. Christie, "Notes on the First Assembly."
31. Borden to Rowell, November 30, 1920, Rowell Papers, vol. 8, file 38.
32. Borden to Rowell, December 14, 1920, ibid.
33. Margaret Prang, N. W. *Rowell: Ontario Nationalist* (Toronto, 1975), pp. 357-58.
34. Appointing order, PC 3018, August 19, 1921, and cable Meighen to Foster and Doherty, July 22, 1921, both in External file 65-1921, vol. 1, sec. 2.
35. Report by Doherty and Perley on Second Assembly (covering letter Perley to Meighen, October 19, 1921), External file 65-A, vol. 4.
36. PC 304, April 26, 1920, covered by Administrator to Colonial Secretary, May 1, 1920, DCER, 3: 409-10.
37. Rowell to Milner, December 24, 1920, ibid., 427-28.
38. Memo by O. D. Skelton, January 21, 1925, ibid., 430-32.
39. Colonial Secretary to Governor General, May 12, 1920; PC 1117, May 19, 1920, both in ibid., 113-14. PRO, CAB 29/28. See Angus Duncan Gilbert, "The Political Influence of Imperialist Thought in Canada, 1899–1923" (Ph.D. thesis, University of Toronto, 1974), p. 344.
40. Documents on External file 65-1921, vol. 1, sec. 1, RG 25, G-1, vol. 1286.
41. Minutes, DCER, 3: 417-26.
42. Ibid., 421.

43. *League of Nations: The Records of the First Assembly. Meetings of the Committees*, First Committee, p. 35.
44. DCER, 3: 421. Papers on External file 65-1921, RG 25, G 1, vol. 1286.
45. DCER, 3: 420-21.
46. Ibid., 428-30.
47. Smuts to Lloyd George (copy), April 2, 1920, PAC, RG 25, G 1, file 42, vol. 1255. Other correspondence, DCER, 3: 153-62.
48. DCER, 3: 161-62.
49. November 26, 1920, Meighen Papers, PAC, file 97, folios 017530-31.
50. Meighen's copy in King Papers.
51. Cmd. 1474, August 1921.
52. Ibid., pp. 3-5 (British House of Commons, July 11, 1921).
53. Christie, "Meeting of the Prime Ministers of the Empire in London, June 1921," copy in Borden Papers, vol. 41 (covering letter April 23, 1921).
54. *Debates*, House of Commons, April 25, 1921, p. 2504.
55. Ibid., April 27, 1921, p. 2640.
56. Ibid., March 4, 1921, p. 564.
57. Ibid., April 27, 1921, p. 2641.
58. Ibid., pp. 2634, 2679-80.
59. Ibid., April 25 and 27, 1921.
60. Ibid., April 27, 1921, p. 2630.
61. Milner to Governor General, January 28, 1921, Meighen Papers, file 97, folio 017533.
62. *Debates*, House of Commons, April 25, 1921, pp. 2504-05. Christie, "Meeting of Prime Ministers . . . "
63. A. R. M. Lower, ed., "Loring Christie and the Genesis of the Washington Conference of 1921–1922," CHR, March 1966. Bothwell, "Loring Christie," p. 298.
64. Pencilled "Rough notes written at sea on return from Geneva and London January 1921 LCC," External file 680-1920, "Anglo-Japanese Alliance" (RG 25, G 1, vol. 1270). These and other papers on this file were transferred from the Christie Papers.
65. Published in Lower, "Loring Christie and the Genesis of the Washington Conference."
66. DCER, 3: 162-63.
67. Michael G. Fry, *Illusions of Security: North Atlantic Diplomacy 1918–22* (Toronto, 1972), p. 102.
68. "Report of the Anglo-Japanese Alliance Committee," in Rohan Butler and J. P. T. Bury, eds., *Documents on British Foreign Policy, 1919–1939*, First Series, 14 (London, 1966), pp. 221-27.
69. Fry, *Illusions of Security*, pp. 102-03.
70. February 26, 1921, DCER, 3: 163-64.
71. Bothwell, "Loring Christie," p. 302 (Christie memo of March 3, 1921).
72. Governor General to Colonial Secretary, April 1, 1921, DCER, 3: 166-67; Colonial Secretary to Governor General, April 26, 1921, ibid., 168. Lampson memorandum, April 8, 1921, *Documents on British Foreign Policy*, First

Series, 14: 271-76. Cabinet decisions, Ian H. Nish, *Alliance in Decline: A Study in Anglo-Japanese Relations, 1908–23* (London, 1972), pp. 328-30.

73. See *Conference of Prime Ministers . . . Summary of Proceedings and Documents*, Cmd. 1474, August 1921; and *Stenographic Notes of a Meeting of Representatives of the United Kingdom, the Dominions and India* (King Papers, folios C61828 *ff*.). Extracts from these documents, Stacey, *The Arts of War and Peace*, pp. 387-410.
74. Cmd. 1474, p. 9.
75. Ibid., p. 6.
76. *Stenographic Notes*, 22nd Meeting (July 11), p. 21. Cf. 23rd Meeting (July 12), p. 5.
77. Ibid., 6th Meeting, June 24, p. 3.
78. Ibid., p. 7, and cf. ibid., 22nd Meeting, July 11, p. 7 *ff*.
79. Cmd. 1474, pp. 3-5.
80. *Debates*, House of Commons, April 27, 1921, pp. 2639-40.
81. Ibid., p. 2657.
82. See, e.g., editorial in *Ottawa Journal*, May 26, 1921.
83. *Speech Delivered by the Rt. Hon. W. M. Hughes . . . in the Federal House of Representatives, Melbourne on Thursday 7th of April 1921 . . .* (copy in External file 680-1920).
84. *Stenographic Notes of a Meeting . . .*, 2nd Meeting, June 21.
85. Ibid., 10th and 11th Meetings, June 29.
86. Ibid., 12th Meeting, June 30.
87. Colonial Secretary to Governor General, June 24, 1920, DCER, 3: 156.
88. *Stenographic Notes . . .*, 8th Meeting, June 28, p. 11.
89. PRO, CAB 23/26, folios 99-105, Conclusions of Cabinet Meeting June 30, 1921, PAC, microfilm B-3847. Nish, *Alliance in Decline*, pp. 335-37.
90. *Stenographic Notes . . .*, 12th Meeting, June 30. Frances Stevenson's diary, quoted in Lord Beaverbrook, *The Decline and Fall of Lloyd George . . .* (London, 1963), p. 81.
91. Conclusions of Cabinet Meeting, note 89 above. Nish, *Alliance in Decline*, pp. 335-36.
92. *Stenographic Notes . . .*, 9th Meeting, June 29, p. 8.
93. Ibid., 13th Meeting, July 1 (afternoon), Appendix (B); 20th Meeting, July 8.
94. Ibid., 12th Meeting, July 1 (morning).
95. Nish, *Alliance in Decline*, pp. 343-51.
96. Cmd. 1474, p. 5.
97. *Stenographic Notes . . .*, 11th Meeting, June 30, and 12th Meeting, July 1.
98. J. B. Brebner, "Canada, the Anglo-Japanese Alliance and the Washington Conference," *Political Science Quarterly*, March, 1935.
99. Nish, *Alliance in Decline*, pp. 351-53.
100. DCER, 3: 484-86. This and other documents preliminary to the conference are in *Foreign Relations of the United States*, 1921, 1: 18-86.
101. Prime Minister of South Africa to Prime Minister of Canada, October 19, 1921, DCER, 3: 489.
102. Ibid., 482-90.

103. *Conference on the Limitation of Armament held at Washington November 12, 1921, to February 6, 1922: Report of the Canadian Delegate including Treaties and Resolutions* (Sessional Papers, Canada, 1922, No. 47). Extracts in Stacey, *The Arts of War and Peace*, 410-18.
104. Treaties in *Report of the Canadian Delegate* . . . They are also conveniently accessible in *Treaties and Agreements affecting Canada . . . in force between His Majesty and the United States of America*, pp. 475-504,
105. There are two versions of the minutes of the British Empire Delegation: the contemporary mimeographed one (in External files, PAC, RG 25, F 1, vol. 919, file 38) and the later printed one (in Borden Papers, vol. 119, file OC 612). See also Borden's various reports, DCER, 3: 490-513.
106. *Report of the Canadian Delegate . . .*, para. 113.
107. Nish, *Alliance in Decline*, pp. 354-67.
108. Telegram to Ambassador at Washington quoted in Colonial Secretary to Govenor General, October 3, 1921, DCER, 3: 487-88.
109. Nish, *Alliance in Decline*, pp. 368-69.
110. Ibid., p. 370.
111. Borden's "Notes . . . Upon the Disarmament Conference at Washington . . ." are really a diary (copies in Borden Papers, vols. 297 and 347). His private diary, kept in French, continues separately, but is rarely informative. Fry, *Illusions of Security*, pp. 164-65.
112. Nish, *Alliance in Decline*, pp. 370-73. Treaty in Sessional Paper No. 47, 1921, pp. 208-11.
113. Minutes of British Empire Delegation, December 7 and 9, 1921.
114. Gwendolen M. Carter, *The British Commonwealth and International Security: The Role of the Dominions, 1919–1939* (Toronto, 1947), p. 53. Nish, *Alliance in Decline*, pp. 373-74. Borden to Meighen, December 10, 1921, DCER, 3: 505.
115. Nish, *Alliance in Decline*, p. 369. Treaties in Sessional Paper No. 47, 1921.
116. Thomas A. Bailey, A *Diplomatic History of the American People* (New York, 1940), chapter 41. Carter, *British Commonwealth*, pp. 55-57. Borden memorandum, November 14, 1921; Sir James Lougheed (Acting Prime Minister) to Borden, November 23, 1921; Borden to Lougheed, November 28, 1921; Meighen to Borden, December 6, 1921, DCER, 3: 491-503.
117. Borden "Notes . . . ," December 9, 1921. Cf. Borden's private diary, same date, and "Notes" of November 15, 1921. Minutes of British Empire Delegation, December 9, 1921. Stephen Roskill, *Hankey, Man of Secrets* (London, 1972), 2: 246-68. Cf. the same author's *Naval Policy Between the Wars* (London, 1968), 1: 318-22. Documents in Butler and Bury, eds., *Documents on British Foreign Policy*, First Series, 14: 544 *ff*. Treaty, Sessional Paper No. 47, 1921.
118. Borden to King, December 26, 1921; King to Borden, January 3, 1922, DCER, 3: 506-07.
119. King Diary, January 28, 1922.
120. Ibid. King to Borden, January 28, 1922, DCER, 3: 509-10.

121. Borden to King, January 31, 1922, ibid., 511. King Diary, January 31, 1922. Christie memorandum, "The Naval Treaty," n.d., RG 25, F 1, vol. 916, file 19.
122. King to Borden, and Borden to King, both February 2, 1922, DCER, 3: 512-13.
123. Order-in-council re naval treaty, PC 1393, July 3, 1922, ibid., 513-14.
124. *Report of the Canadian Delegate.*

INDEX